SPEED GRAPHER スピードグラファー

GRAPHER

Volume 1

Written and Illustrated by
Tomozo & Yusuke Kozaki

TOKYOPOP®

HAMBURG // LONDON // LOS ANGELES // TOKYO

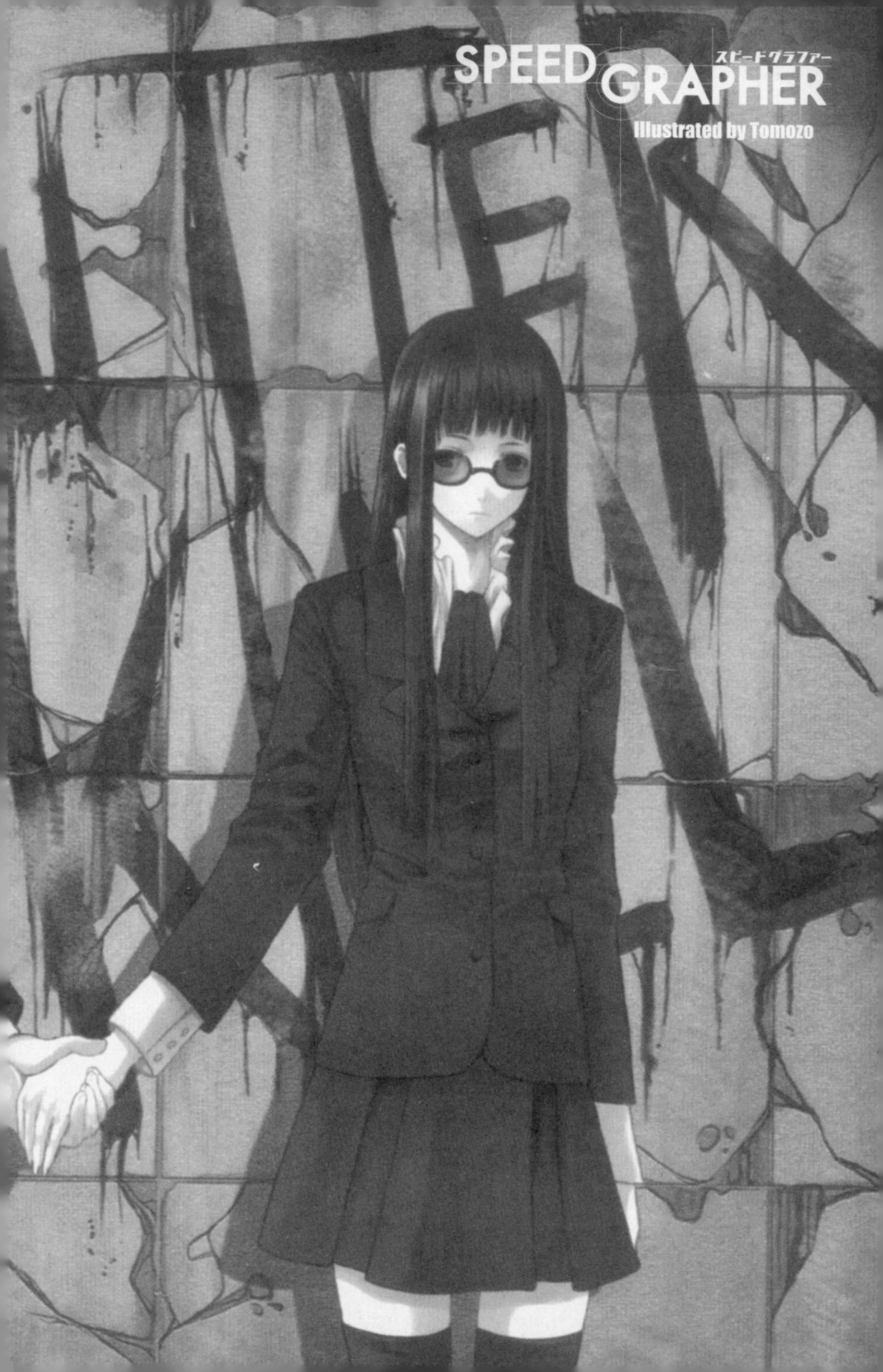
SPEED GRAPHER
スピードグラファー
Illustrated by Tomozo

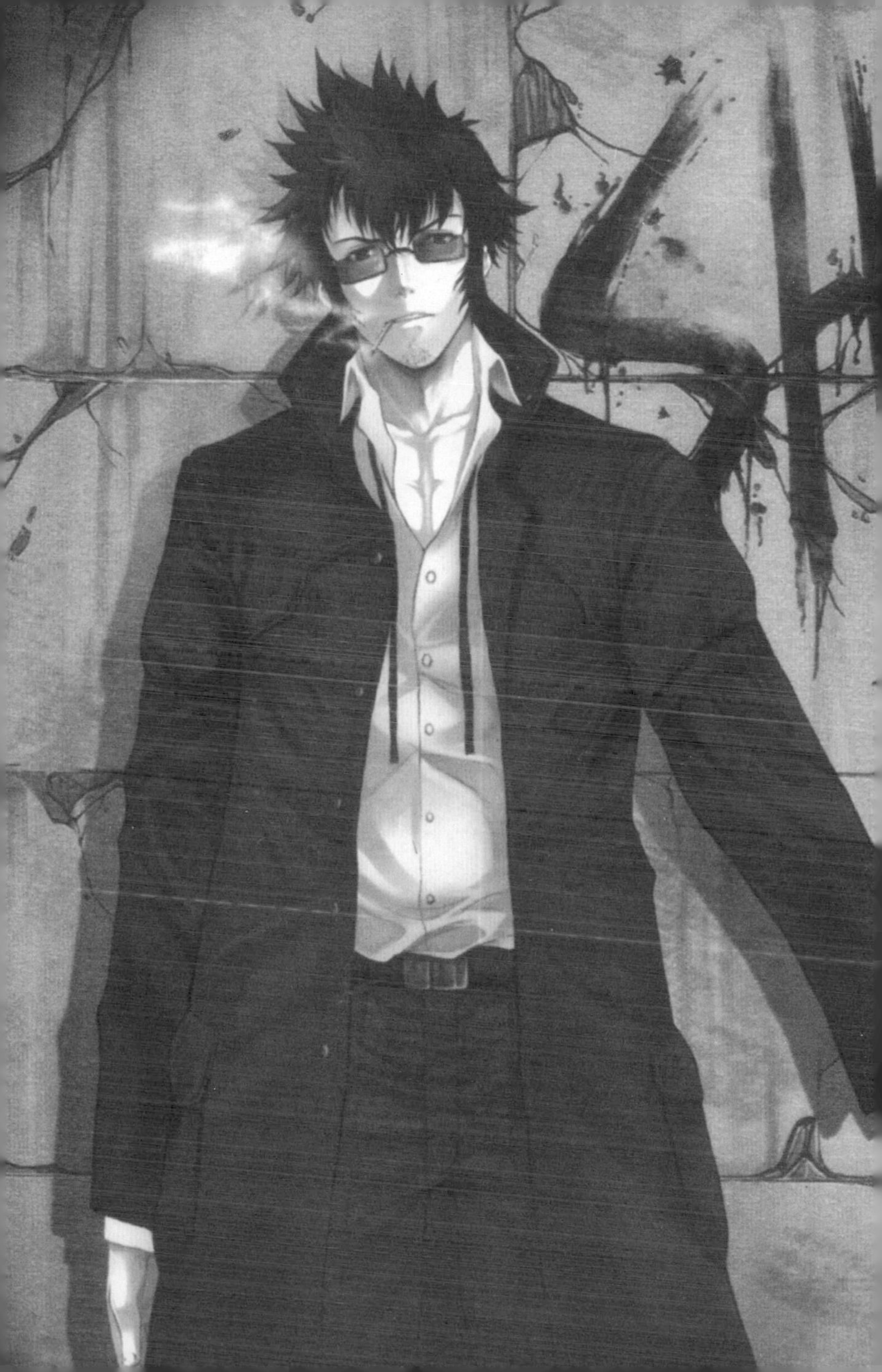

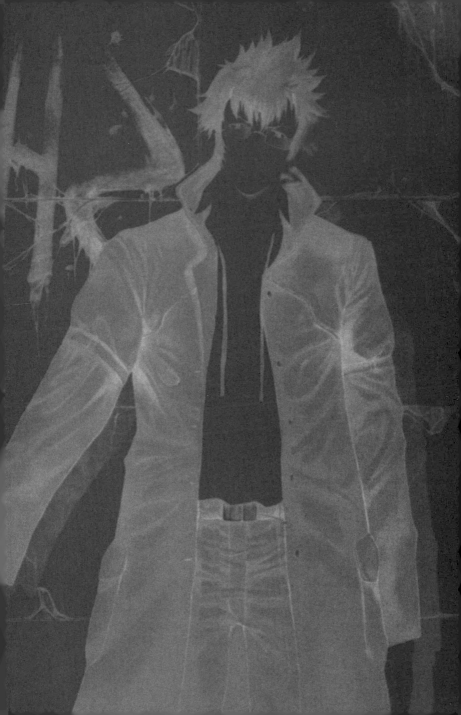

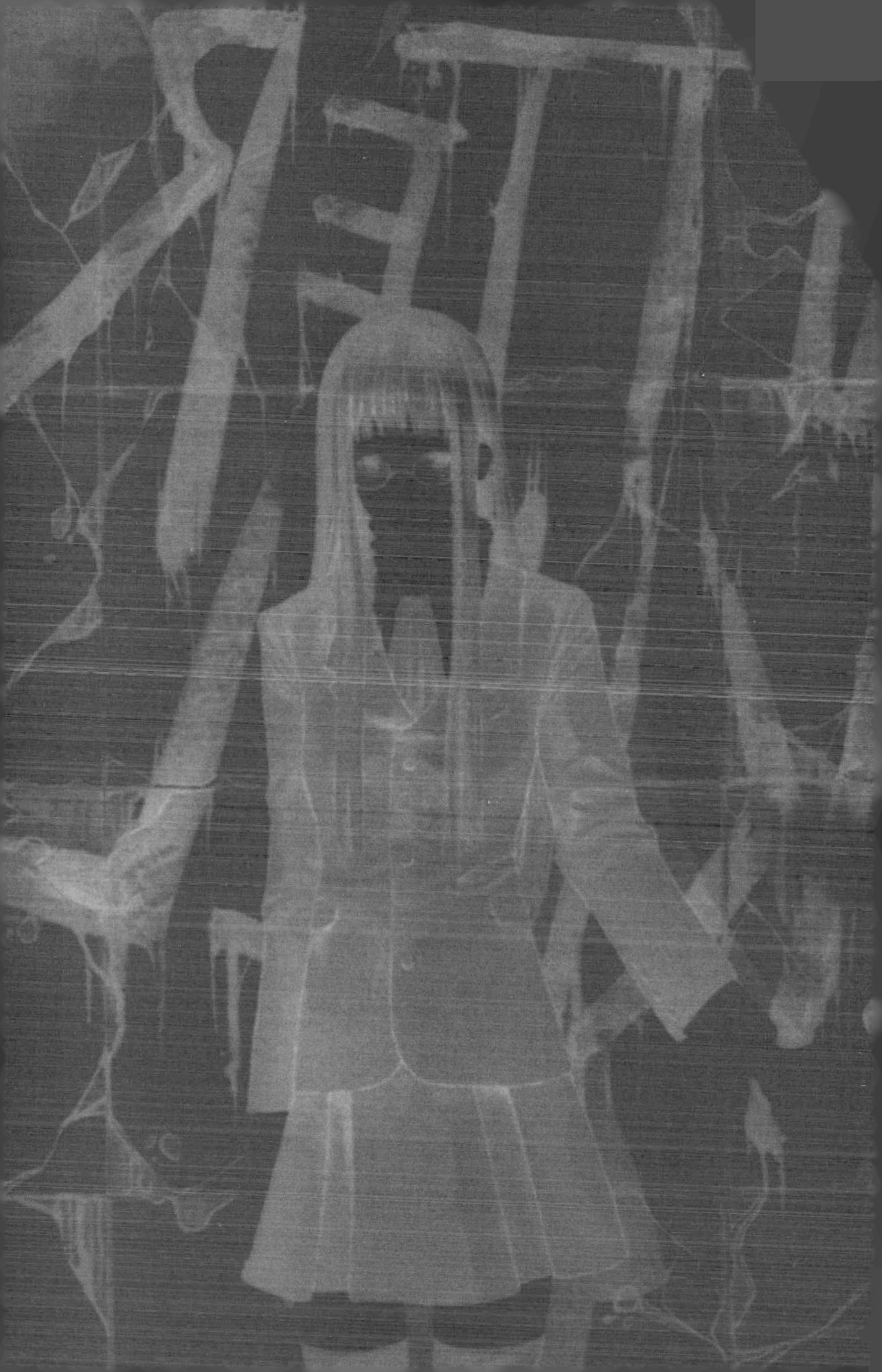

Speed Grapher - MANGA Volume 1
Written and Illustrated by Tomozo & Yusuke Kozaki

Translation - Satsuki Yamashita
English Adaptation - Clint Bickham
Retouch and Lettering - Star Print Brokers
Production Artist - Vicente Rivera, Jr.
Cover Design - Colin Graham

Editor - Nikhil Burman
Digital Imaging Manager - Chris Buford
Pre-Production Supervisor - Vicente Rivera, Jr.
Production Specialist - Lucas Rivera
Managing Editor - Vy Nguyen
Art Director - Al-Insan Lashley
Editor-in-Chief - Rob Tokar
Publisher - Mike Kiley
President and C.O.O. - John Parker
C.E.O. and Chief Creative Officer - Stu Levy

A 🔘 **TOKYOPOP** Manga

TOKYOPOP and 🔘 are trademarks or registered trademarks of TOKYOPOP Inc.

TOKYOPOP Inc.
5900 Wilshire Blvd. Suite 2000
Los Angeles, CA 90036

E-mail: info@TOKYOPOP.com
Come visit us online at www.TOKYOPOP.com

ISBN: 978-1-4278-1186-8

First TOKYOPOP printing: September 2008
10 9 8 7 6 5 4 3 2 1
Printed in the USA

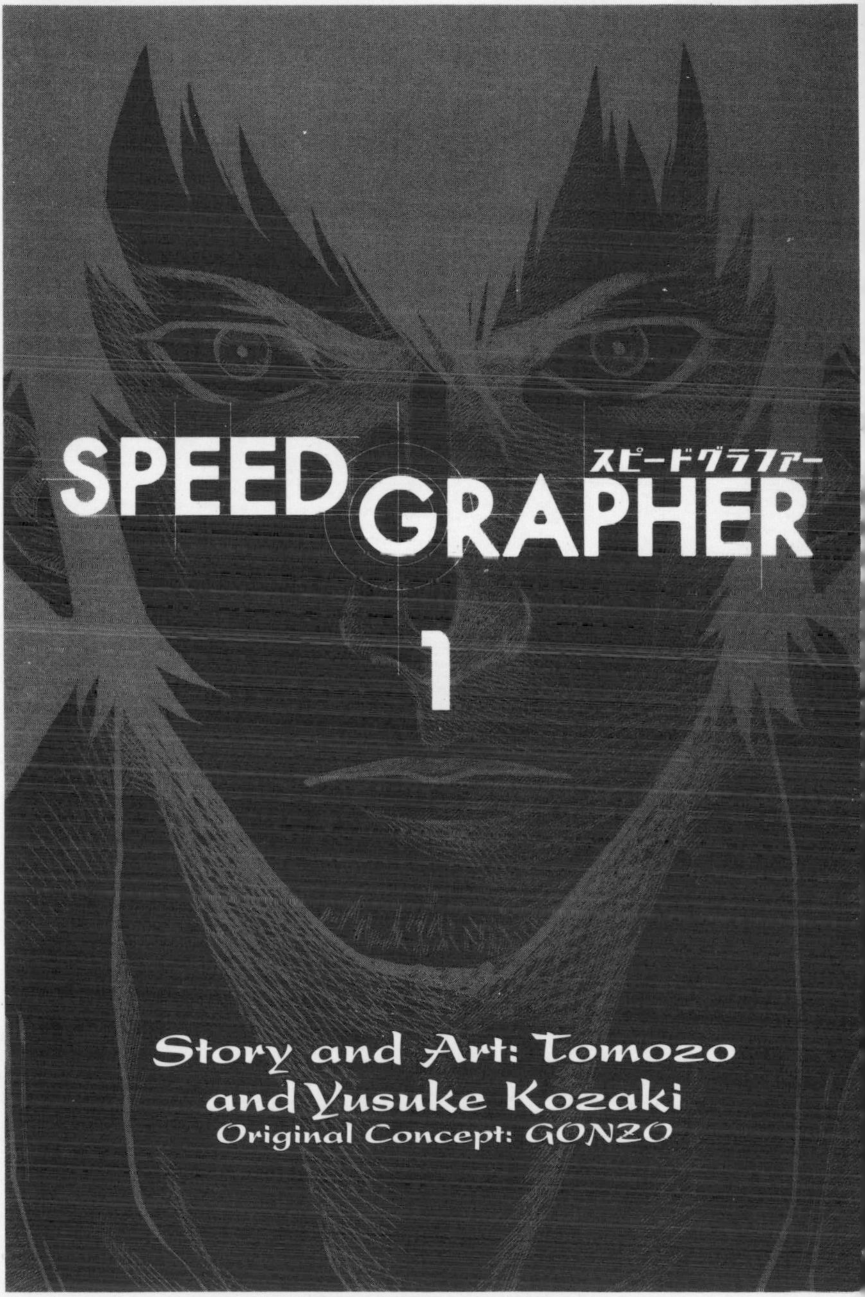

SPEED GRAPHER

スピードグラファー

1

Story and Art: Tomozo and Yusuke Kozaki

Original Concept: GONZO

Design : **stereotypeprodukts**

CONTENTS

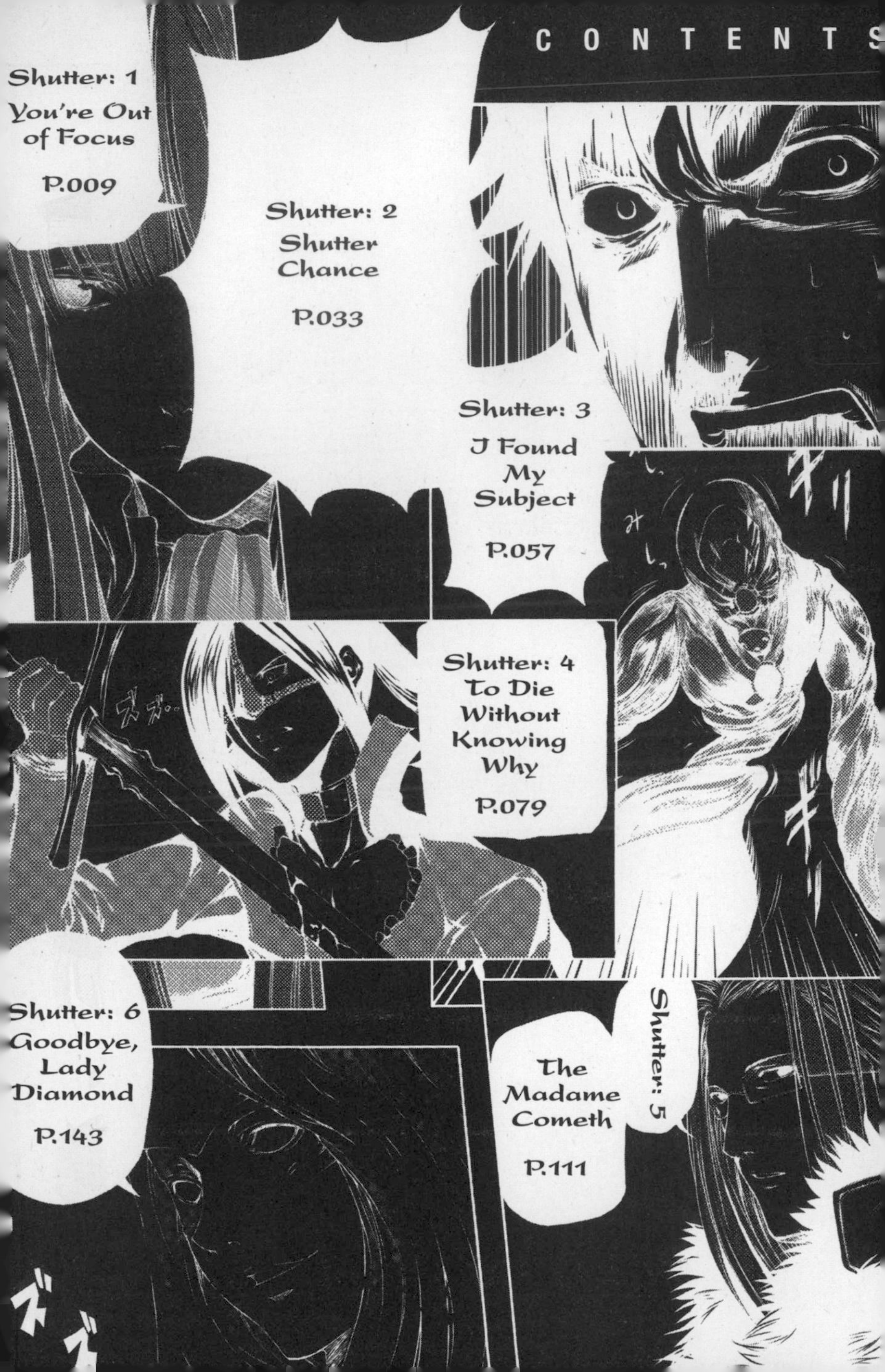

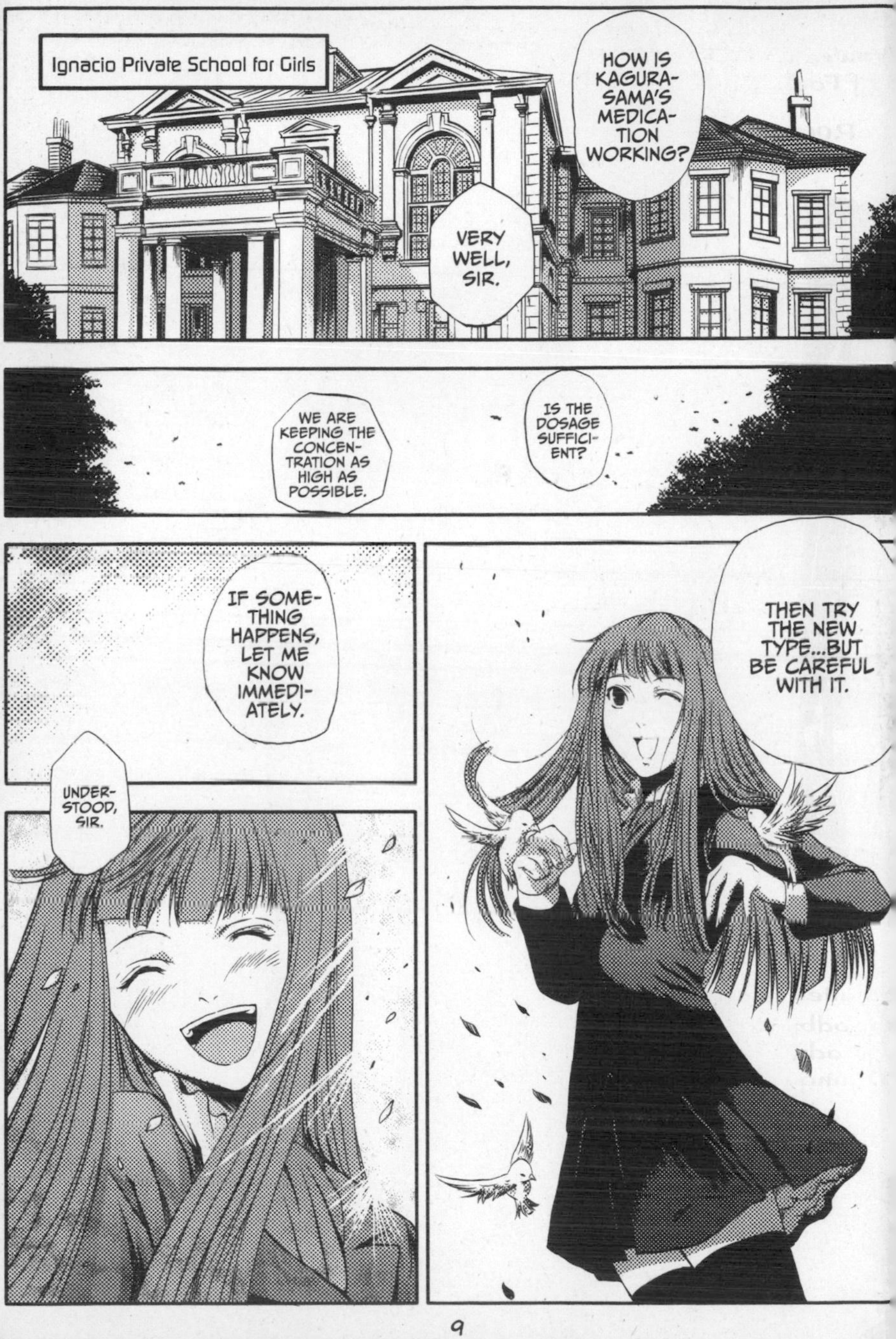
Ignacio Private School for Girls
HOW IS KAGURA-SAMA'S MEDICATION WORKING?
VERY WELL, SIR.
IS THE DOSAGE SUFFICIENT?
WE ARE KEEPING THE CONCENTRATION AS HIGH AS POSSIBLE.
THEN TRY THE NEW TYPE...BUT BE CAREFUL WITH IT.
IF SOMETHING HAPPENS, LET ME KNOW IMMEDIATELY.
UNDERSTOOD, SIR.

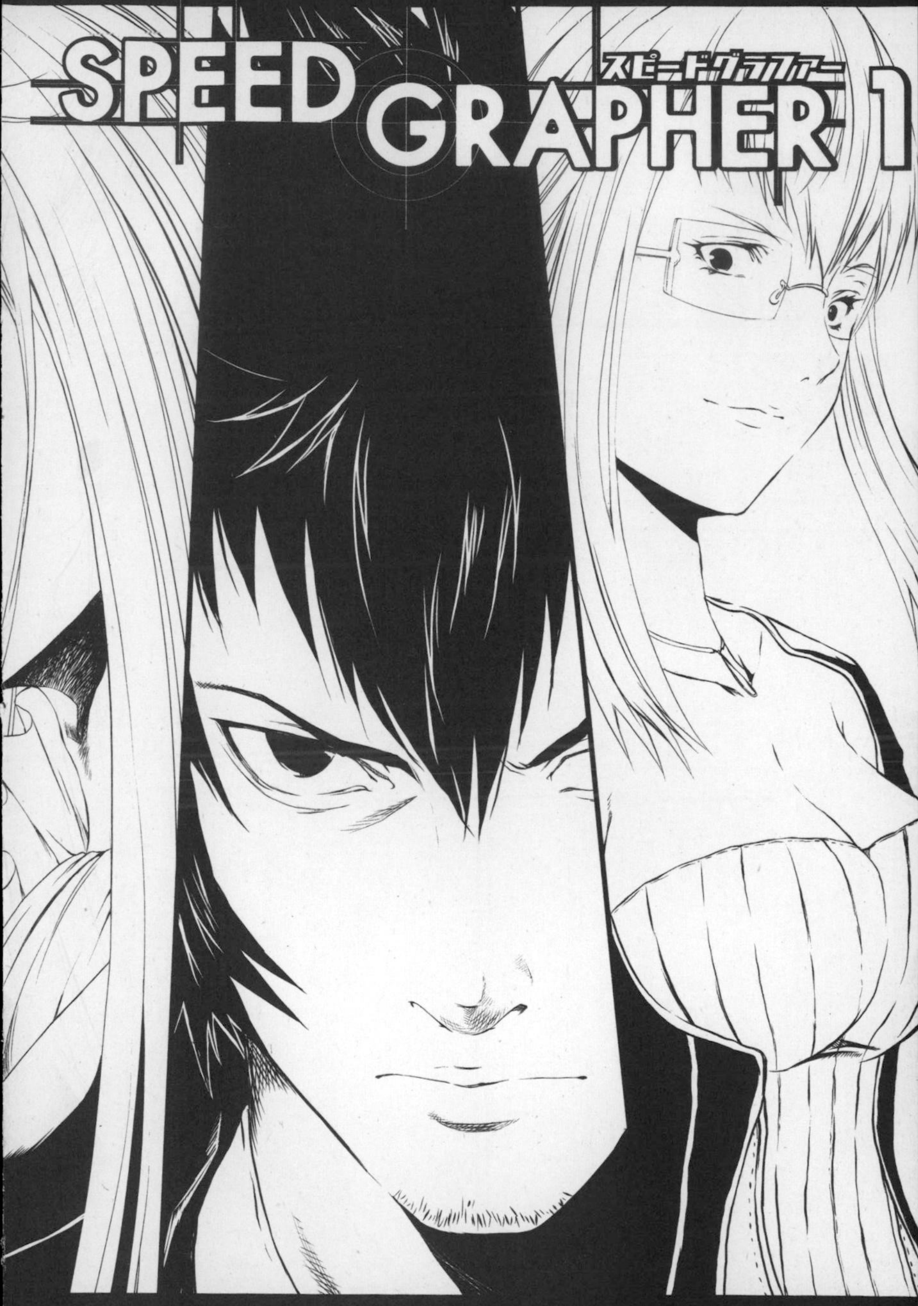
SPEED GRAPHER 1
スピードグラファー

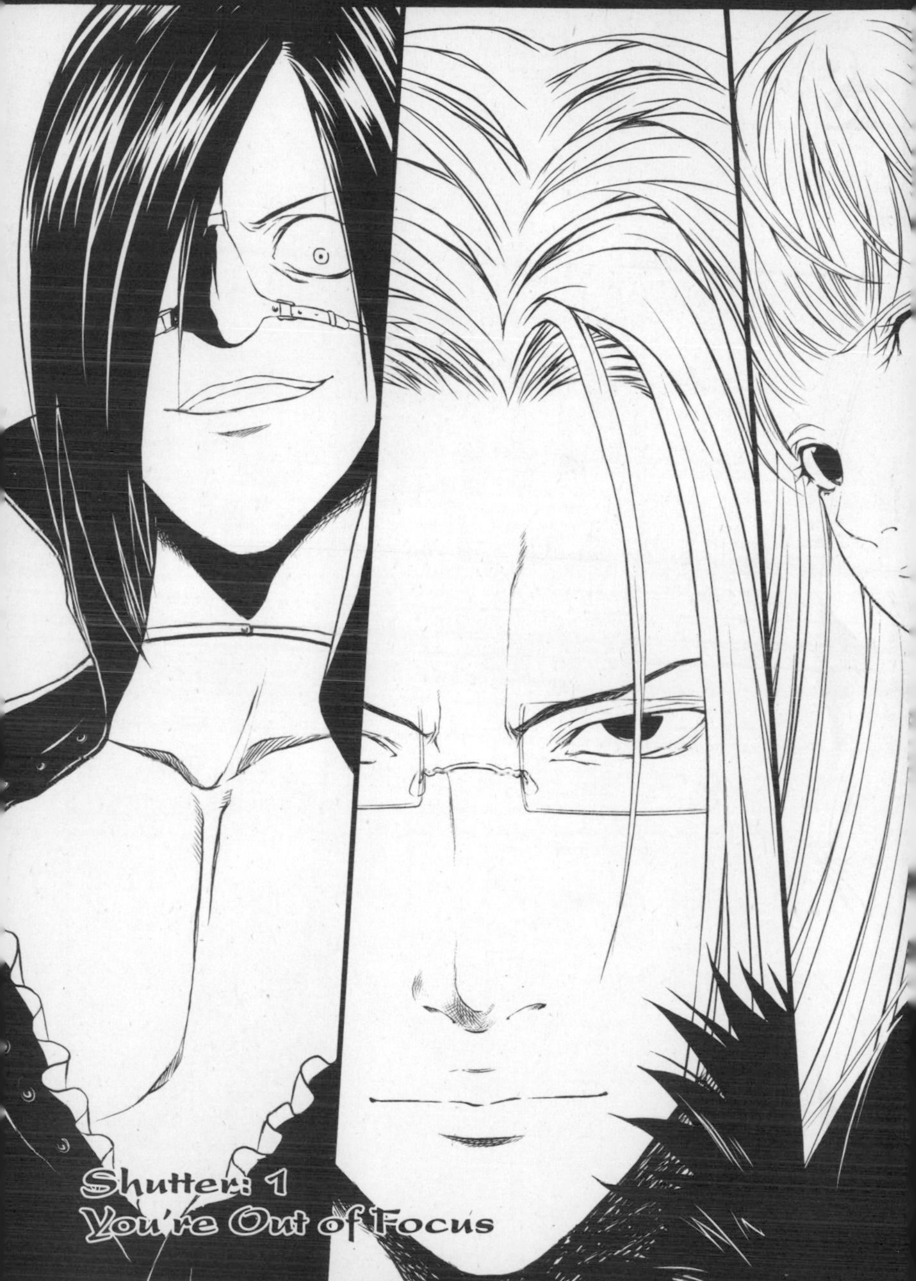
Shutter: 1
You're Out of Focus

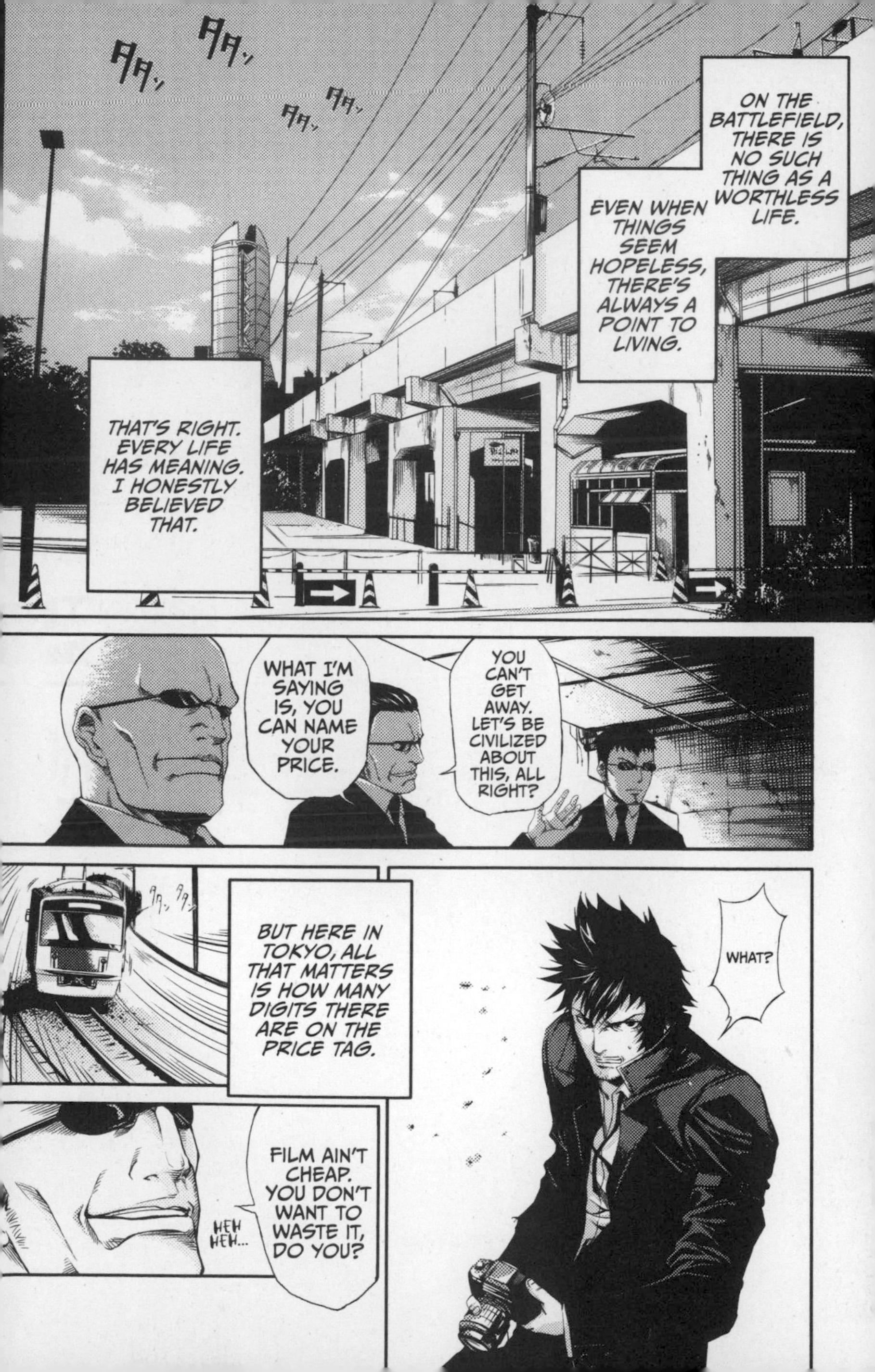
ON THE BATTLEFIELD, THERE IS NO SUCH THING AS A WORTHLESS LIFE.
EVEN WHEN THINGS SEEM HOPELESS, THERE'S ALWAYS A POINT TO LIVING.
THAT'S RIGHT. EVERY LIFE HAS MEANING. I HONESTLY BELIEVED THAT.
YOU CAN'T GET AWAY. LET'S BE CIVILIZED ABOUT THIS, ALL RIGHT?
WHAT I'M SAYING IS, YOU CAN NAME YOUR PRICE.
WHAT?
BUT HERE IN TOKYO, ALL THAT MATTERS IS HOW MANY DIGITS THERE ARE ON THE PRICE TAG.
FILM AIN'T CHEAP. YOU DON'T WANT TO WASTE IT, DO YOU?
HEH HEH...

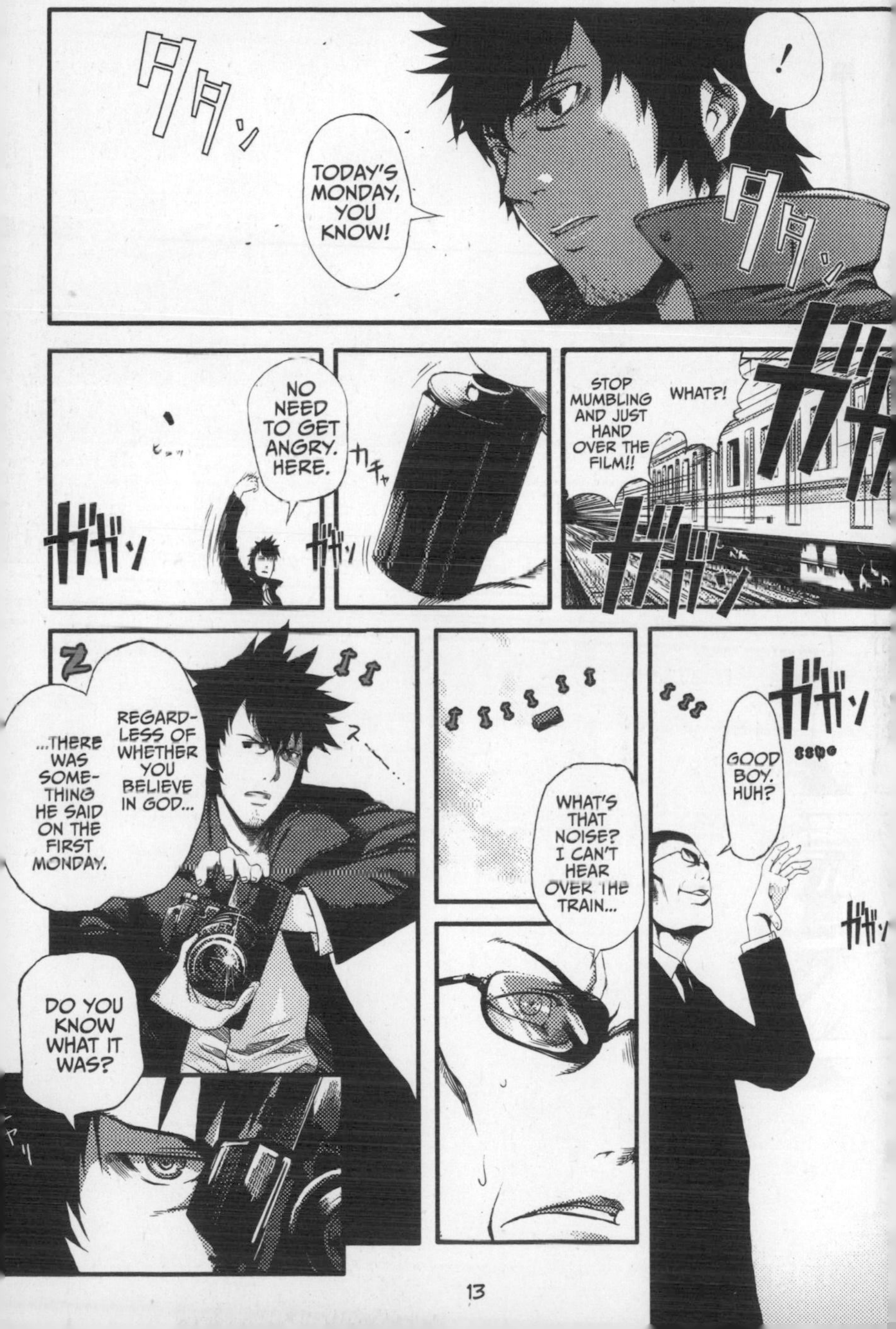
!
TODAY'S MONDAY, YOU KNOW!
WHAT?!
STOP MUMBLING AND JUST HAND OVER THE FILM!!
NO NEED TO GET ANGRY. HERE.
GOOD BOY. HUH?
WHAT'S THAT NOISE? I CAN'T HEAR OVER THE TRAIN...
REGARDLESS OF WHETHER YOU BELIEVE IN GOD...
...THERE WAS SOMETHING HE SAID ON THE FIRST MONDAY.
DO YOU KNOW WHAT IT WAS?

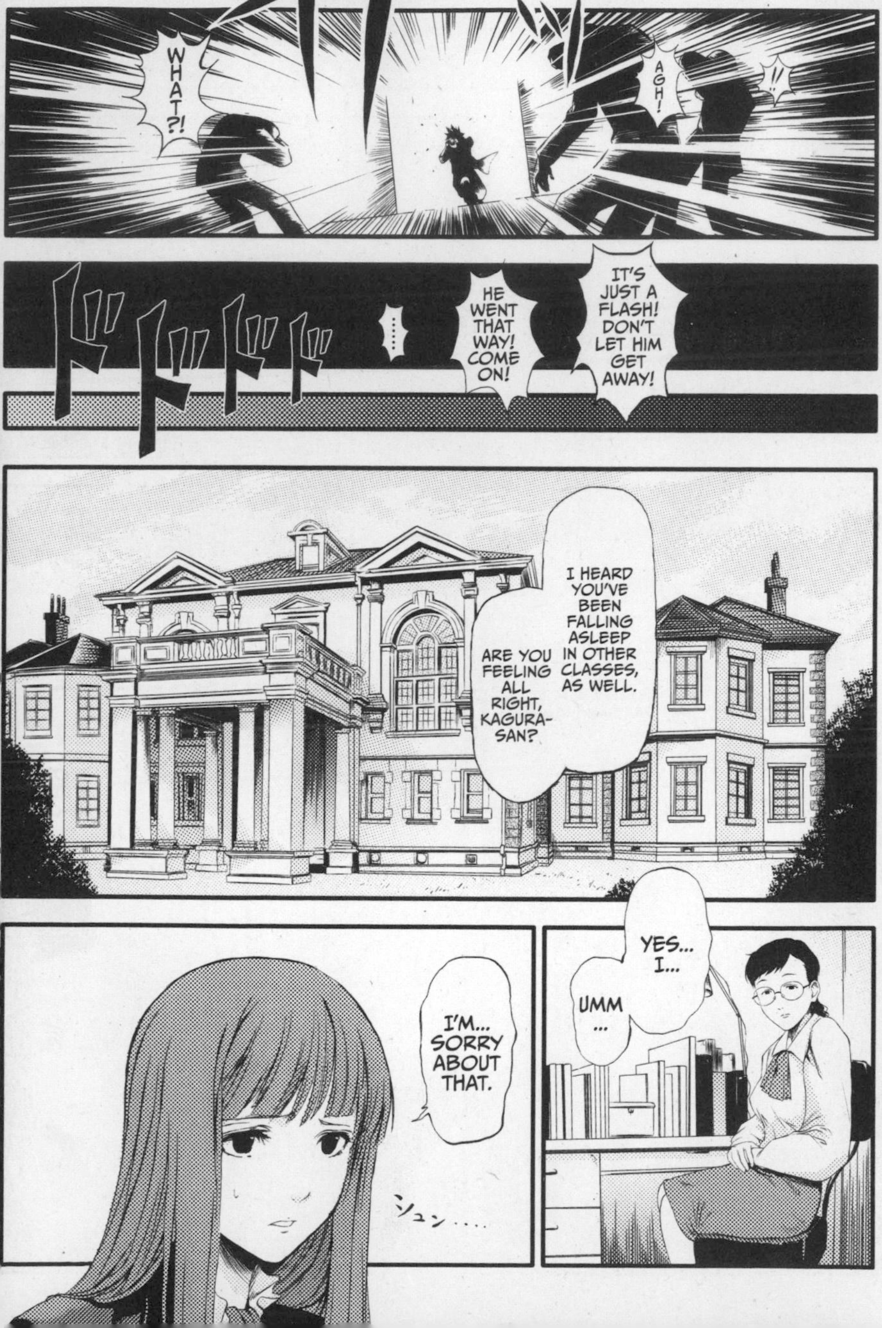
!!
AGH!
WHAT?!
IT'S JUST A FLASH! DON'T LET HIM GET AWAY!
HE WENT THAT WAY! COME ON!
......
ドドドドド
I HEARD YOU'VE BEEN FALLING ASLEEP IN OTHER CLASSES, AS WELL.
ARE YOU FEELING ALL RIGHT, KAGURA-SAN?
YES... I...
UMM ...
I'M... SORRY ABOUT THAT.
シュン....

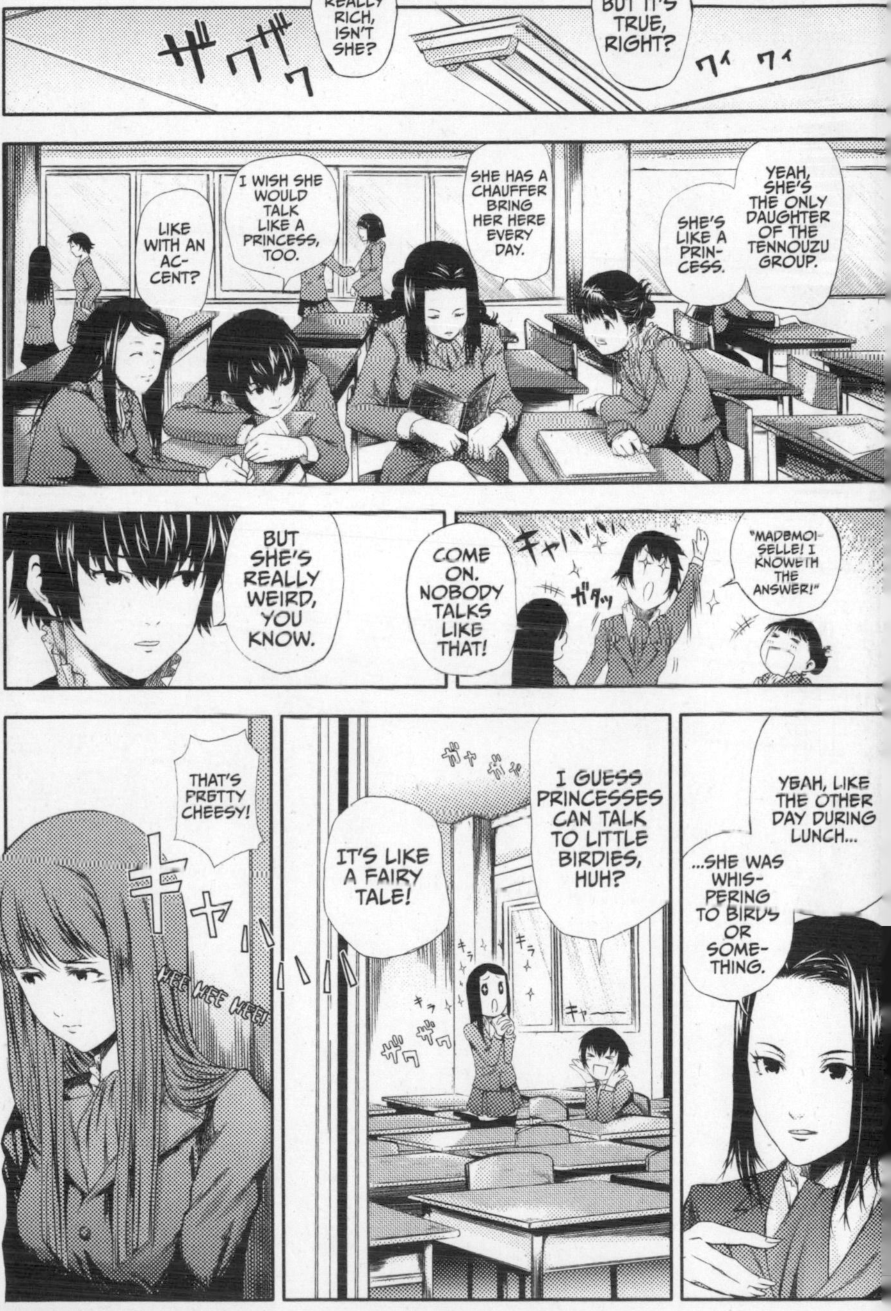
ワイ ワイ
BUT IT'S TRUE, RIGHT?
SHE'S REALLY RICH, ISN'T SHE?
ザワザワ
YEAH, SHE'S THE ONLY DAUGHTER OF THE TENNOUZU GROUP.
SHE'S LIKE A PRINCESS.
SHE HAS A CHAUFFER BRING HER HERE EVERY DAY.
I WISH SHE WOULD TALK LIKE A PRINCESS, TOO.
LIKE WITH AN ACCENT?
"MADEMOISELLE! I KNOWETH THE ANSWER!"
キャハハ
ガタッ
COME ON. NOBODY TALKS LIKE THAT!
BUT SHE'S REALLY WEIRD, YOU KNOW.
YEAH, LIKE THE OTHER DAY DURING LUNCH...
...SHE WAS WHISPERING TO BIRDS OR SOMETHING.
ガヤガヤ
I GUESS PRINCESSES CAN TALK TO LITTLE BIRDIES, HUH?
IT'S LIKE A FAIRY TALE!
キラ キラ
キラ
ザワザワ
キャー
THAT'S PRETTY CHEESY!
キャハハ
HEE HEE HEE!

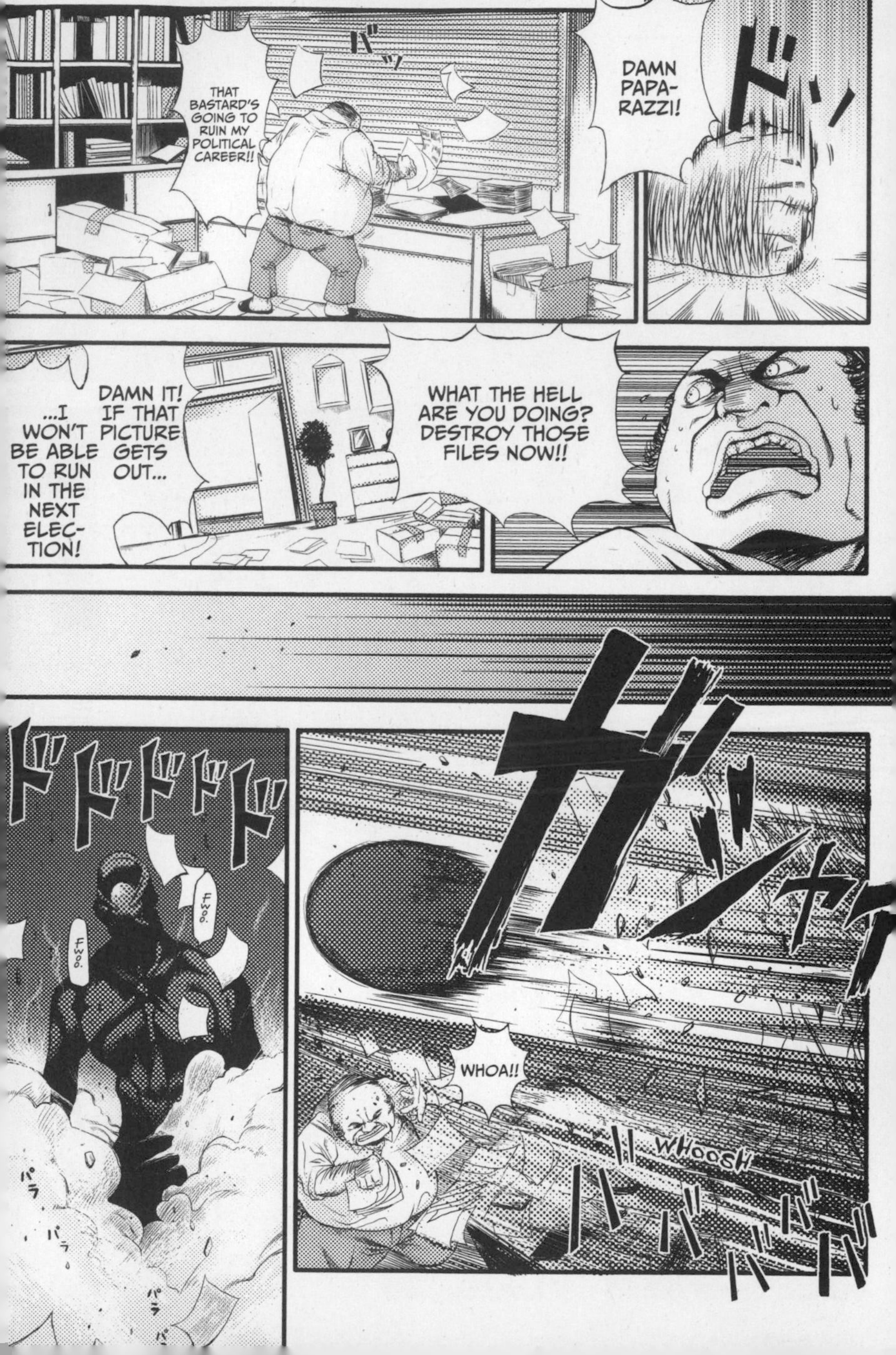
DAMN PAPA-RAZZI!
THAT BASTARD'S GOING TO RUIN MY POLITICAL CAREER!!
WHAT THE HELL ARE YOU DOING? DESTROY THOSE FILES NOW!!
DAMN IT! IF THAT PICTURE GETS OUT...
...I WON'T BE ABLE TO RUN IN THE NEXT ELEC-TION!
WHOA!!
WHOOSH
ドドドドドド
Fwoo.
Fwoo.
パラ
パラ

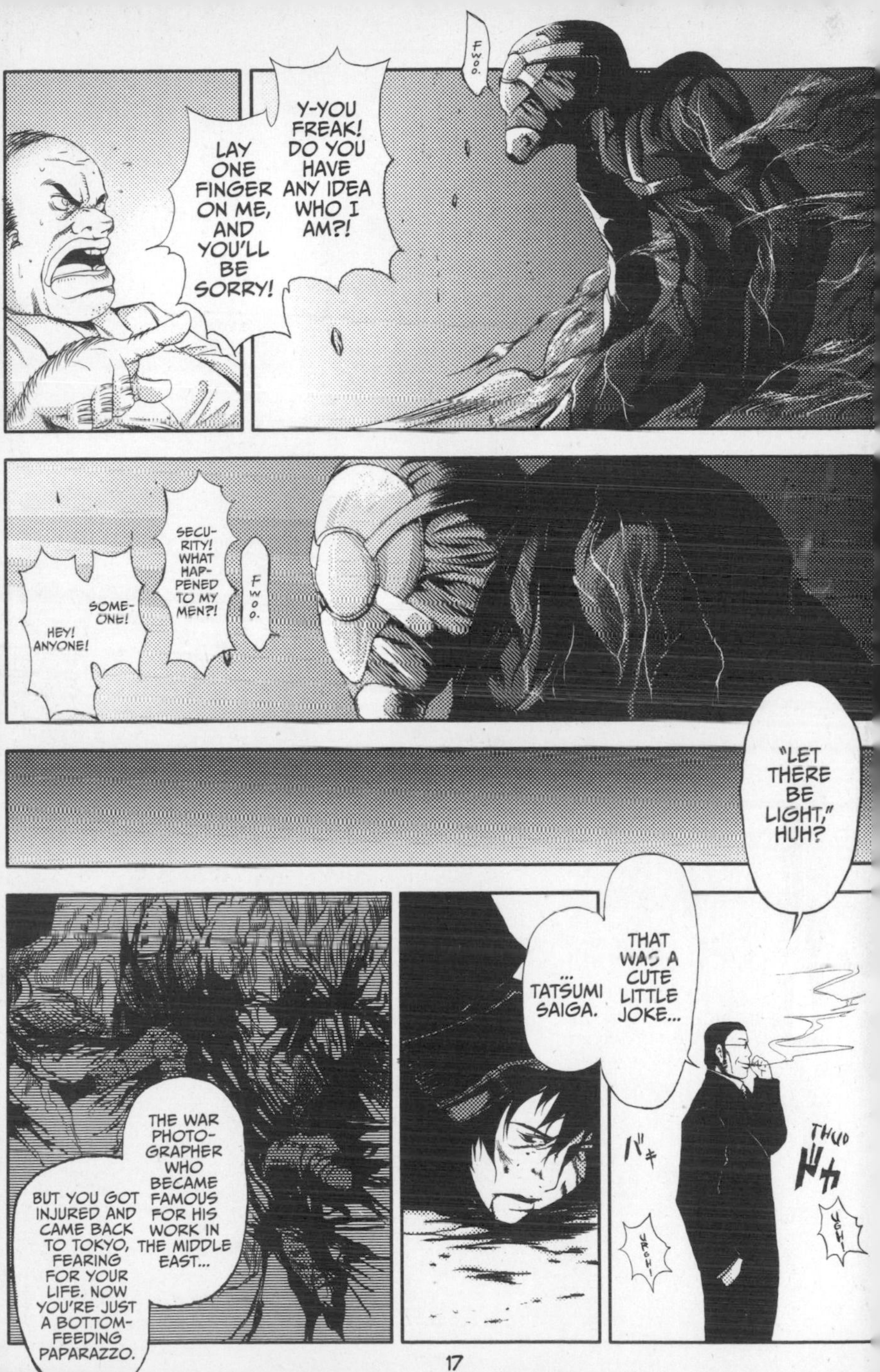
FWOO.
Y-YOU FREAK! DO YOU HAVE ANY IDEA WHO I AM?!
LAY ONE FINGER ON ME, AND YOU'LL BE SORRY!
FWOO.
SECURITY! WHAT HAPPENED TO MY MEN?!
SOMEONE!
HEY! ANYONE!
"LET THERE BE LIGHT," HUH?
THUD
ドカ
UGH!
THAT WAS A CUTE LITTLE JOKE...
バキ
URGH!
... TATSUMI SAIGA.
THE WAR PHOTOGRAPHER WHO BECAME FAMOUS FOR HIS WORK IN THE MIDDLE EAST...
BUT YOU GOT INJURED AND CAME BACK TO TOKYO, FEARING FOR YOUR LIFE. NOW YOU'RE JUST A BOTTOM-FEEDING PAPARAZZO.

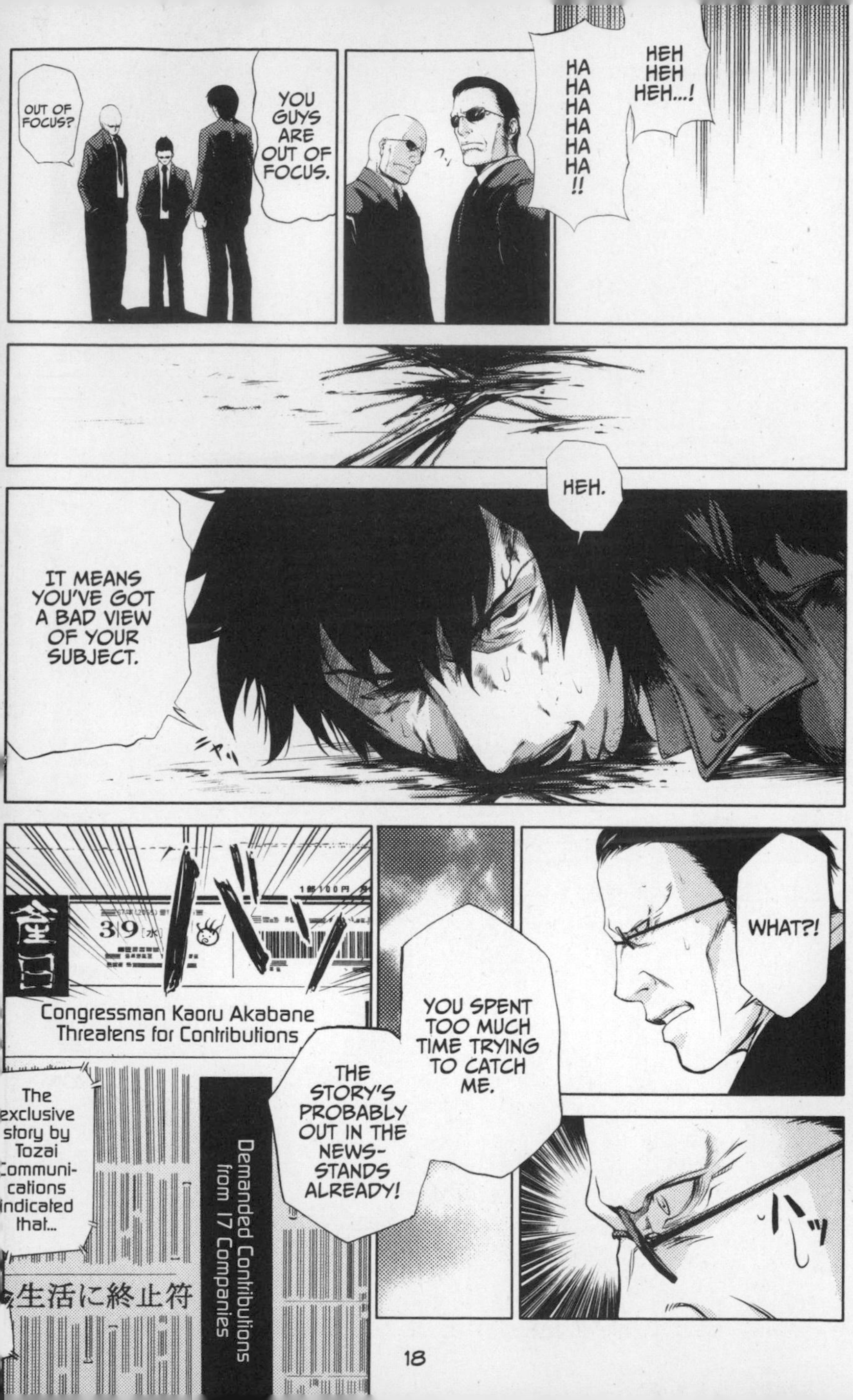
HEH HEH HEH...!
HA HA HA HA HA HA!!
YOU GUYS ARE OUT OF FOCUS.
OUT OF FOCUS?
HEH.
IT MEANS YOU'VE GOT A BAD VIEW OF YOUR SUBJECT.
WHAT?!
ハッ
YOU SPENT TOO MUCH TIME TRYING TO CATCH ME.
THE STORY'S PROBABLY OUT IN THE NEWS-STANDS ALREADY!
1部100円
3 9 水
Congressman Kaoru Akabane Threatens for Contributions
Demanded Contributions from 17 Companies
The exclusive story by Tozai Communications indicated that...
生活に終止符

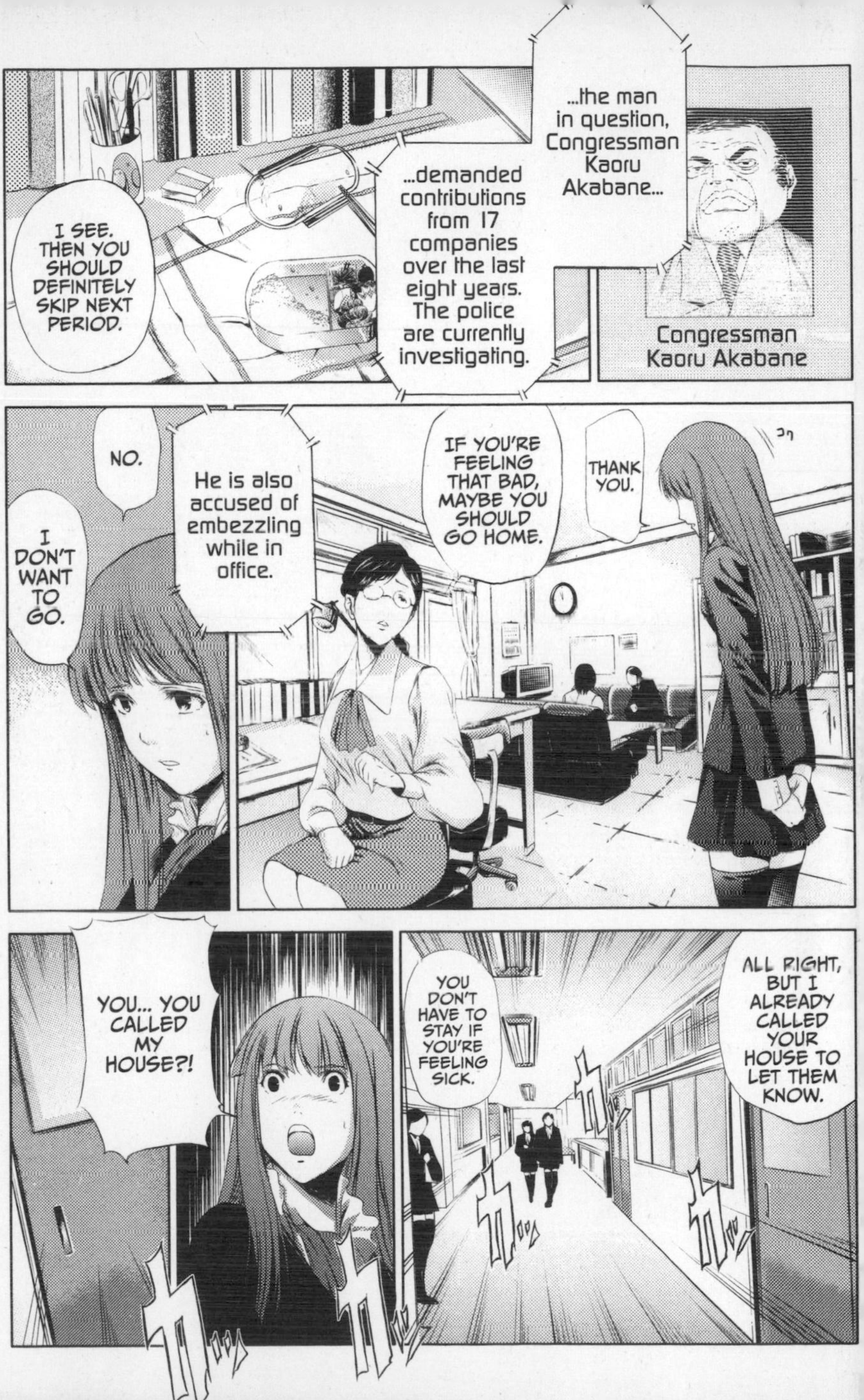
...the man in question, Congressman Kaoru Akabane...
Congressman Kaoru Akabane
...demanded contributions from 17 companies over the last eight years. The police are currently investigating.
I SEE. THEN YOU SHOULD DEFINITELY SKIP NEXT PERIOD.
THANK YOU.
IF YOU'RE FEELING THAT BAD, MAYBE YOU SHOULD GO HOME.
He is also accused of embezzling while in office.
NO.
I DON'T WANT TO GO.
ALL RIGHT, BUT I ALREADY CALLED YOUR HOUSE TO LET THEM KNOW.
YOU DON'T HAVE TO STAY IF YOU'RE FEELING SICK.
YOU... YOU CALLED MY HOUSE?!

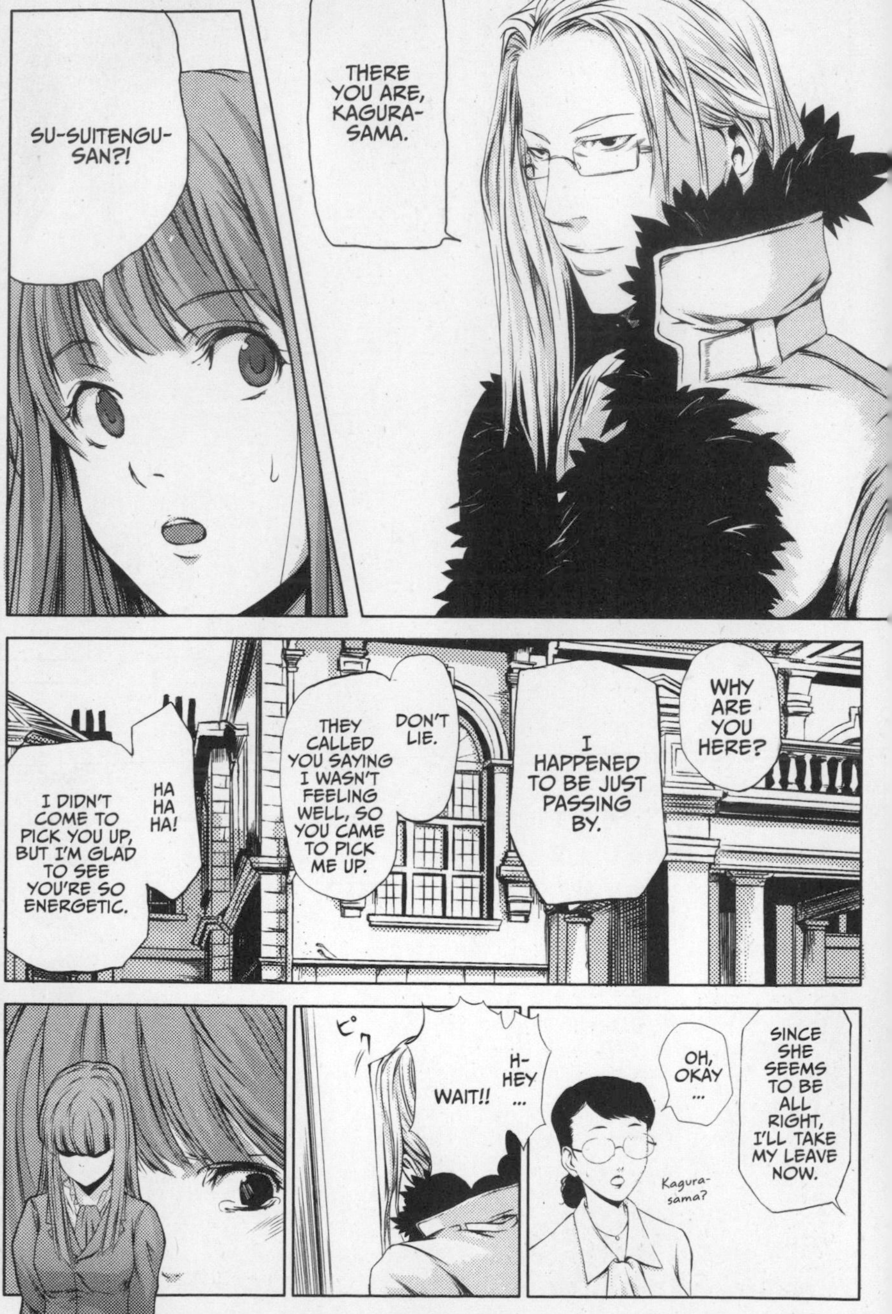
THERE YOU ARE, KAGURA-SAMA.
SU-SUITENGU-SAN?!
WHY ARE YOU HERE?
I HAPPENED TO BE JUST PASSING BY.
DON'T LIE.
THEY CALLED YOU SAYING I WASN'T FEELING WELL, SO YOU CAME TO PICK ME UP.
HA HA HA!
I DIDN'T COME TO PICK YOU UP, BUT I'M GLAD TO SEE YOU'RE SO ENERGETIC.
SINCE SHE SEEMS TO BE ALL RIGHT, I'LL TAKE MY LEAVE NOW.
OH, OKAY ...
Kagura-sama?
ピク
H-HEY ...
WAIT!!

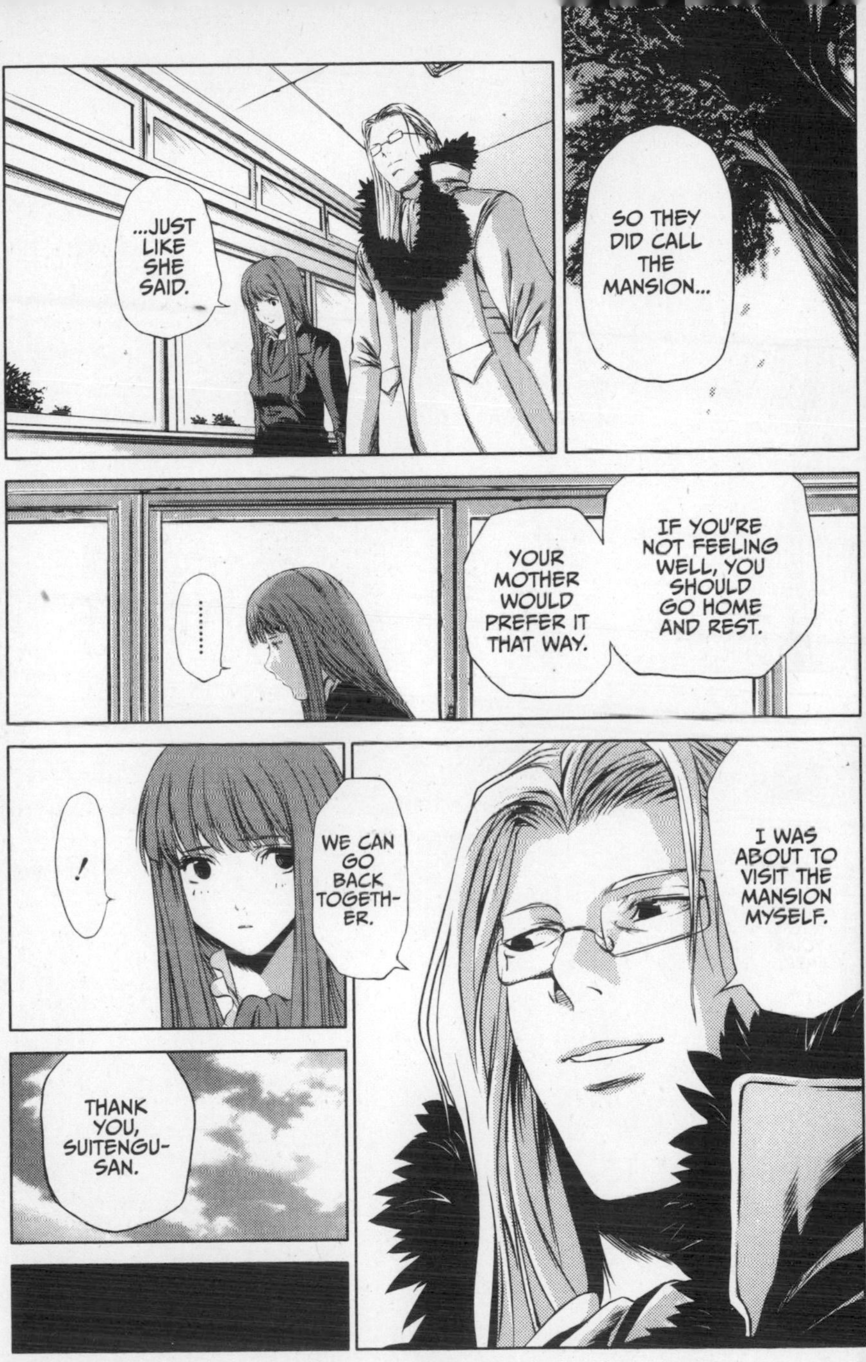
SO THEY DID CALL THE MANSION...
...JUST LIKE SHE SAID.
IF YOU'RE NOT FEELING WELL, YOU SHOULD GO HOME AND REST.
YOUR MOTHER WOULD PREFER IT THAT WAY.
......
I WAS ABOUT TO VISIT THE MANSION MYSELF.
WE CAN GO BACK TOGETH-ER.
!
THANK YOU, SUITENGU-SAN.

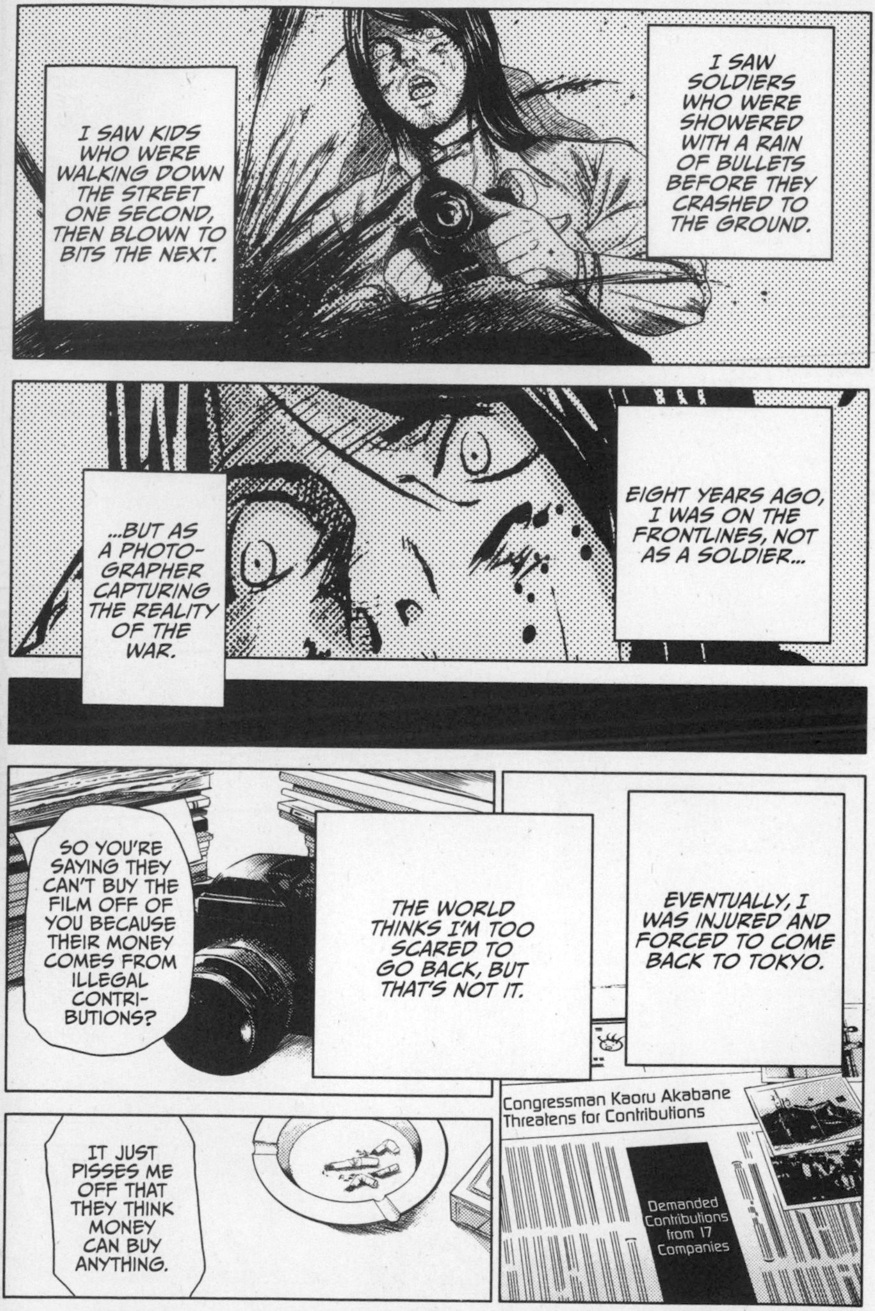
I SAW SOLDIERS WHO WERE SHOWERED WITH A RAIN OF BULLETS BEFORE THEY CRASHED TO THE GROUND.
I SAW KIDS WHO WERE WALKING DOWN THE STREET ONE SECOND, THEN BLOWN TO BITS THE NEXT.
EIGHT YEARS AGO, I WAS ON THE FRONTLINES, NOT AS A SOLDIER...
...BUT AS A PHOTO-GRAPHER CAPTURING THE REALITY OF THE WAR.
EVENTUALLY, I WAS INJURED AND FORCED TO COME BACK TO TOKYO.
Congressman Kaoru Akabane Threatens for Contributions
Demanded Contributions from 17 Companies
THE WORLD THINKS I'M TOO SCARED TO GO BACK, BUT THAT'S NOT IT.
SO YOU'RE SAYING THEY CAN'T BUY THE FILM OFF OF YOU BECAUSE THEIR MONEY COMES FROM ILLEGAL CONTRI-BUTIONS?
IT JUST PISSES ME OFF THAT THEY THINK MONEY CAN BUY ANYTHING.

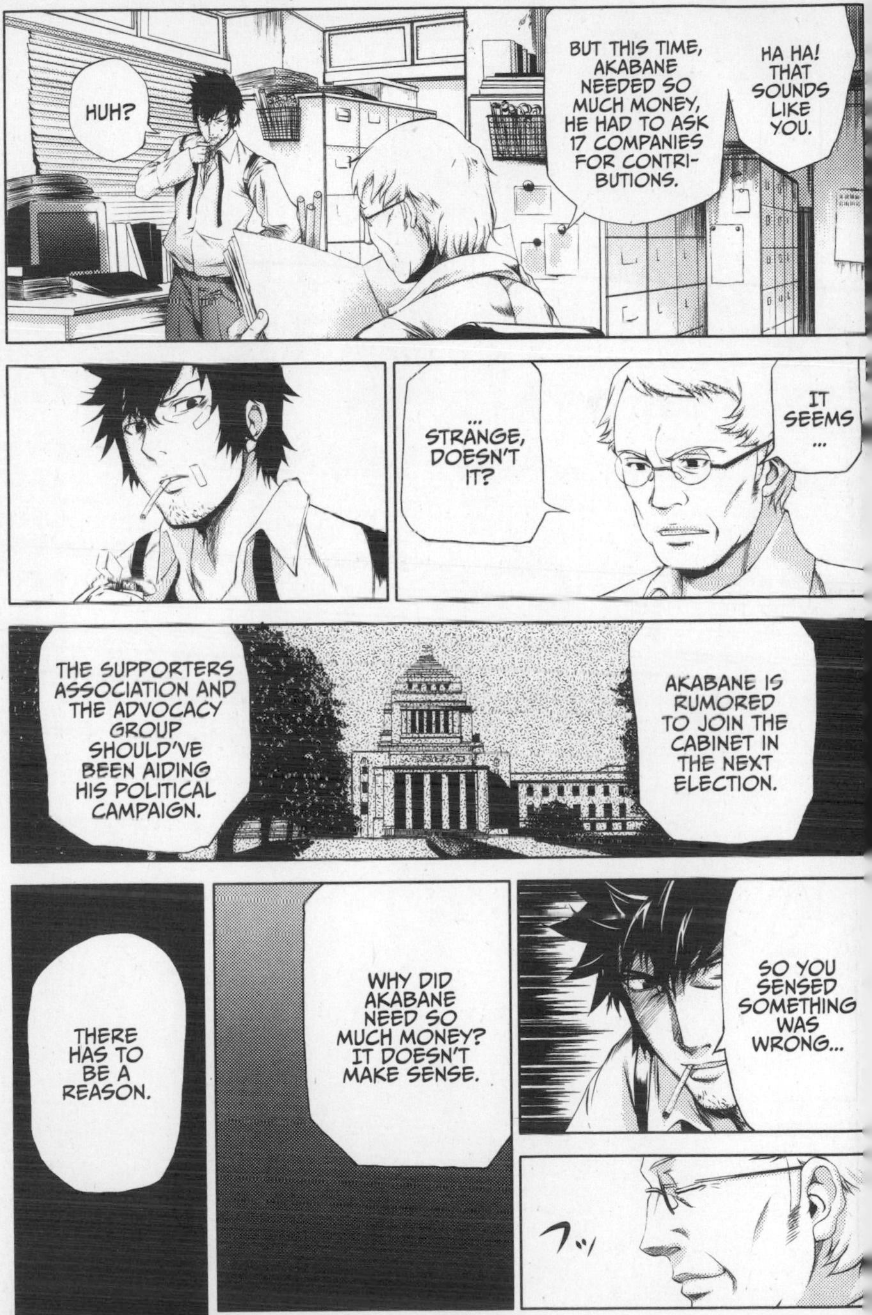
HA HA! THAT SOUNDS LIKE YOU.
BUT THIS TIME, AKABANE NEEDED SO MUCH MONEY, HE HAD TO ASK 17 COMPANIES FOR CONTRI-BUTIONS.
HUH?
IT SEEMS ...
... STRANGE, DOESN'T IT?
AKABANE IS RUMORED TO JOIN THE CABINET IN THE NEXT ELECTION.
THE SUPPORTERS ASSOCIATION AND THE ADVOCACY GROUP SHOULD'VE BEEN AIDING HIS POLITICAL CAMPAIGN.
SO YOU SENSED SOMETHING WAS WRONG...
フッ
WHY DID AKABANE NEED SO MUCH MONEY? IT DOESN'T MAKE SENSE.
THERE HAS TO BE A REASON.

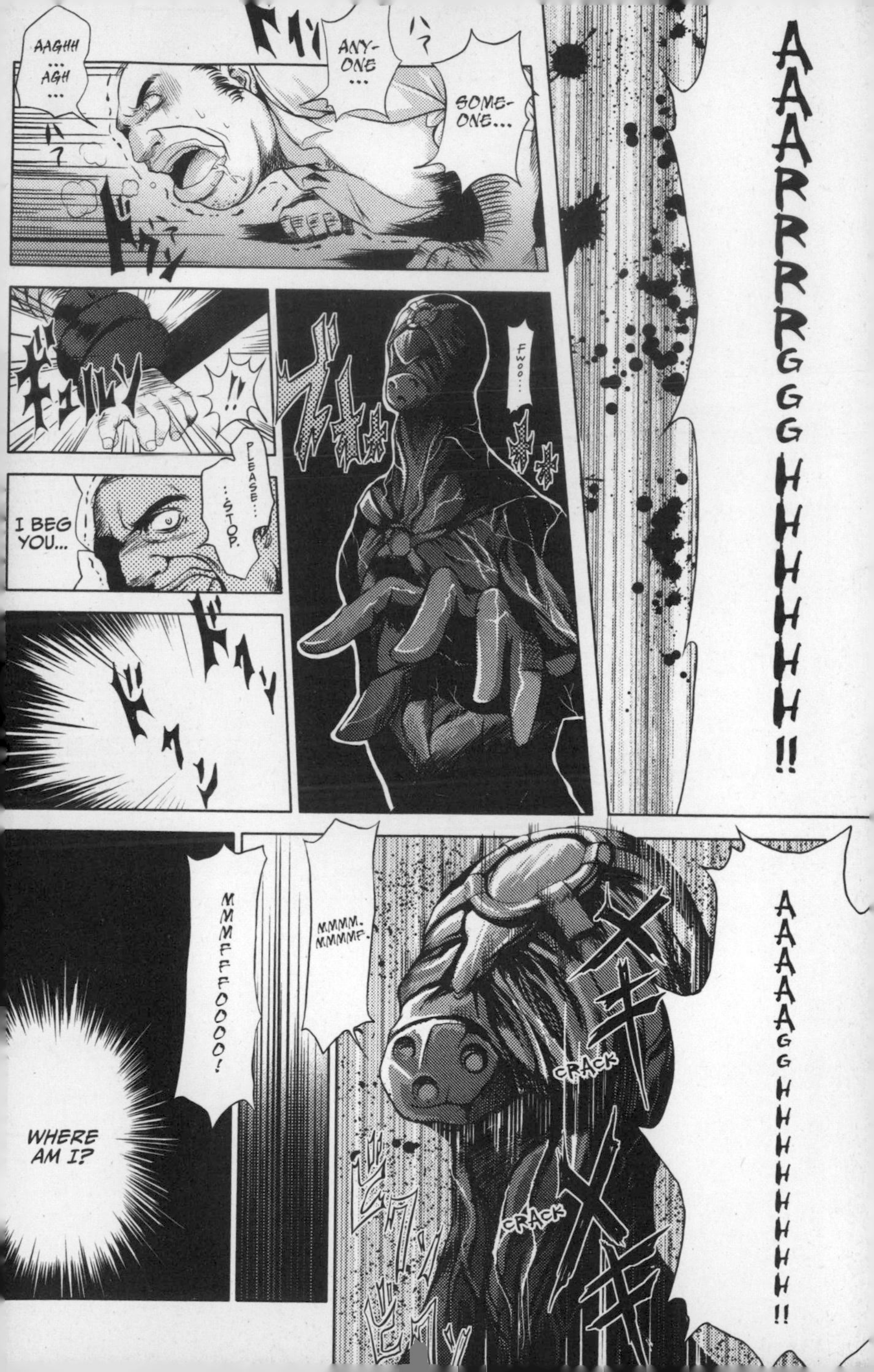
AAARRRRGGGHHHHHHHH!!
SOME-ONE...
ANY-ONE...
AAGHH... AGH...
FWOO...
!!
PLEASE... ...STOP.
I BEG YOU...
AAAAAGGHHHHHHHHH!!
CRACK
CRACK
MMMM. MMMMF.
MMMFFFOOOO!
WHERE AM I?

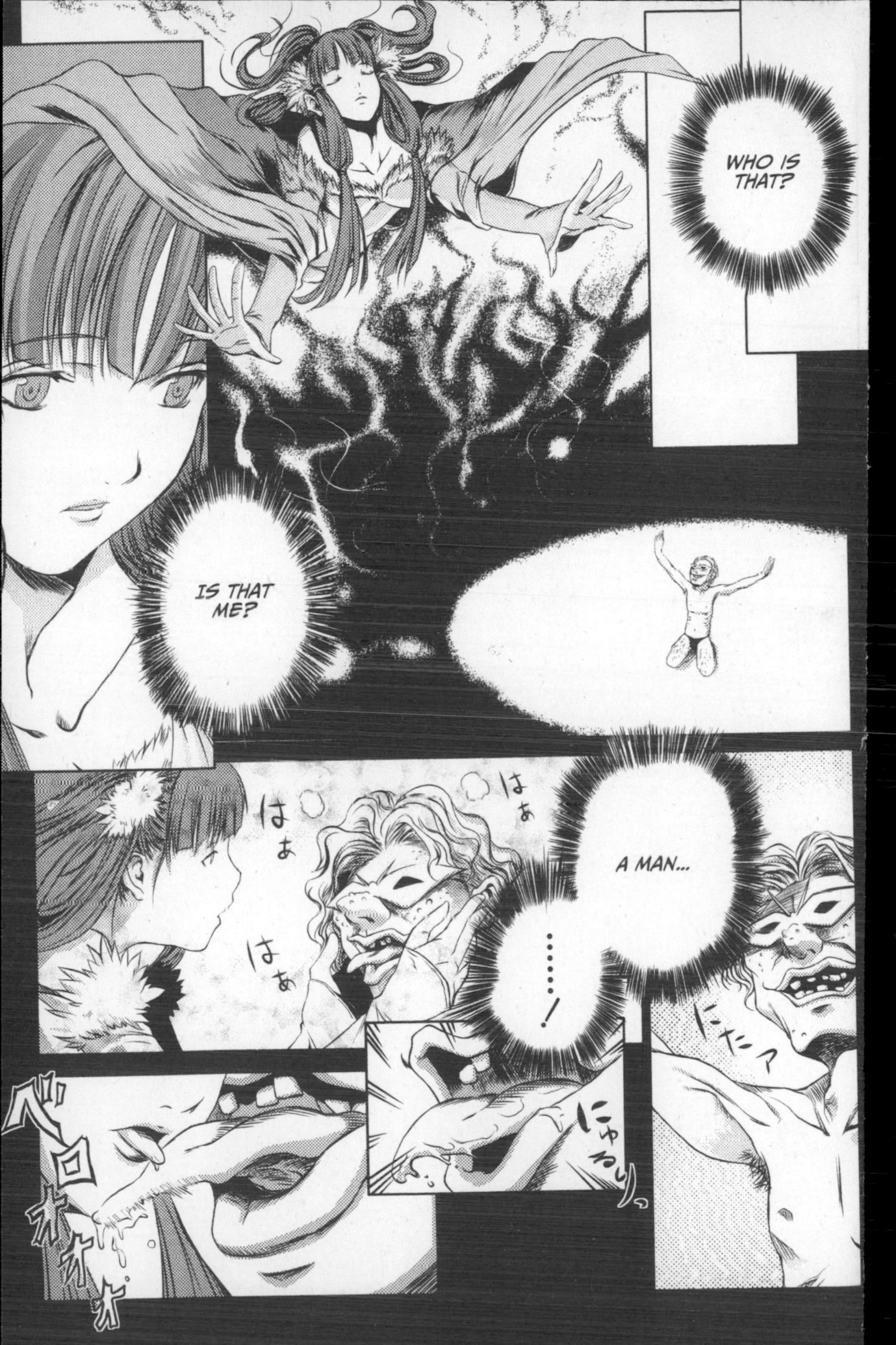
WHO IS THAT?
IS THAT ME?
A MAN...
.....!
はぁ
はぁ
はぁ
にゅるりっ

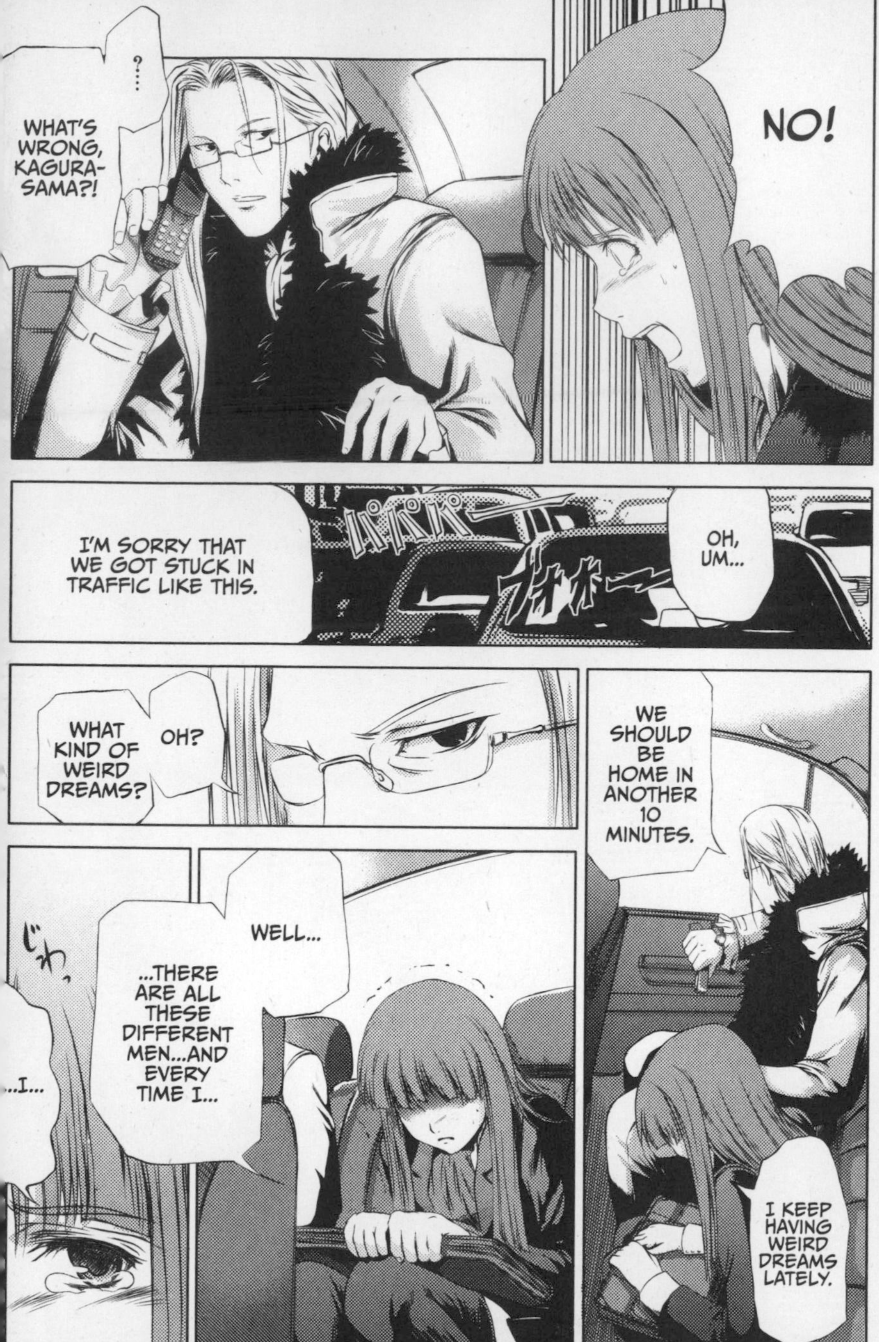
NO!
?.....
WHAT'S WRONG, KAGURA-SAMA?!
OH, UM...
パパパー
ブォオー
I'M SORRY THAT WE GOT STUCK IN TRAFFIC LIKE THIS.
WE SHOULD BE HOME IN ANOTHER 10 MINUTES.
I KEEP HAVING WEIRD DREAMS LATELY.
OH?
WHAT KIND OF WEIRD DREAMS?
WELL...
...THERE ARE ALL THESE DIFFERENT MEN...AND EVERY TIME I...
じわ
...I...

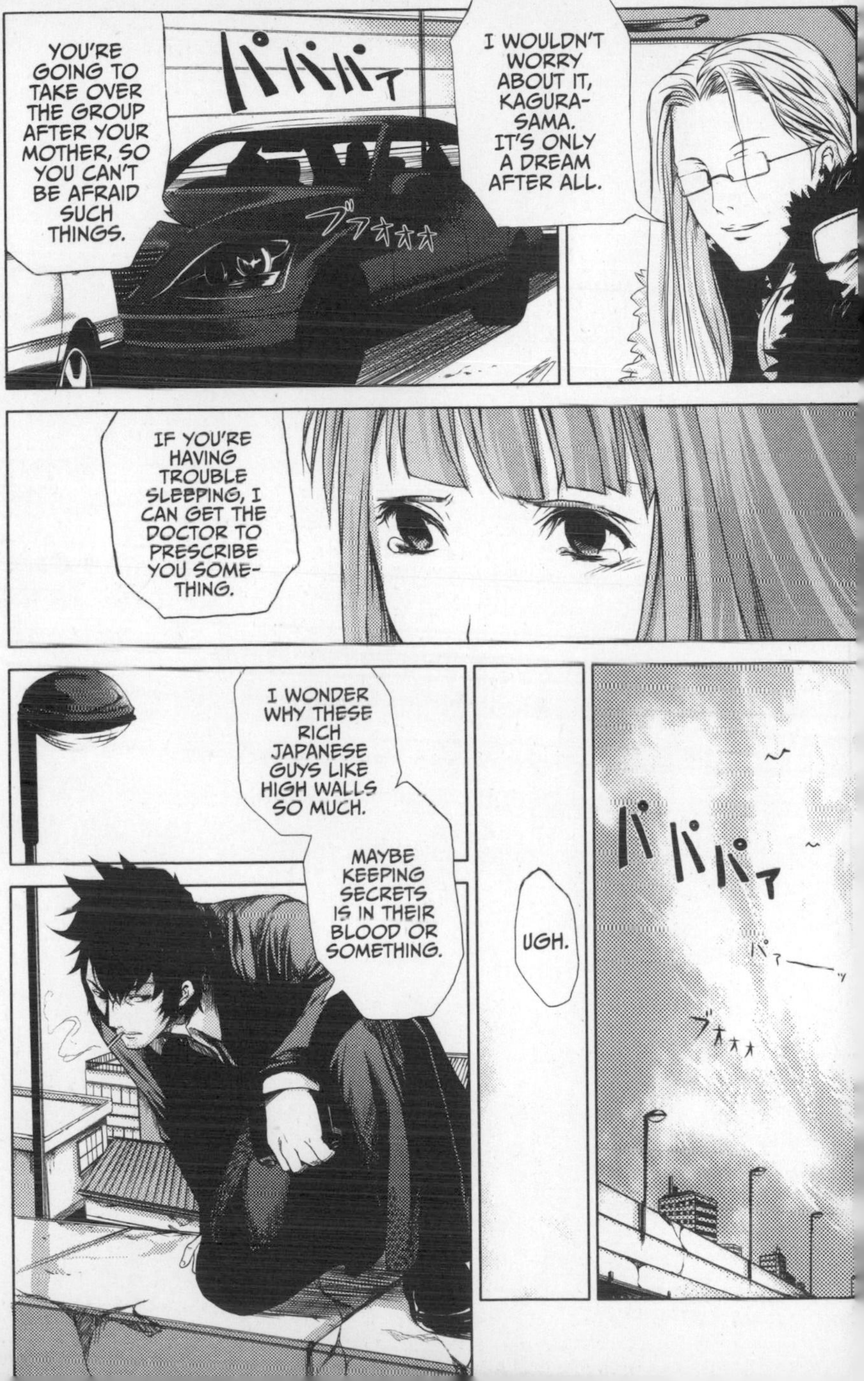
I WOULDN'T WORRY ABOUT IT, KAGURA-SAMA. IT'S ONLY A DREAM AFTER ALL.
パパパァ
ブァオオオ
YOU'RE GOING TO TAKE OVER THE GROUP AFTER YOUR MOTHER, SO YOU CAN'T BE AFRAID SUCH THINGS.
IF YOU'RE HAVING TROUBLE SLEEPING, I CAN GET THE DOCTOR TO PRESCRIBE YOU SOME-THING.
パパパァ
パァーーッ
ブォォォ
UGH.
I WONDER WHY THESE RICH JAPANESE GUYS LIKE HIGH WALLS SO MUCH.
MAYBE KEEPING SECRETS IS IN THEIR BLOOD OR SOMETHING.

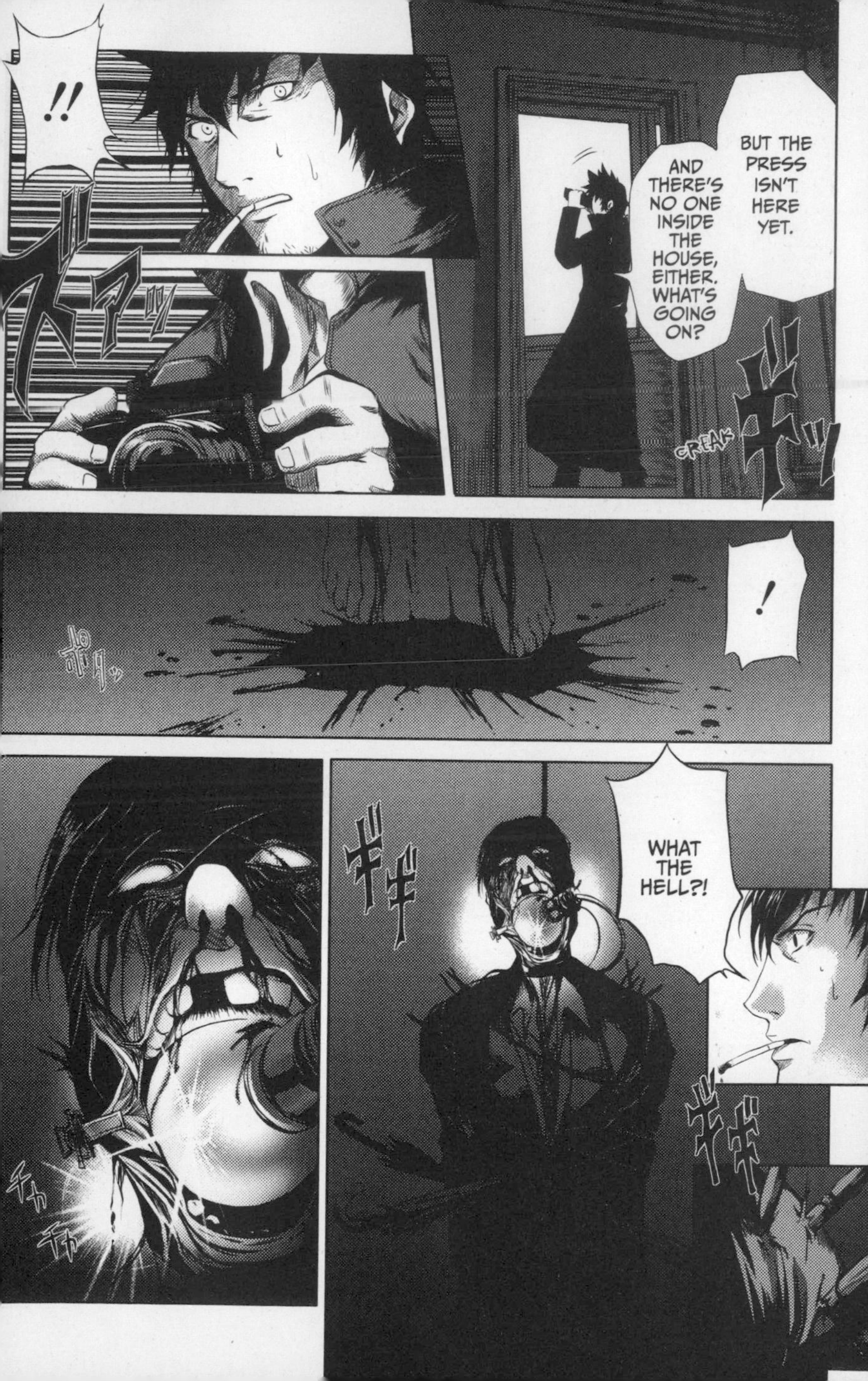
BUT THE PRESS ISN'T HERE YET.
AND THERE'S NO ONE INSIDE THE HOUSE, EITHER. WHAT'S GOING ON?
CREAK
!!
!
WHAT THE HELL?!

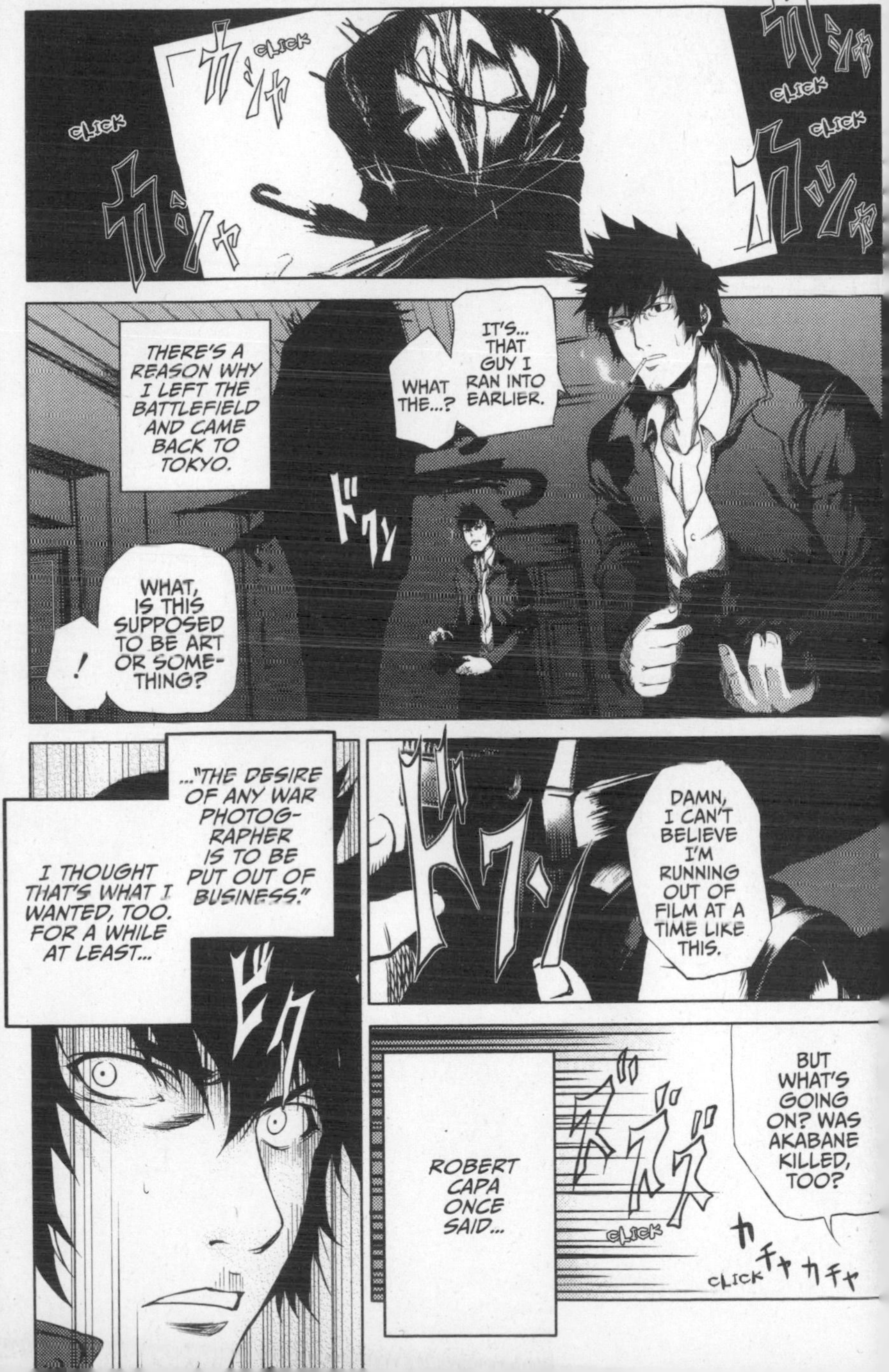
CLICK
CLICK
CLICK
CLICK
IT'S... THAT GUY I RAN INTO EARLIER.
WHAT THE...?
THERE'S A REASON WHY I LEFT THE BATTLEFIELD AND CAME BACK TO TOKYO.
WHAT, IS THIS SUPPOSED TO BE ART OR SOME-THING?
!
DAMN, I CAN'T BELIEVE I'M RUNNING OUT OF FILM AT A TIME LIKE THIS.
BUT WHAT'S GOING ON? WAS AKABANE KILLED, TOO?
CLICK
CLICK
ROBERT CAPA ONCE SAID...
..."THE DESIRE OF ANY WAR PHOTOG-RAPHER IS TO BE PUT OUT OF BUSINESS."
I THOUGHT THAT'S WHAT I WANTED, TOO. FOR A WHILE AT LEAST...

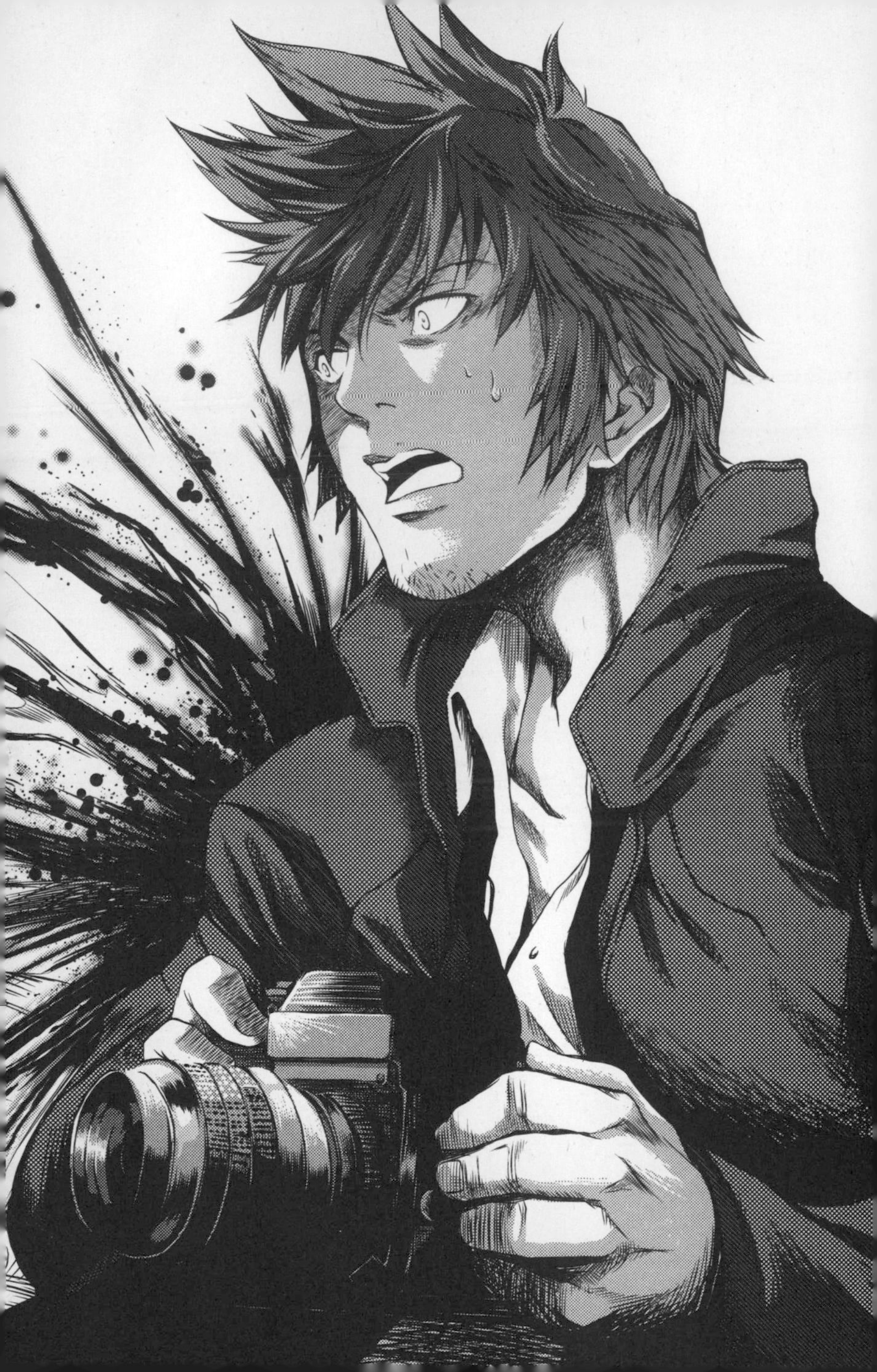

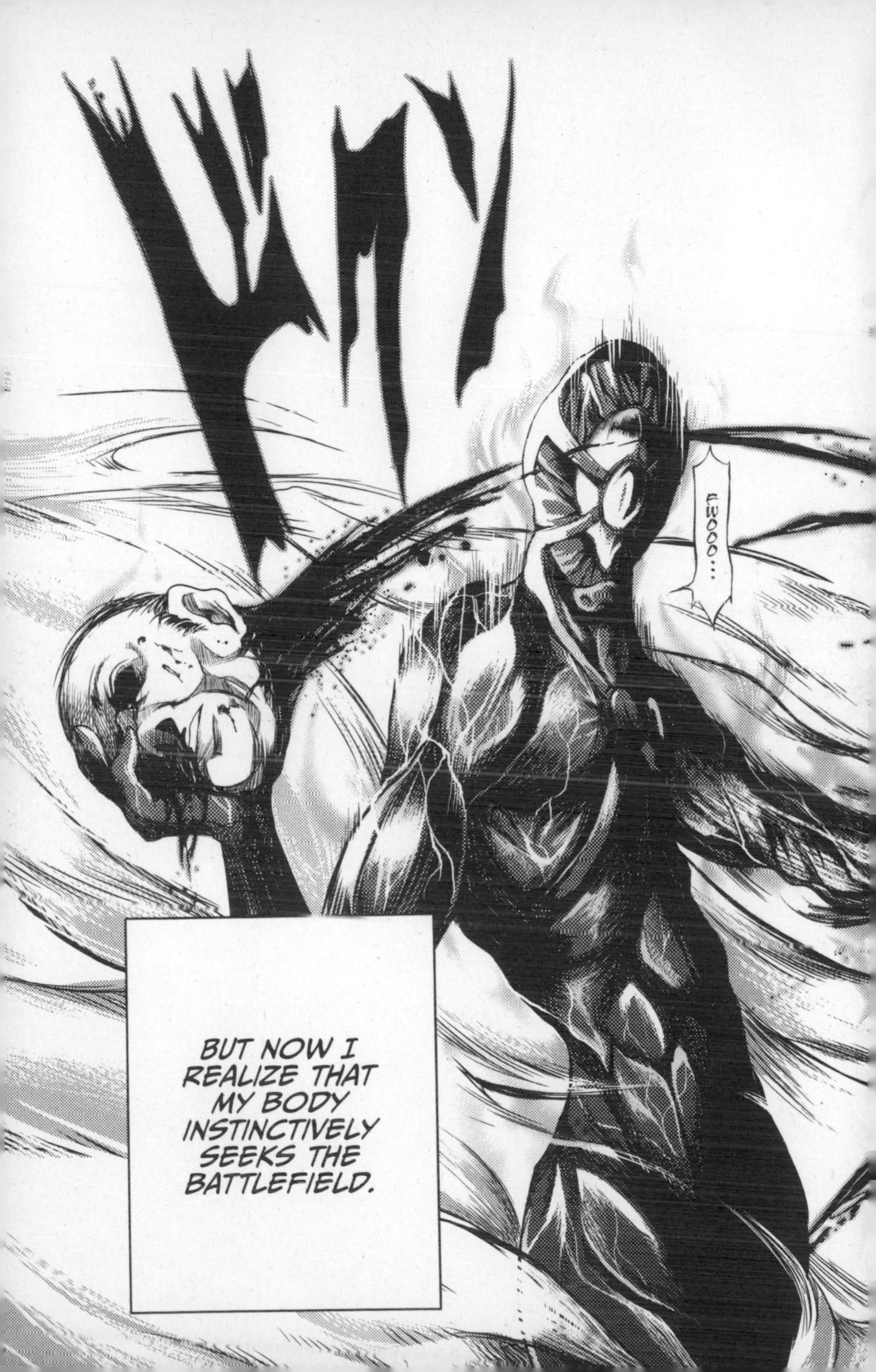
FWOOO...
BUT NOW I REALIZE THAT MY BODY INSTINCTIVELY SEEKS THE BATTLEFIELD.

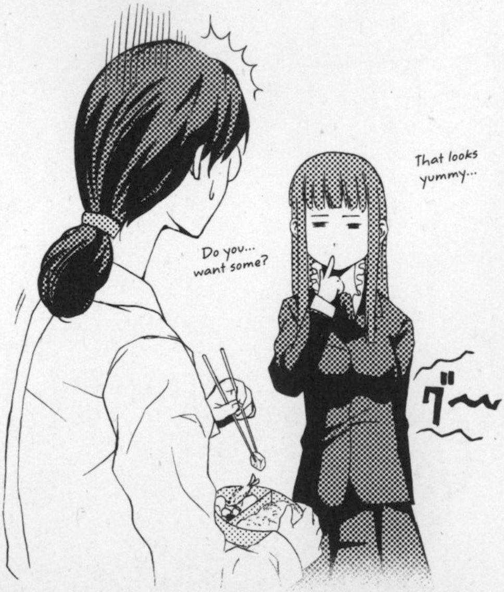
That looks yummy...
グ～
Do you... want some?

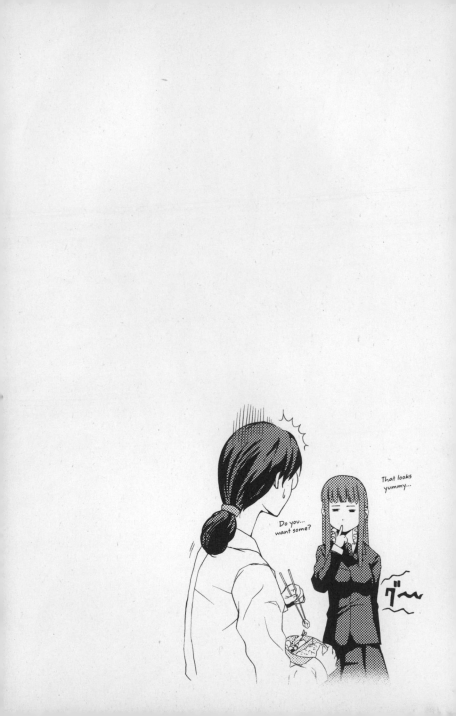

Shutter: 2
Shutter Chance

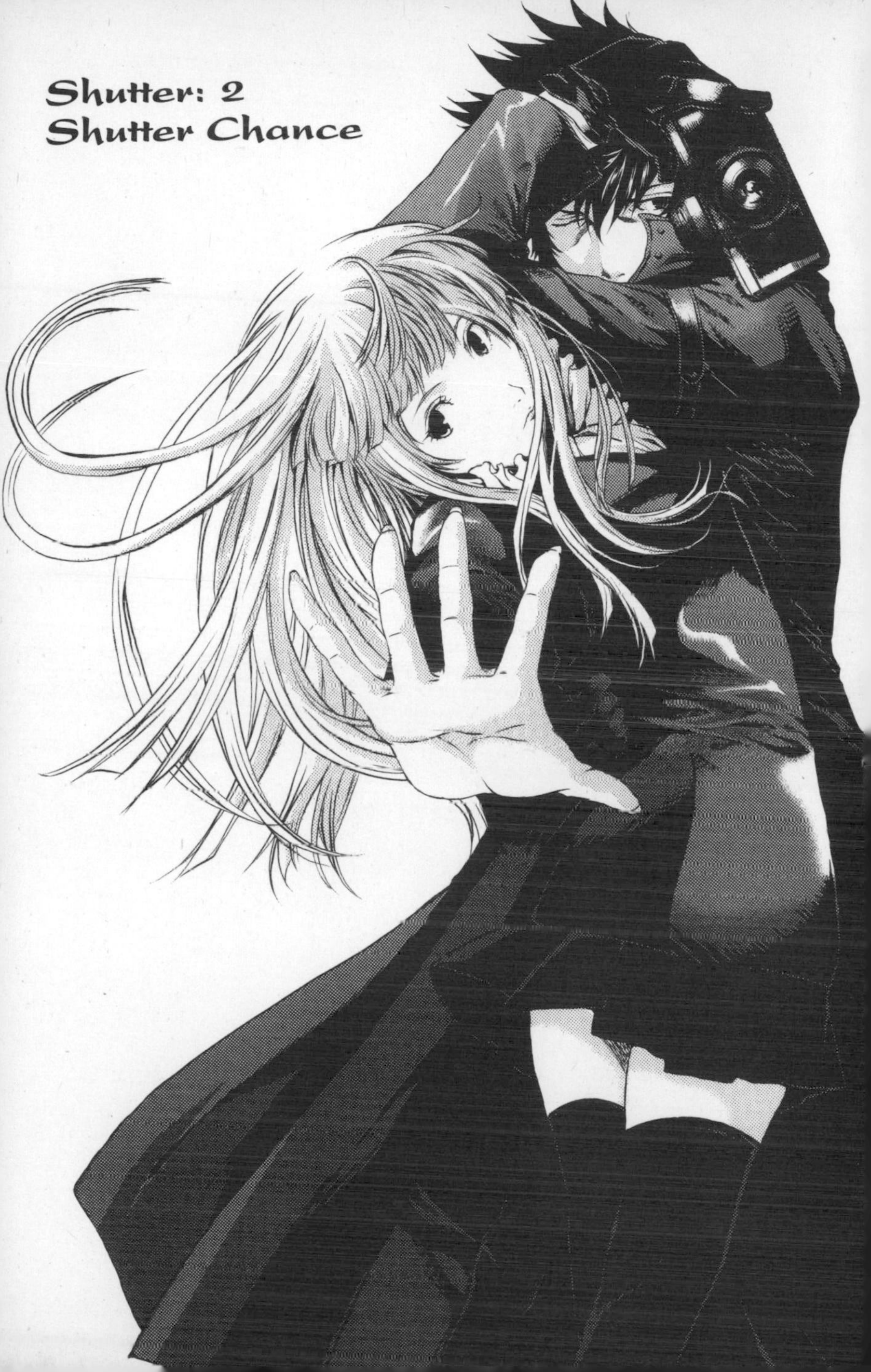

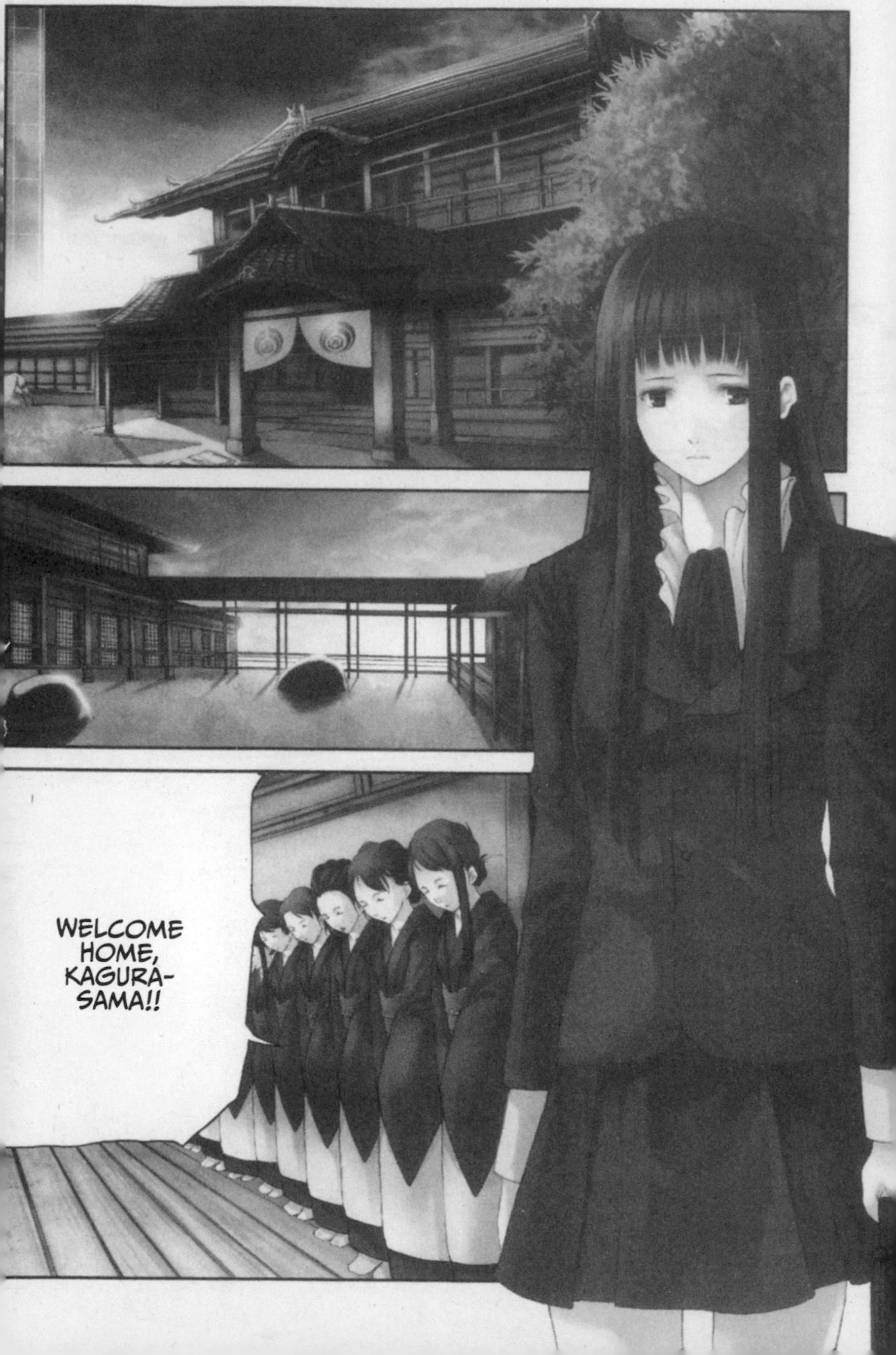
WELCOME HOME, KAGURA-SAMA!!

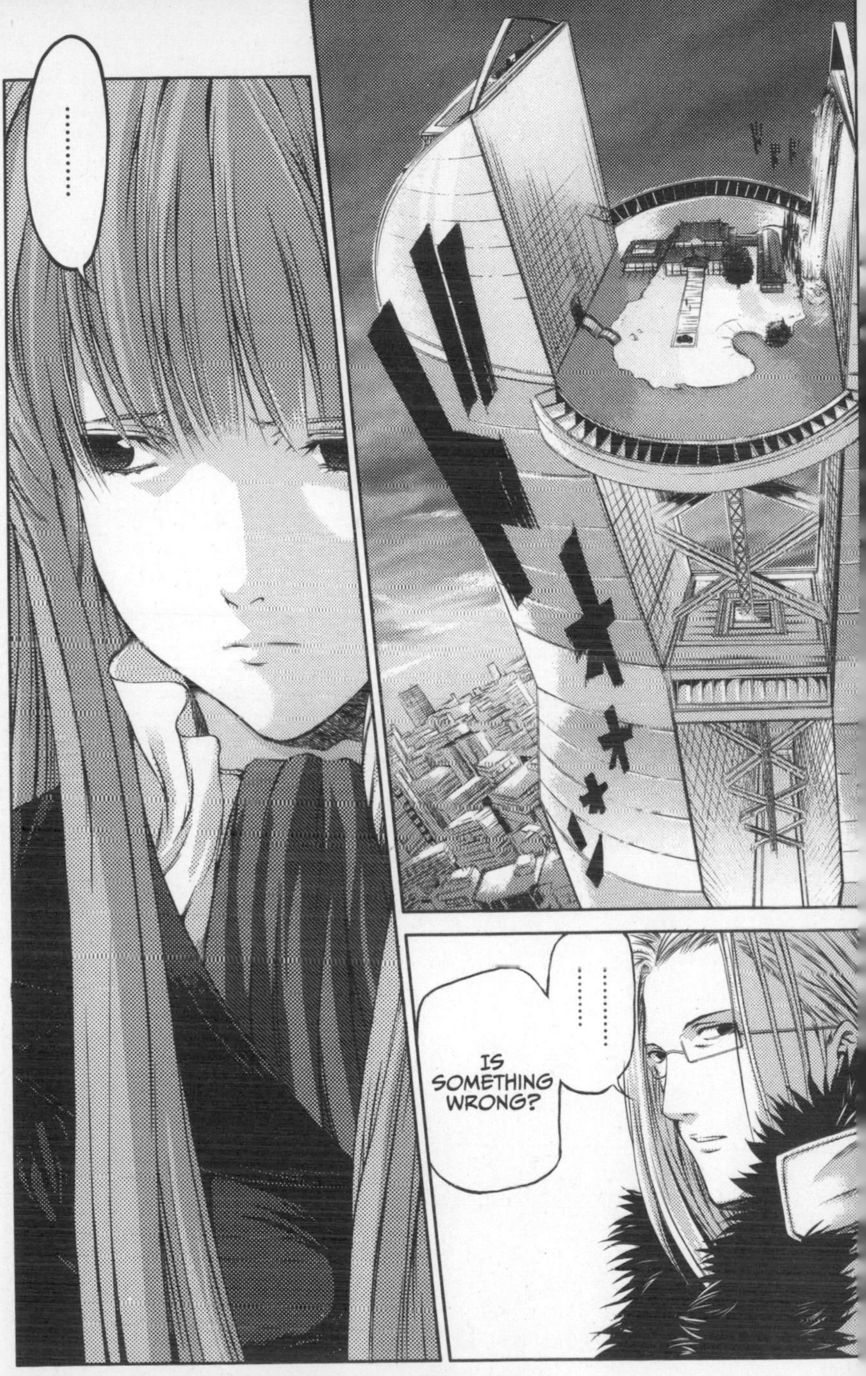
......
IS SOMETHING WRONG?
......

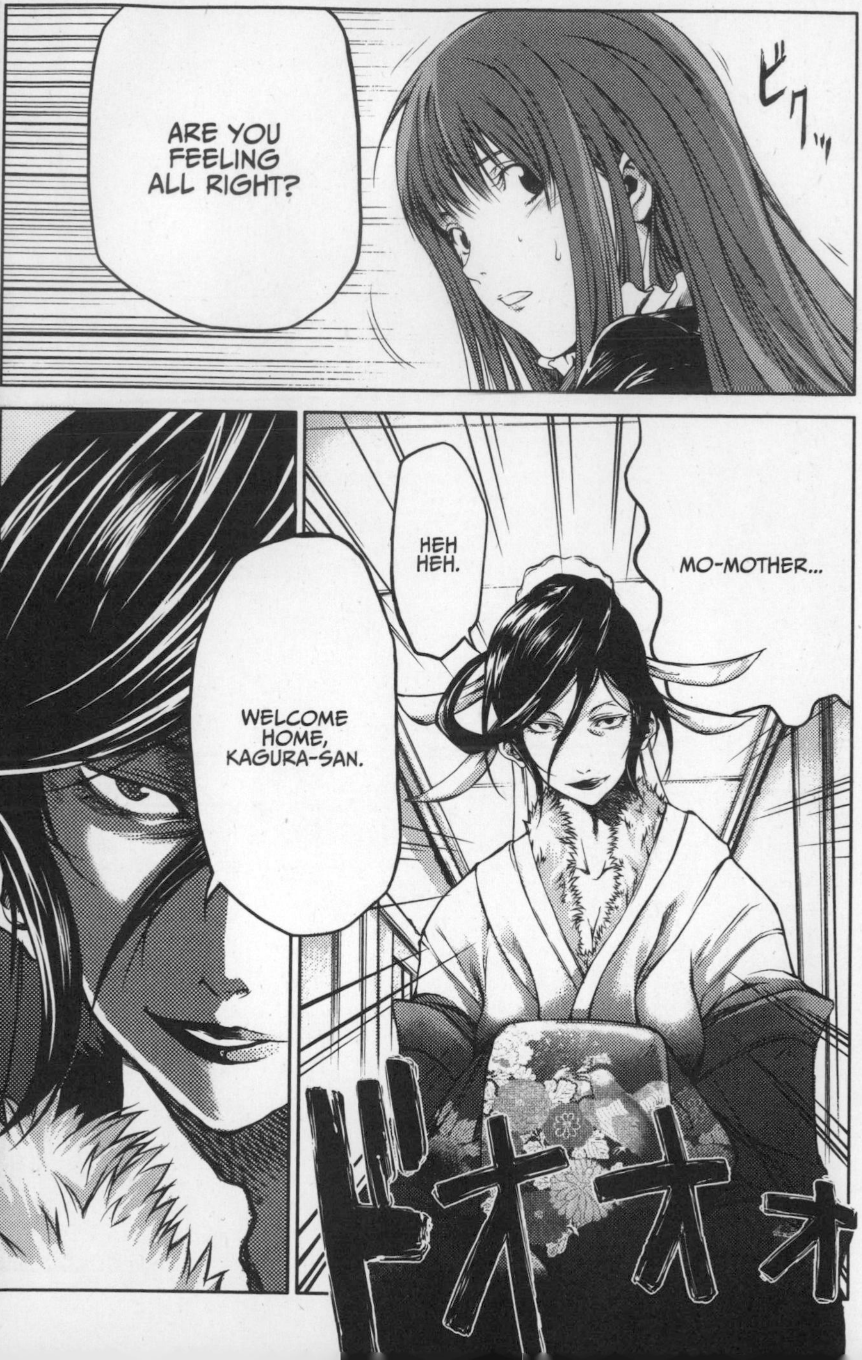
ビクッ
ARE YOU FEELING ALL RIGHT?
MO-MOTHER...
HEH HEH.
WELCOME HOME, KAGURA-SAN.
ドオオォ

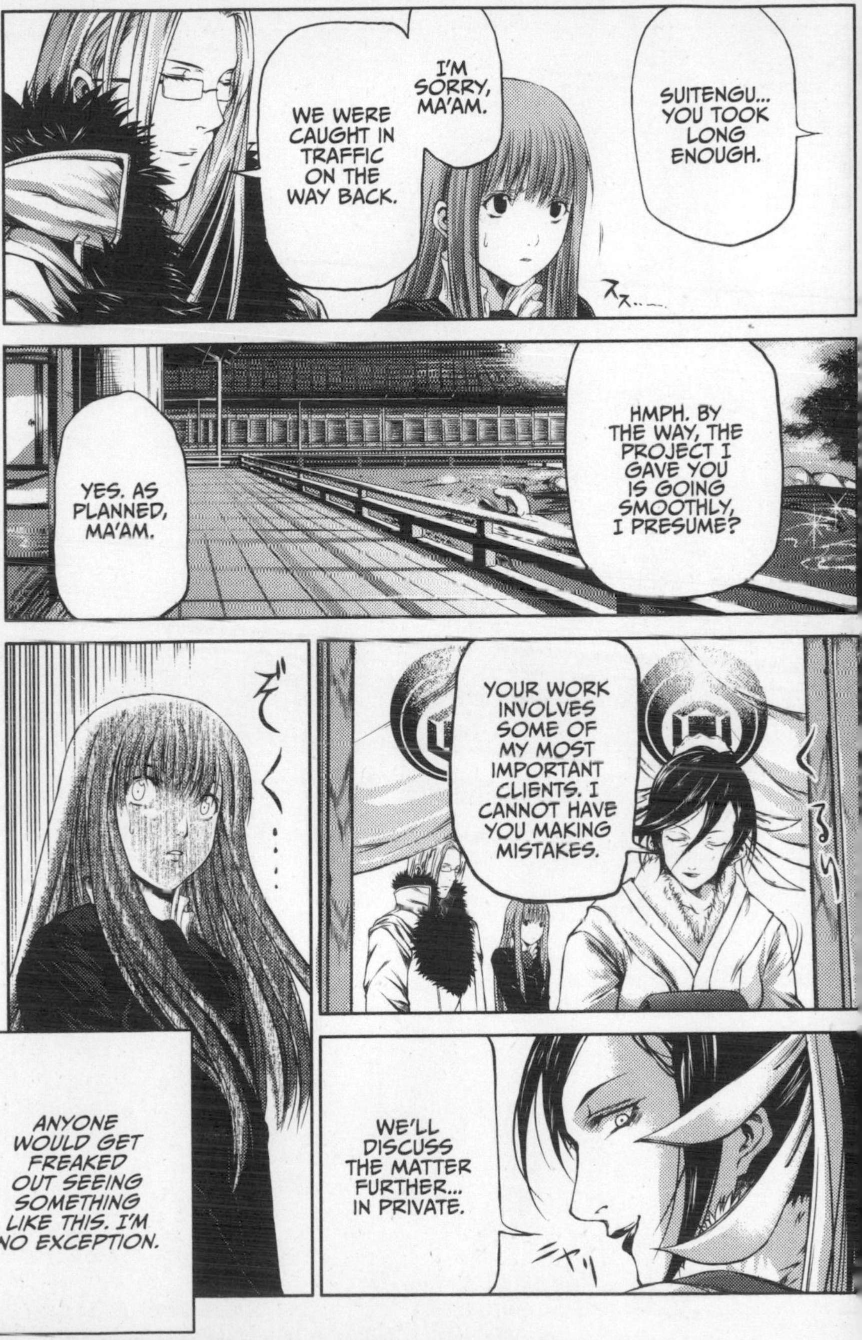
SUITENGU... YOU TOOK LONG ENOUGH.
I'M SORRY, MA'AM.
WE WERE CAUGHT IN TRAFFIC ON THE WAY BACK.
HMPH. BY THE WAY, THE PROJECT I GAVE YOU IS GOING SMOOTHLY, I PRESUME?
YES. AS PLANNED, MA'AM.
YOUR WORK INVOLVES SOME OF MY MOST IMPORTANT CLIENTS. I CANNOT HAVE YOU MAKING MISTAKES.
WE'LL DISCUSS THE MATTER FURTHER... IN PRIVATE.
ANYONE WOULD GET FREAKED OUT SEEING SOMETHING LIKE THIS. I'M NO EXCEPTION.

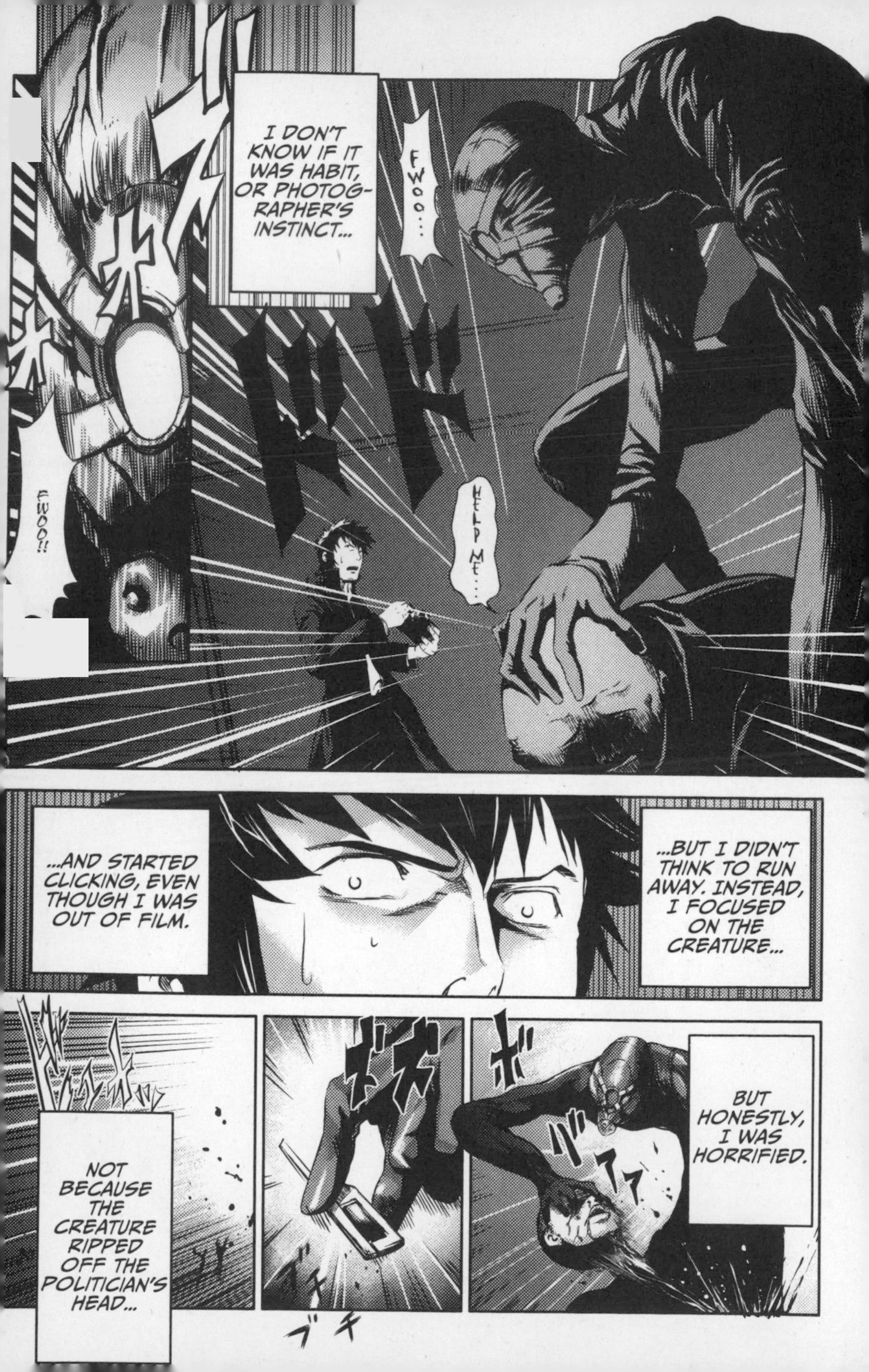
I DON'T KNOW IF IT WAS HABIT, OR PHOTOG-RAPHER'S INSTINCT...
FWOO...
HELP ME...
FWOO!!
...BUT I DIDN'T THINK TO RUN AWAY. INSTEAD, I FOCUSED ON THE CREATURE...
...AND STARTED CLICKING, EVEN THOUGH I WAS OUT OF FILM.
BUT HONESTLY, I WAS HORRIFIED.
NOT BECAUSE THE CREATURE RIPPED OFF THE POLITICIAN'S HEAD...

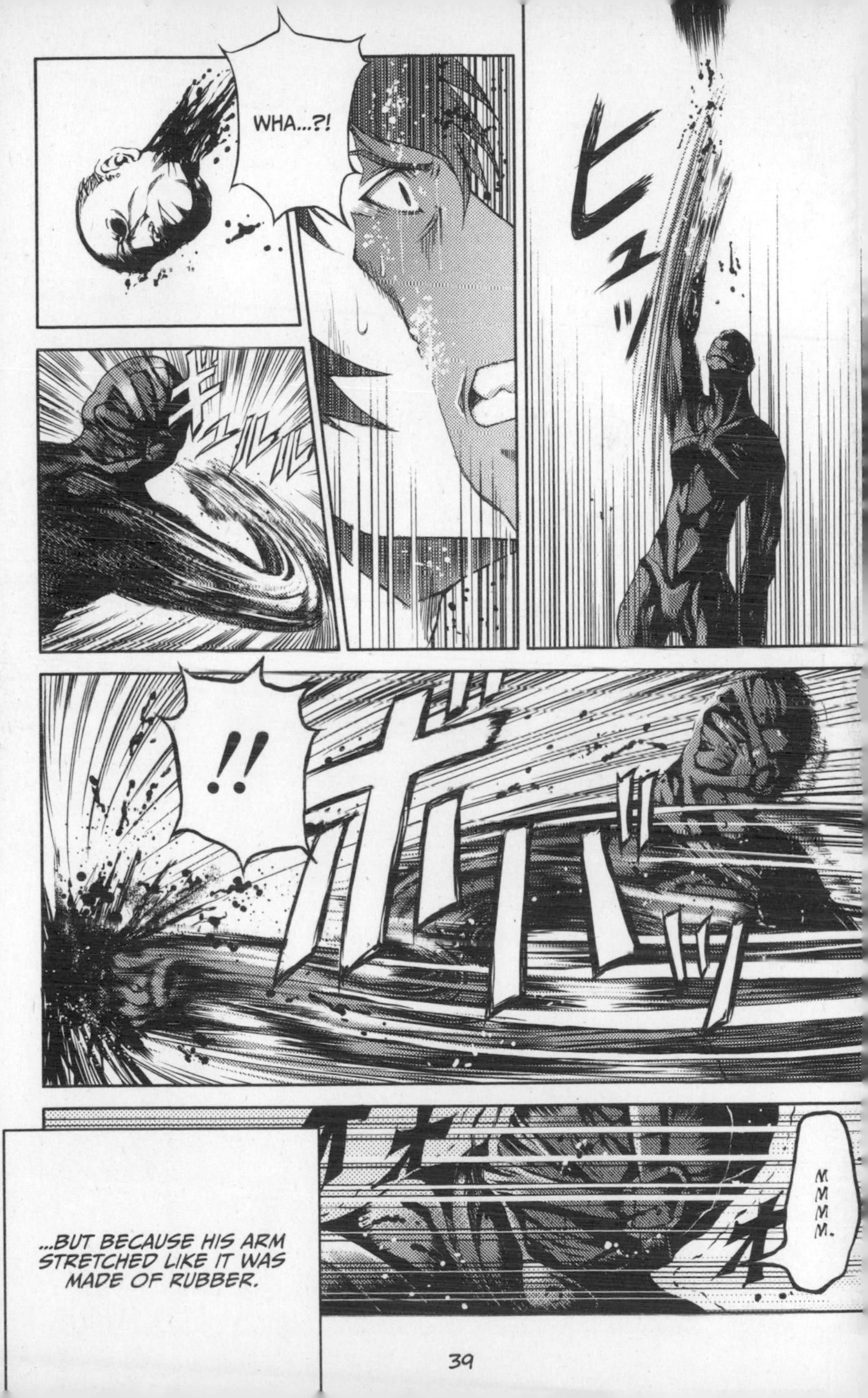
WHA...?!
!!
MMMM.
...BUT BECAUSE HIS ARM STRETCHED LIKE IT WAS MADE OF RUBBER.

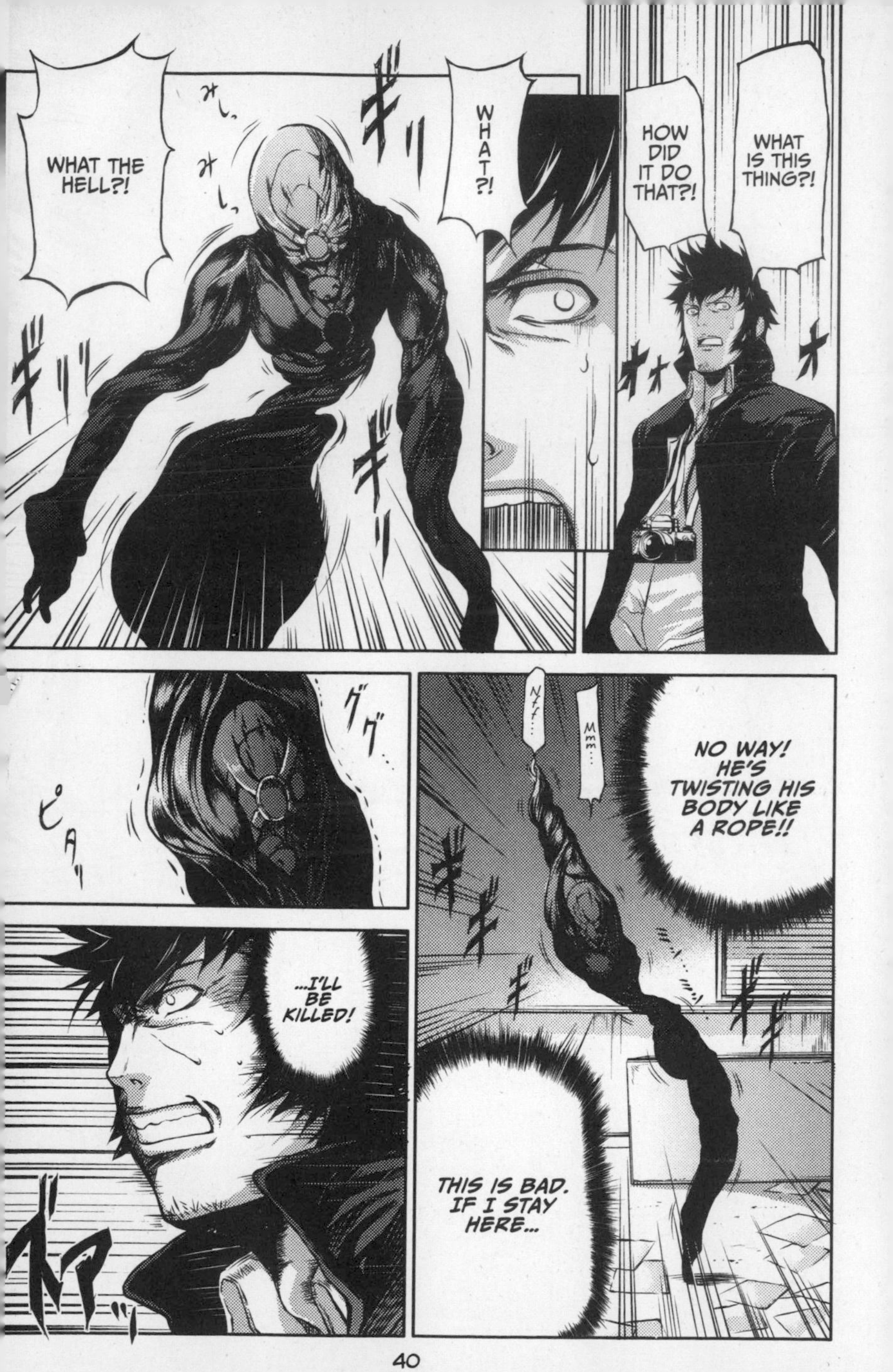
WHAT IS THIS THING?!
HOW DID IT DO THAT?!
WHAT?!
WHAT THE HELL?!
Mmm...
Nff...
NO WAY! HE'S TWISTING HIS BODY LIKE A ROPE!!
THIS IS BAD. IF I STAY HERE...
...I'LL BE KILLED!

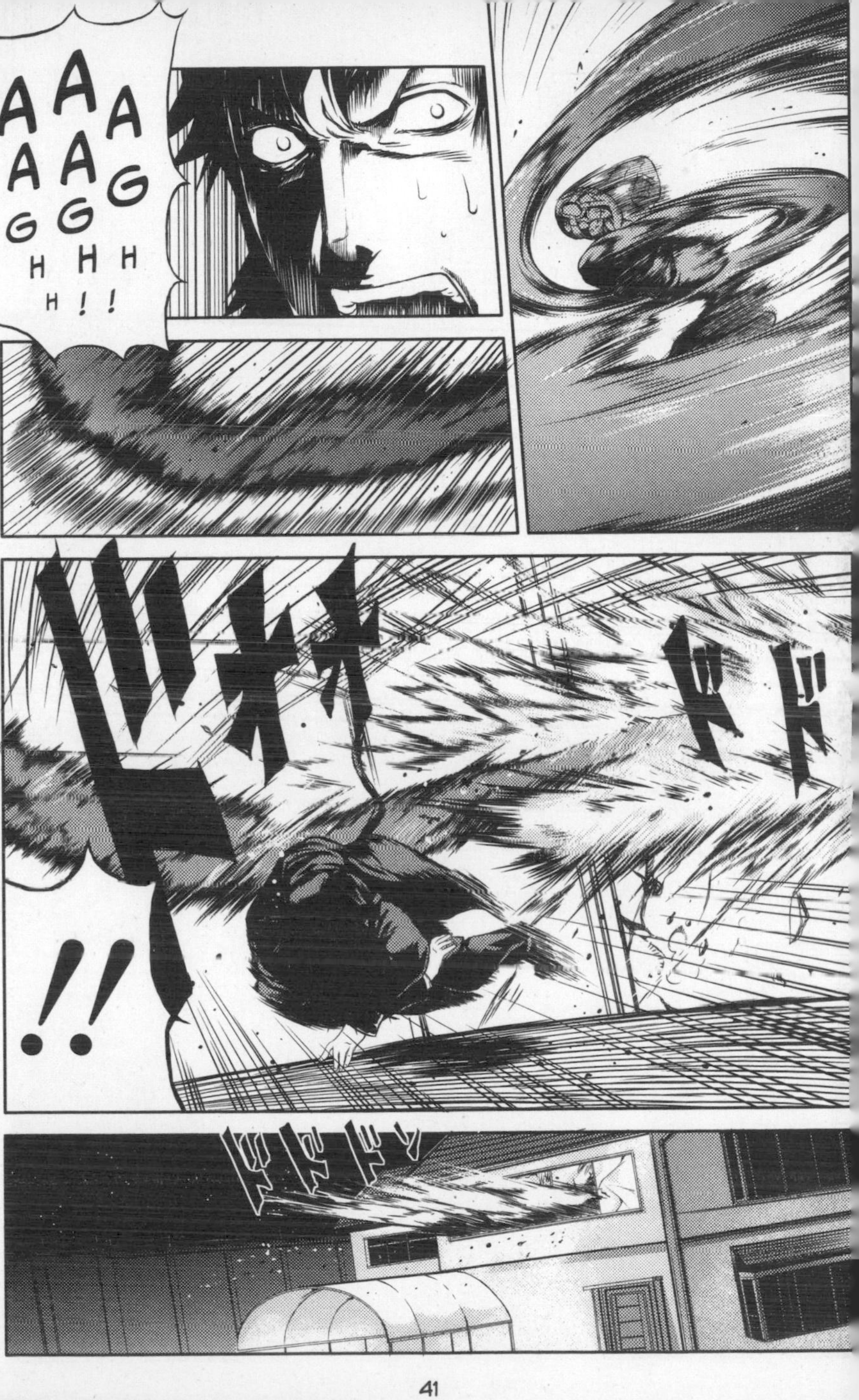
AAAAAGGGHHHH!!
!!

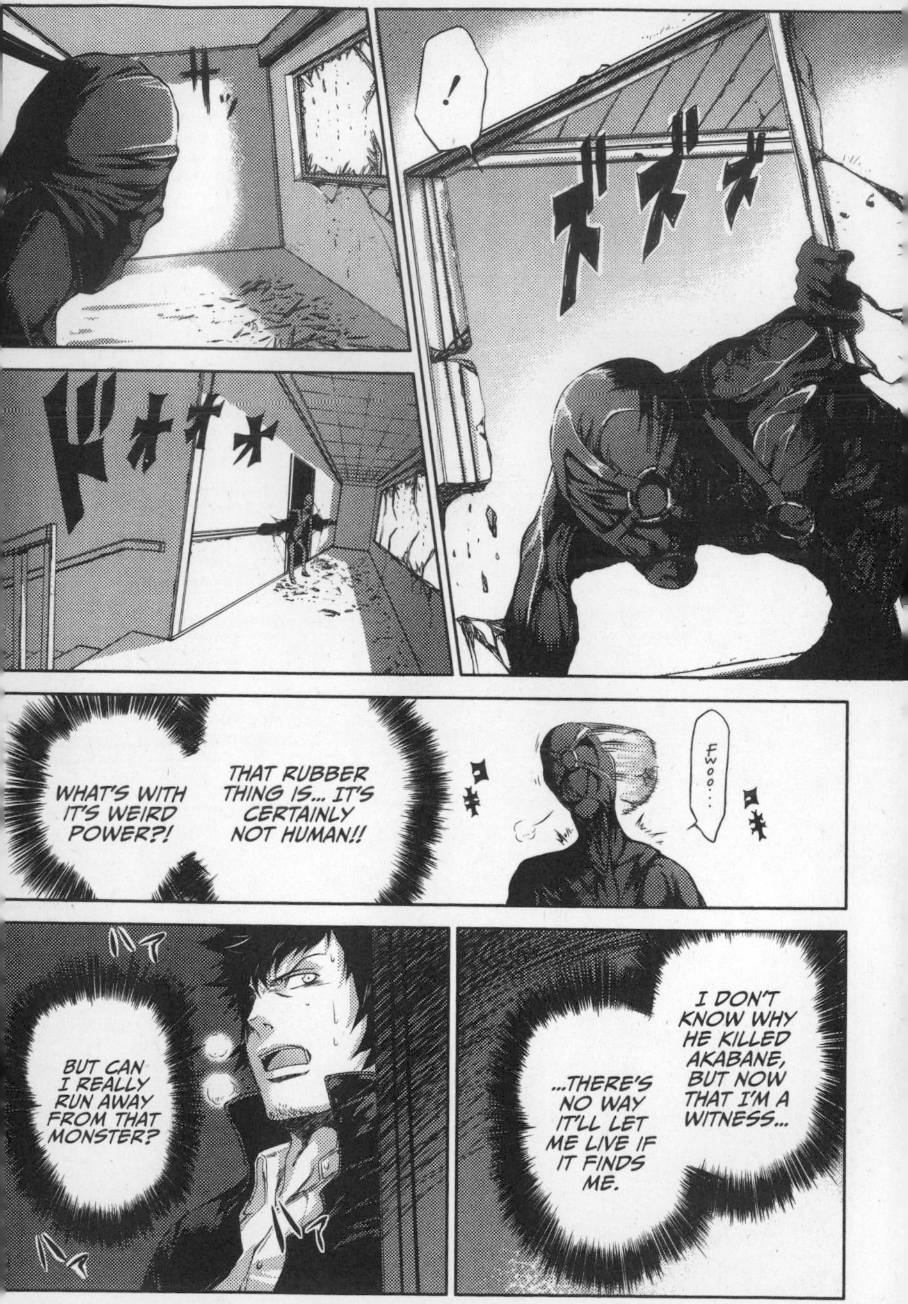
!
Fwoo...
THAT RUBBER THING IS... IT'S CERTAINLY NOT HUMAN!!
WHAT'S WITH IT'S WEIRD POWER?!
I DON'T KNOW WHY HE KILLED AKABANE, BUT NOW THAT I'M A WITNESS...
...THERE'S NO WAY IT'LL LET ME LIVE IF IT FINDS ME.
BUT CAN I REALLY RUN AWAY FROM THAT MONSTER?

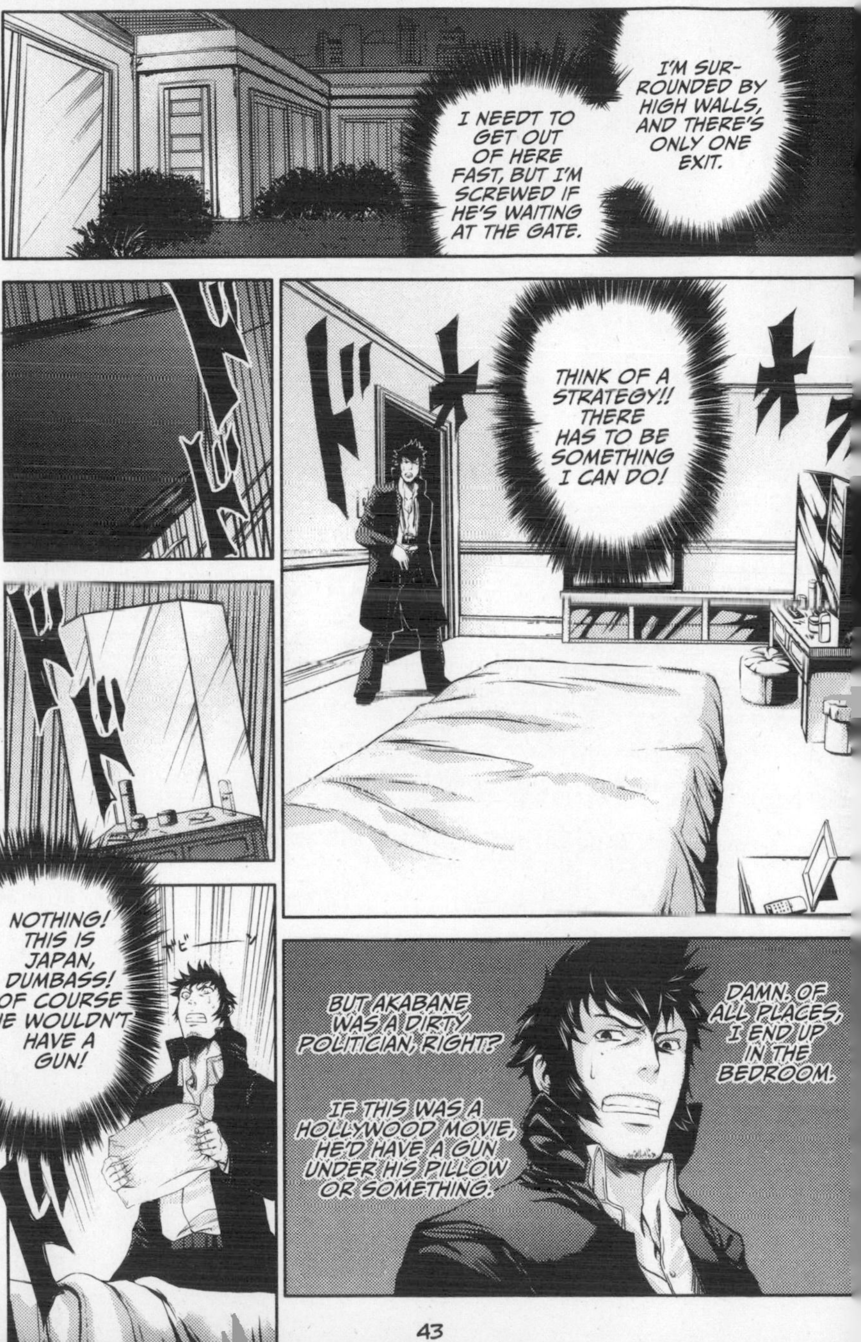
I'M SUR-ROUNDED BY HIGH WALLS, AND THERE'S ONLY ONE EXIT.
I NEEDT TO GET OUT OF HERE FAST, BUT I'M SCREWED IF HE'S WAITING AT THE GATE.
THINK OF A STRATEGY!! THERE HAS TO BE SOMETHING I CAN DO!
DAMN. OF ALL PLACES, I END UP IN THE BEDROOM.
BUT AKABANE WAS A DIRTY POLITICIAN, RIGHT?
IF THIS WAS A HOLLYWOOD MOVIE, HE'D HAVE A GUN UNDER HIS PILLOW OR SOMETHING.
NOTHING! THIS IS JAPAN, DUMBASS! OF COURSE HE WOULDN'T HAVE A GUN!

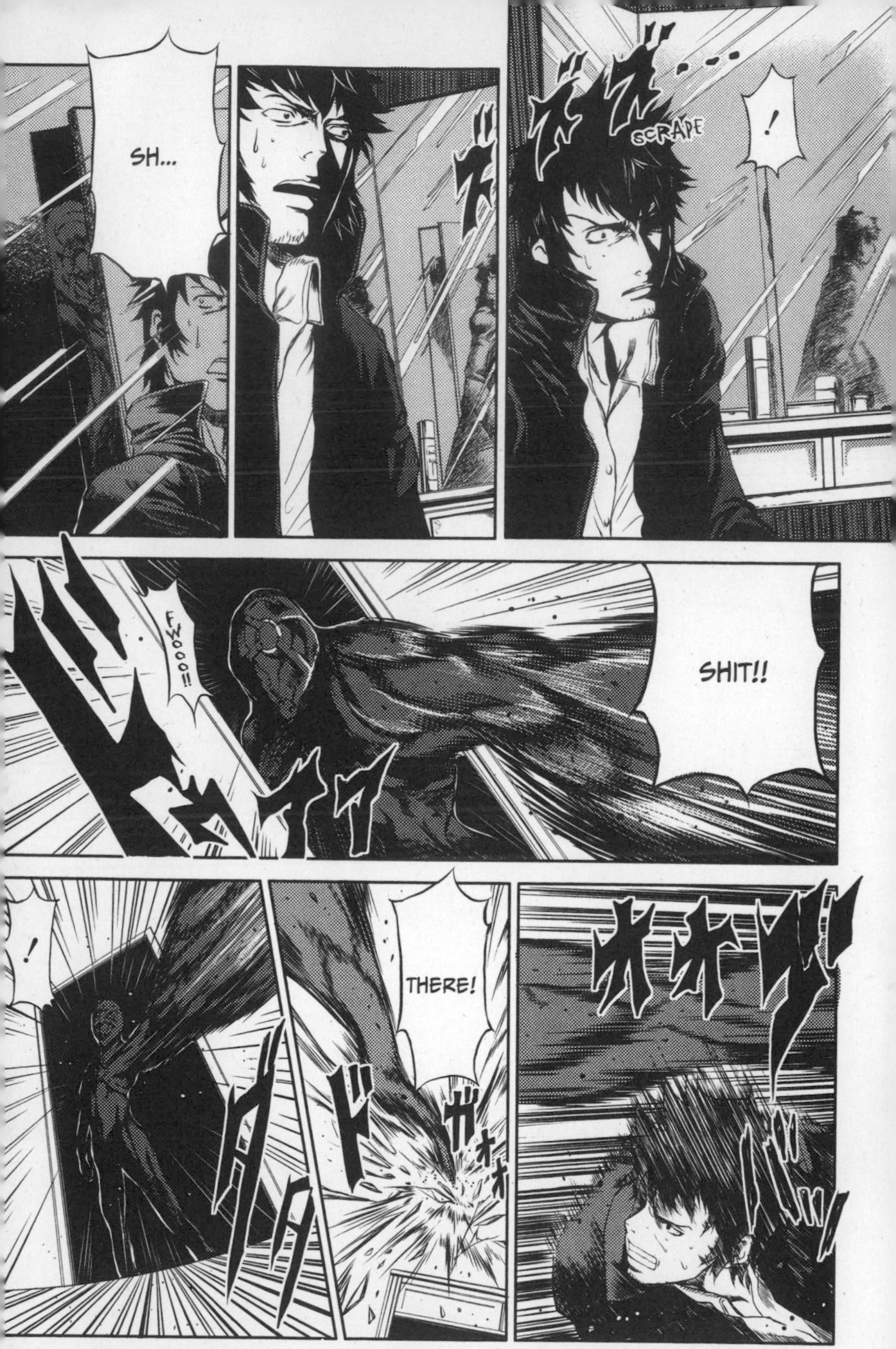

!
SCRAPE
SH...
SHIT!!
FWOOOO!!
THERE!
!

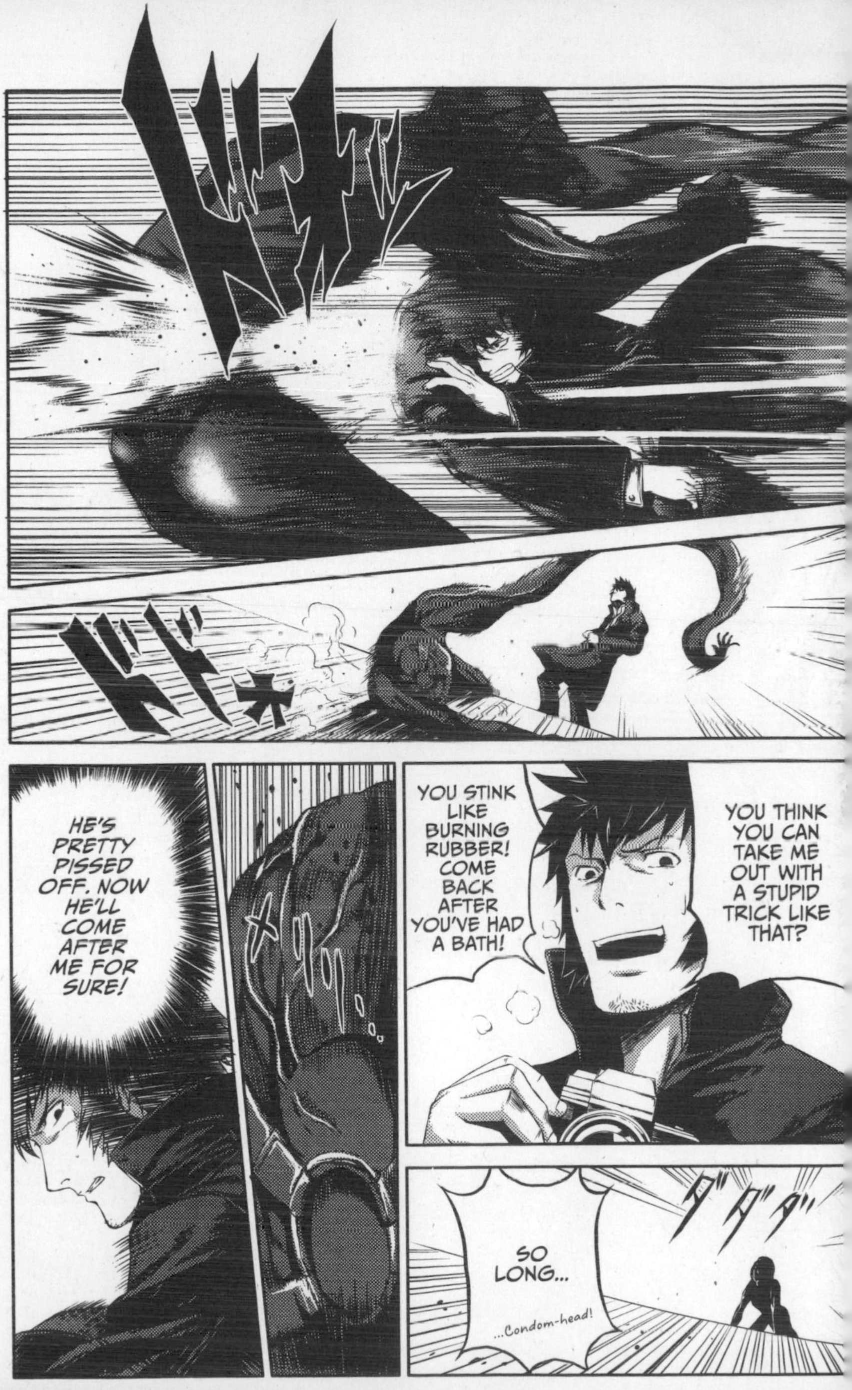
YOU THINK YOU CAN TAKE ME OUT WITH A STUPID TRICK LIKE THAT?
YOU STINK LIKE BURNING RUBBER! COME BACK AFTER YOU'VE HAD A BATH!
SO LONG...
...Condom-head!
HE'S PRETTY PISSED OFF. NOW HE'LL COME AFTER ME FOR SURE!

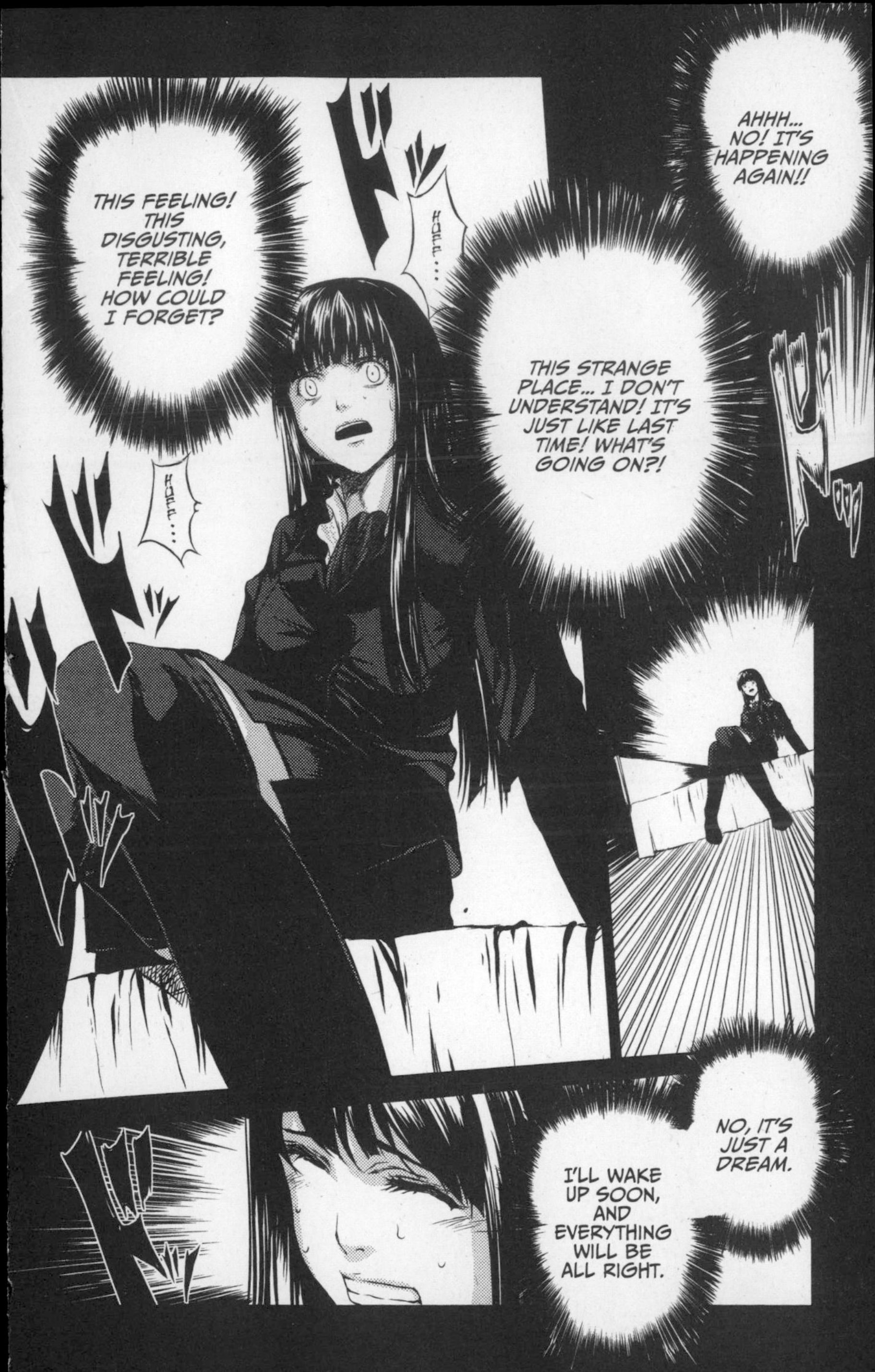
AHHH... NO! IT'S HAPPENING AGAIN!!
THIS STRANGE PLACE... I DON'T UNDERSTAND! IT'S JUST LIKE LAST TIME! WHAT'S GOING ON?!
HUFF...
THIS FEELING! THIS DISGUSTING, TERRIBLE FEELING! HOW COULD I FORGET?
HUFF...
NO, IT'S JUST A DREAM.
I'LL WAKE UP SOON, AND EVERYTHING WILL BE ALL RIGHT.

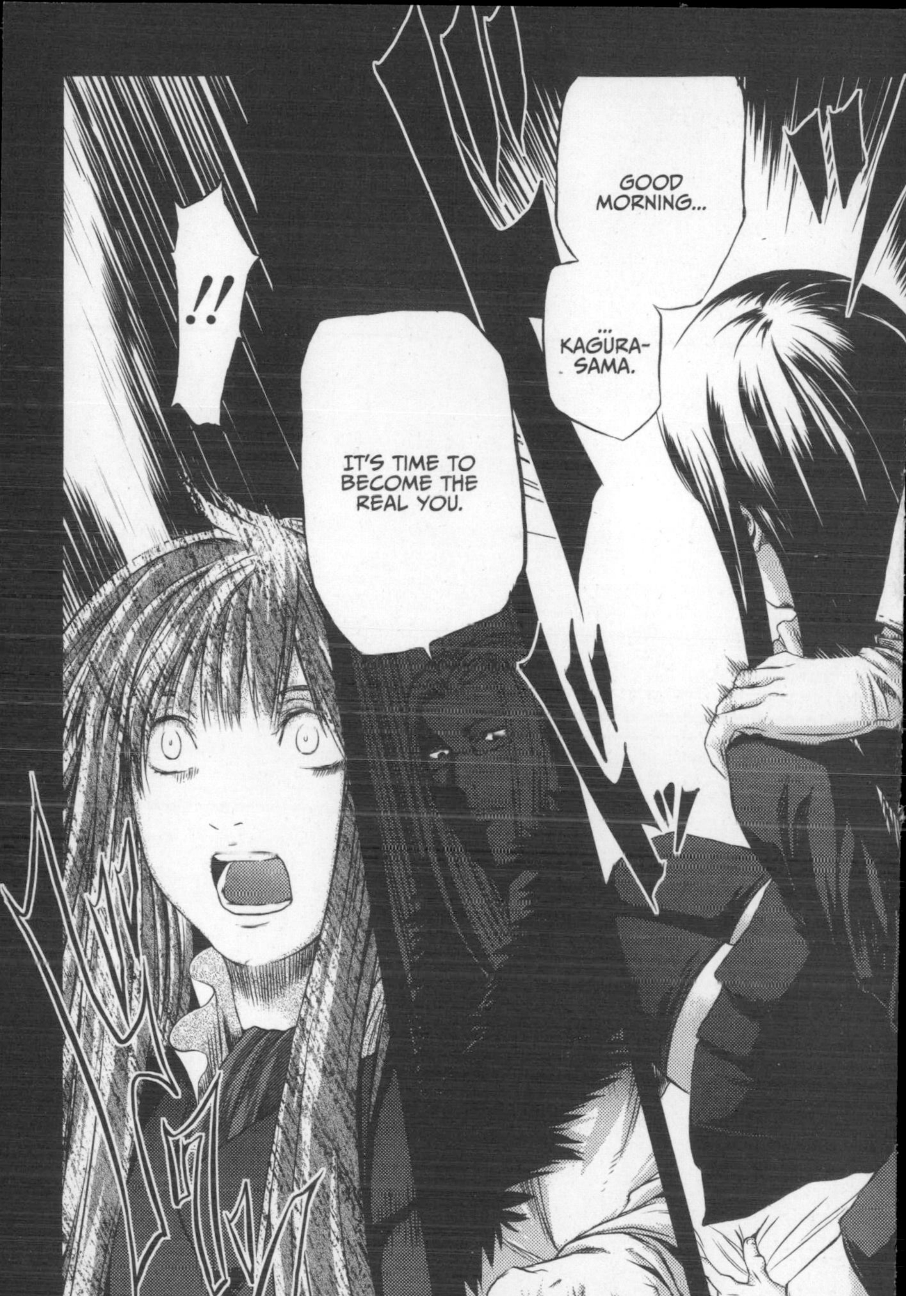
GOOD MORNING...
...KAGÜRA-SAMA.
IT'S TIME TO BECOME THE REAL YOU.
!!

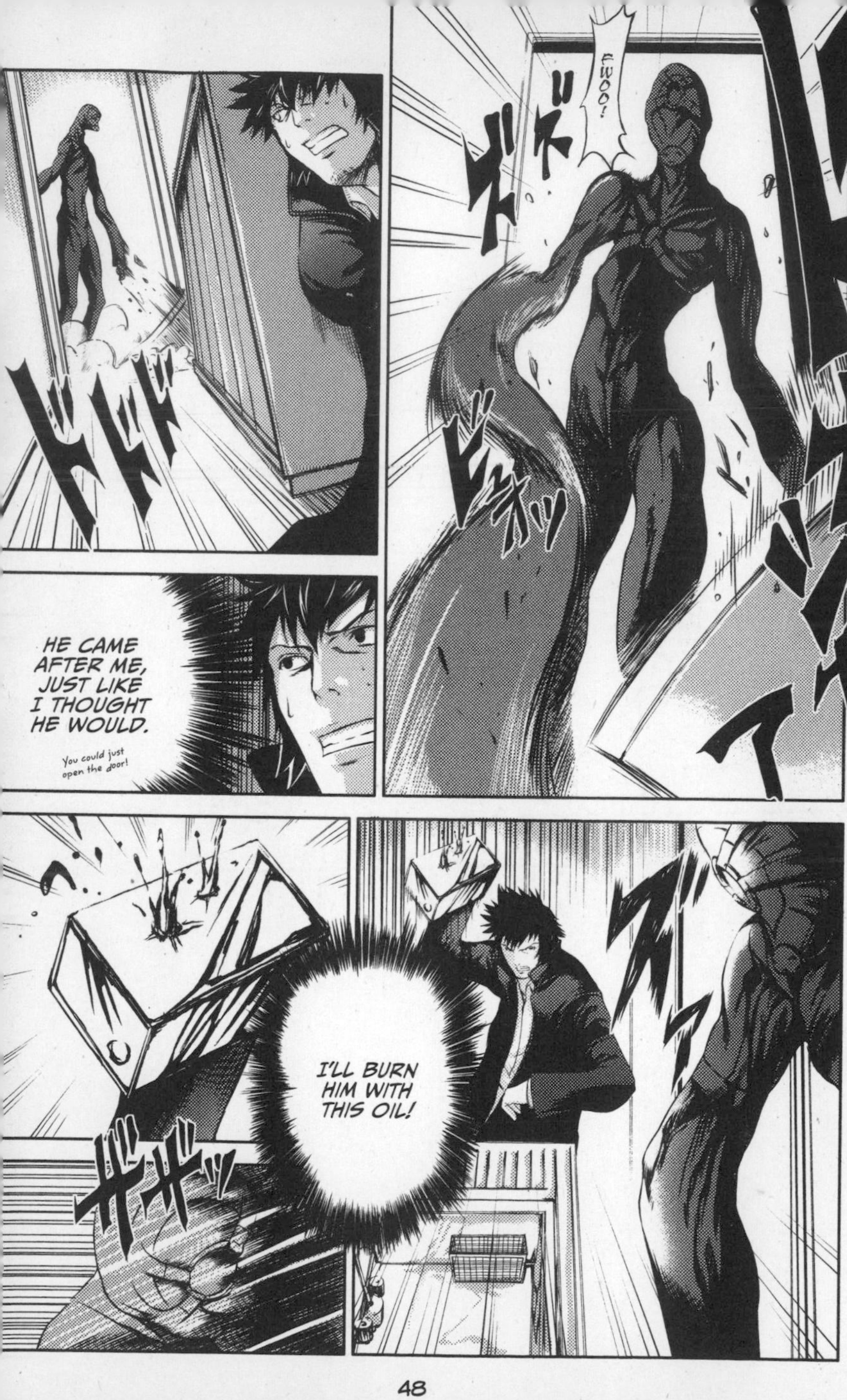
FWOO!
HE CAME AFTER ME, JUST LIKE I THOUGHT HE WOULD.
You could just open the door!
I'LL BURN HIM WITH THIS OIL!

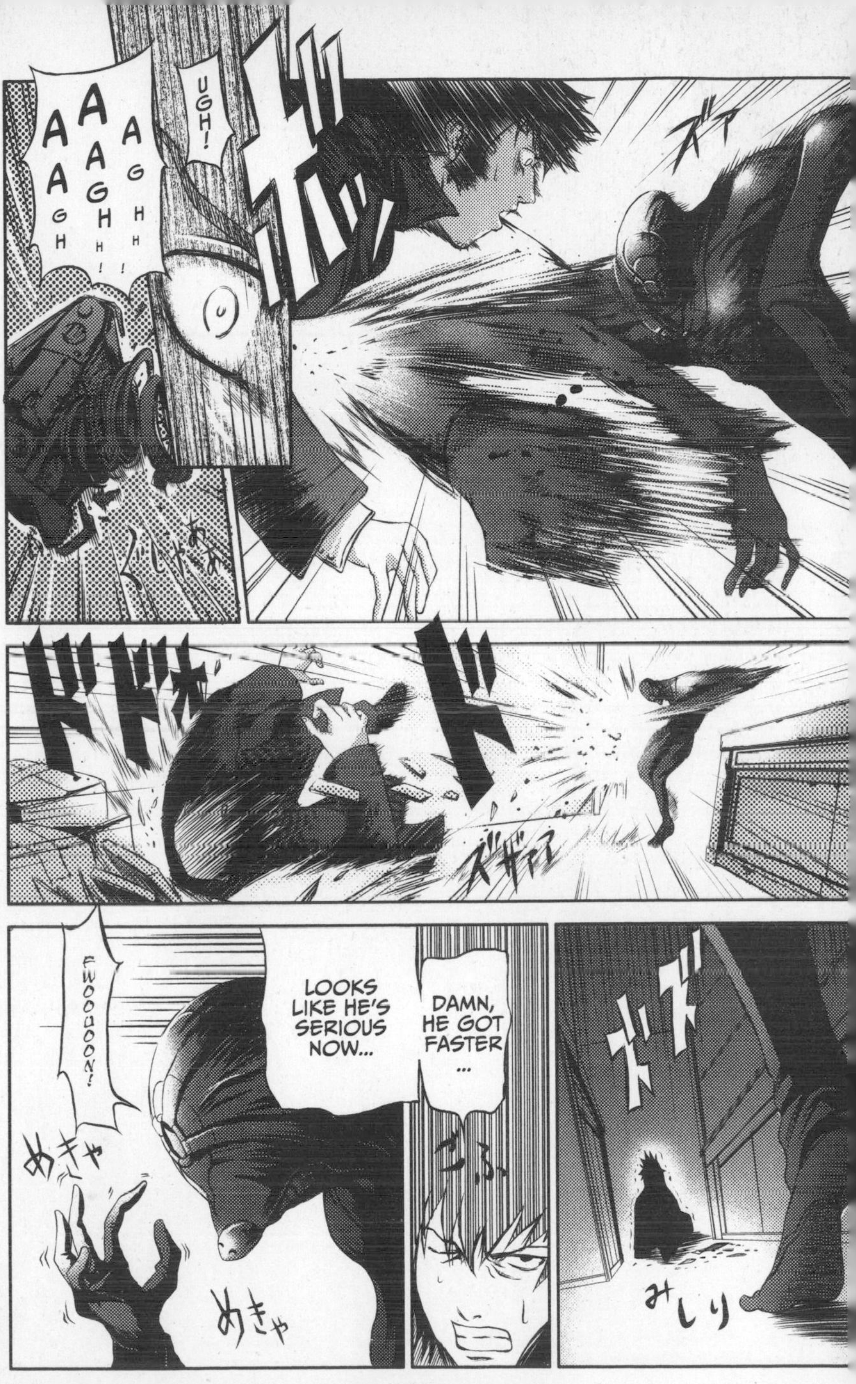
ズァ
UGH!
AGHH!
AAGHH!
AAGH
ぐしゃあ
ド
ズザァア
DAMN, HE GOT FASTER ...
ごふ
LOOKS LIKE HE'S SERIOUS NOW...
FWOOOUOOON!
めきゃ
めきゃ
ズズ
みしり

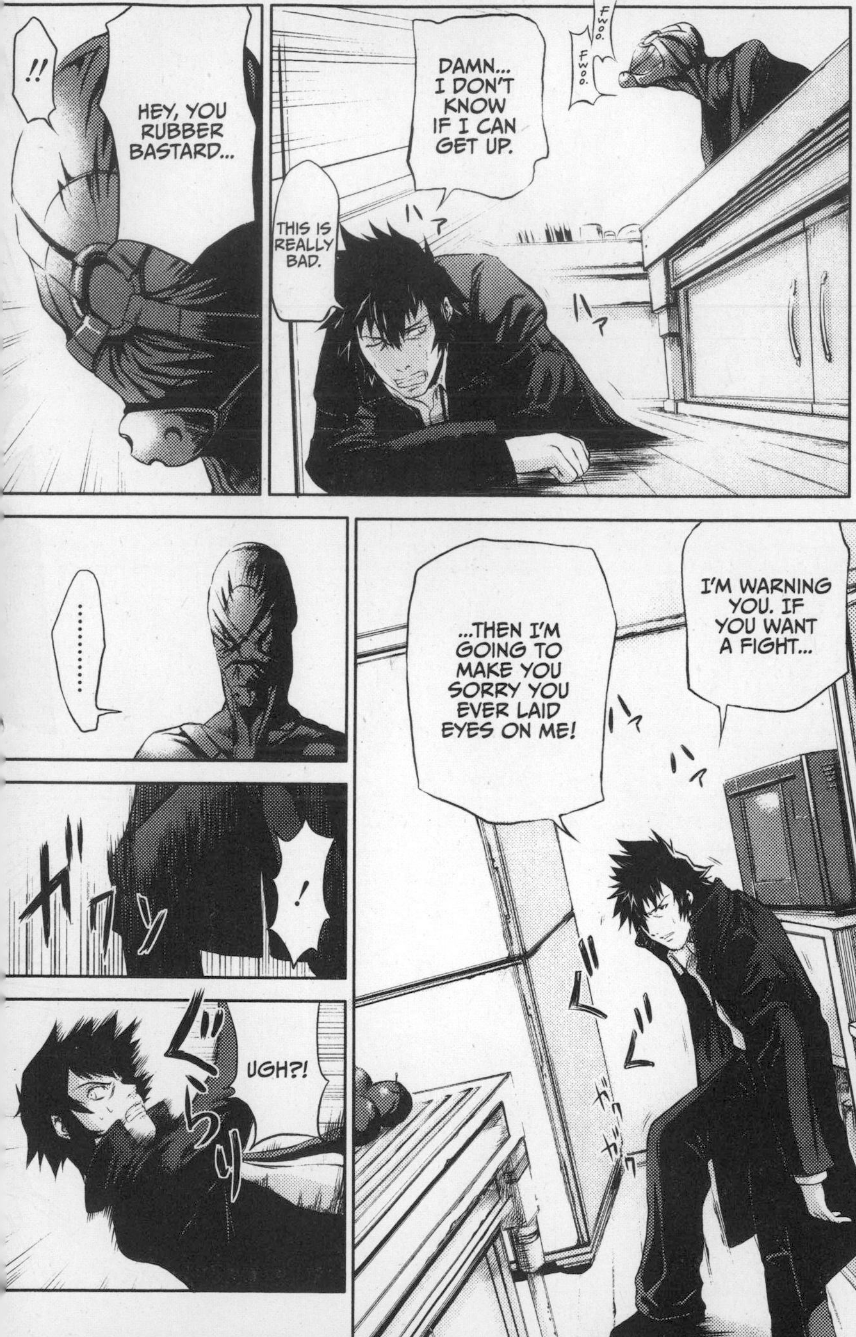
Fwoo.
Fwoo.
DAMN... I DON'T KNOW IF I CAN GET UP.
THIS IS REALLY BAD.
!!
HEY, YOU RUBBER BASTARD...
I'M WARNING YOU. IF YOU WANT A FIGHT...
...THEN I'M GOING TO MAKE YOU SORRY YOU EVER LAID EYES ON ME!
......
!
UGH?!

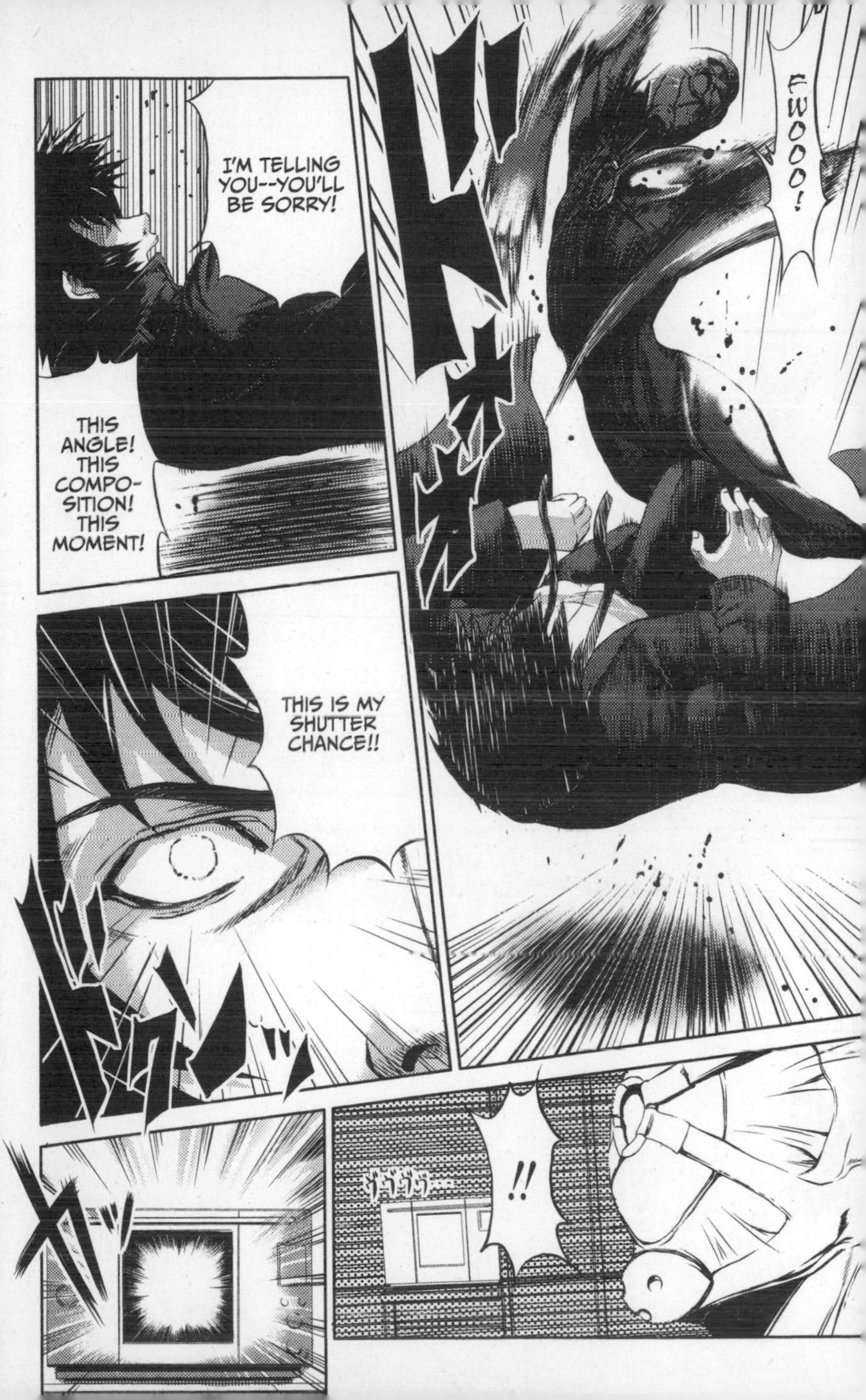
FWOOOO!
I'M TELLING YOU--YOU'LL BE SORRY!
THIS ANGLE! THIS COMPOSITION! THIS MOMENT!
THIS IS MY SHUTTER CHANCE!!
!!

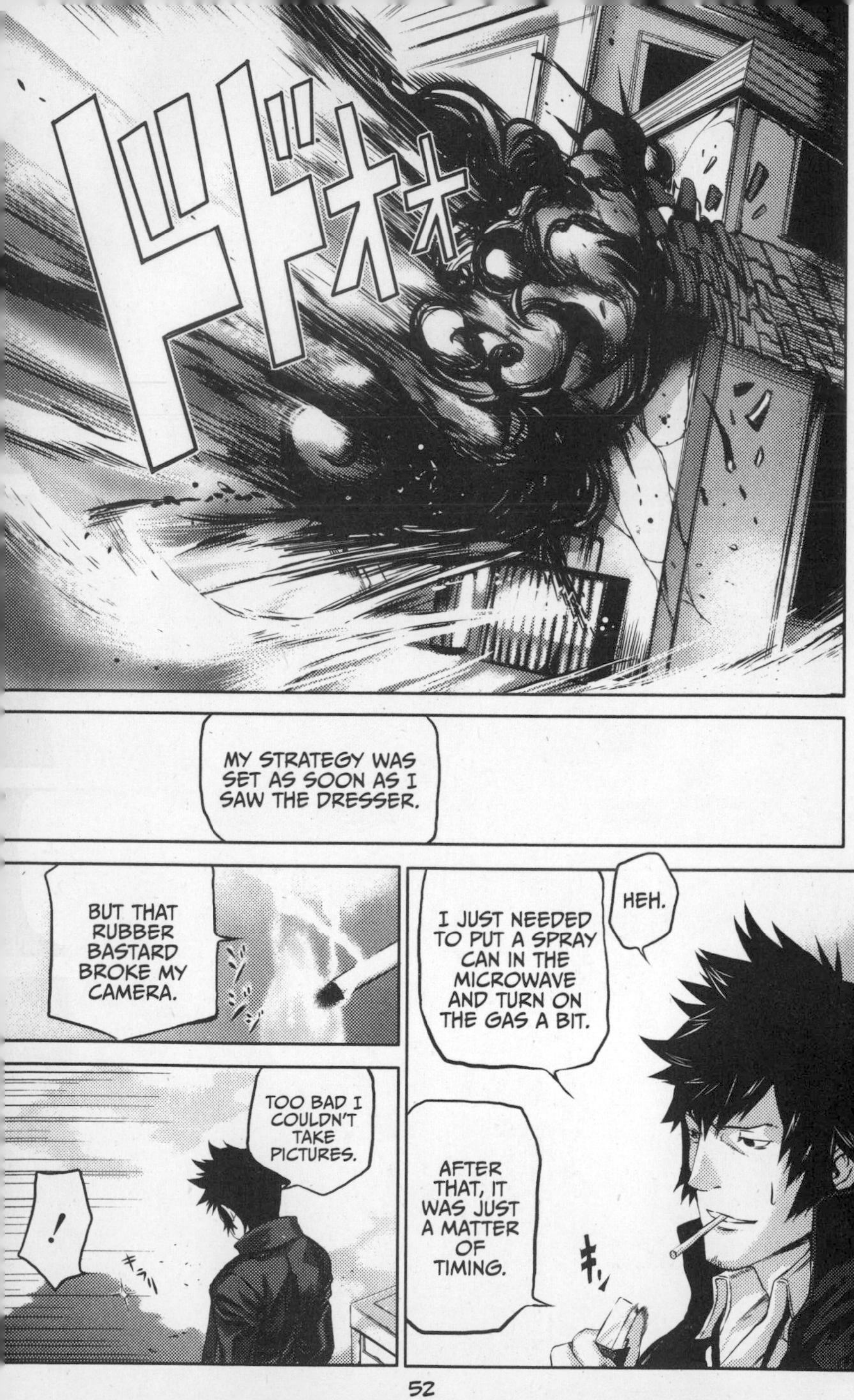
ドドオオ
MY STRATEGY WAS SET AS SOON AS I SAW THE DRESSER.
HEH.
I JUST NEEDED TO PUT A SPRAY CAN IN THE MICROWAVE AND TURN ON THE GAS A BIT.
AFTER THAT, IT WAS JUST A MATTER OF TIMING.
キッ
BUT THAT RUBBER BASTARD BROKE MY CAMERA.
TOO BAD I COULDN'T TAKE PICTURES.
!
キラッ

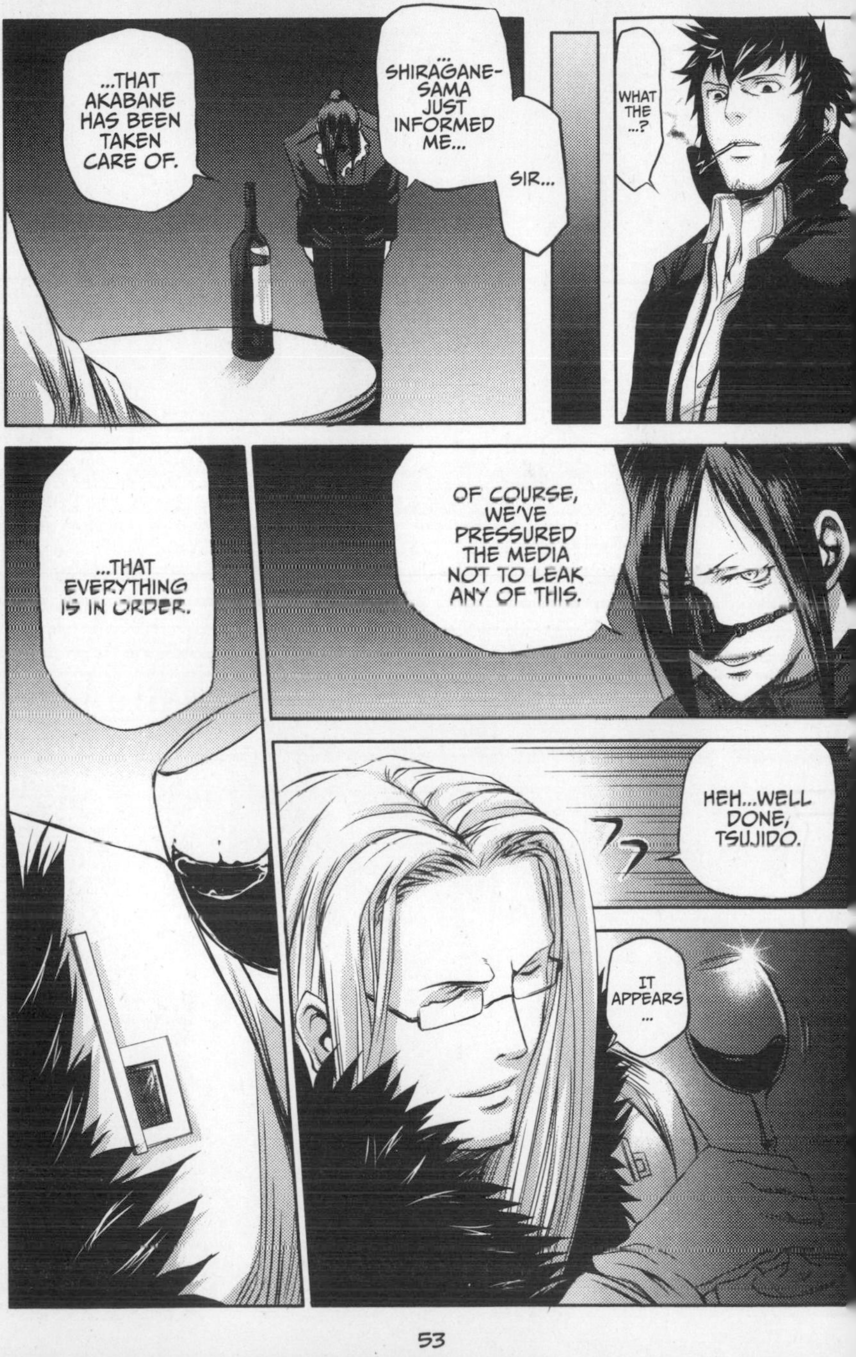
WHAT THE ...?
SIR...
... SHIRAGANE-SAMA JUST INFORMED ME...
...THAT AKABANE HAS BEEN TAKEN CARE OF.
OF COURSE, WE'VE PRESSURED THE MEDIA NOT TO LEAK ANY OF THIS.
HEH...WELL DONE, TSUJIDO.
IT APPEARS ...
...THAT EVERYTHING IS IN ORDER.

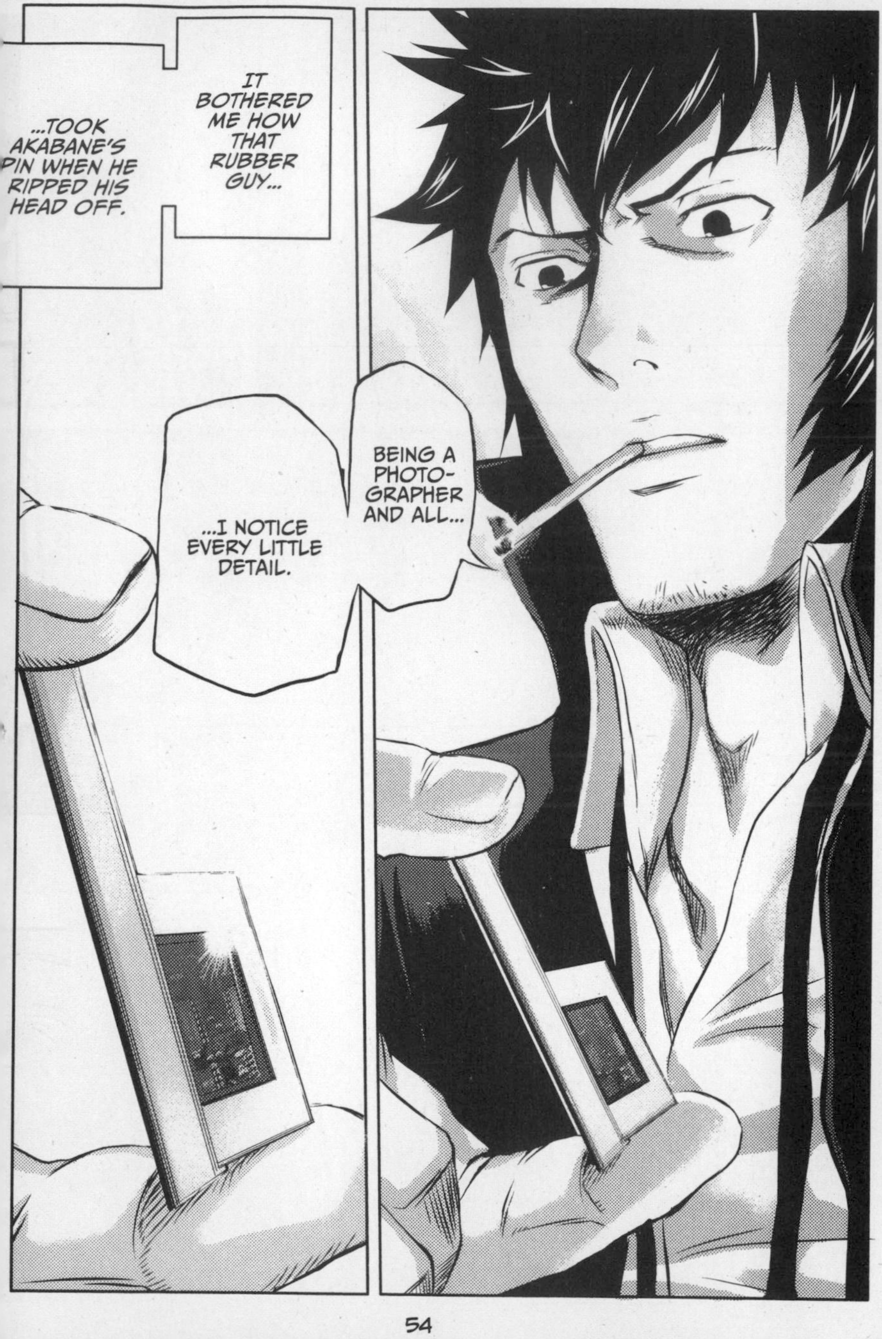
BEING A PHOTO-GRAPHER AND ALL...
...I NOTICE EVERY LITTLE DETAIL.
IT BOTHERED ME HOW THAT RUBBER GUY...
...TOOK AKABANE'S PIN WHEN HE RIPPED HIS HEAD OFF.

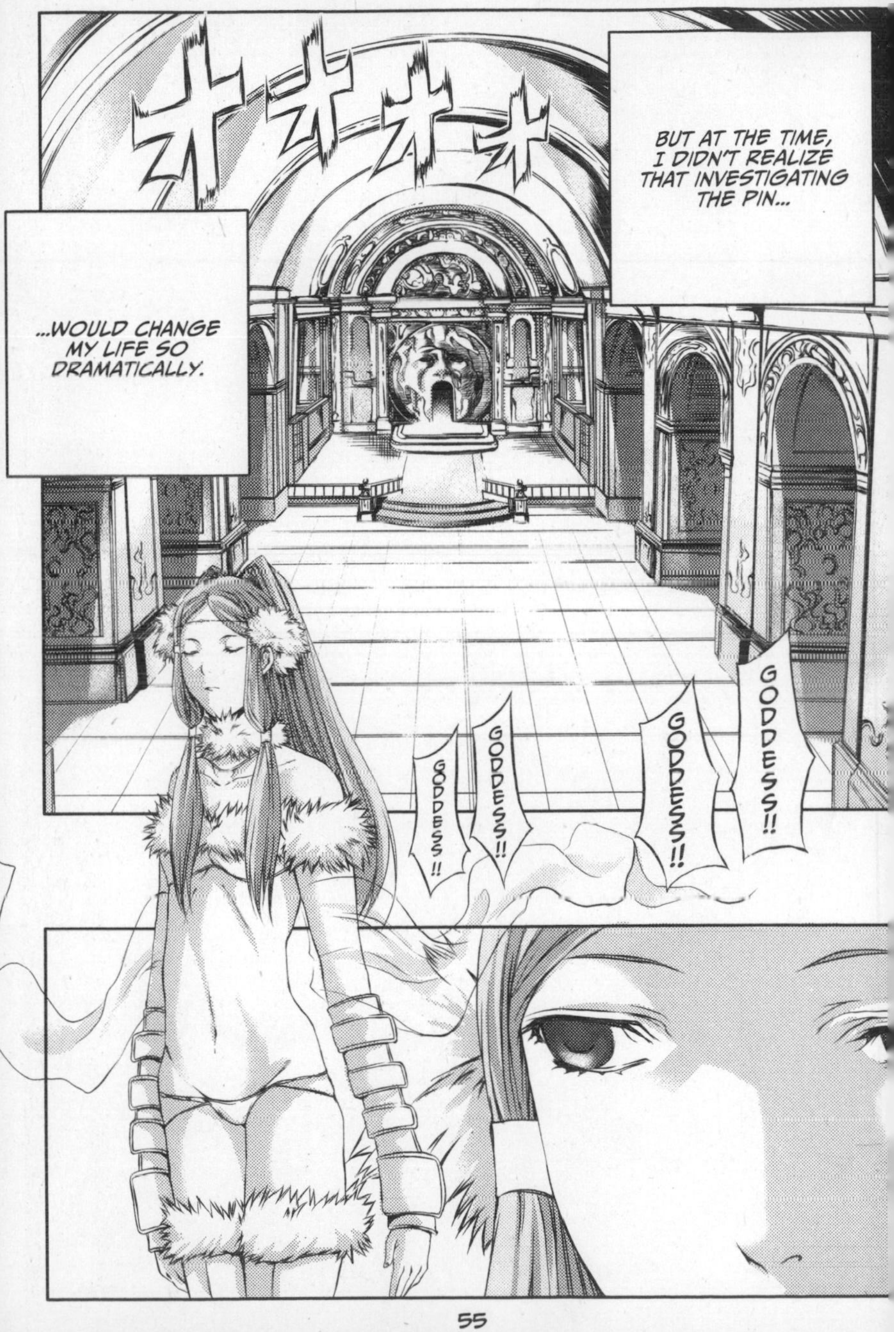
BUT AT THE TIME, I DIDN'T REALIZE THAT INVESTIGATING THE PIN...
...WOULD CHANGE MY LIFE SO DRAMATICALLY.
オオオオ
GODDESS!!
GODDESS!!
GODDESS!!
GODDESS!!

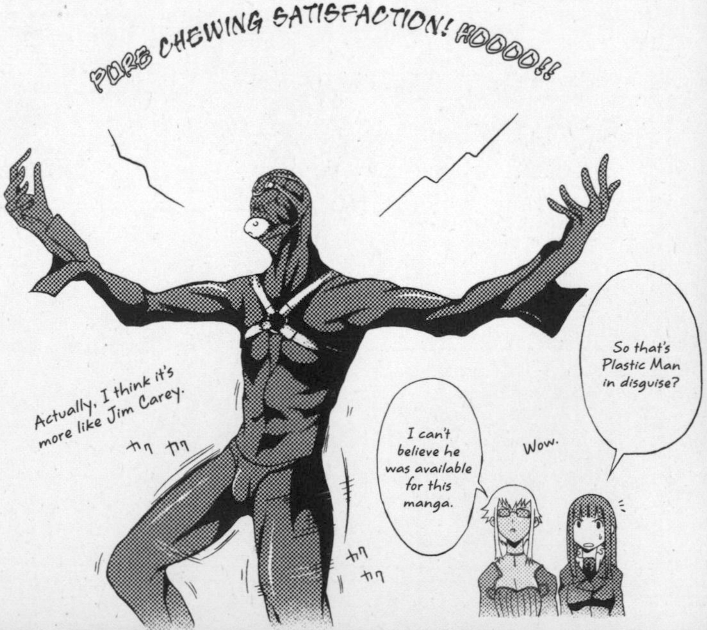
PURE CHEWING SATISFACTION! HOOOOO!!
So that's Plastic Man in disguise?
Wow.
I can't believe he was available for this manga.
Actually, I think it's more like Jim Carey.

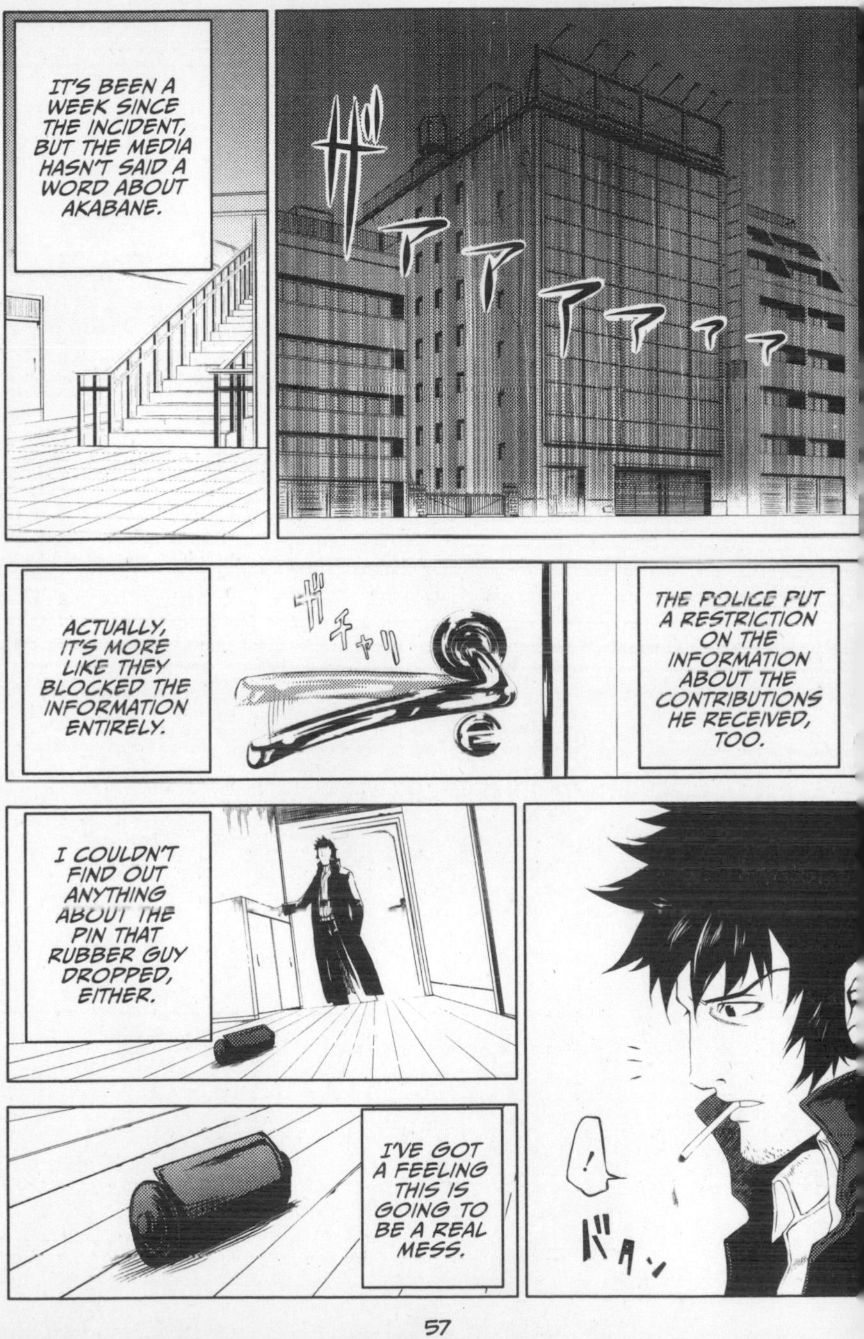
ザァァァァァァ
IT'S BEEN A WEEK SINCE THE INCIDENT, BUT THE MEDIA HASN'T SAID A WORD ABOUT AKABANE.
THE POLICE PUT A RESTRICTION ON THE INFORMATION ABOUT THE CONTRIBUTIONS HE RECEIVED, TOO.
ガチャリ
ACTUALLY, IT'S MORE LIKE THEY BLOCKED THE INFORMATION ENTIRELY.
!
バタン
I COULDN'T FIND OUT ANYTHING ABOUT THE PIN THAT RUBBER GUY DROPPED, EITHER.
I'VE GOT A FEELING THIS IS GOING TO BE A REAL MESS.

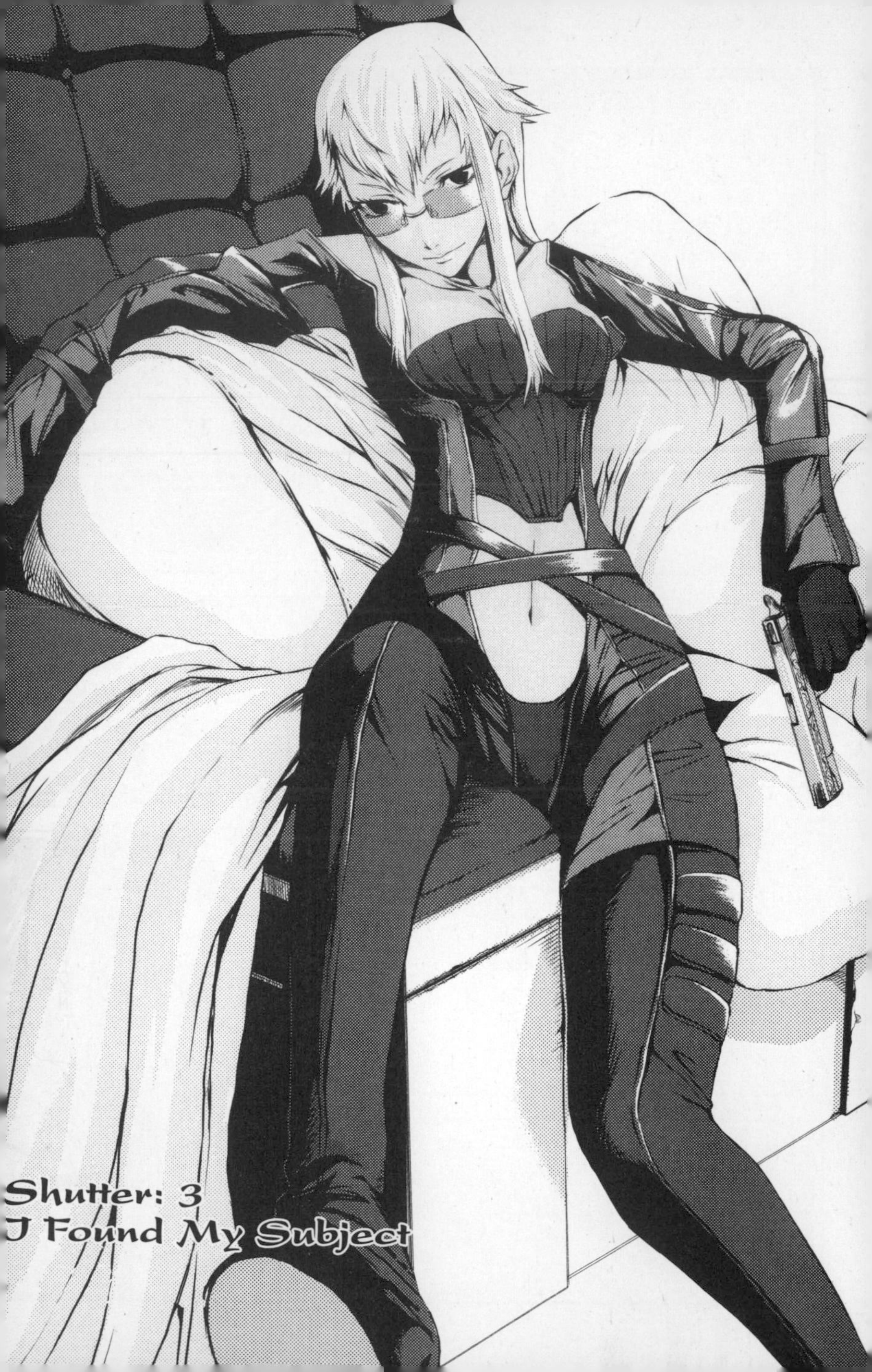
Shutter: 3
I Found My Subject

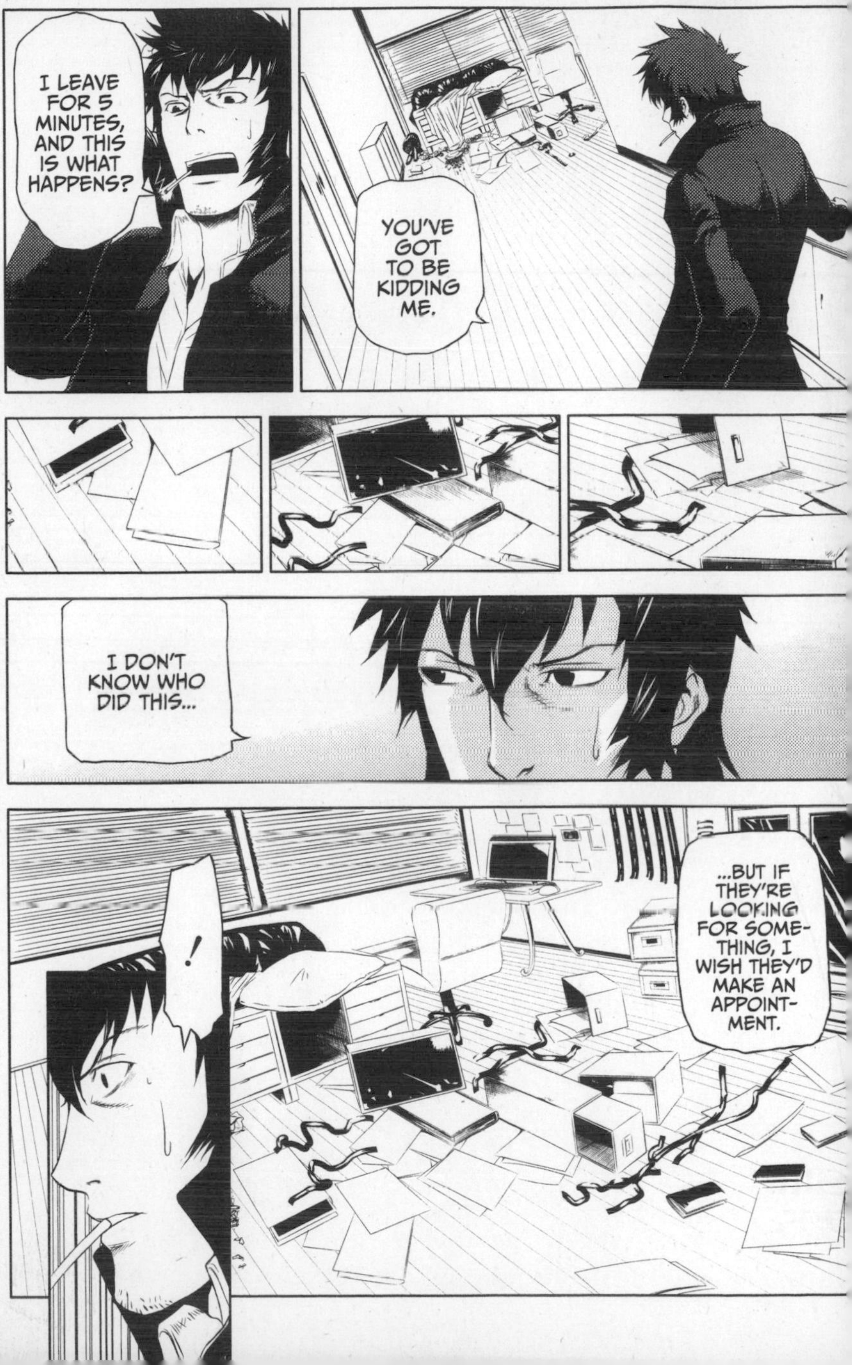
YOU'VE GOT TO BE KIDDING ME.
I LEAVE FOR 5 MINUTES, AND THIS IS WHAT HAPPENS?
I DON'T KNOW WHO DID THIS...
...BUT IF THEY'RE LOOKING FOR SOME-THING, I WISH THEY'D MAKE AN APPOINT-MENT.
!

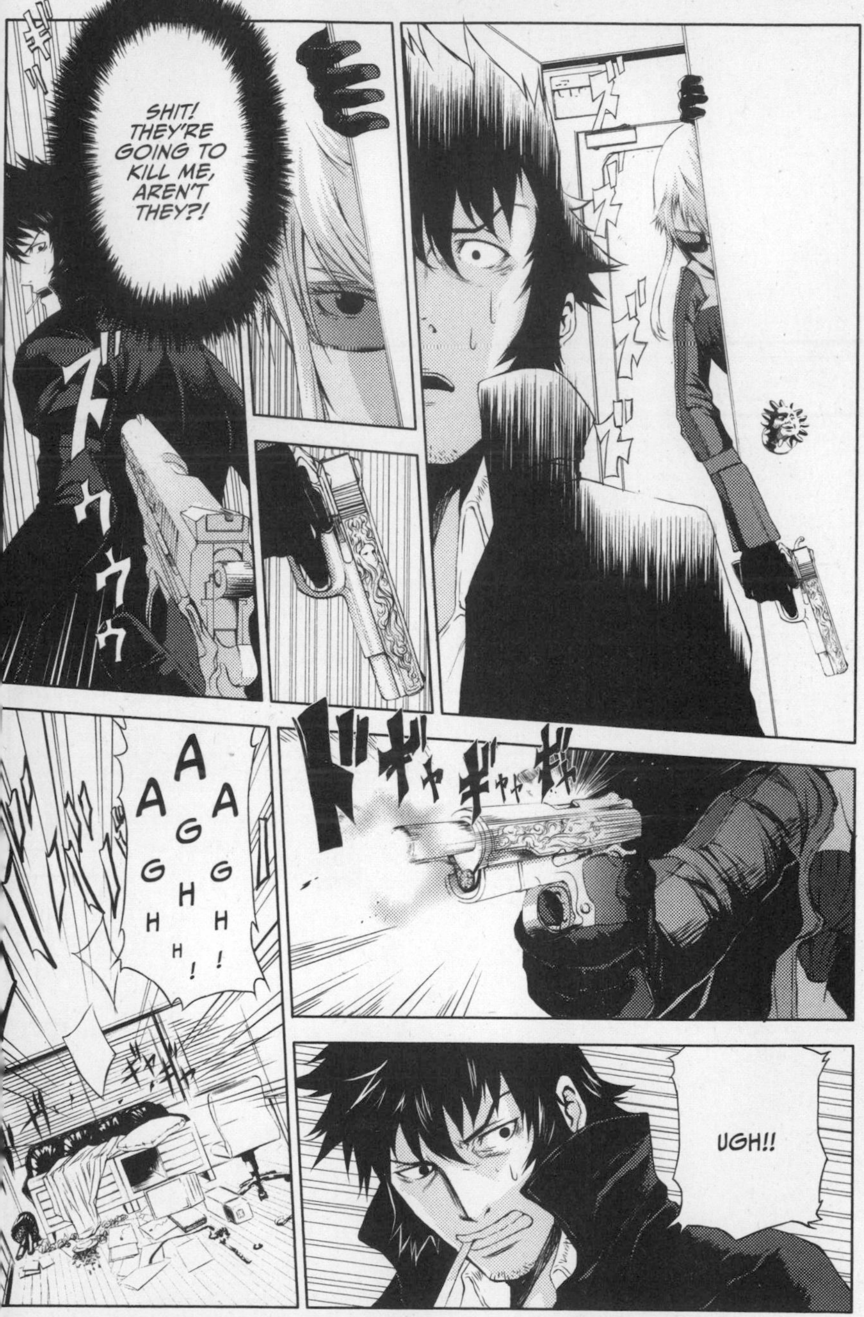
SHIT! THEY'RE GOING TO KILL ME, AREN'T THEY?!
AAGGHHH! AAGGHH!
UGH!!

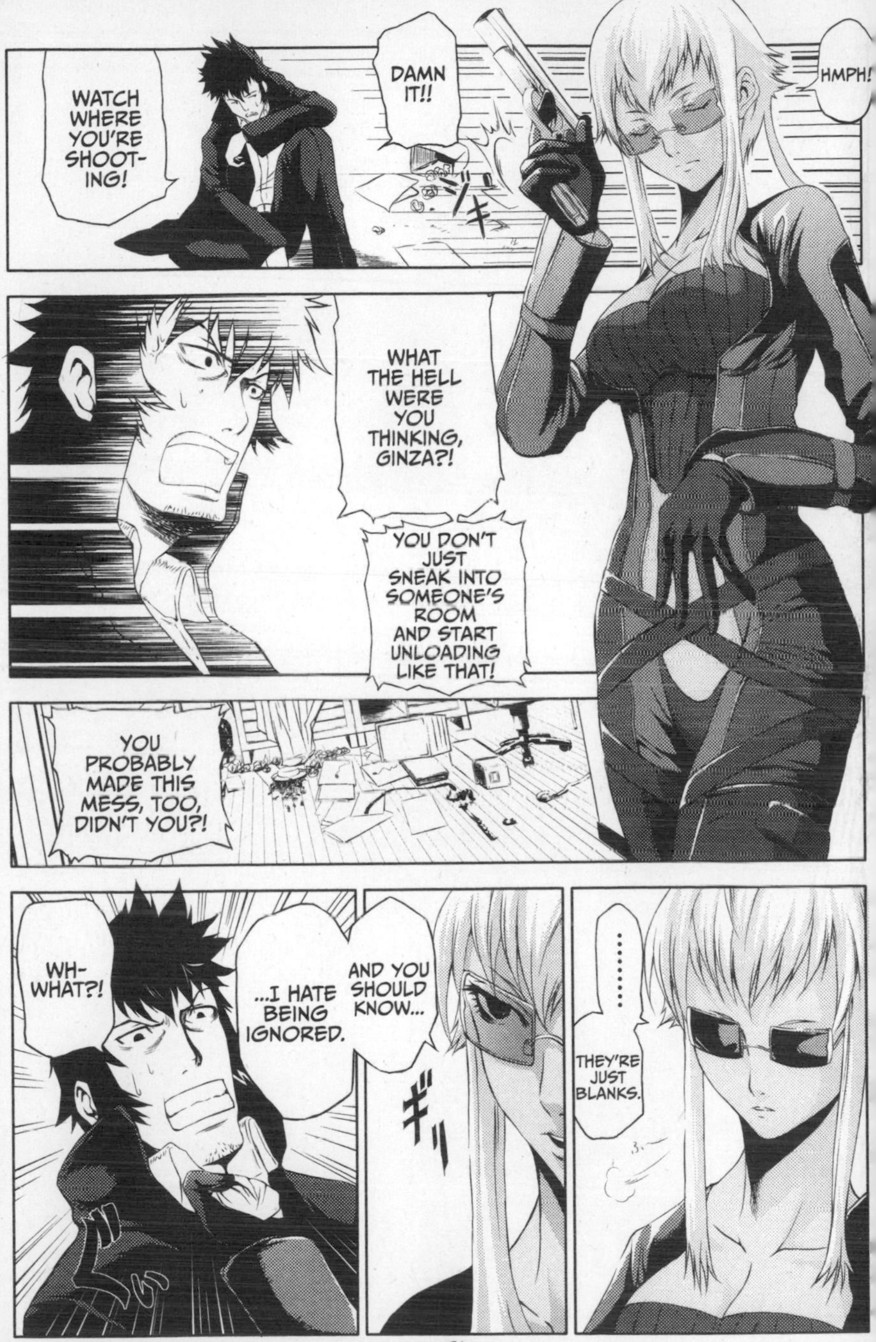
HMPH!
DAMN IT!!
WATCH WHERE YOU'RE SHOOT-ING!
WHAT THE HELL WERE YOU THINKING, GINZA?!
YOU DON'T JUST SNEAK INTO SOMEONE'S ROOM AND START UNLOADING LIKE THAT!
YOU PROBABLY MADE THIS MESS, TOO, DIDN'T YOU?!
......
THEY'RE JUST BLANKS.
AND YOU SHOULD KNOW...
...I HATE BEING IGNORED.
ギリ
WH-WHAT?!

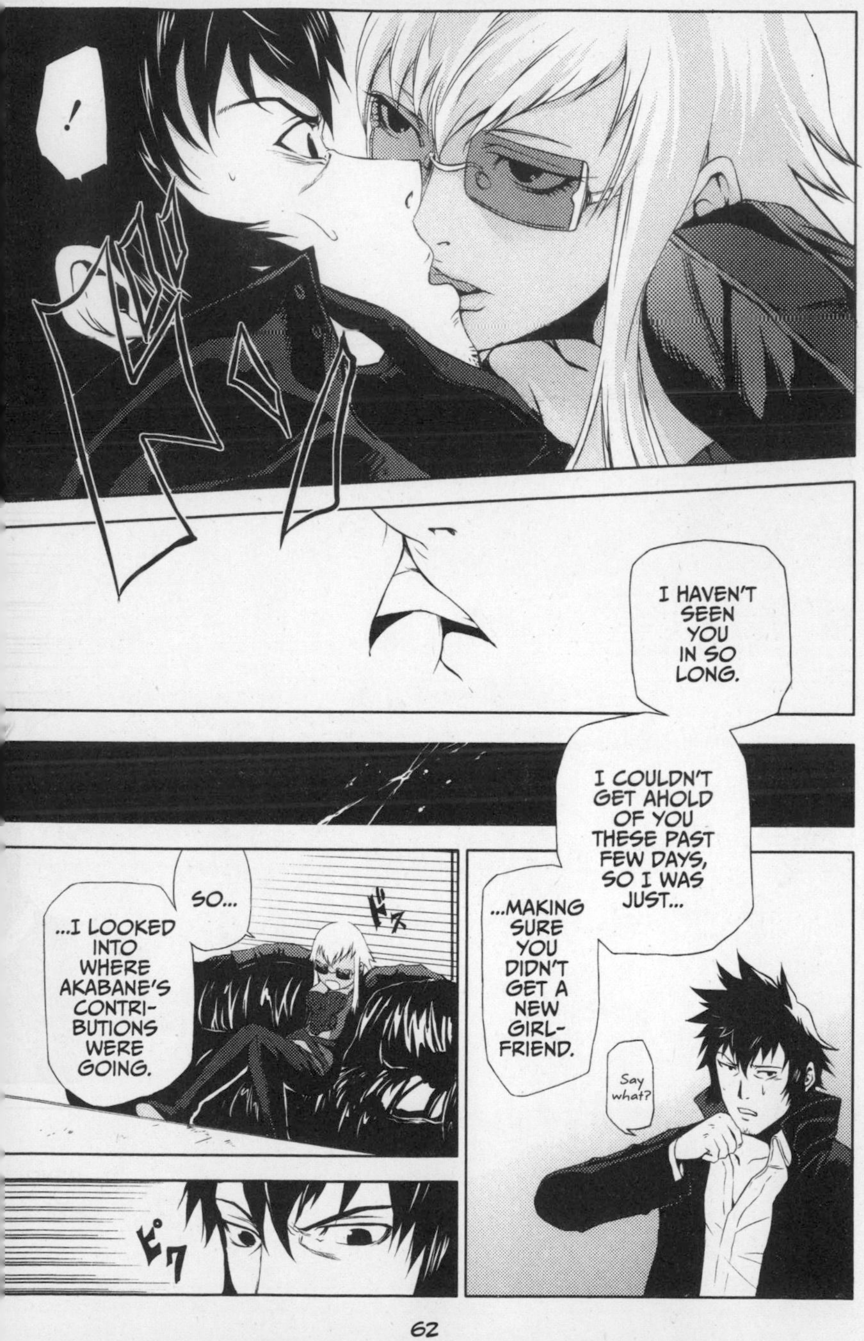
!
I HAVEN'T SEEN YOU IN SO LONG.
I COULDN'T GET AHOLD OF YOU THESE PAST FEW DAYS, SO I WAS JUST...
...MAKING SURE YOU DIDN'T GET A NEW GIRL-FRIEND.
Say what?
SO...
...I LOOKED INTO WHERE AKABANE'S CONTRI-BUTIONS WERE GOING.
ドス
ピク

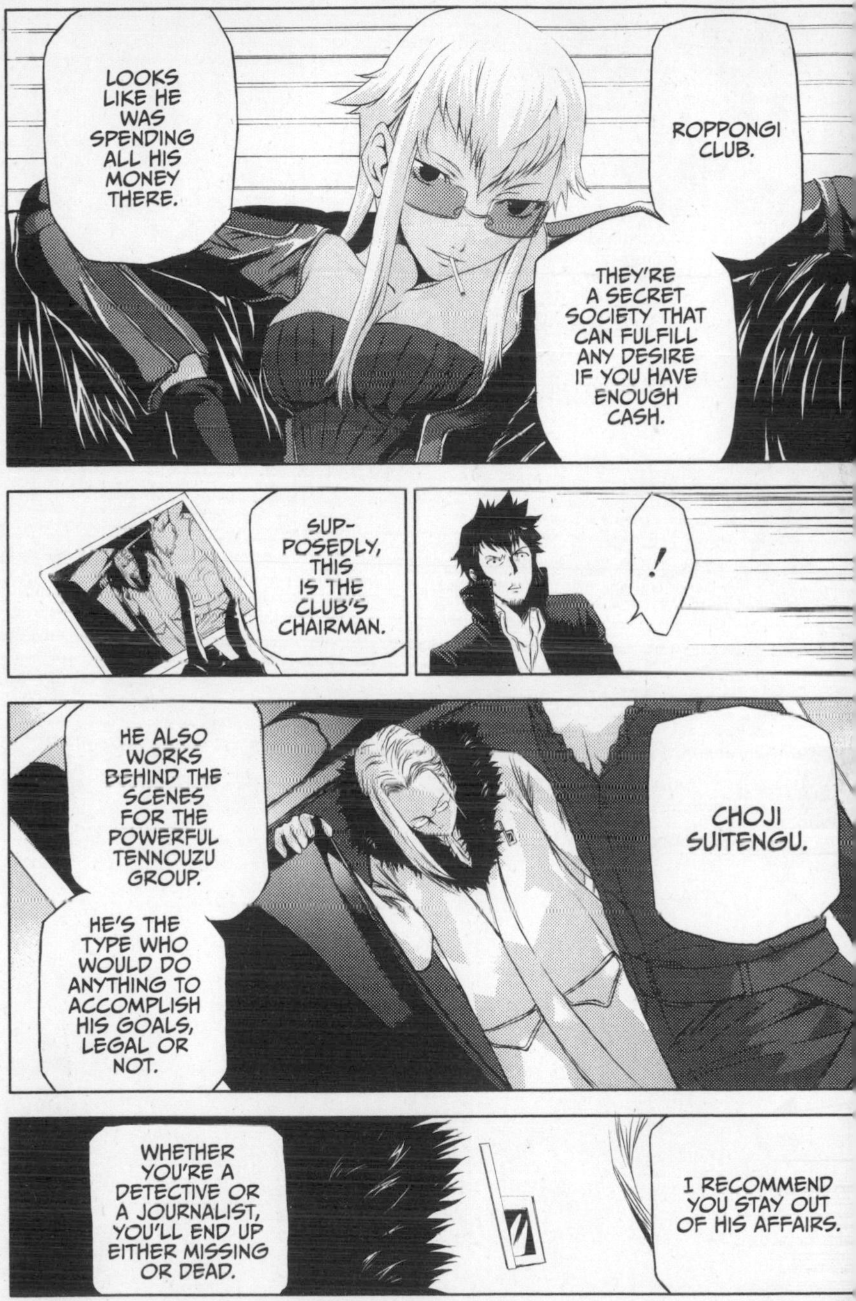
ROPPONGI CLUB.
LOOKS LIKE HE WAS SPENDING ALL HIS MONEY THERE.
THEY'RE A SECRET SOCIETY THAT CAN FULFILL ANY DESIRE IF YOU HAVE ENOUGH CASH.
!
SUP-POSEDLY, THIS IS THE CLUB'S CHAIRMAN.
CHOJI SUITENGU.
HE ALSO WORKS BEHIND THE SCENES FOR THE POWERFUL TENNOUZU GROUP.
HE'S THE TYPE WHO WOULD DO ANYTHING TO ACCOMPLISH HIS GOALS, LEGAL OR NOT.
I RECOMMEND YOU STAY OUT OF HIS AFFAIRS.
WHETHER YOU'RE A DETECTIVE OR A JOURNALIST, YOU'LL END UP EITHER MISSING OR DEAD.

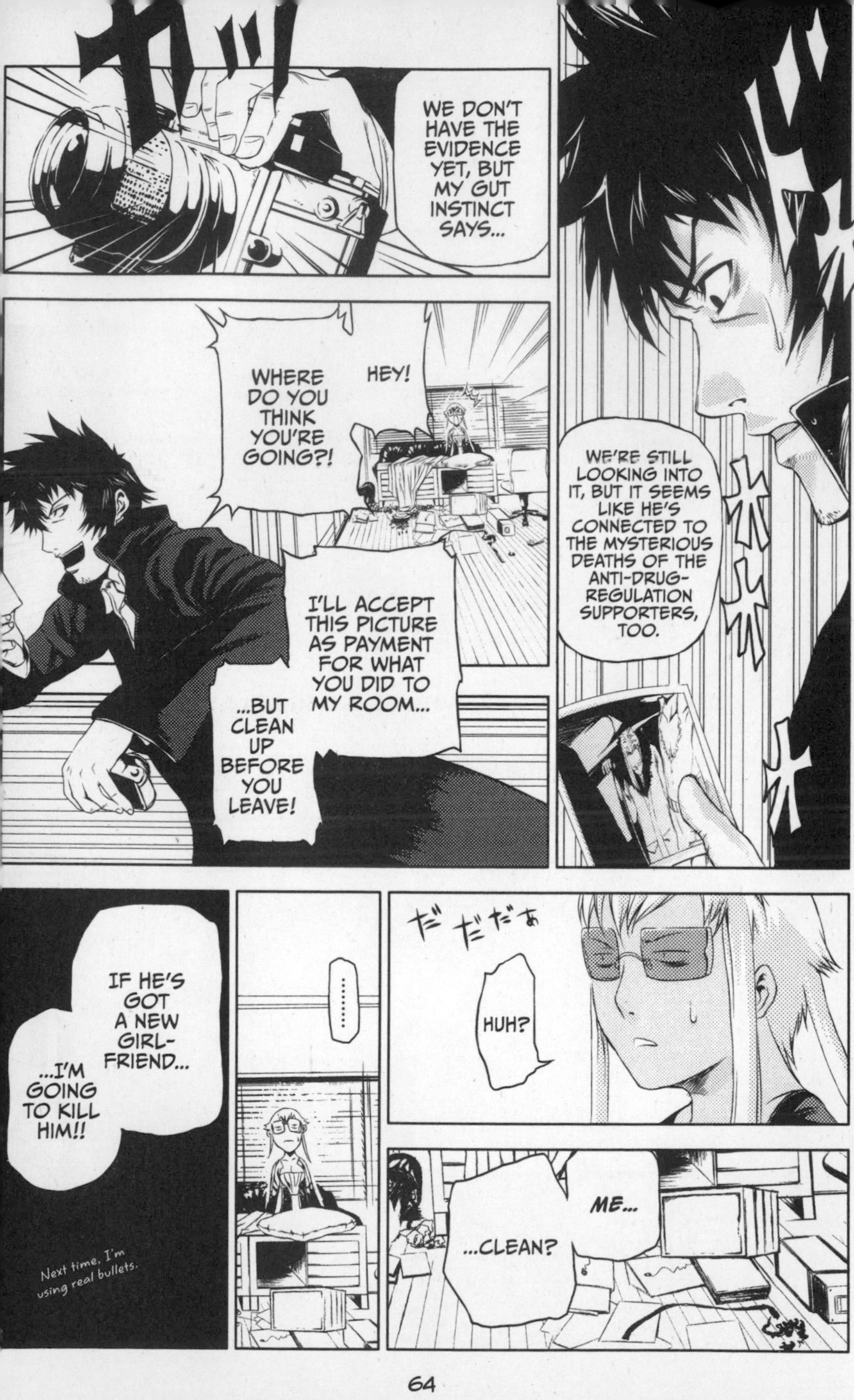
WE'RE STILL LOOKING INTO IT, BUT IT SEEMS LIKE HE'S CONNECTED TO THE MYSTERIOUS DEATHS OF THE ANTI-DRUG-REGULATION SUPPORTERS, TOO.
カッ!
WE DON'T HAVE THE EVIDENCE YET, BUT MY GUT INSTINCT SAYS...
HEY!
WHERE DO YOU THINK YOU'RE GOING?!
I'LL ACCEPT THIS PICTURE AS PAYMENT FOR WHAT YOU DID TO MY ROOM...
...BUT CLEAN UP BEFORE YOU LEAVE!
だだだぁ
HUH?
ME...
...CLEAN?
....
IF HE'S GOT A NEW GIRL-FRIEND...
...I'M GOING TO KILL HIM!!
Next time, I'm using real bullets.

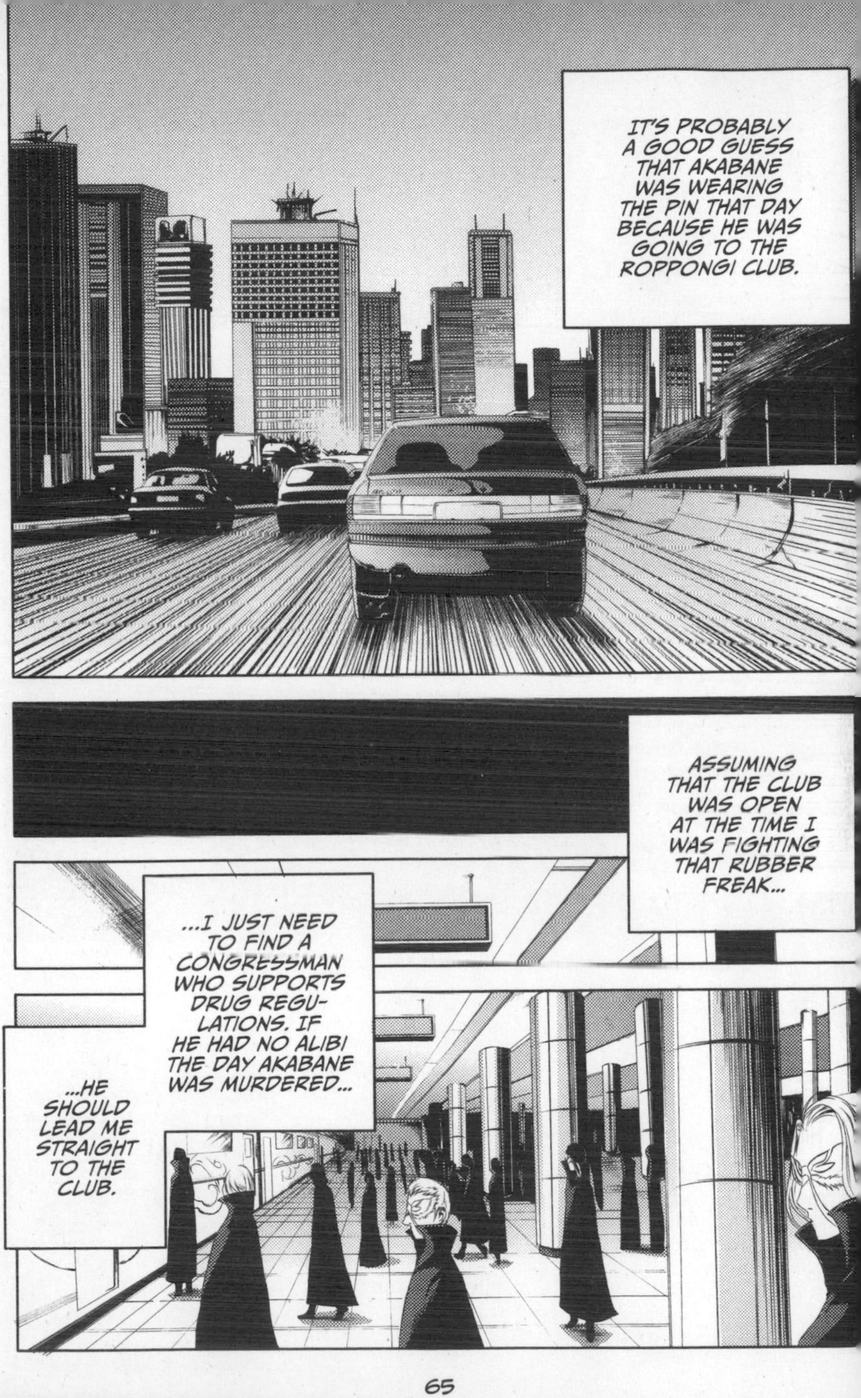
IT'S PROBABLY A GOOD GUESS THAT AKABANE WAS WEARING THE PIN THAT DAY BECAUSE HE WAS GOING TO THE ROPPONGI CLUB.
ASSUMING THAT THE CLUB WAS OPEN AT THE TIME I WAS FIGHTING THAT RUBBER FREAK...
...I JUST NEED TO FIND A CONGRESSMAN WHO SUPPORTS DRUG REGU-LATIONS. IF HE HAD NO ALIBI THE DAY AKABANE WAS MURDERED...
...HE SHOULD LEAD ME STRAIGHT TO THE CLUB.

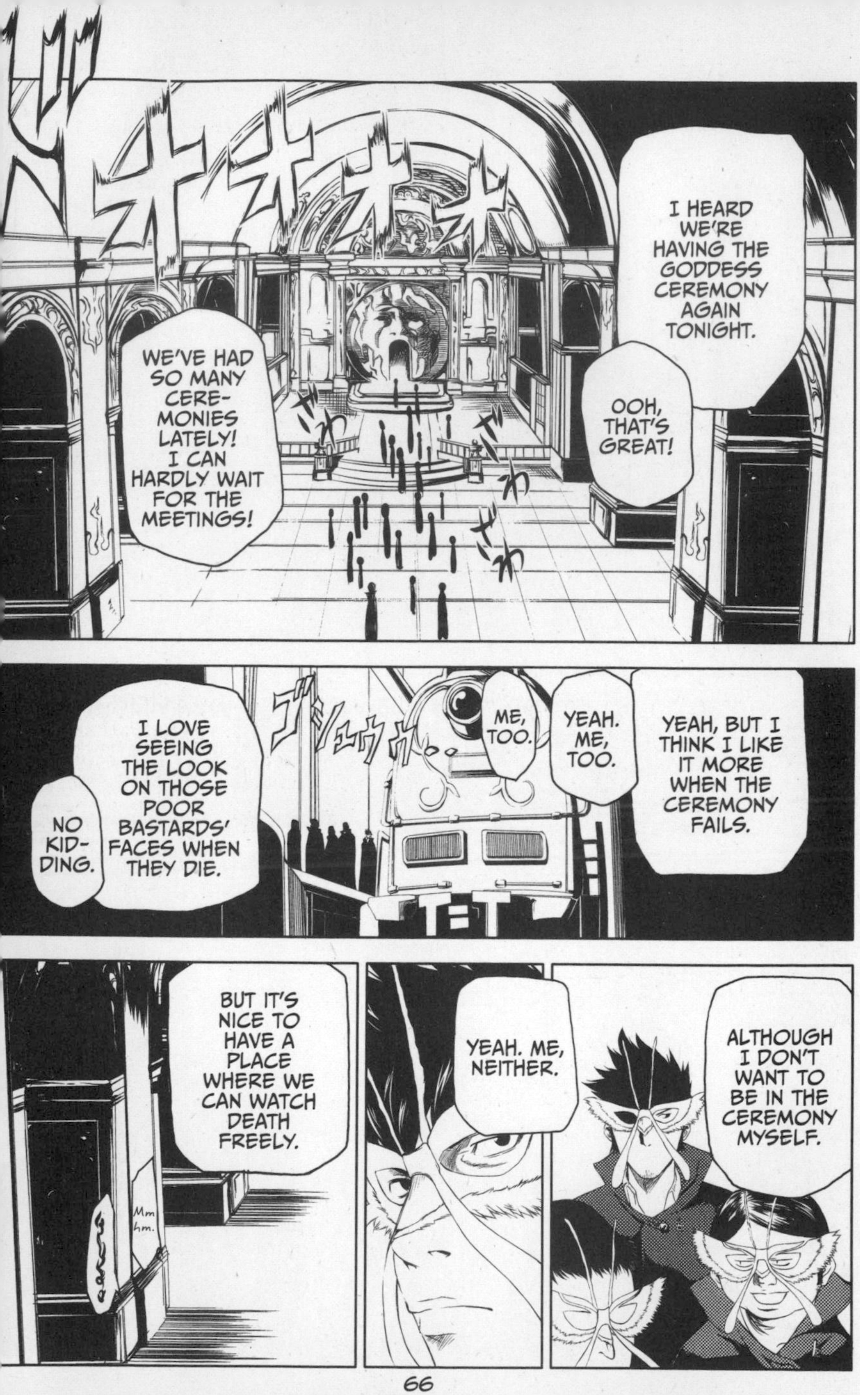
I HEARD WE'RE HAVING THE GODDESS CEREMONY AGAIN TONIGHT.
OOH, THAT'S GREAT!
WE'VE HAD SO MANY CERE-MONIES LATELY! I CAN HARDLY WAIT FOR THE MEETINGS!
YEAH, BUT I THINK I LIKE IT MORE WHEN THE CEREMONY FAILS.
YEAH. ME, TOO.
ME, TOO.
I LOVE SEEING THE LOOK ON THOSE POOR BASTARDS' FACES WHEN THEY DIE.
NO KID-DING.
ALTHOUGH I DON'T WANT TO BE IN THE CEREMONY MYSELF.
YEAH. ME, NEITHER.
BUT IT'S NICE TO HAVE A PLACE WHERE WE CAN WATCH DEATH FREELY.
Mm hm.

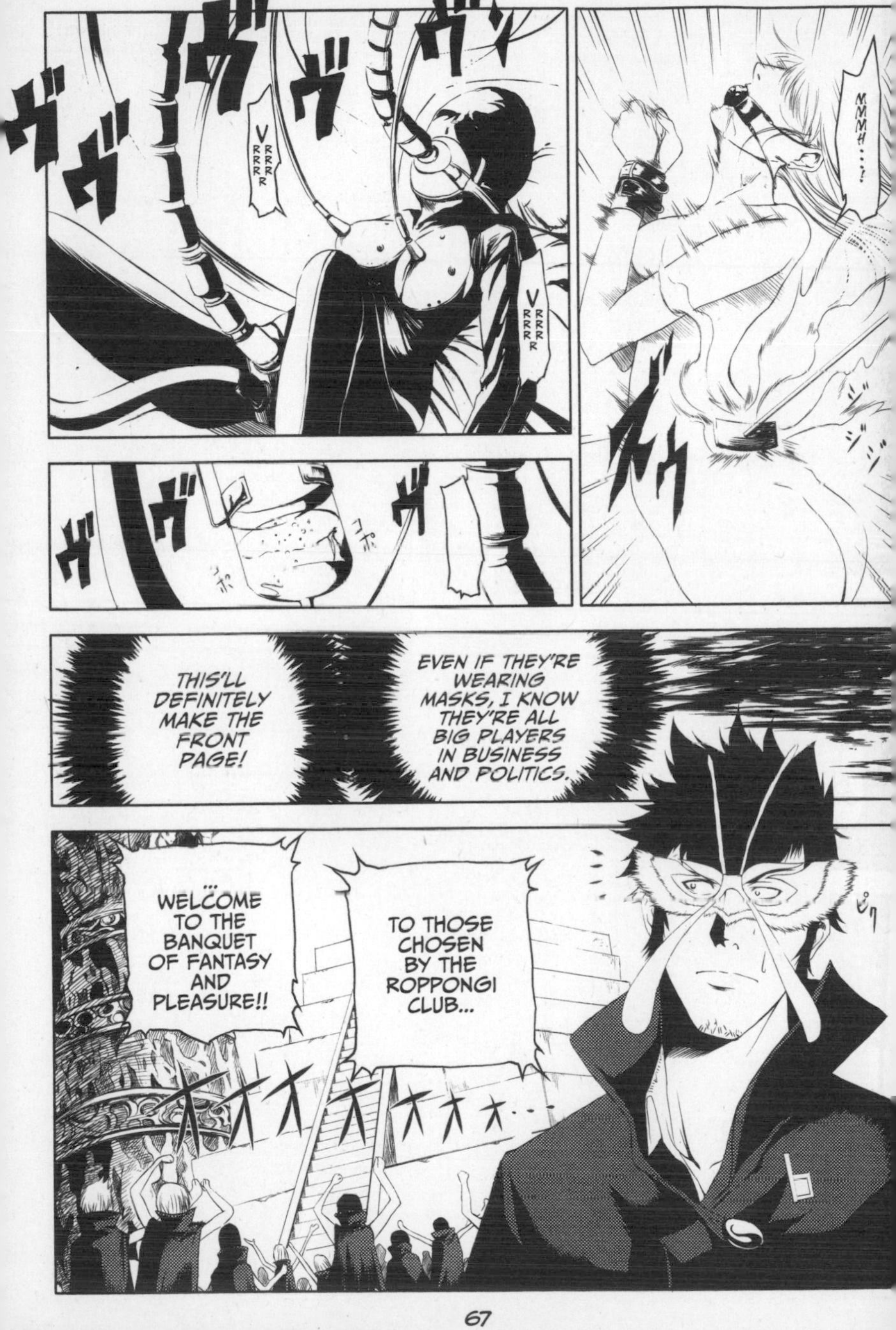
MMMH...?!
VRRRRRR
VRRRRRR
EVEN IF THEY'RE WEARING MASKS, I KNOW THEY'RE ALL BIG PLAYERS IN BUSINESS AND POLITICS.
THIS'LL DEFINITELY MAKE THE FRONT PAGE!
TO THOSE CHOSEN BY THE ROPPONGI CLUB...
...WELCOME TO THE BANQUET OF FANTASY AND PLEASURE!!

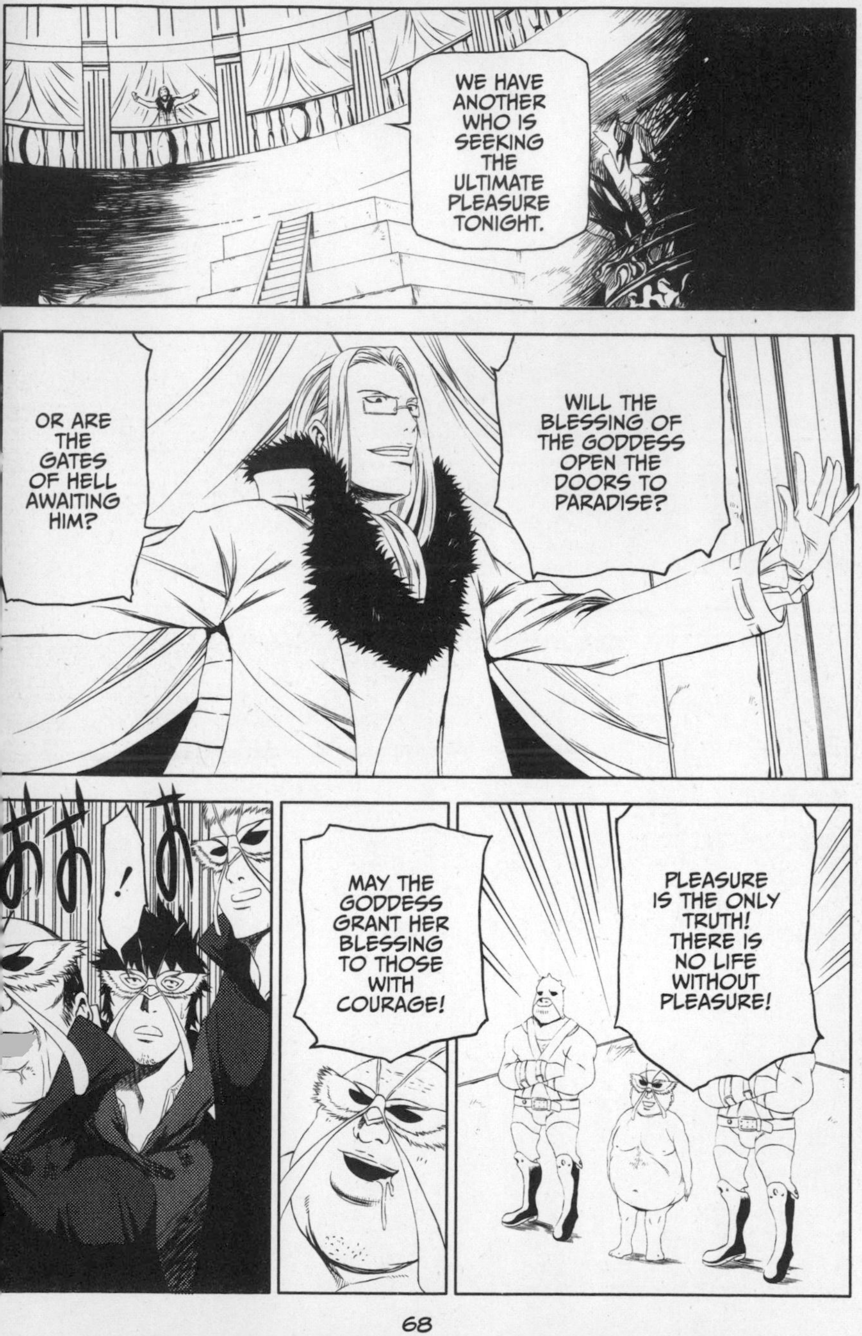
WE HAVE ANOTHER WHO IS SEEKING THE ULTIMATE PLEASURE TONIGHT.
WILL THE BLESSING OF THE GODDESS OPEN THE DOORS TO PARADISE?
OR ARE THE GATES OF HELL AWAITING HIM?
PLEASURE IS THE ONLY TRUTH! THERE IS NO LIFE WITHOUT PLEASURE!
MAY THE GODDESS GRANT HER BLESSING TO THOSE WITH COURAGE!
おおお
!

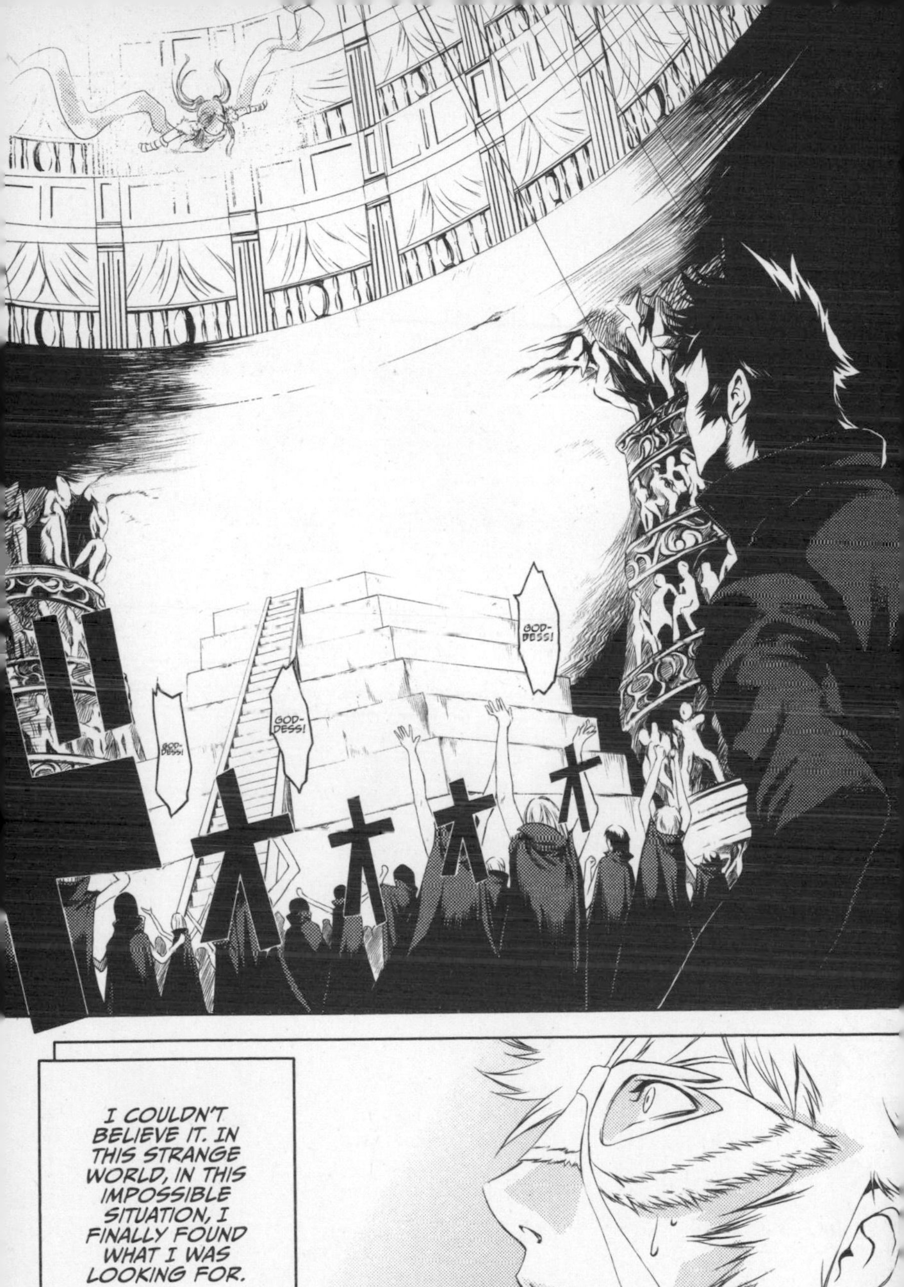
GOD-DESS!
GOD-DESS!
GOD-DESS!
I COULDN'T BELIEVE IT. IN THIS STRANGE WORLD, IN THIS IMPOSSIBLE SITUATION, I FINALLY FOUND WHAT I WAS LOOKING FOR.

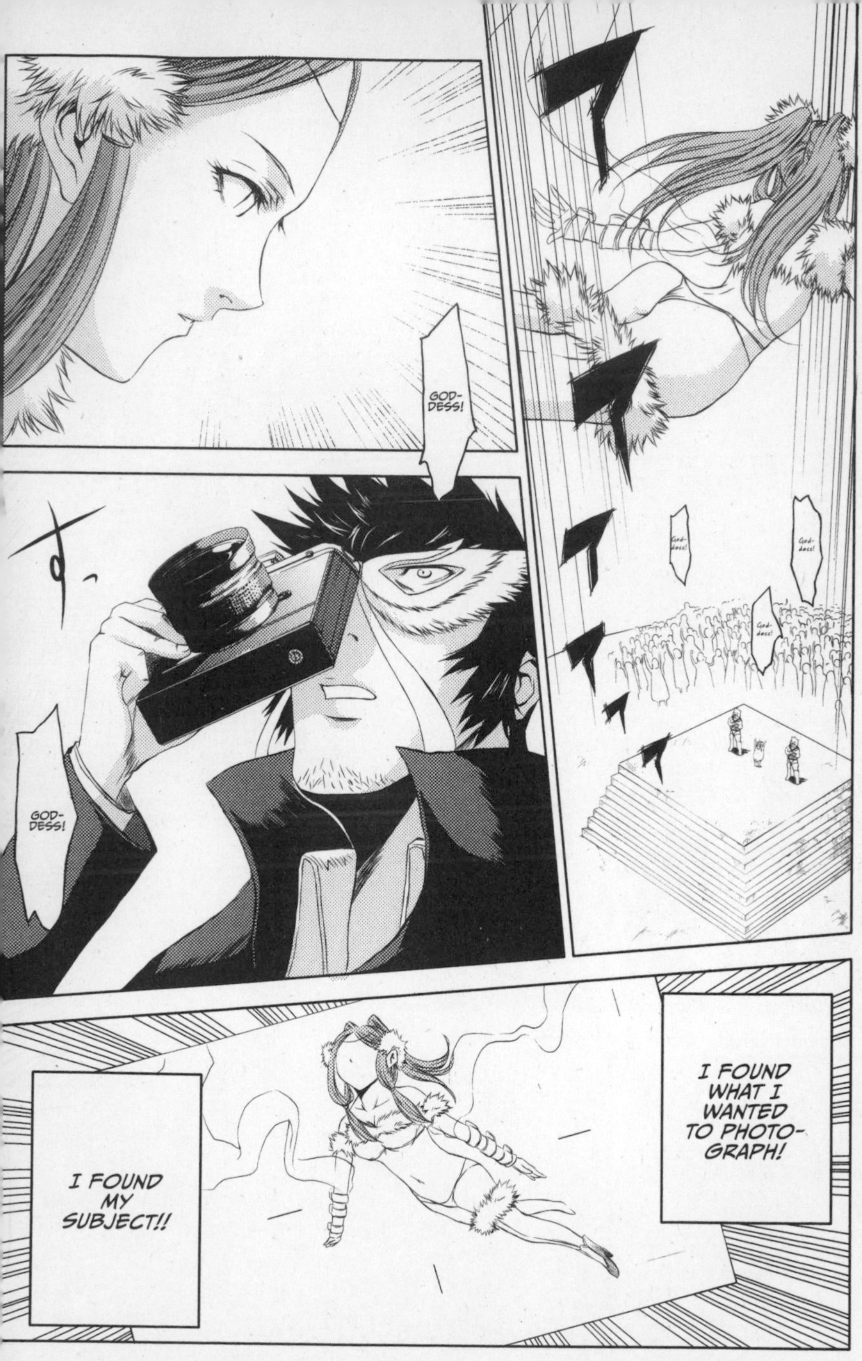
God-dess!
God-dess!
God-dess!
GOD-DESS!
GOD-DESS!
I FOUND WHAT I WANTED TO PHOTO-GRAPH!
I FOUND MY SUBJECT!!

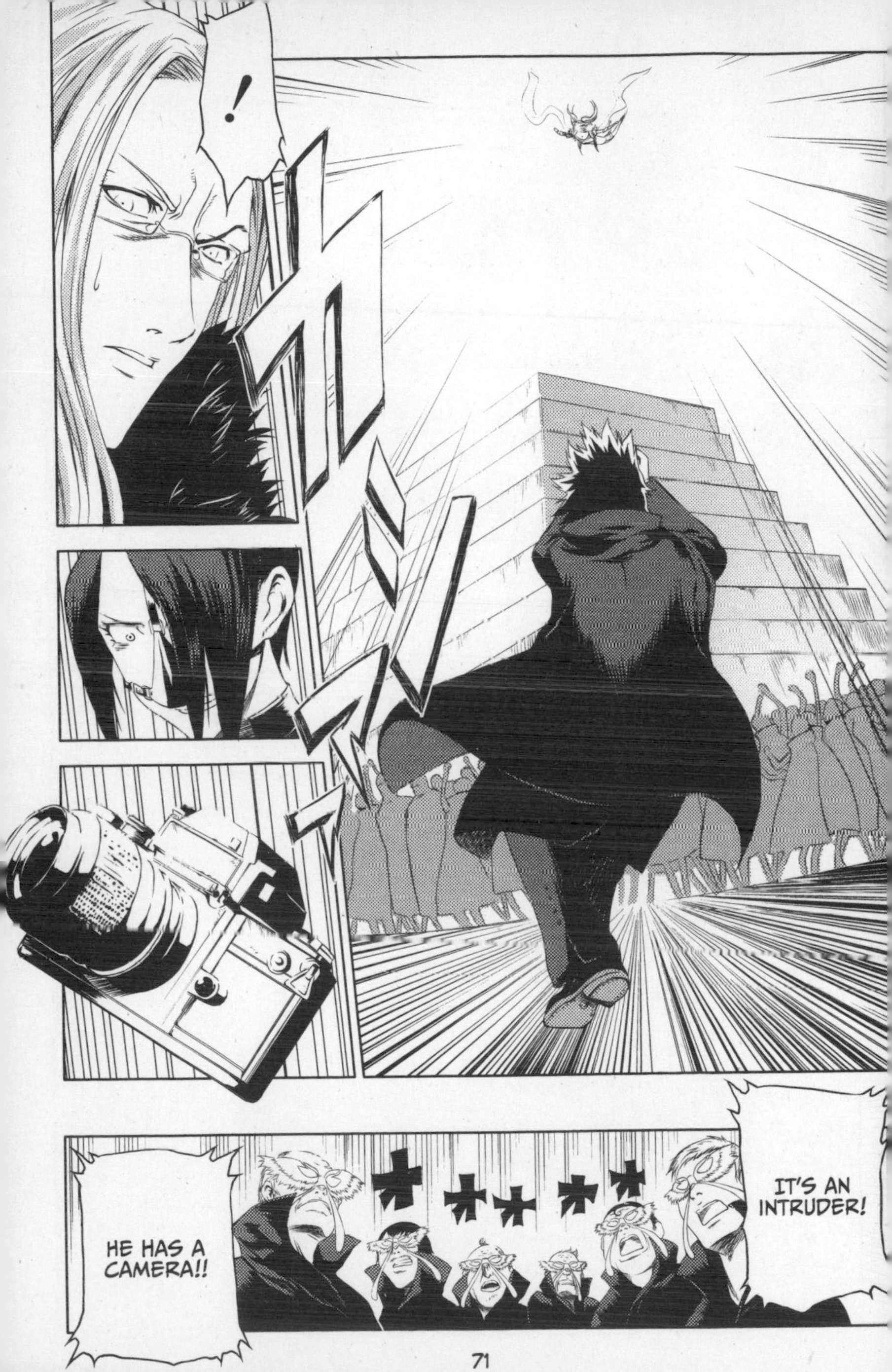
!
IT'S AN INTRUDER!
HE HAS A CAMERA!!

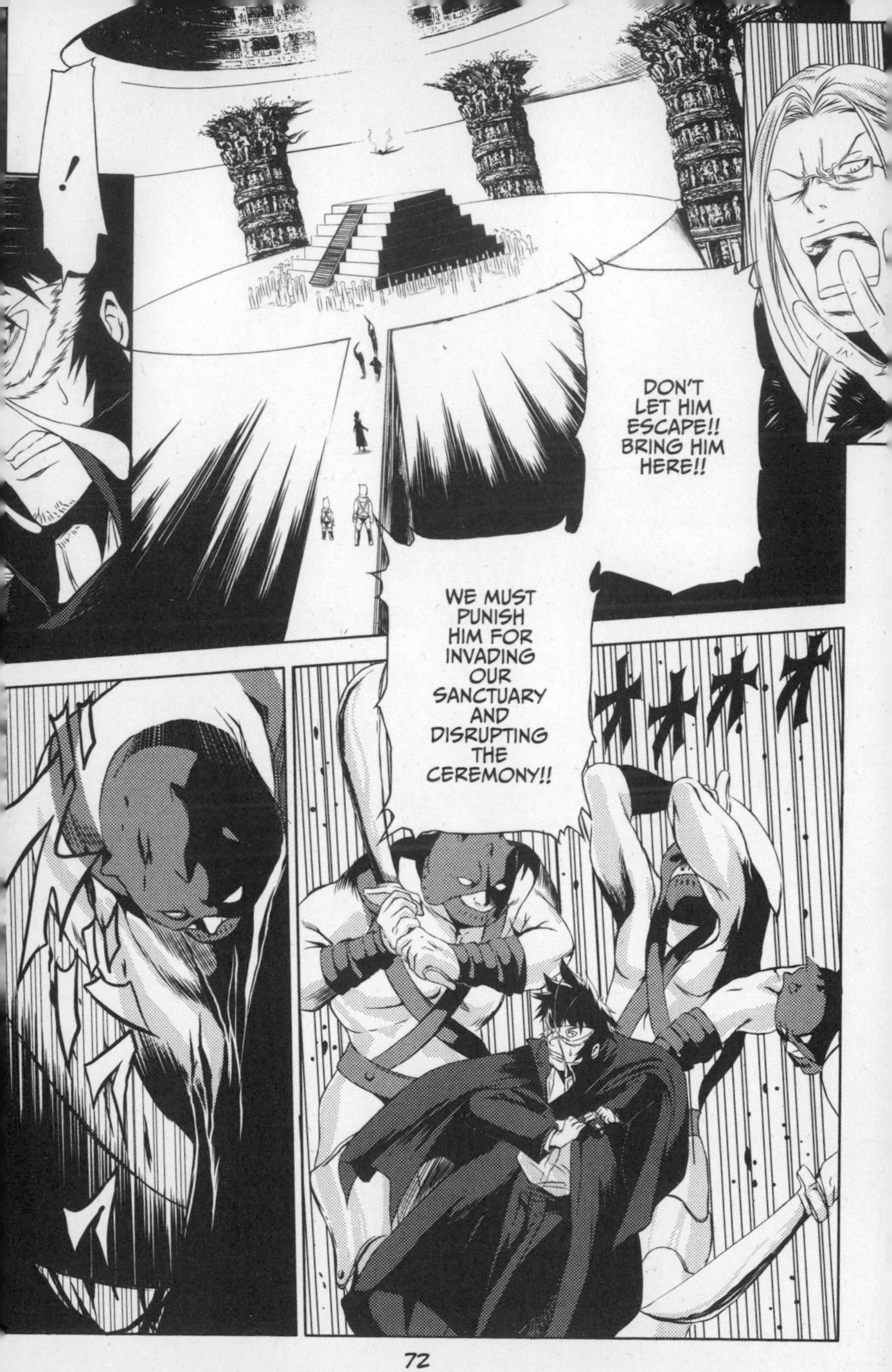
DON'T LET HIM ESCAPE!! BRING HIM HERE!!
!
WE MUST PUNISH HIM FOR INVADING OUR SANCTUARY AND DISRUPTING THE CEREMONY!!
オオオオ

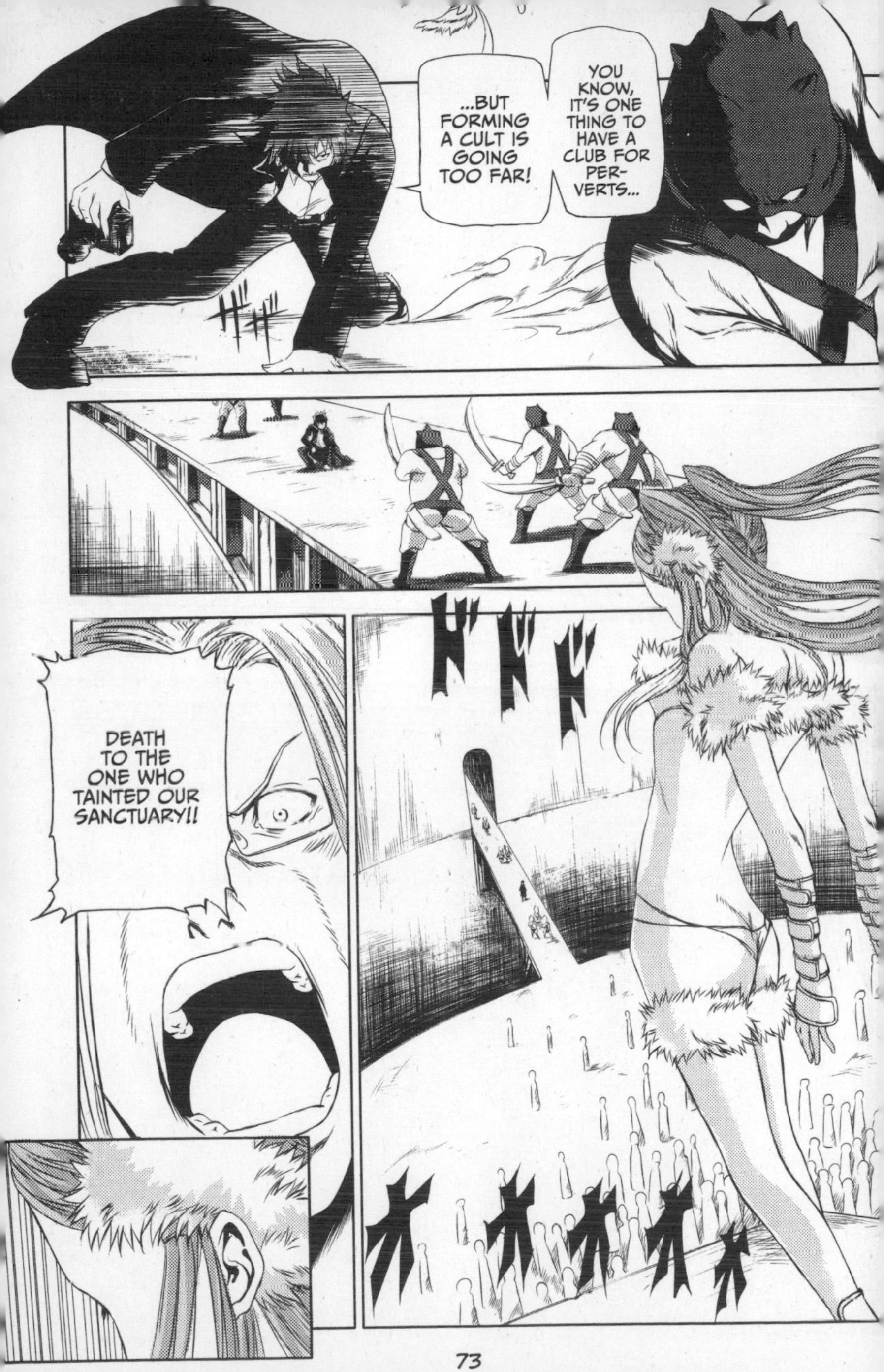
YOU KNOW, IT'S ONE THING TO HAVE A CLUB FOR PER-VERTS...
...BUT FORMING A CULT IS GOING TOO FAR!
DEATH TO THE ONE WHO TAINTED OUR SANCTUARY!!

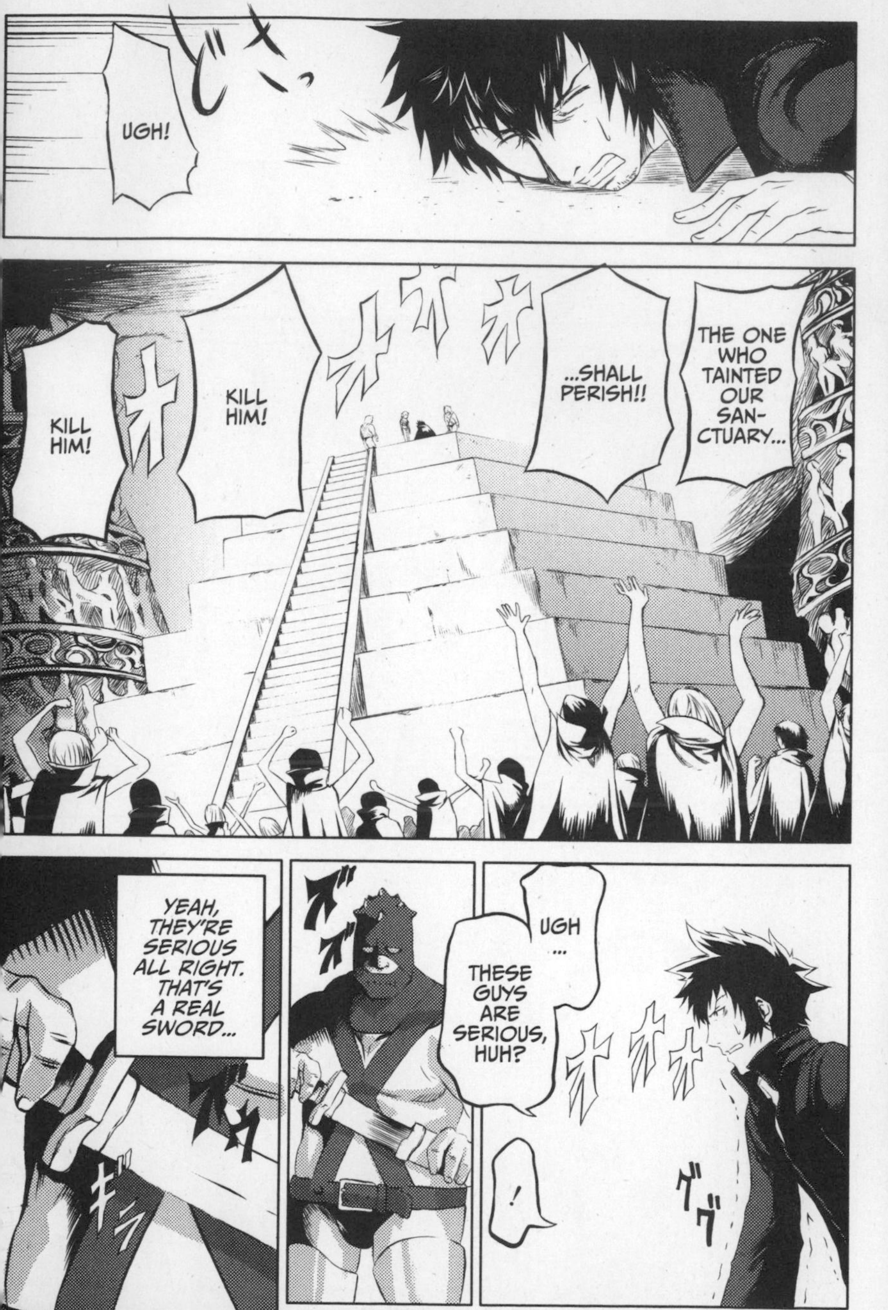
UGH!
THE ONE WHO TAINTED OUR SANCTUARY...
...SHALL PERISH!!
KILL HIM!
KILL HIM!
UGH ... THESE GUYS ARE SERIOUS, HUH?
!
YEAH, THEY'RE SERIOUS ALL RIGHT. THAT'S A REAL SWORD...

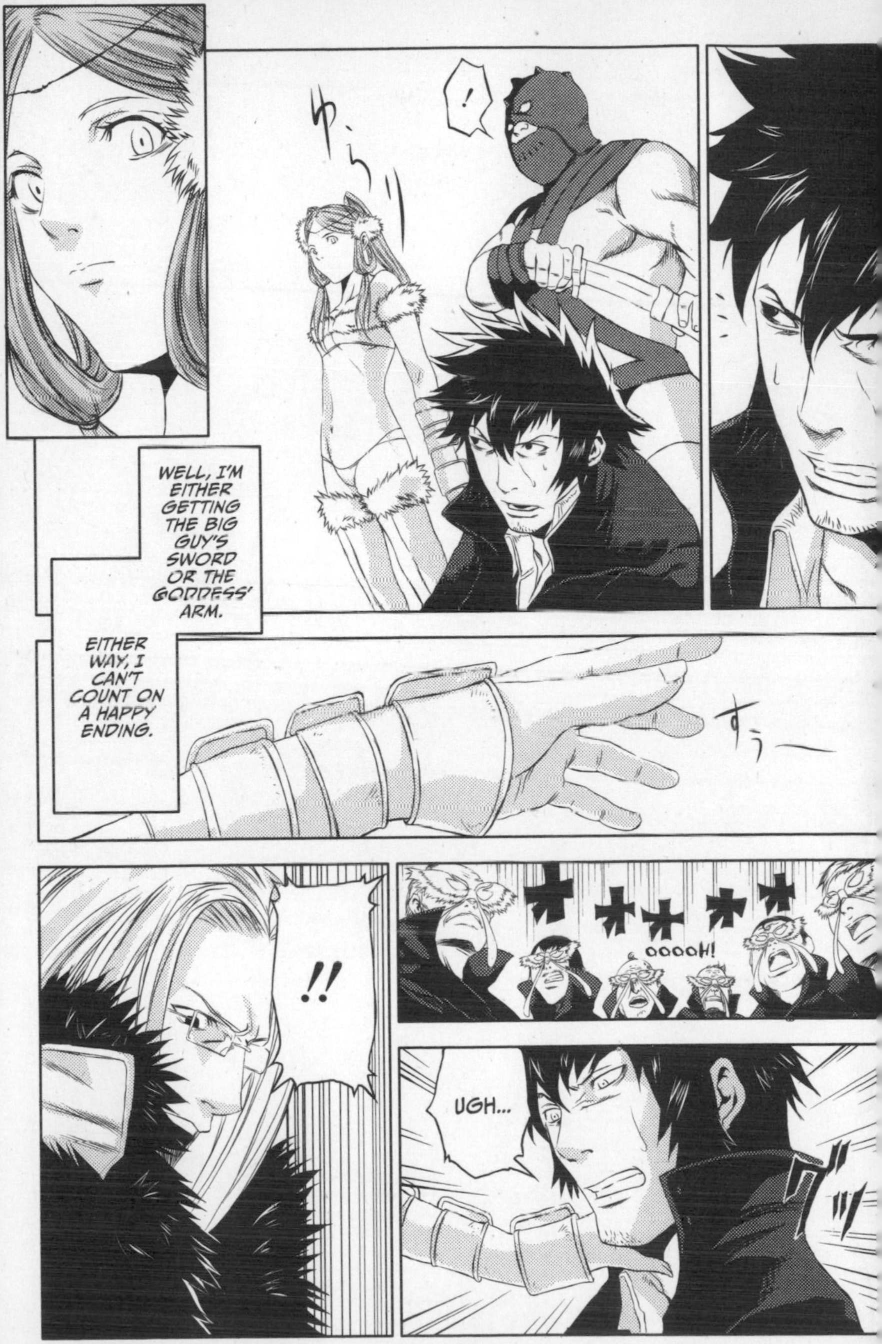
ゆら
!
WELL, I'M EITHER GETTING THE BIG GUY'S SWORD OR THE GODDESS' ARM.
EITHER WAY, I CAN'T COUNT ON A HAPPY ENDING.
すぅー
OOOOH!
UGH...
!!

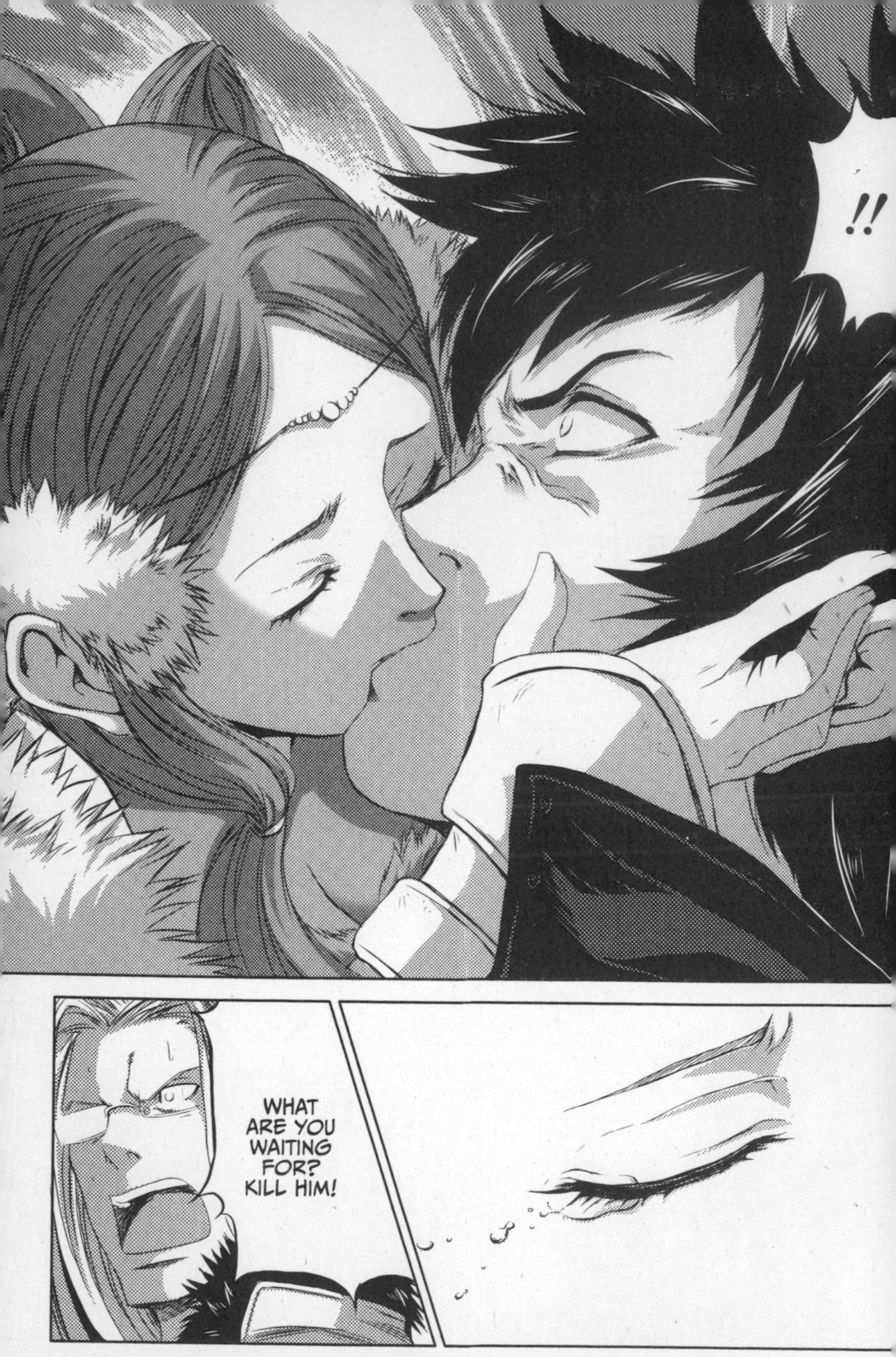
!!
WHAT ARE YOU WAITING FOR? KILL HIM!

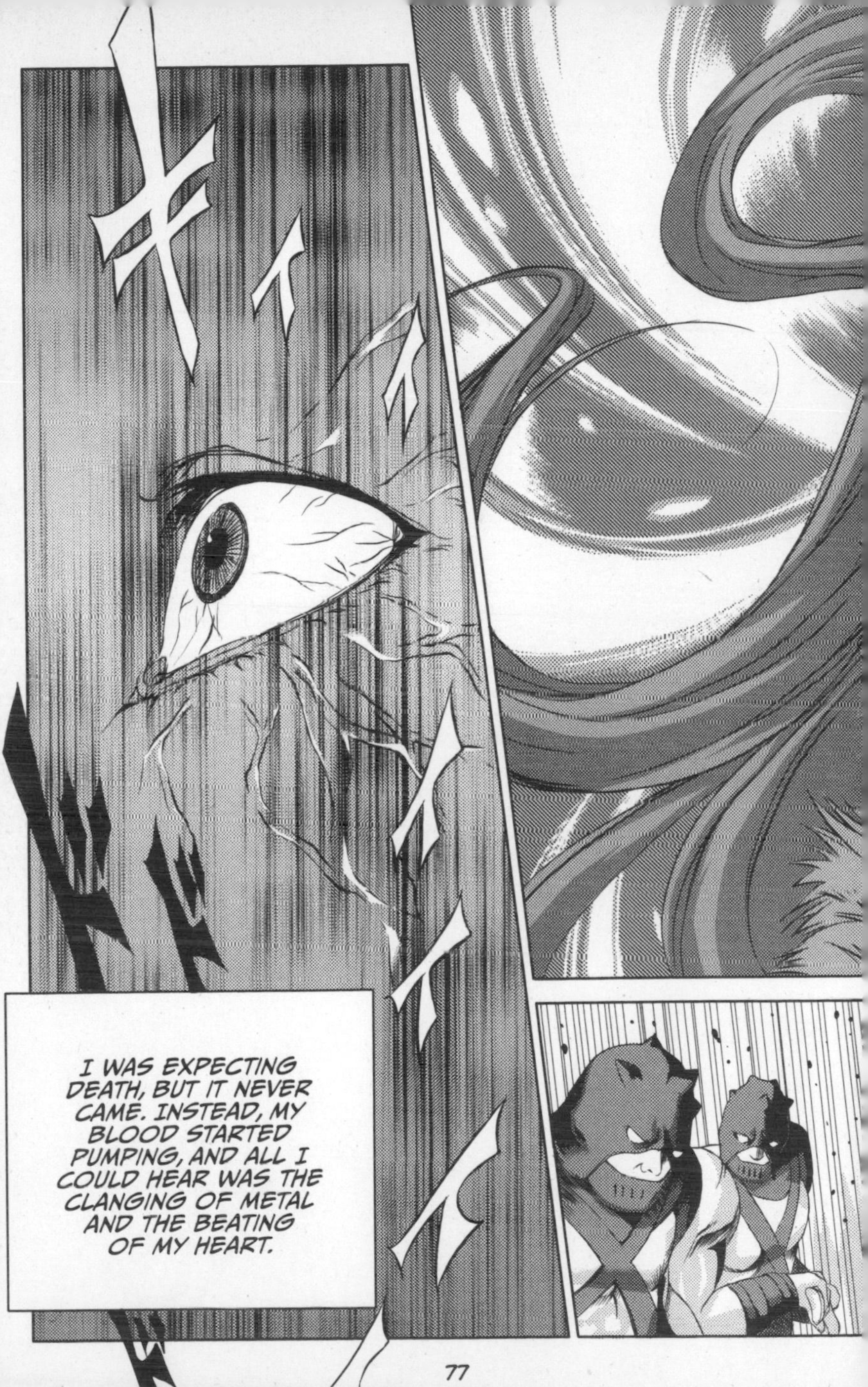
I WAS EXPECTING DEATH, BUT IT NEVER CAME. INSTEAD, MY BLOOD STARTED PUMPING, AND ALL I COULD HEAR WAS THE CLANGING OF METAL AND THE BEATING OF MY HEART.

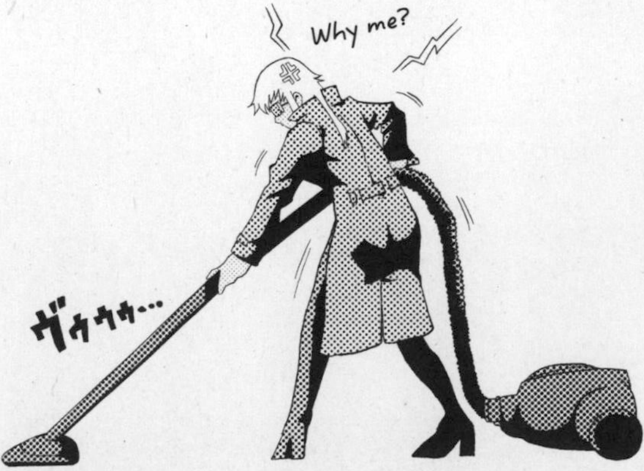
Why me?
ヴゥゥゥ…

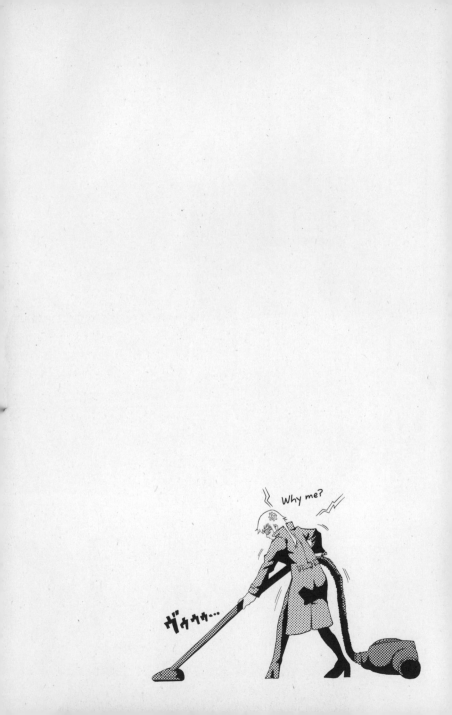

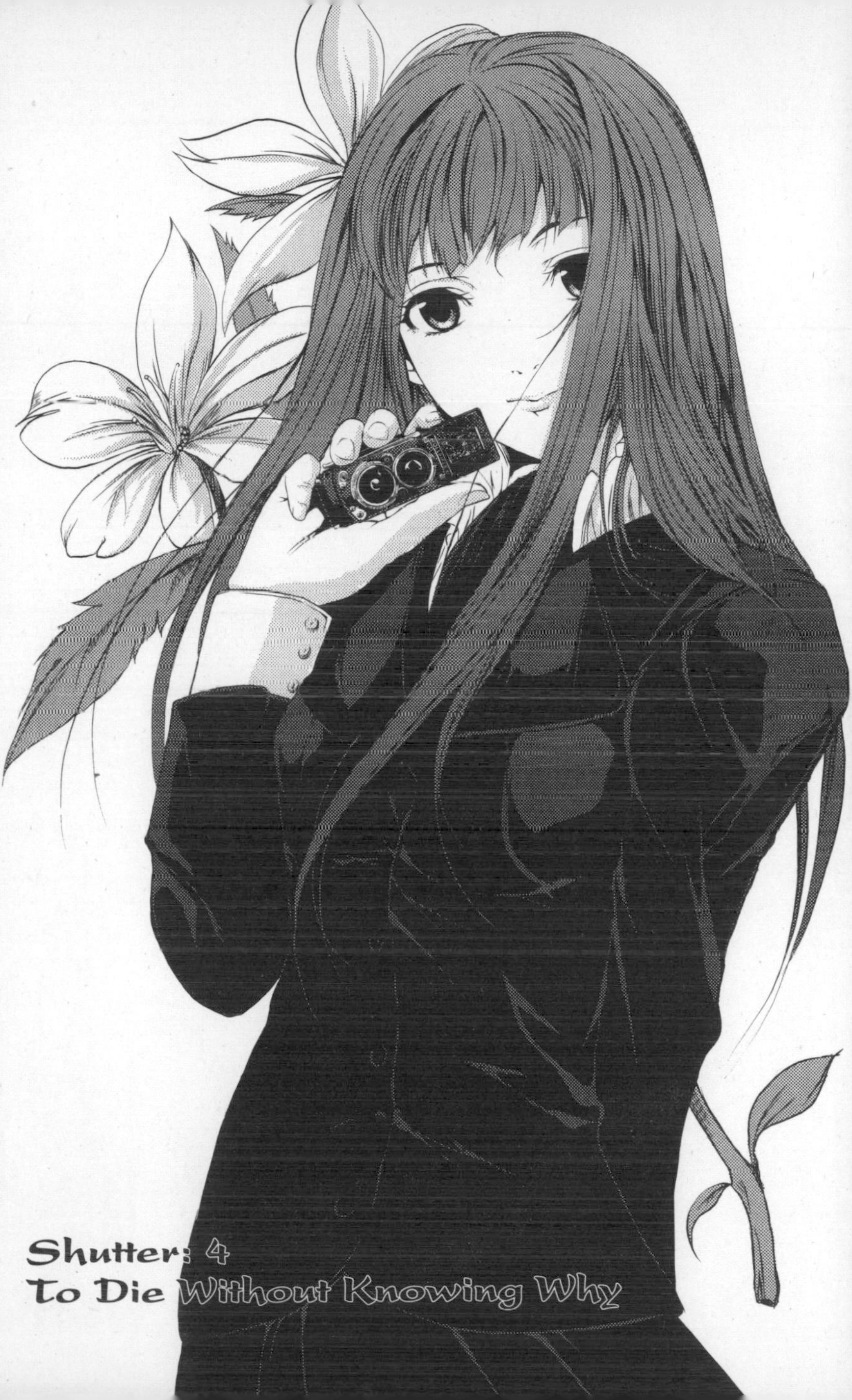

Shutter: 4
To Die Without Knowing Why

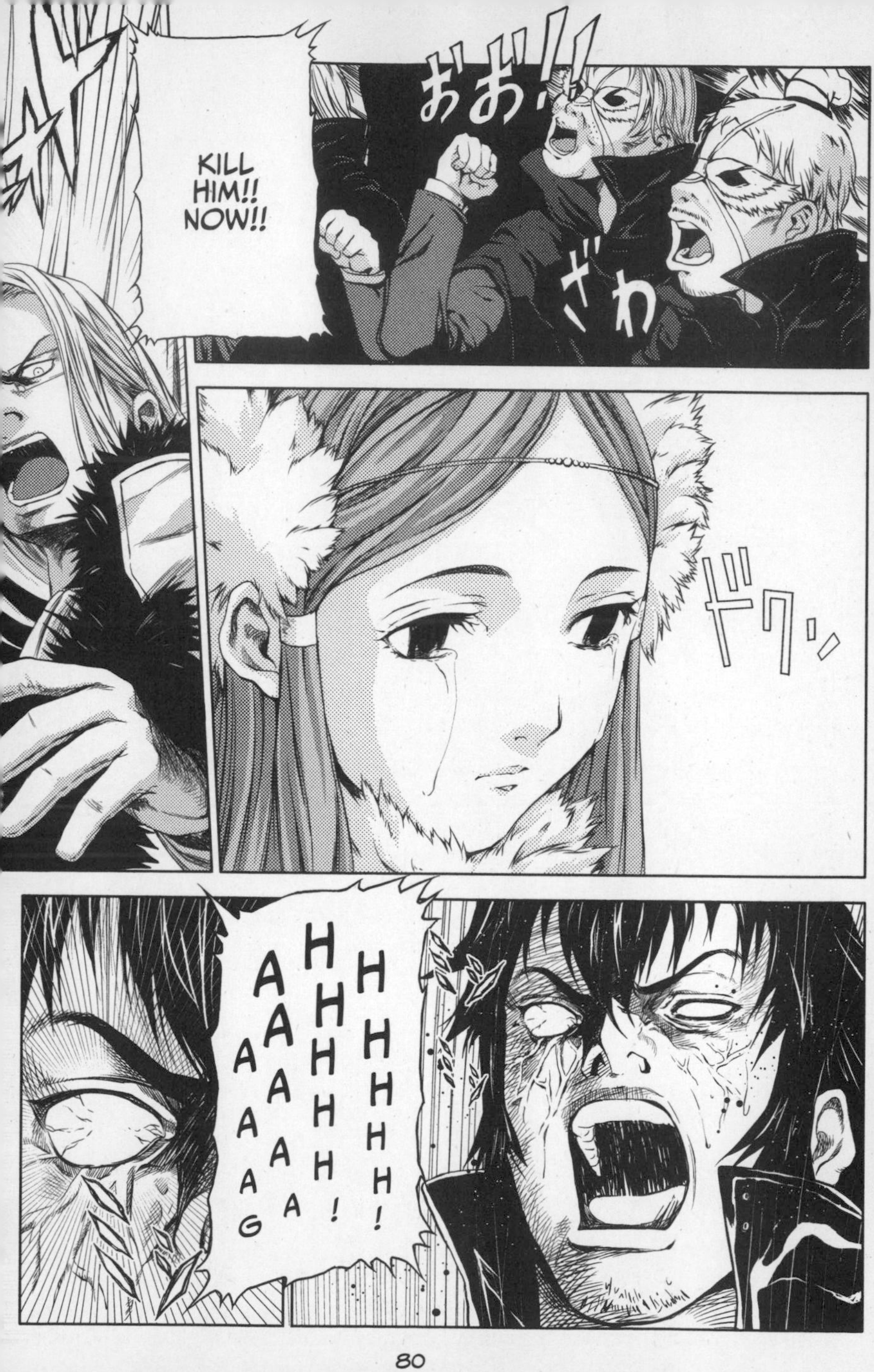
おお!!
ざわ
KILL HIM!! NOW!!
ドクッ
AAAAG
AAAAA
HHHHH!
HHHHH!

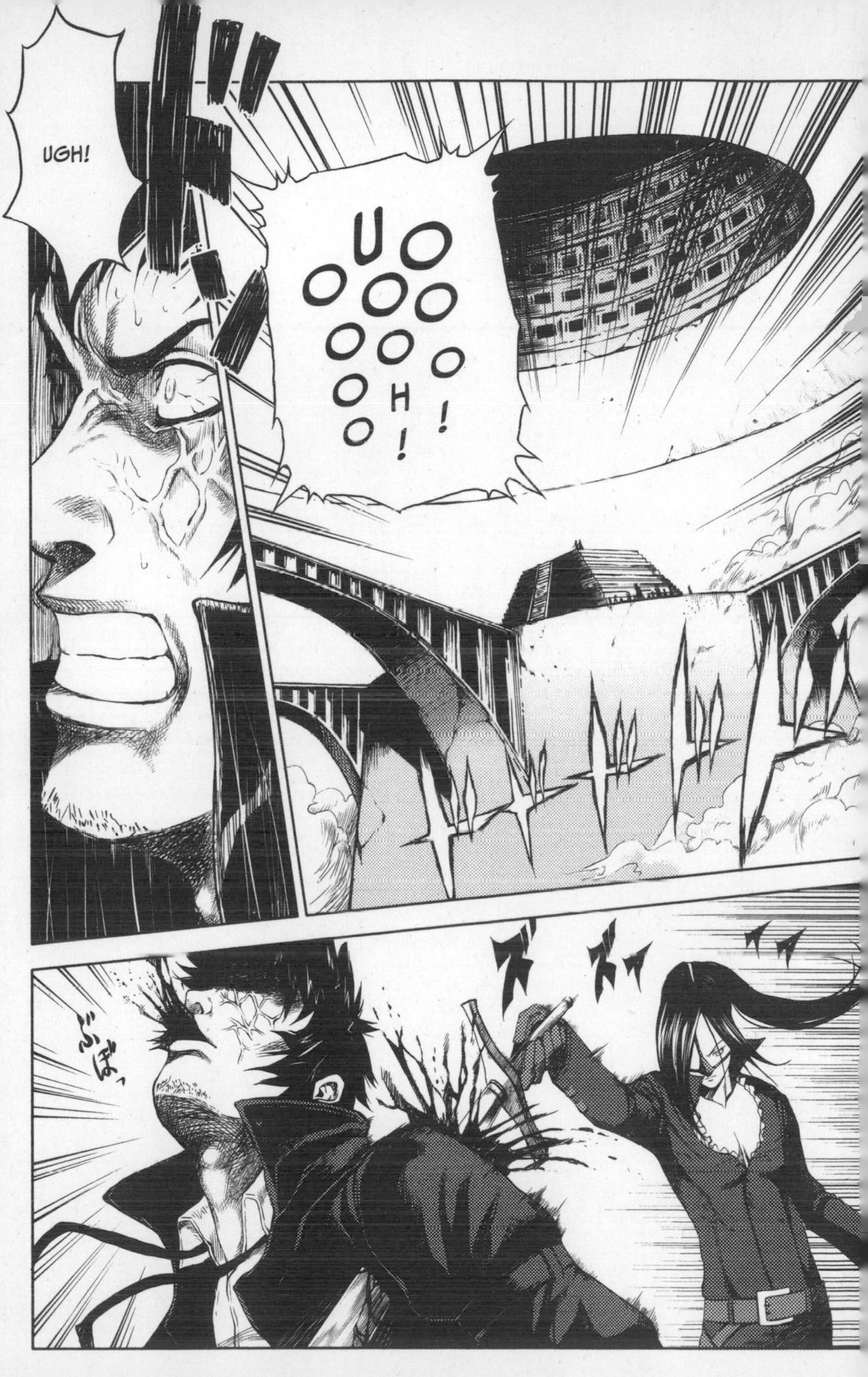
UOOOOOOOOOH!!
UGH!
ズズァ
ぶぼっ

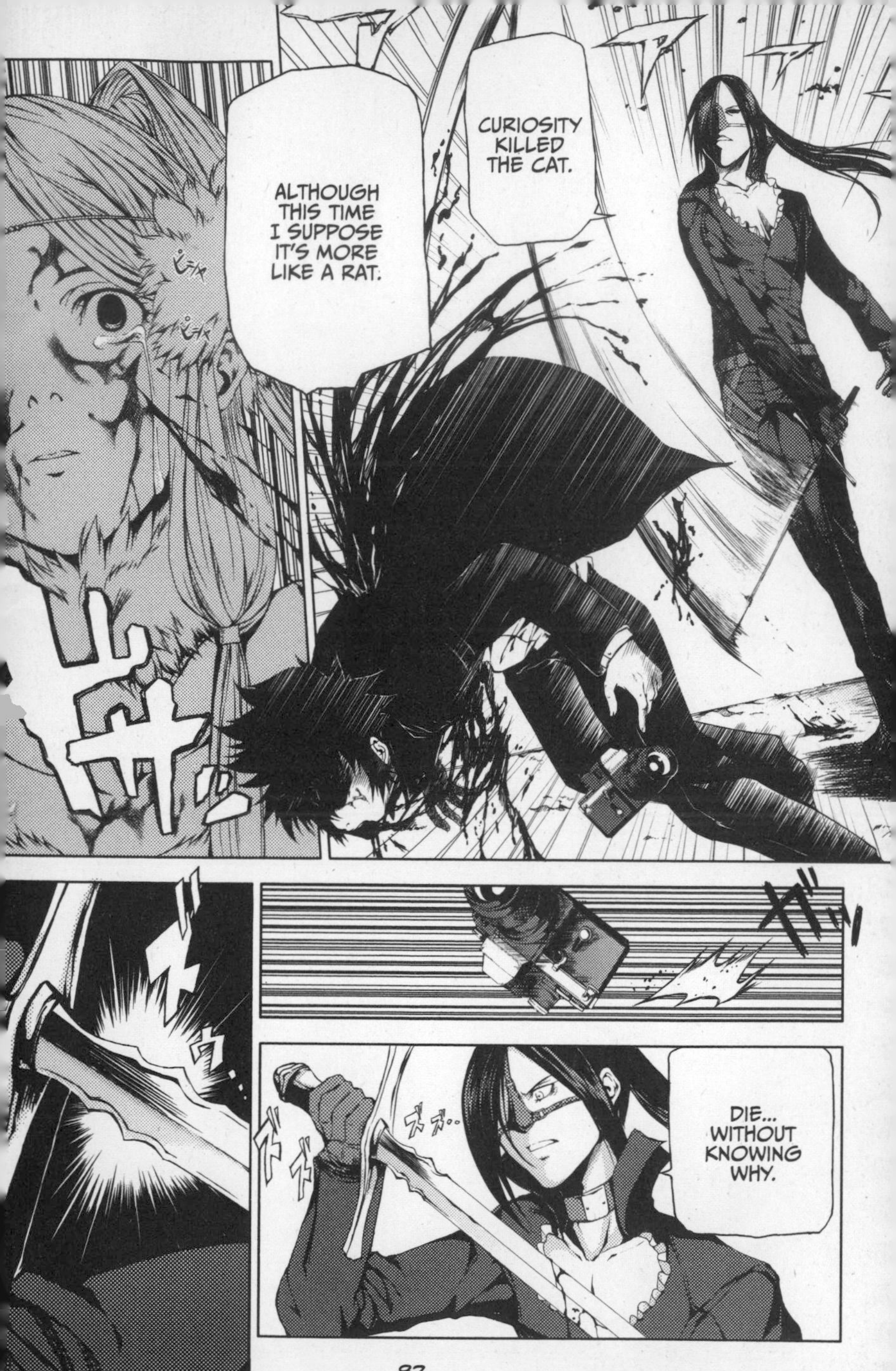
CURIOSITY KILLED THE CAT.
ALTHOUGH THIS TIME I SUPPOSE IT'S MORE LIKE A RAT.
DIE... WITHOUT KNOWING WHY.

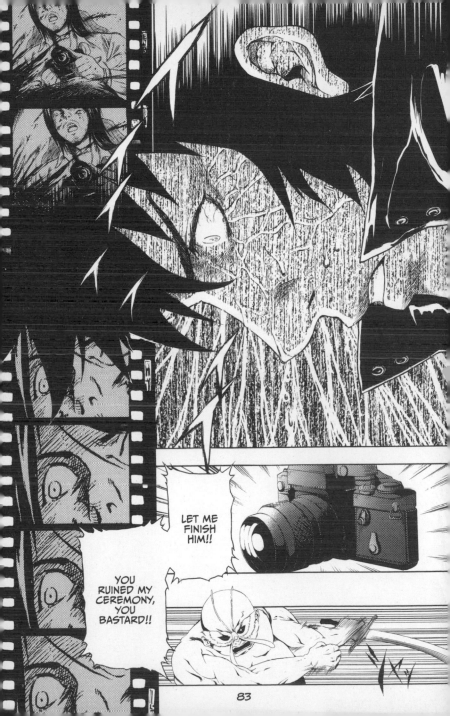

LET ME FINISH HIM!!

YOU RUINED MY CEREMONY, YOU BASTARD!!

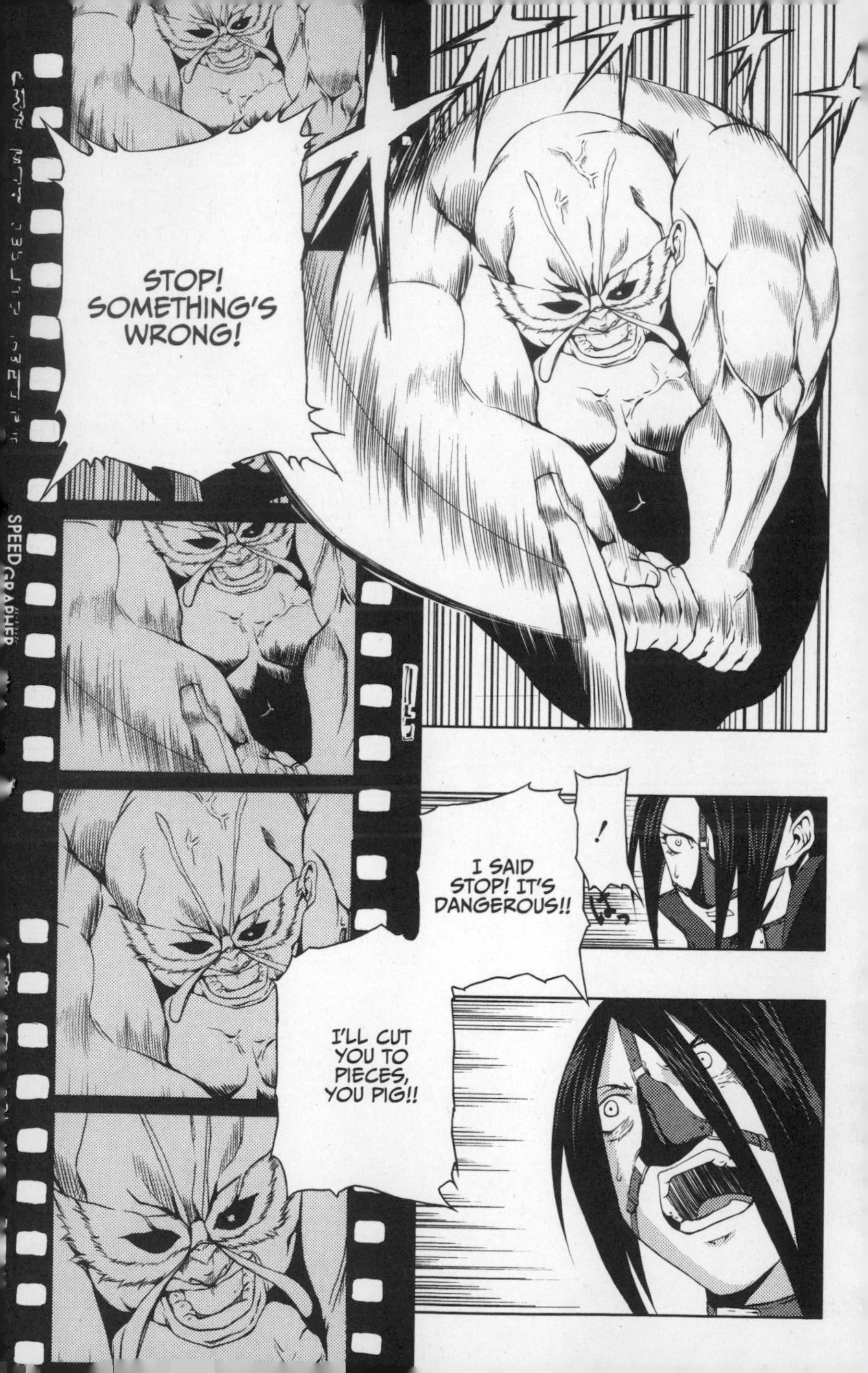
STOP! SOMETHING'S WRONG!
!
I SAID STOP! IT'S DANGEROUS!!
I'LL CUT YOU TO PIECES, YOU PIG!!
SPEED GRAPHER

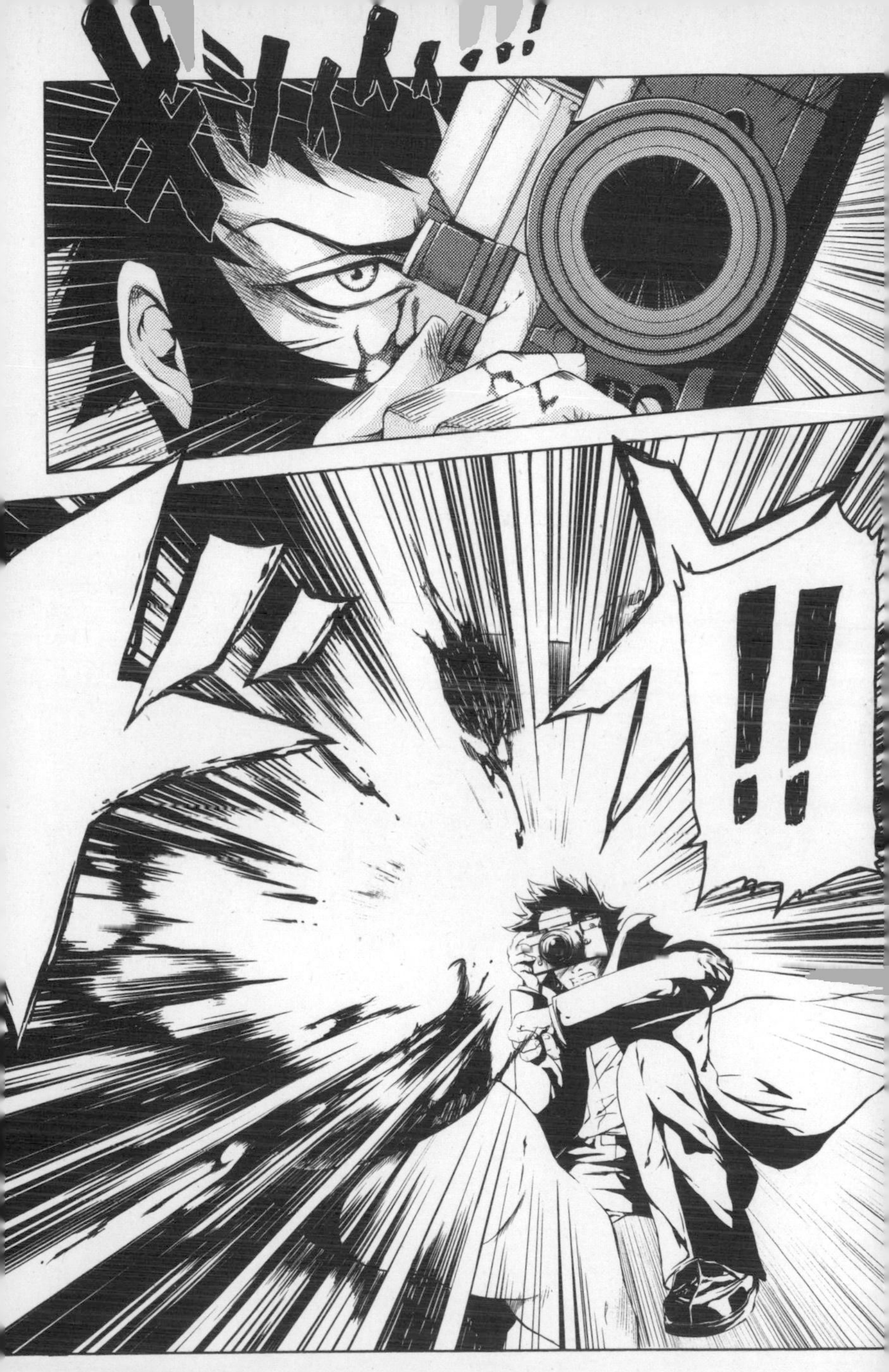

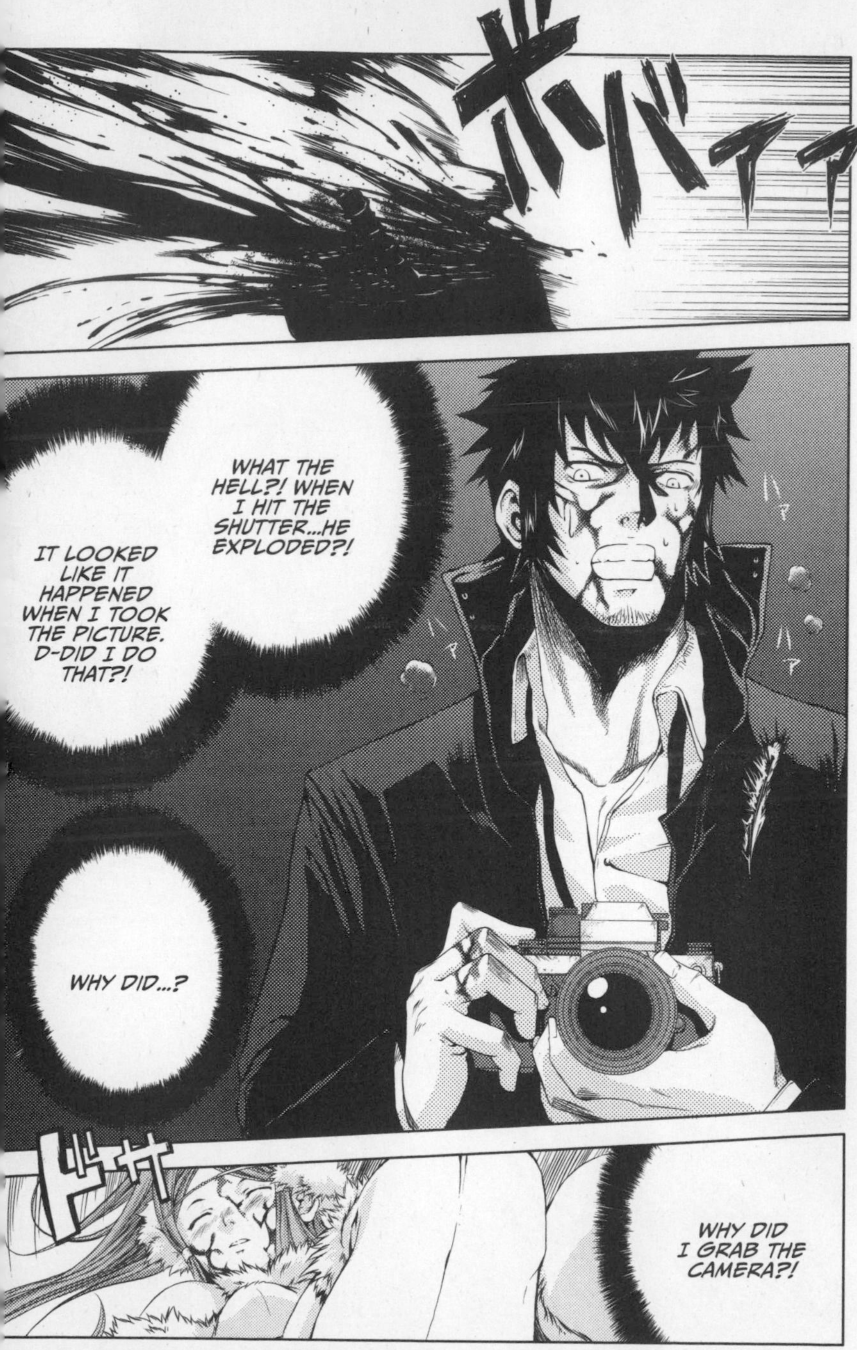
ボバァァ
WHAT THE HELL?! WHEN I HIT THE SHUTTER...HE EXPLODED?!
IT LOOKED LIKE IT HAPPENED WHEN I TOOK THE PICTURE. D-DID I DO THAT?!
WHY DID...?
WHY DID I GRAB THE CAMERA?!

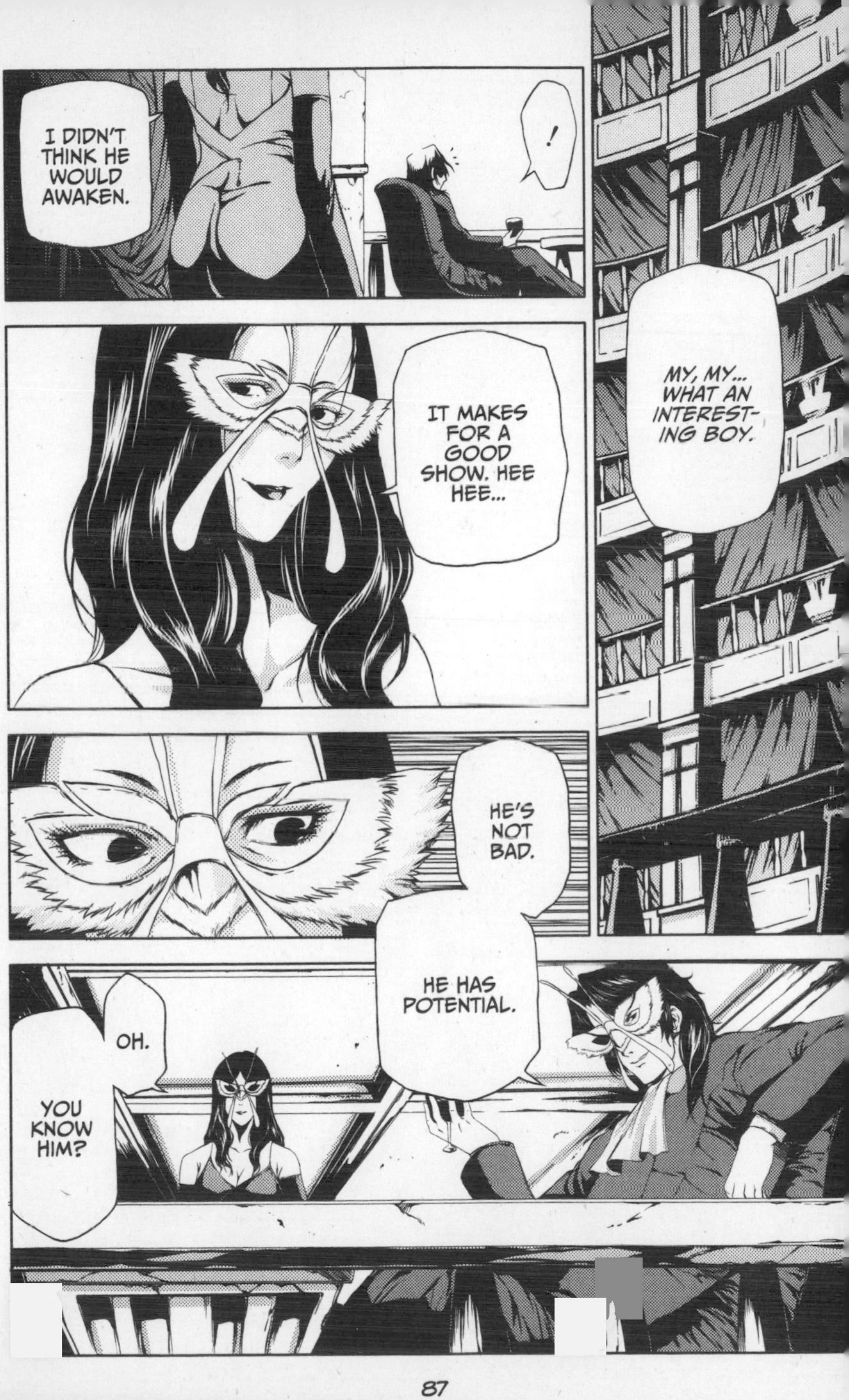
MY, MY... WHAT AN INTERESTING BOY.
!
I DIDN'T THINK HE WOULD AWAKEN.
IT MAKES FOR A GOOD SHOW. HEE HEE...
HE'S NOT BAD.
HE HAS POTENTIAL.
OH.
YOU KNOW HIM?

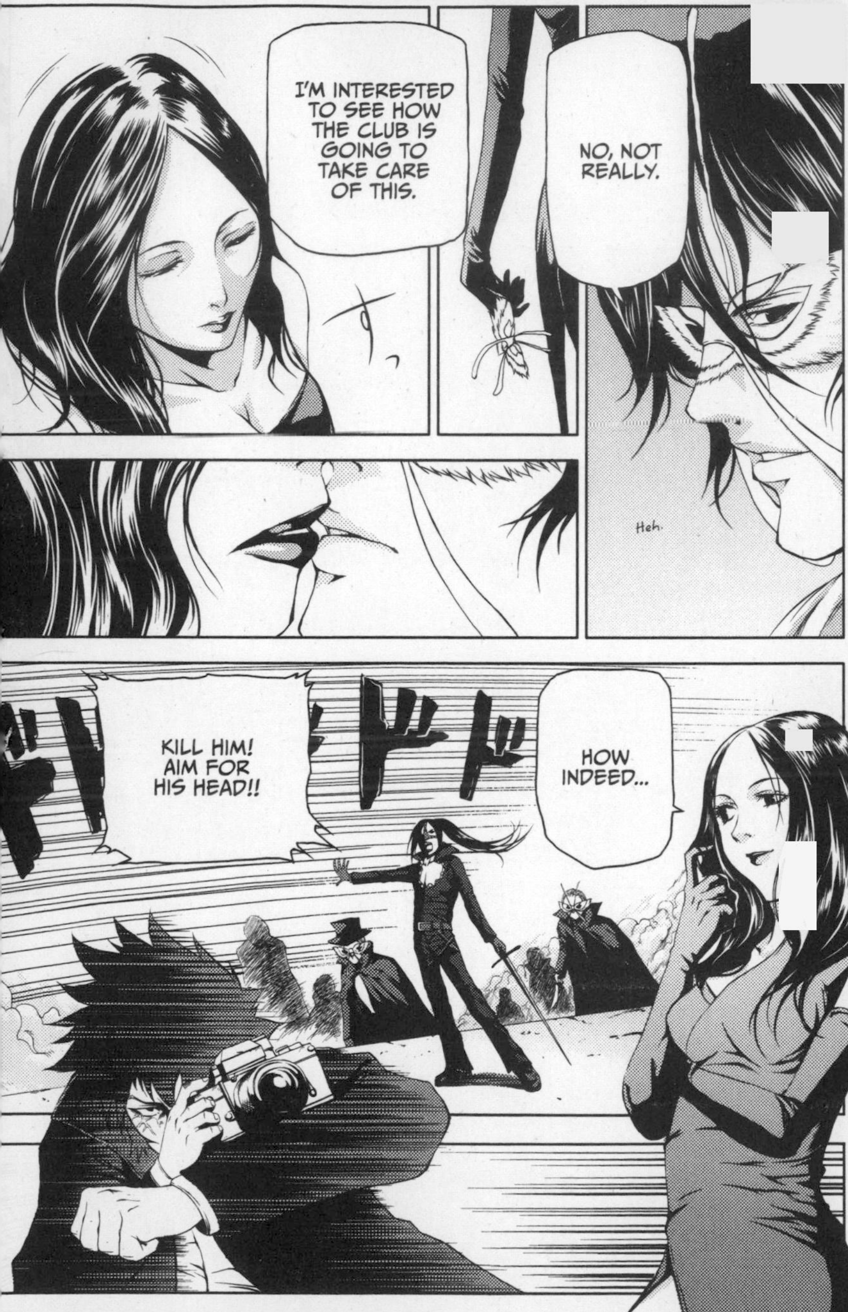
NO, NOT REALLY.
Heh.
I'M INTERESTED TO SEE HOW THE CLUB IS GOING TO TAKE CARE OF THIS.
HOW INDEED...
KILL HIM! AIM FOR HIS HEAD!!

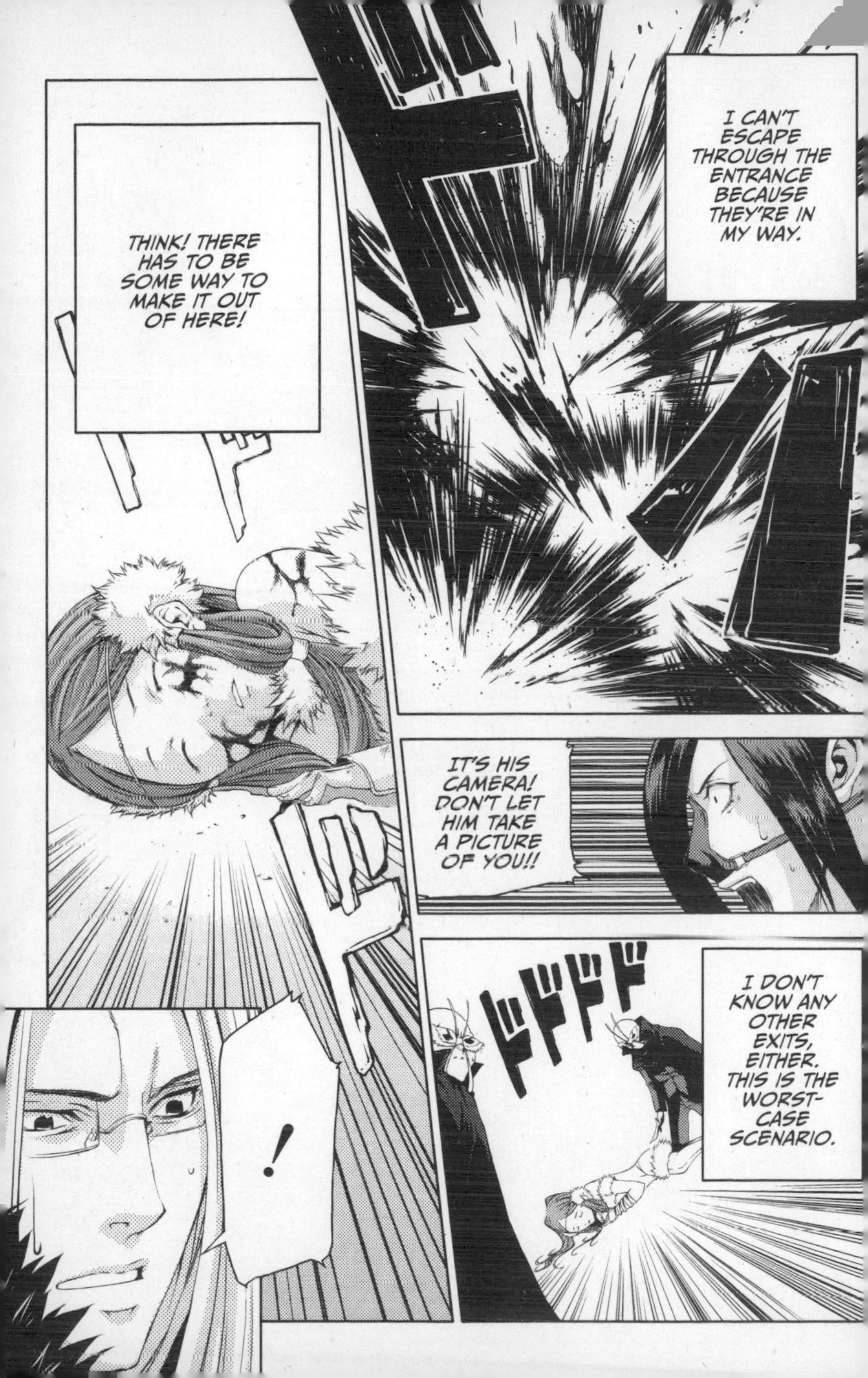
I CAN'T ESCAPE THROUGH THE ENTRANCE BECAUSE THEY'RE IN MY WAY.
IT'S HIS CAMERA! DON'T LET HIM TAKE A PICTURE OF YOU!!
ドドドド
I DON'T KNOW ANY OTHER EXITS, EITHER. THIS IS THE WORST-CASE SCENARIO.
THINK! THERE HAS TO BE SOME WAY TO MAKE IT OUT OF HERE!
!

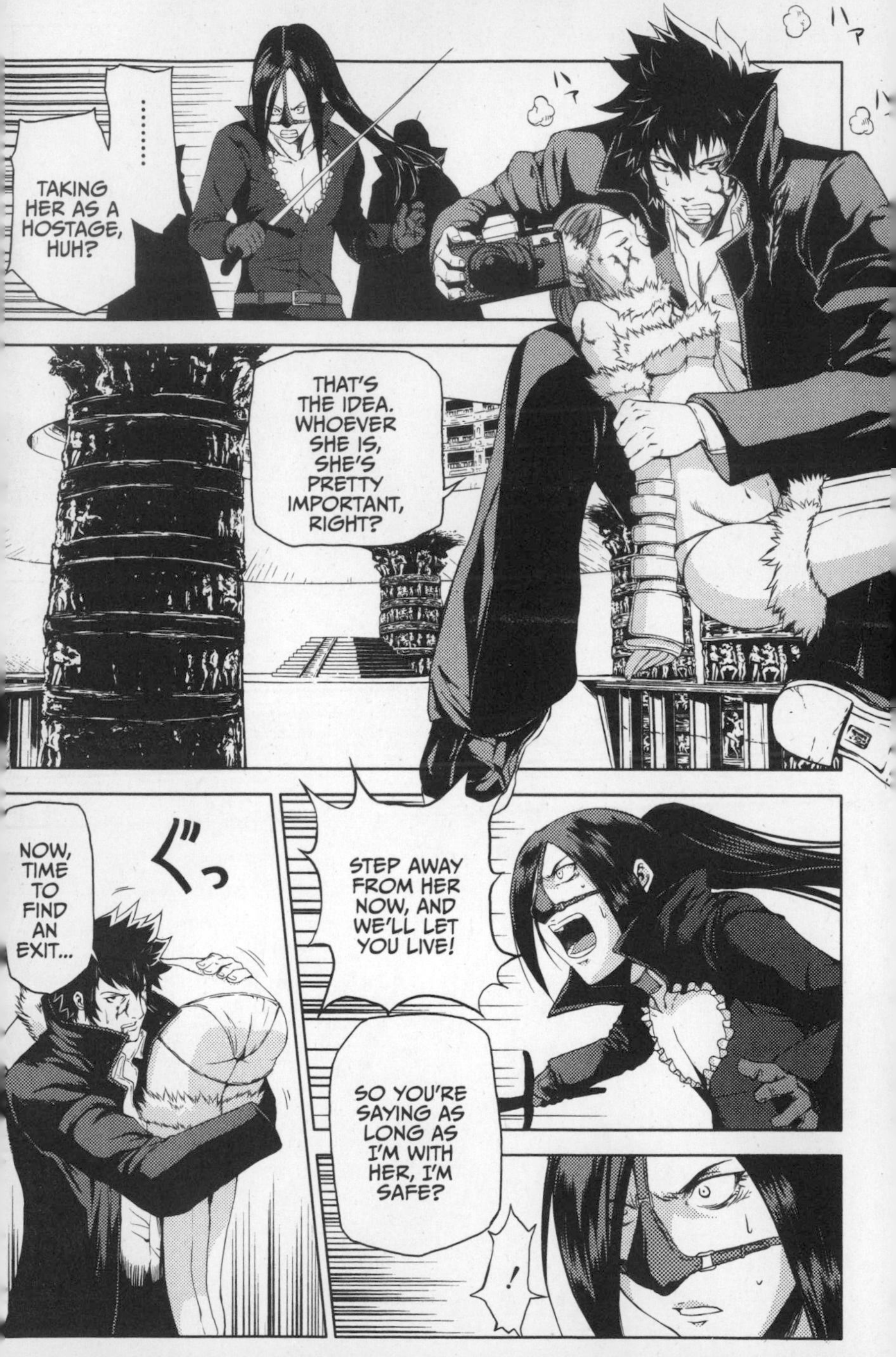
ハァ
ハァ
ハァ
……
TAKING HER AS A HOSTAGE, HUH?
THAT'S THE IDEA. WHOEVER SHE IS, SHE'S PRETTY IMPORTANT, RIGHT?
STEP AWAY FROM HER NOW, AND WE'LL LET YOU LIVE!
SO YOU'RE SAYING AS LONG AS I'M WITH HER, I'M SAFE?
!
ぐっ
NOW, TIME TO FIND AN EXIT...

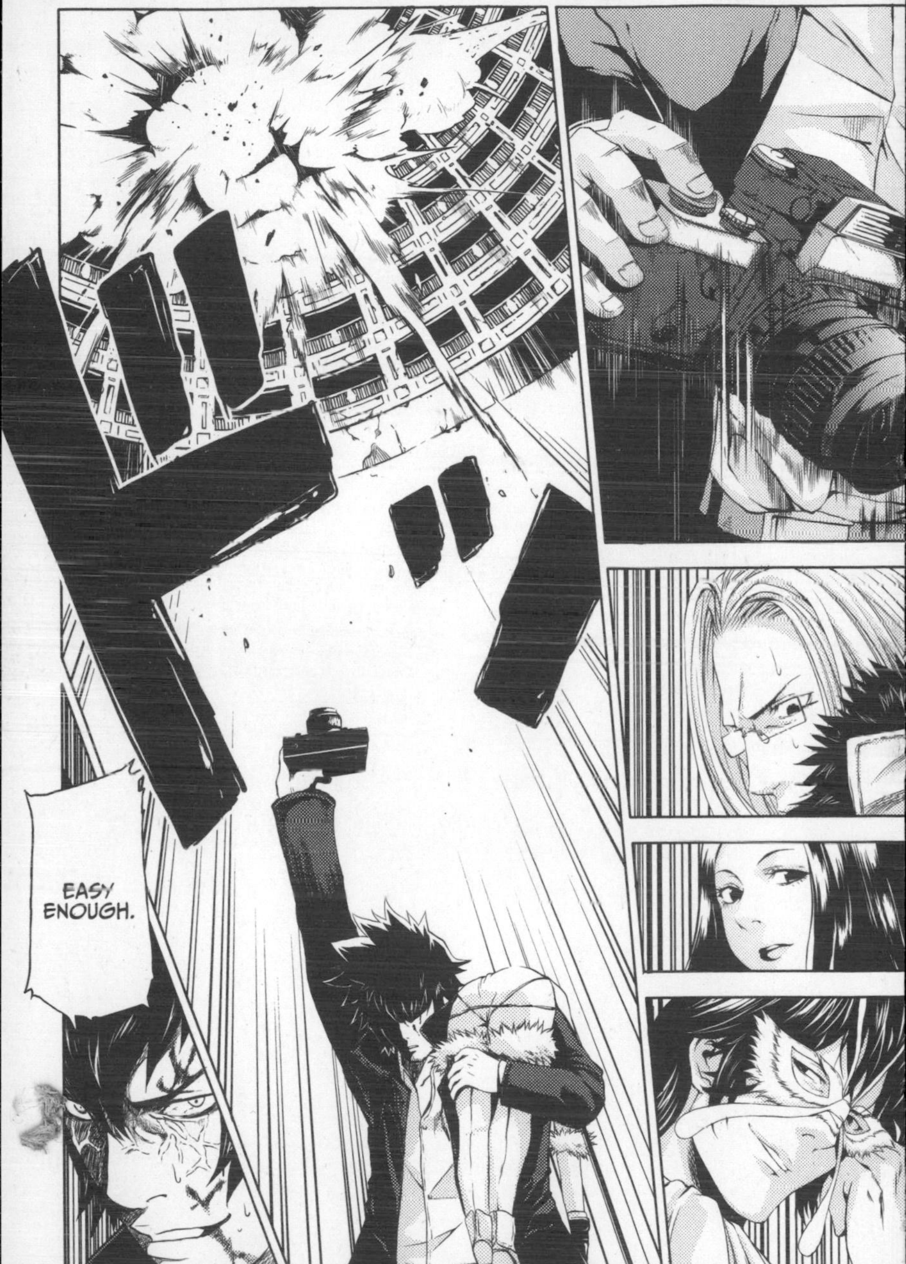
EASY ENOUGH.

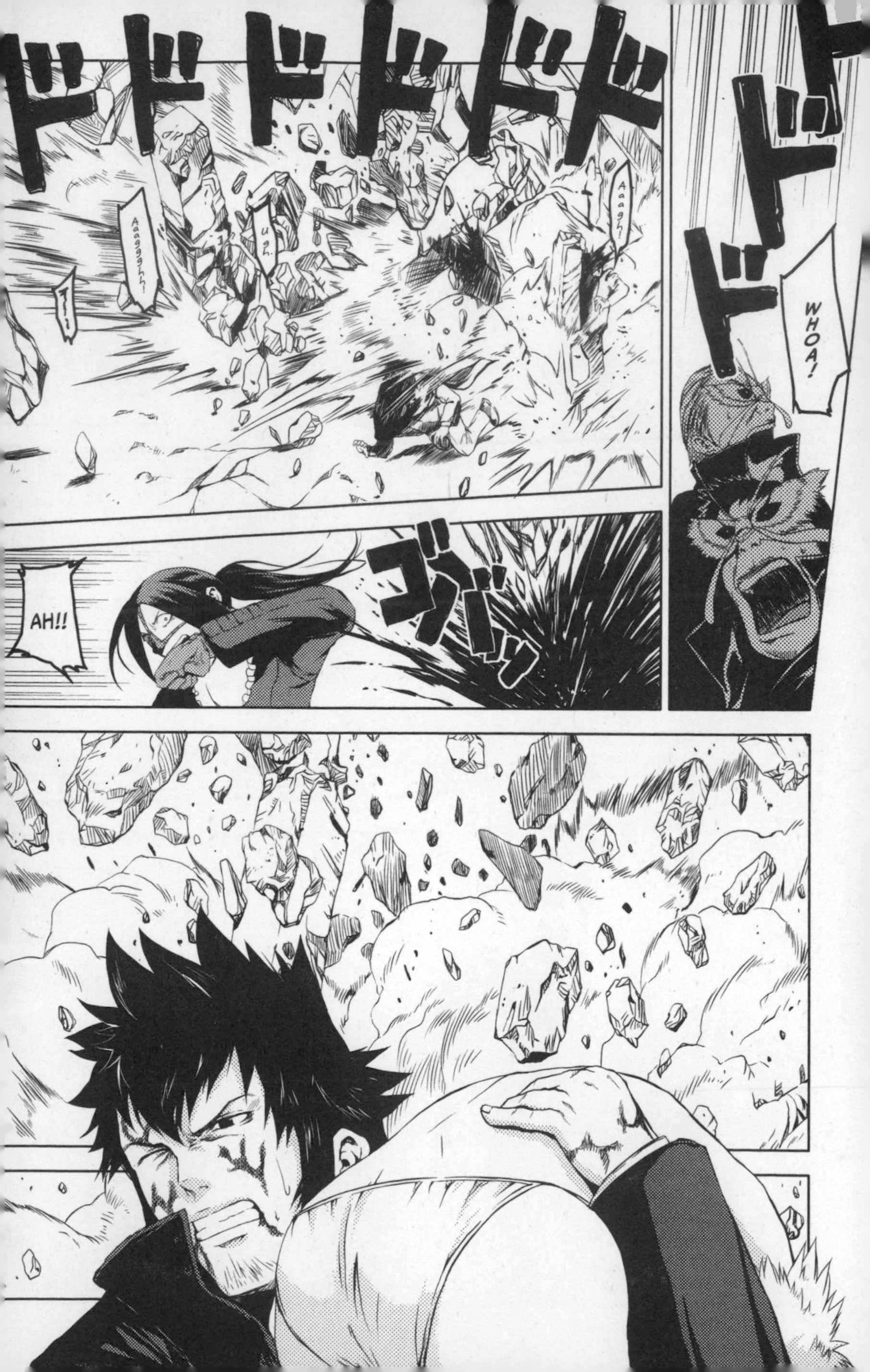
ドドド
WHOA!
ドドドドドド
Aaaagh!
Ugh.
Aaaggghhh!
ゴバッ
AH!!

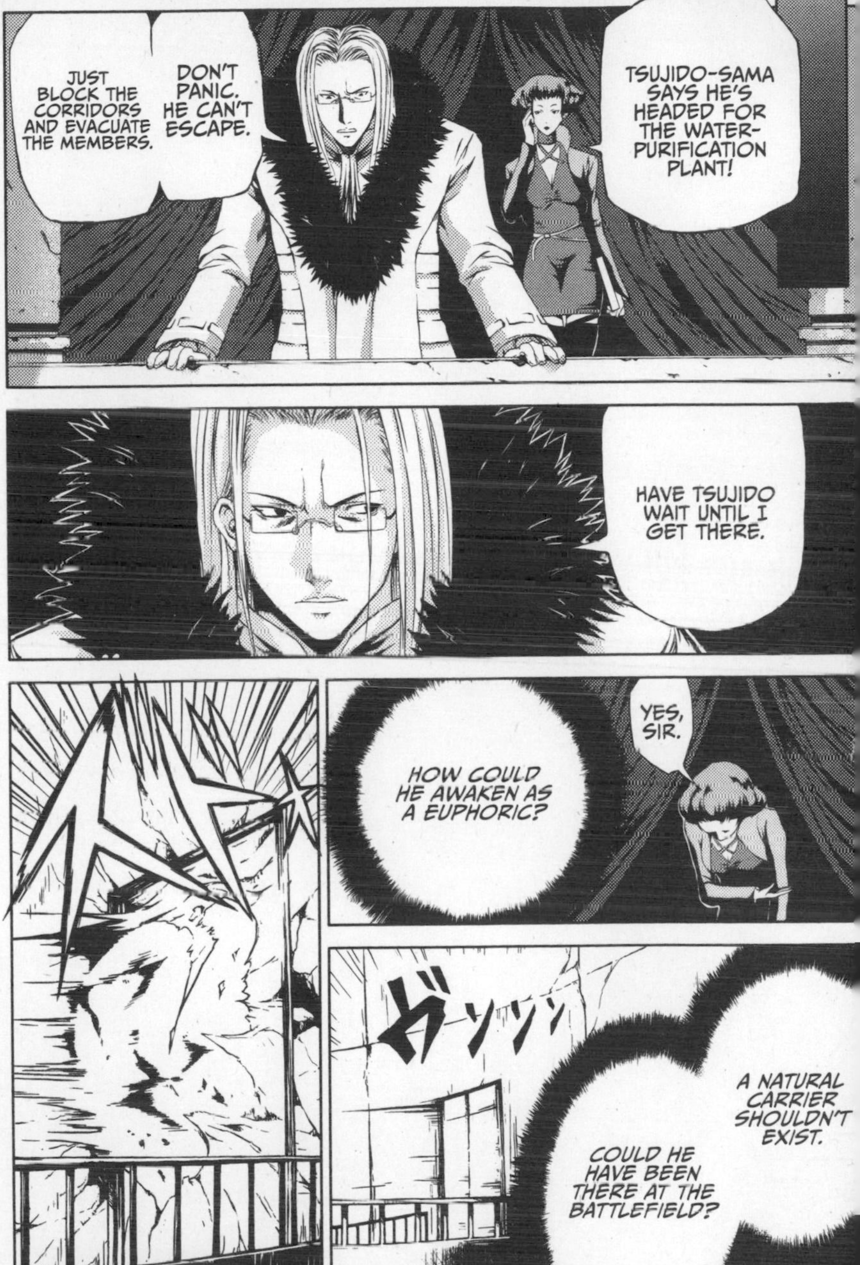
TSUJIDO-SAMA SAYS HE'S HEADED FOR THE WATER-PURIFICATION PLANT!
DON'T PANIC. HE CAN'T ESCAPE.
JUST BLOCK THE CORRIDORS AND EVACUATE THE MEMBERS.
HAVE TSUJIDO WAIT UNTIL I GET THERE.
YES, SIR.
HOW COULD HE AWAKEN AS A EUPHORIC?
ガッッッ
A NATURAL CARRIER SHOULDN'T EXIST.
COULD HE HAVE BEEN THERE AT THE BATTLEFIELD?

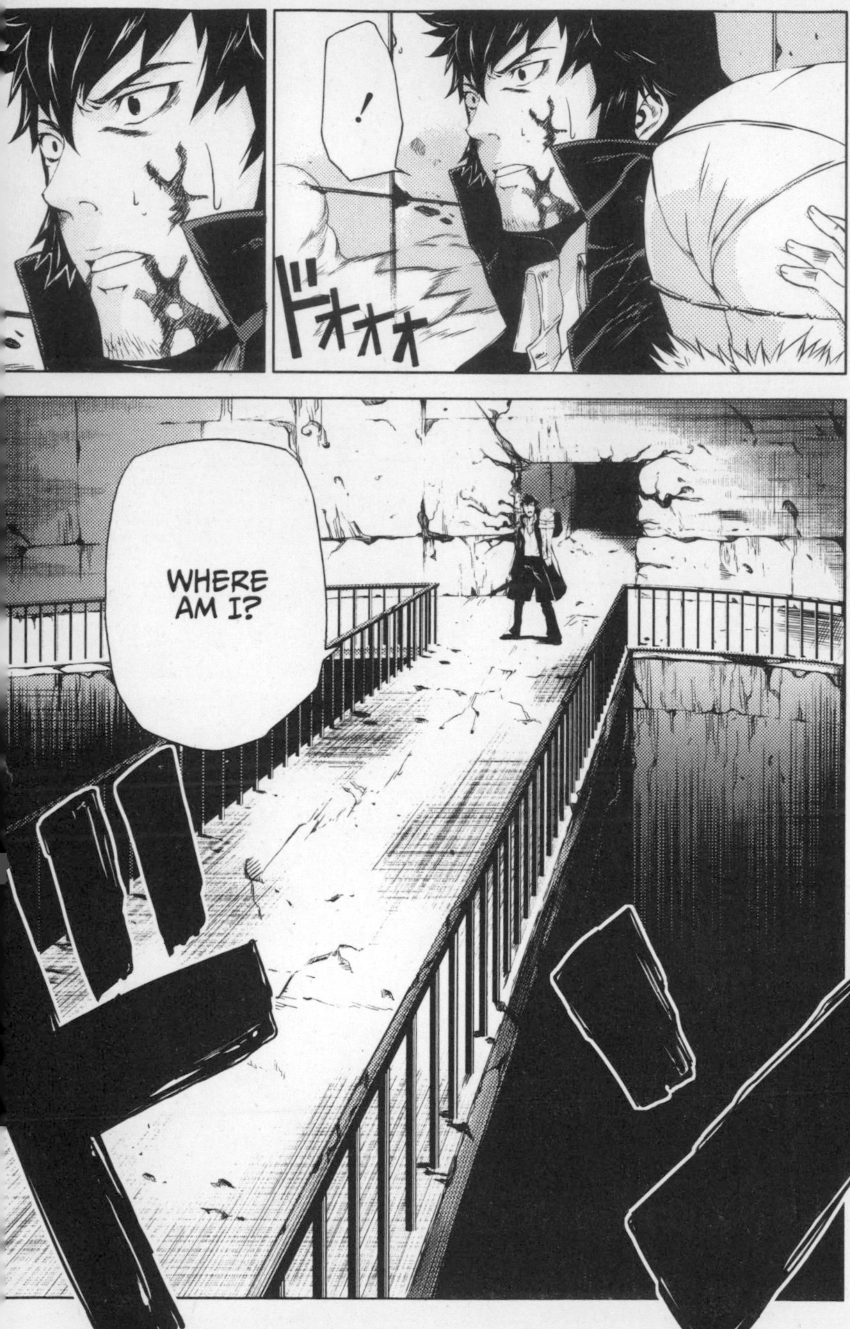
!
ドオオオ
WHERE AM I?

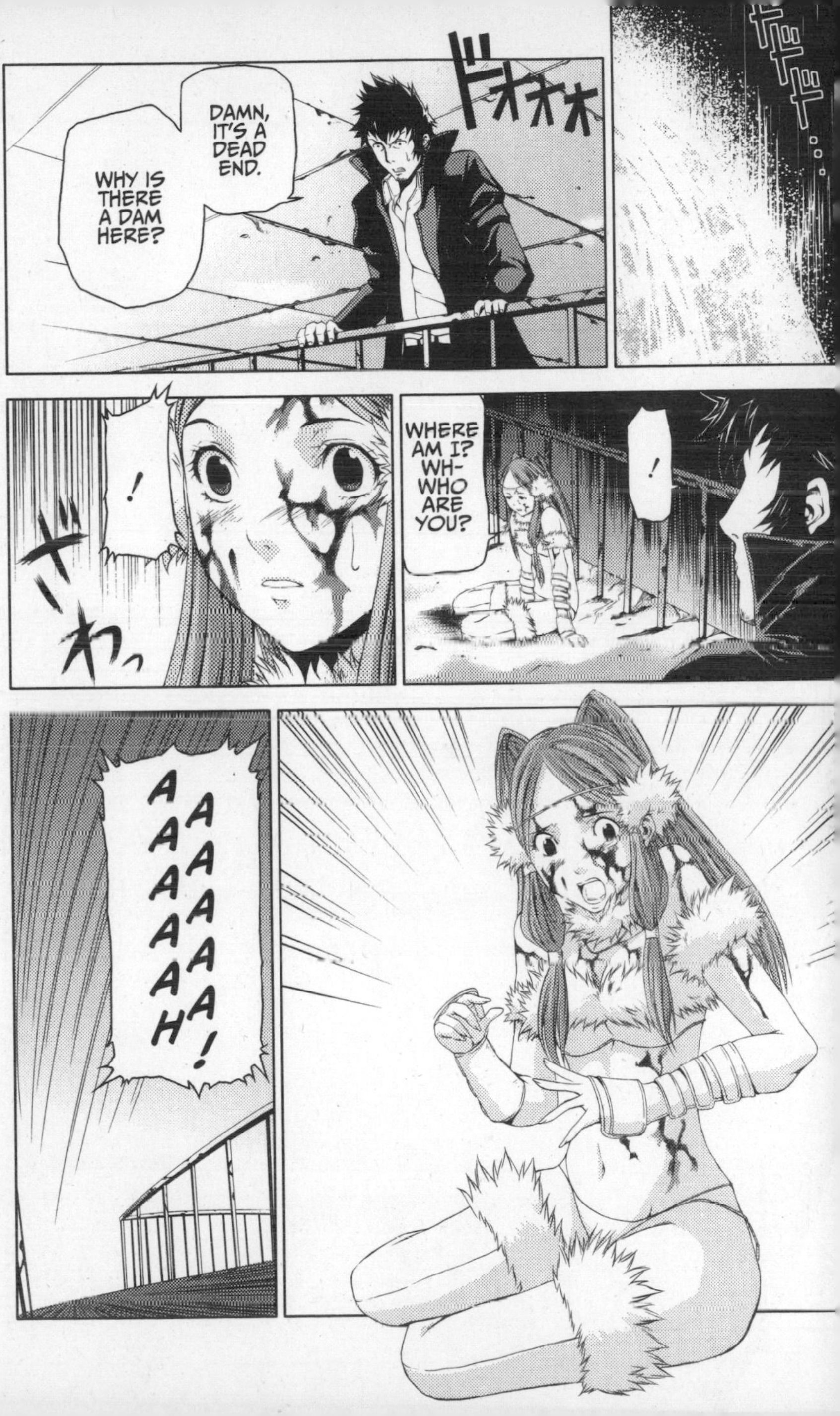
ドオオオ
DAMN, IT'S A DEAD END.
WHY IS THERE A DAM HERE?
!
WHERE AM I? WH-WHO ARE YOU?
!
AAAAAAAAAAAH!

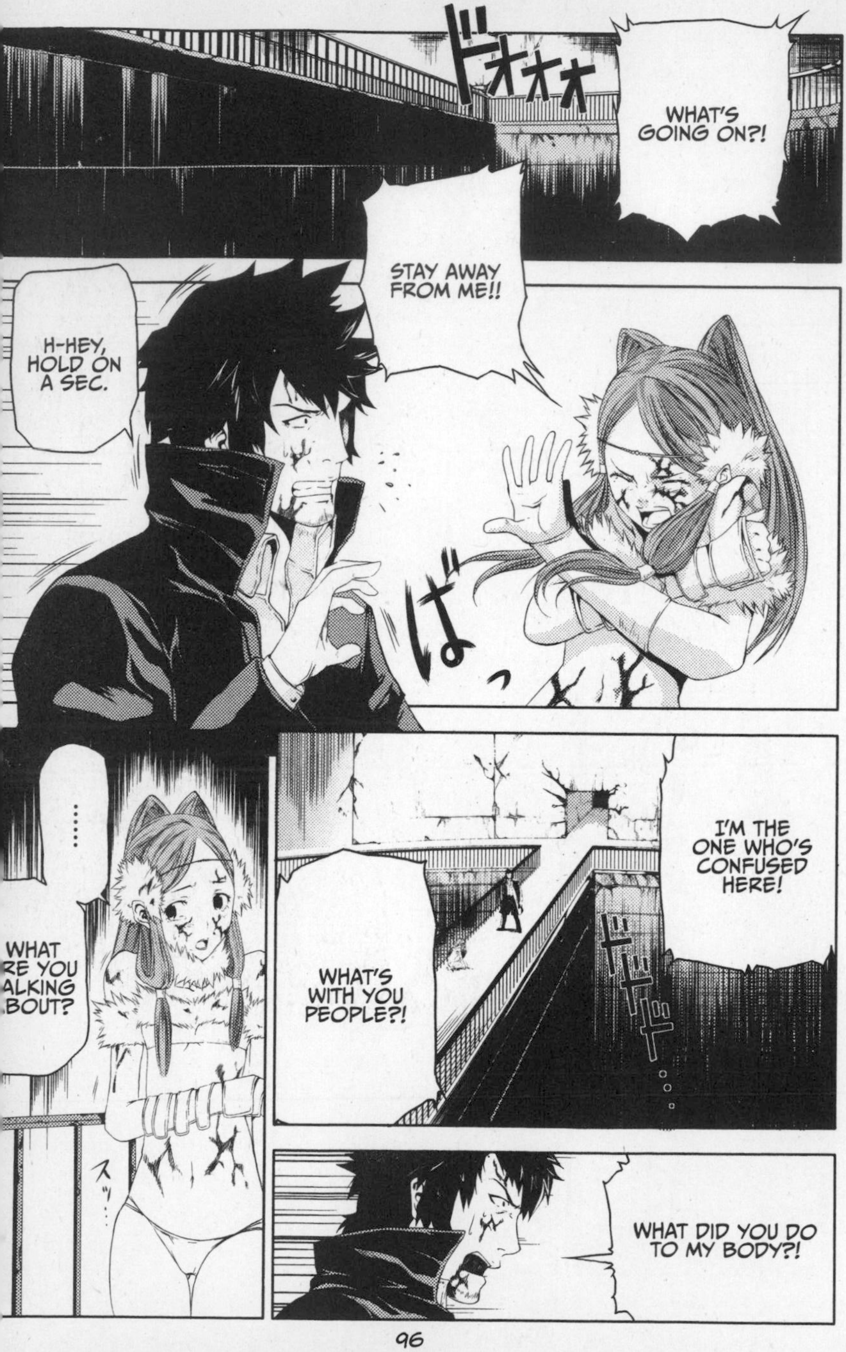
ドオオオ
WHAT'S GOING ON?!
STAY AWAY FROM ME!!
H-HEY, HOLD ON A SEC.
ぱっ
I'M THE ONE WHO'S CONFUSED HERE!
WHAT'S WITH YOU PEOPLE?!
ドドド
WHAT DID YOU DO TO MY BODY?!
......
WHAT RE YOU ALKING BOUT?
スッ...

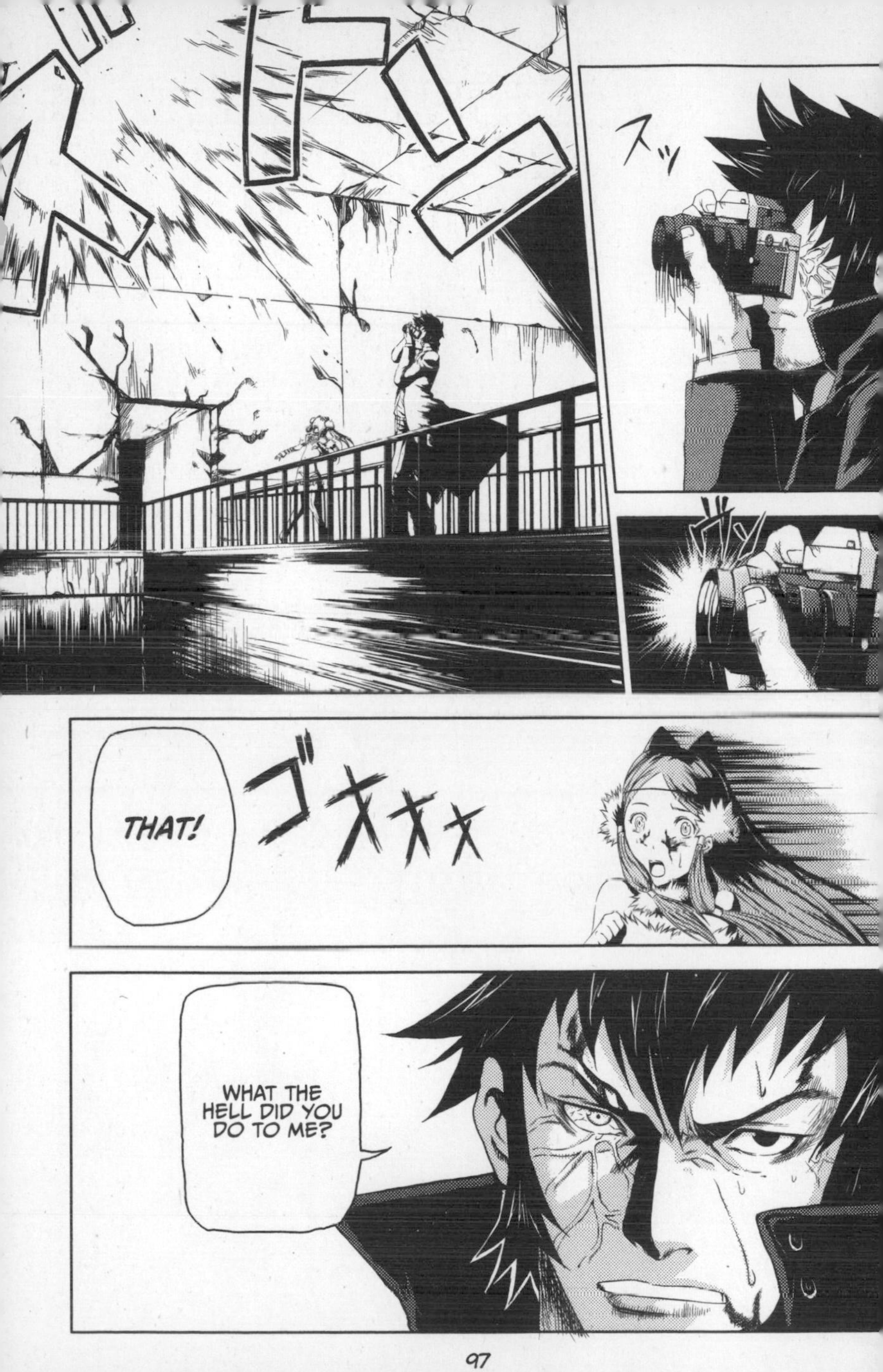

スッ
ゴォォォ
THAT!
WHAT THE HELL DID YOU DO TO ME?

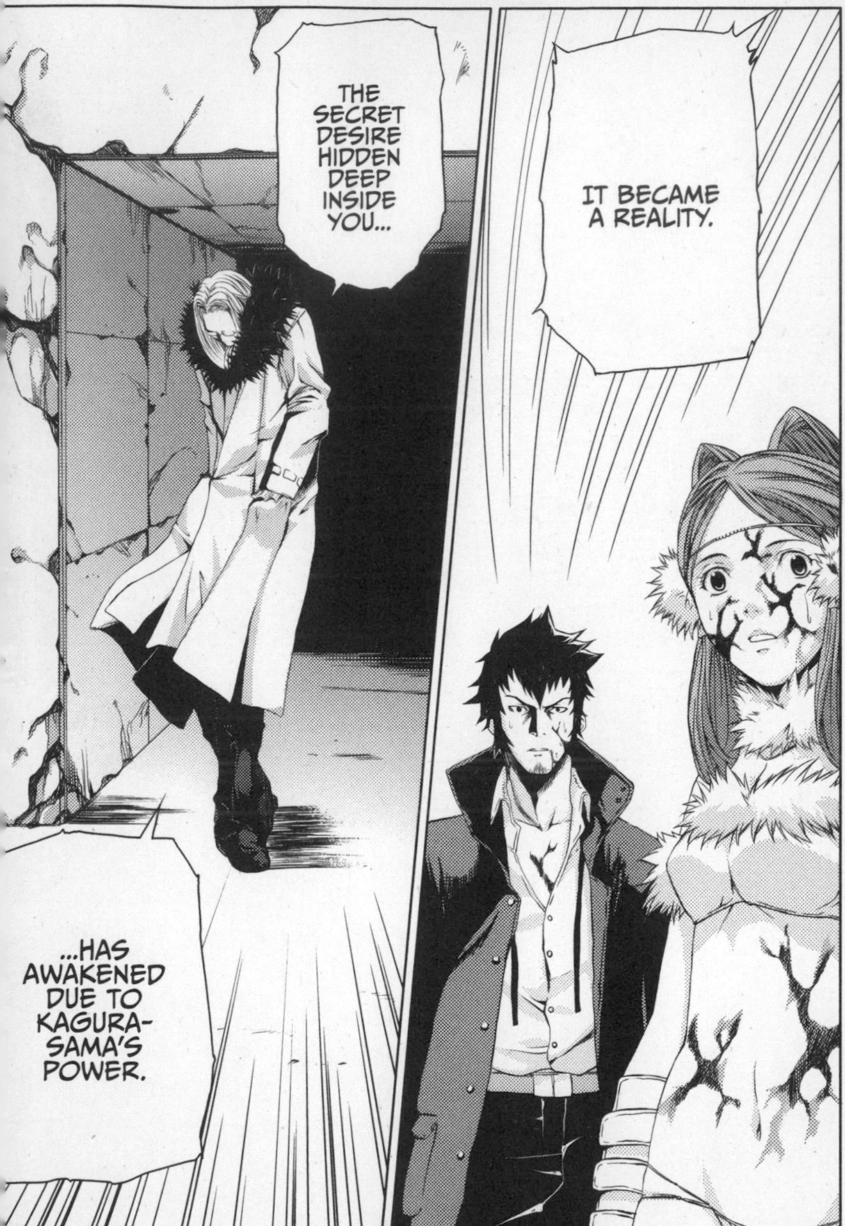
IT BECAME A REALITY.
THE SECRET DESIRE HIDDEN DEEP INSIDE YOU...
...HAS AWAKENED DUE TO KAGURA-SAMA'S POWER.

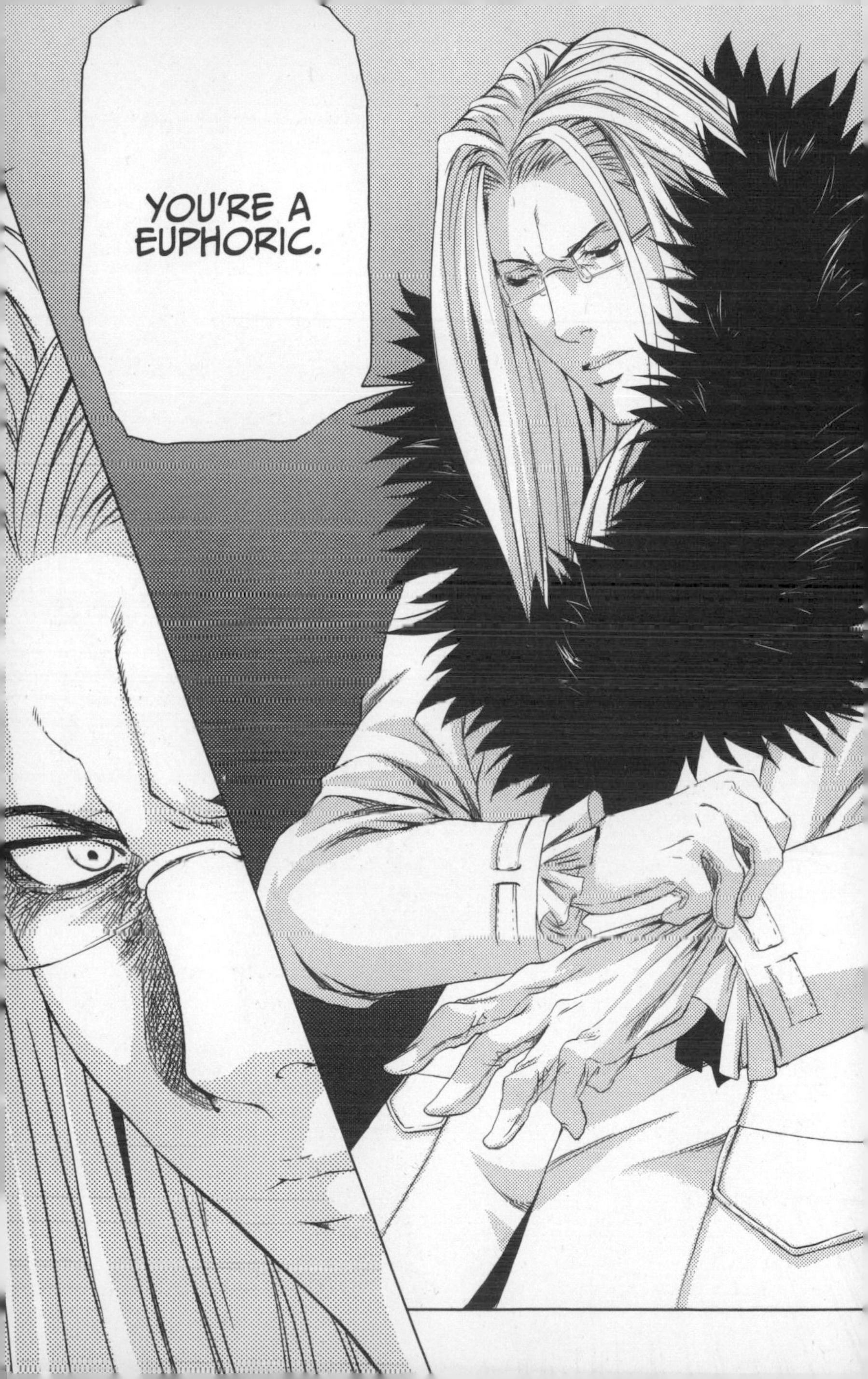
YOU'RE A EUPHORIC.

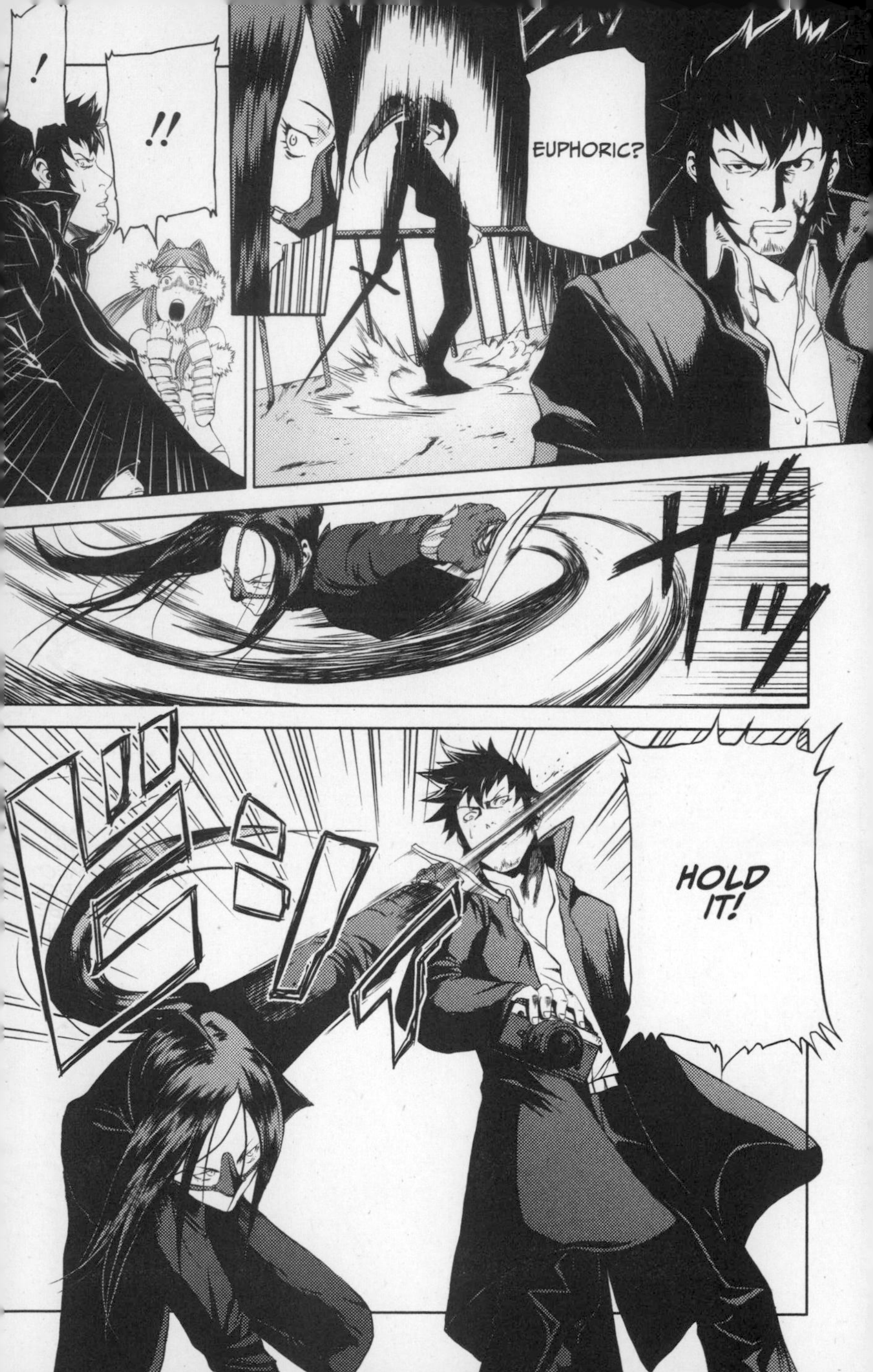
EUPHORIC?
!!
!
HOLD IT!

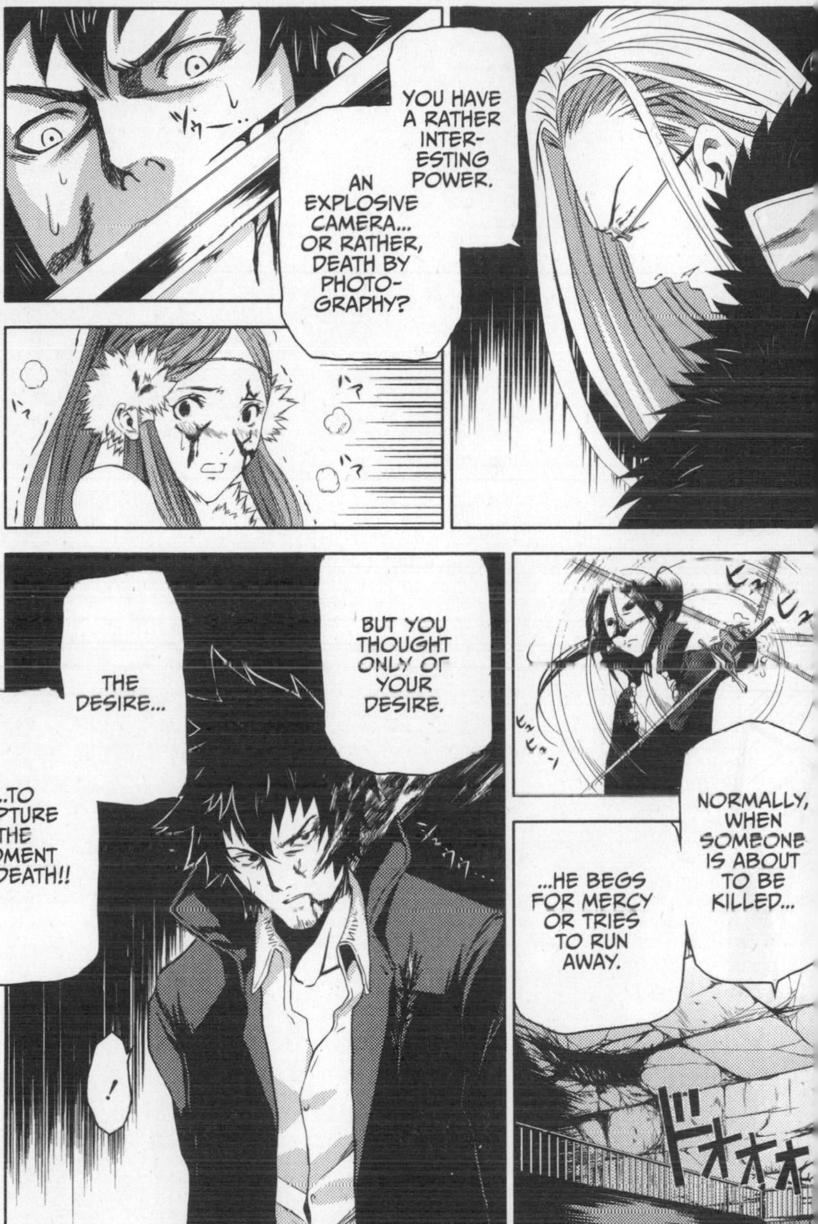
YOU HAVE A RATHER INTER-ESTING POWER.
AN EXPLOSIVE CAMERA... OR RATHER, DEATH BY PHOTO-GRAPHY?
NORMALLY, WHEN SOMEONE IS ABOUT TO BE KILLED...
...HE BEGS FOR MERCY OR TRIES TO RUN AWAY.
BUT YOU THOUGHT ONLY OF YOUR DESIRE.
THE DESIRE...
...TO CAPTURE THE MOMENT OF DEATH!!
!

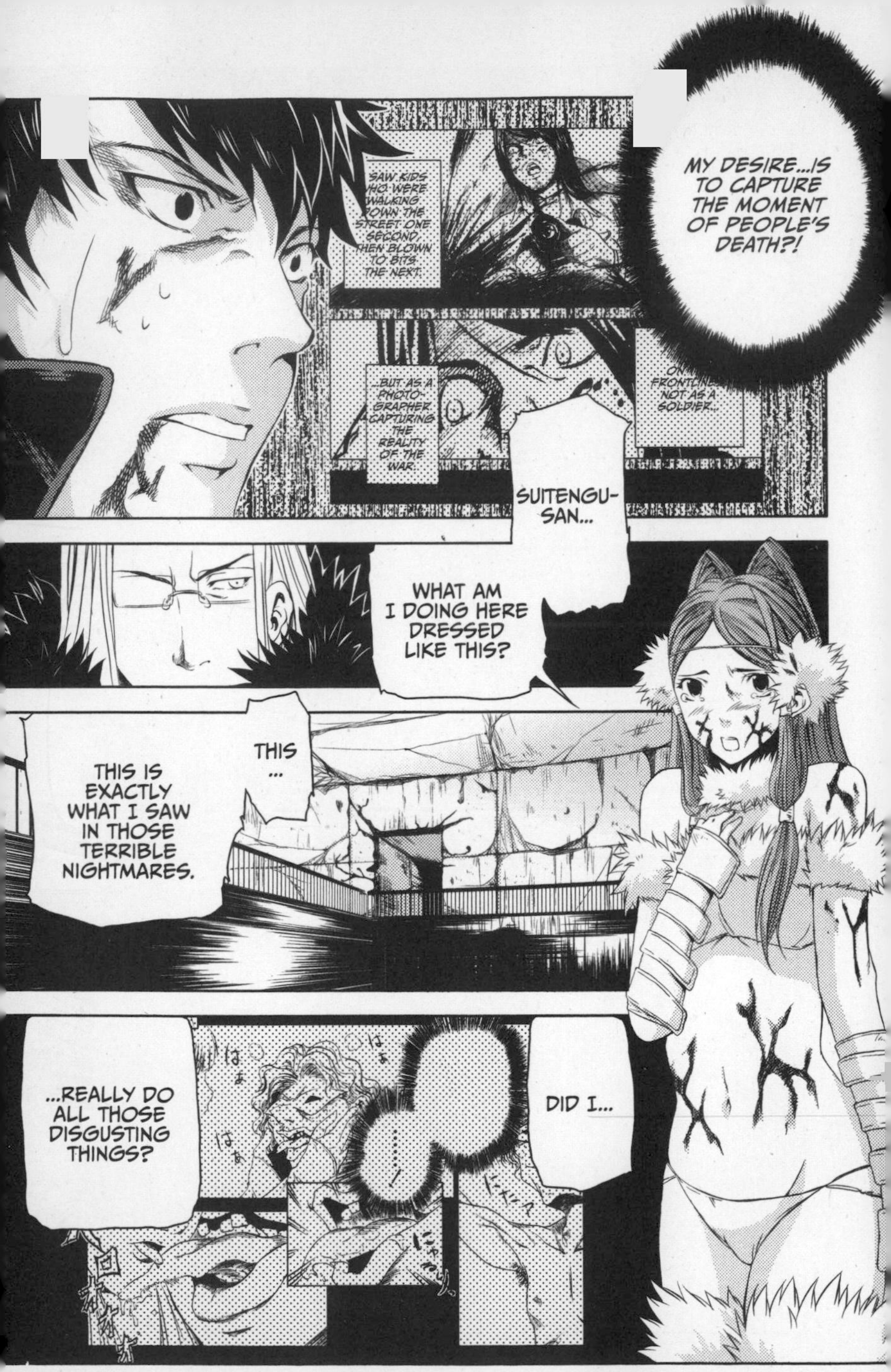
MY DESIRE...IS TO CAPTURE THE MOMENT OF PEOPLE'S DEATH?!
SAW KIDS WHO WERE WALKING DOWN THE STREET ONE SECOND, THEN BLOWN TO BITS THE NEXT.
ON FRONTLINES NOT AS A SOLDIER...
...BUT AS A PHOTO-GRAPHER CAPTURING THE REALITY OF THE WAR.
SUITENGU-SAN...
WHAT AM I DOING HERE DRESSED LIKE THIS?
THIS ...
THIS IS EXACTLY WHAT I SAW IN THOSE TERRIBLE NIGHTMARES.
DID I...
...REALLY DO ALL THOSE DISGUSTING THINGS?

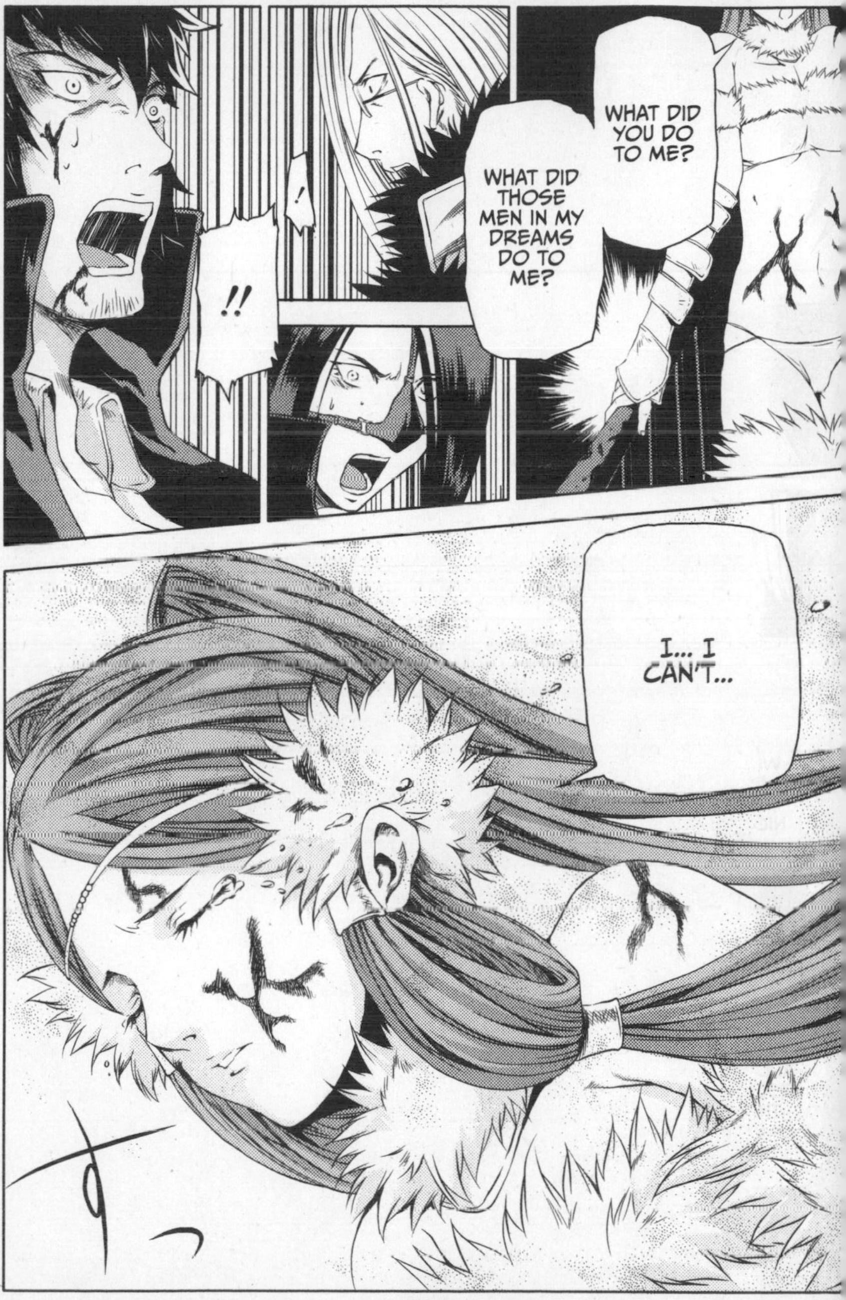
WHAT DID YOU DO TO ME?
WHAT DID THOSE MEN IN MY DREAMS DO TO ME?
!
!!
I... I CAN'T...

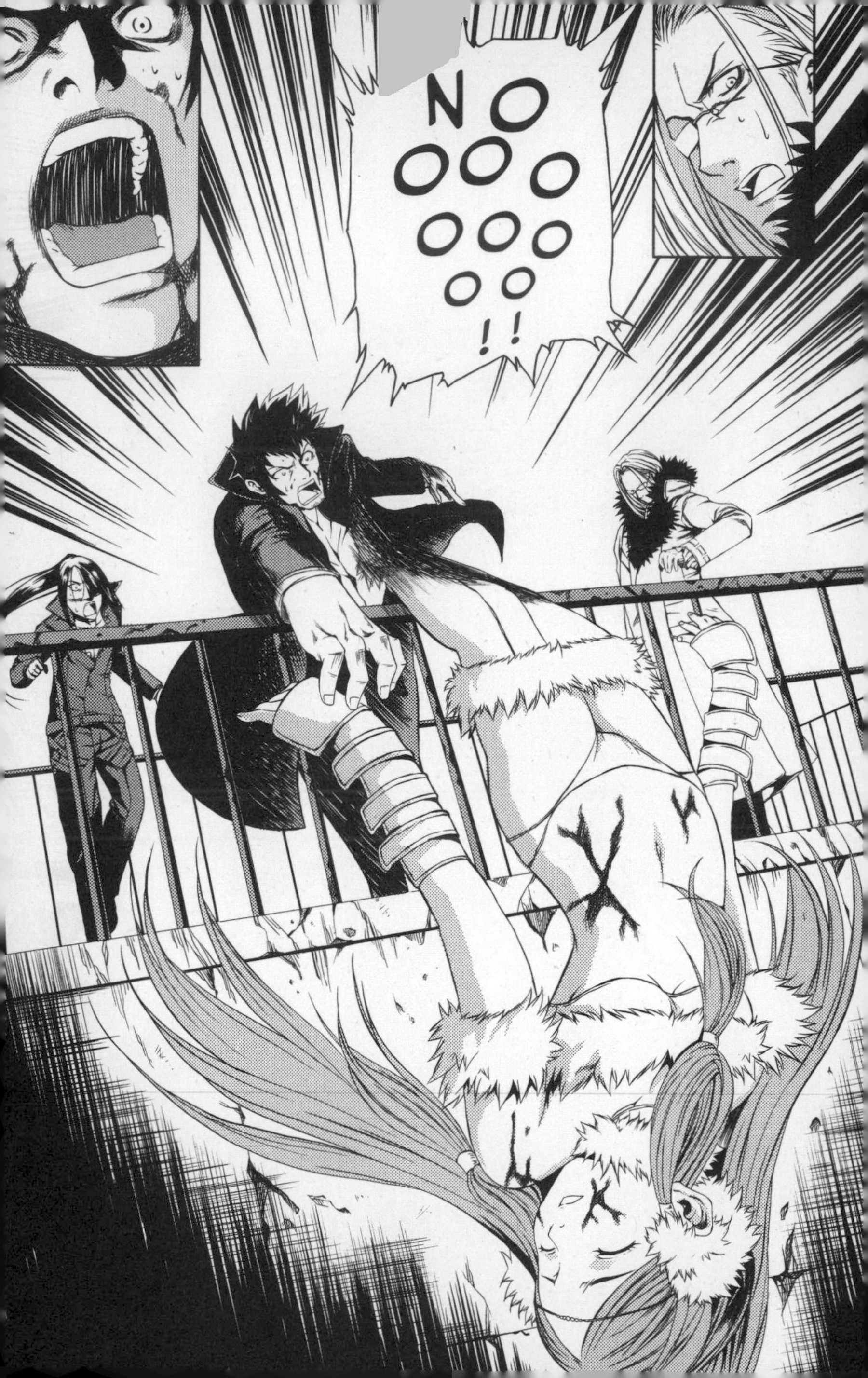
NOOOOOOOOO!!

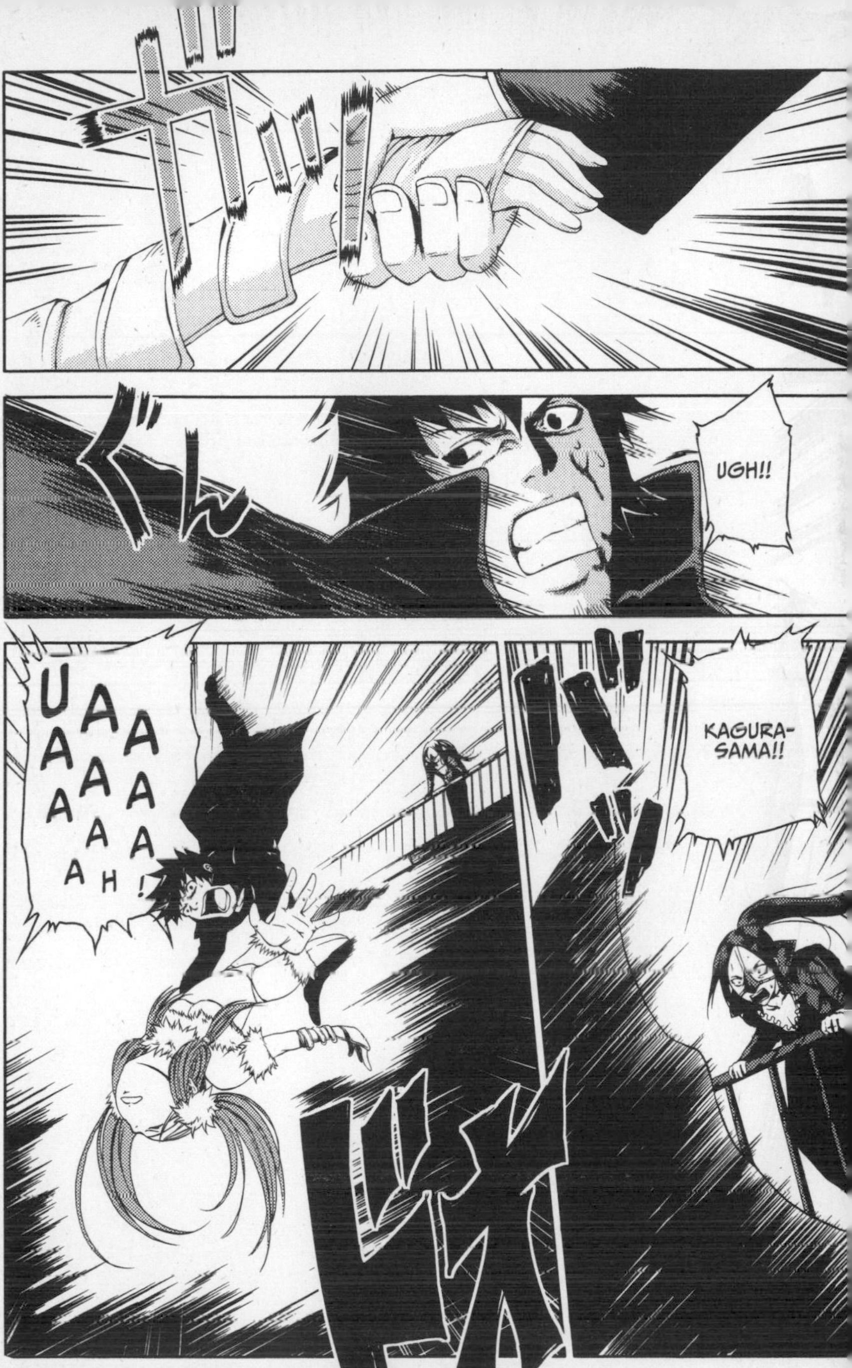
UGH!!
KAGURA-SAMA!!
UAAAAAAAAAAH!

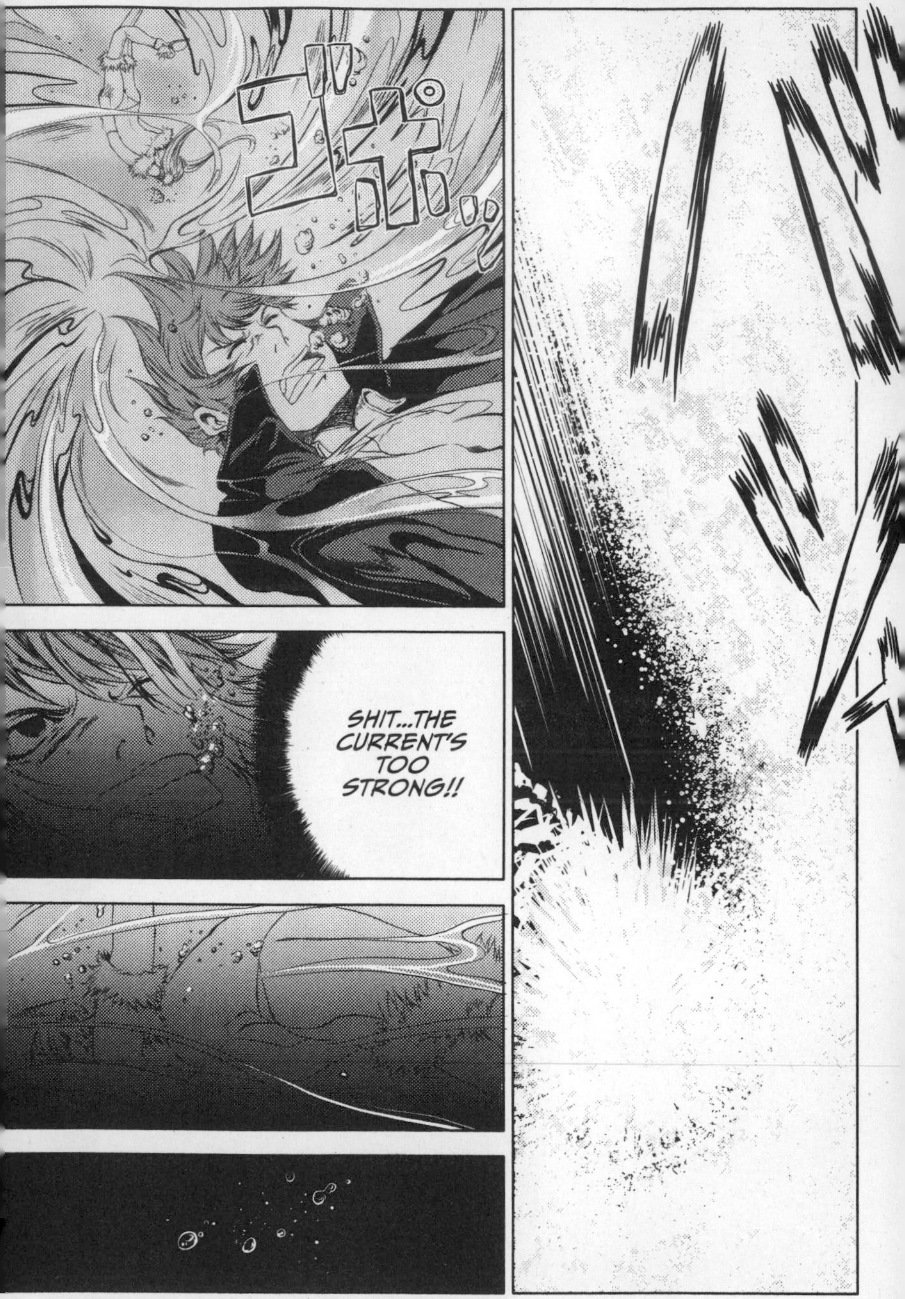
SHIT...THE CURRENT'S TOO STRONG!!

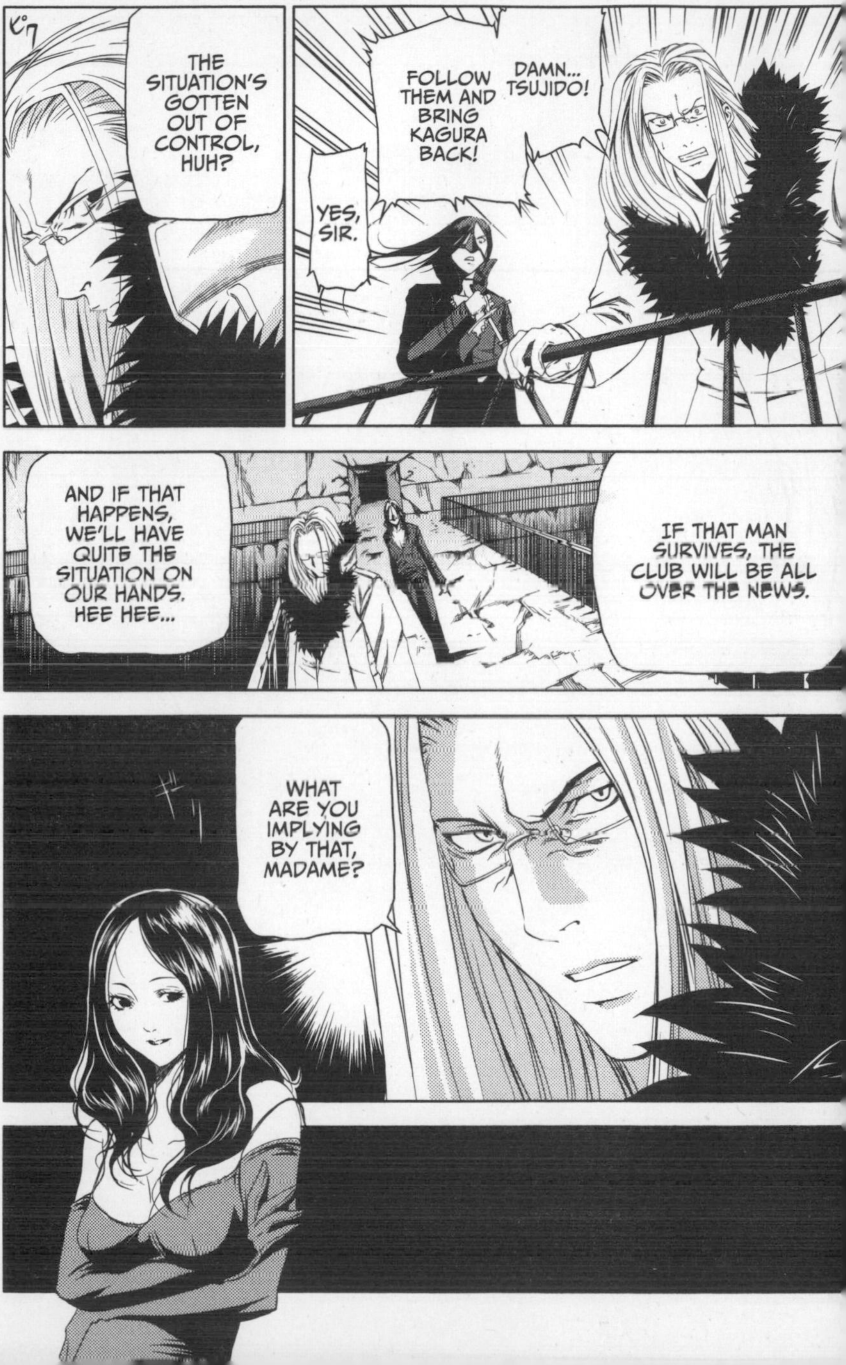
DAMN... TSUJIDO!
FOLLOW THEM AND BRING KAGURA BACK!
YES, SIR.
ピク
THE SITUATION'S GOTTEN OUT OF CONTROL, HUH?
IF THAT MAN SURVIVES, THE CLUB WILL BE ALL OVER THE NEWS.
AND IF THAT HAPPENS, WE'LL HAVE QUITE THE SITUATION ON OUR HANDS. HEE HEE...
WHAT ARE YOU IMPLYING BY THAT, MADAME?

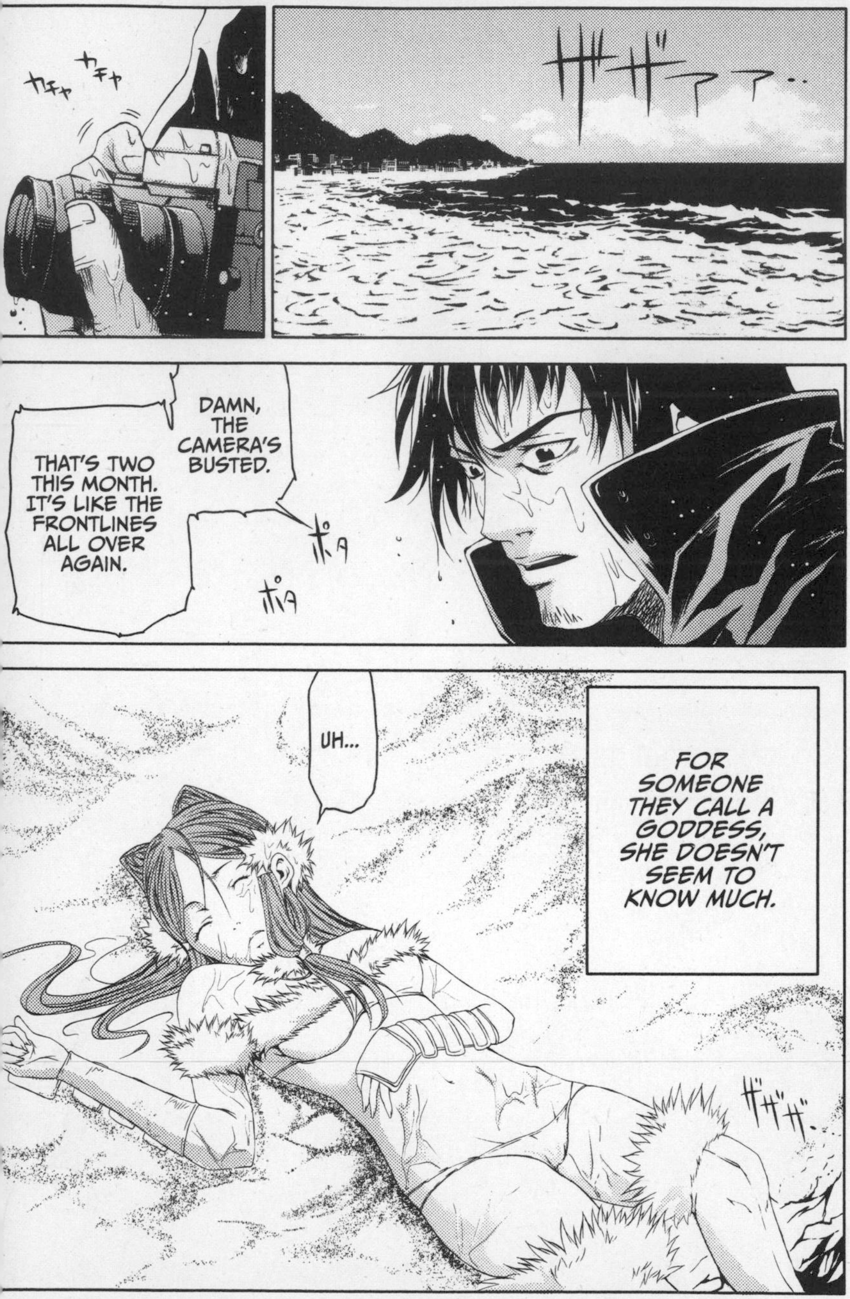
ザザアア‥
カチャ
カチャ
DAMN, THE CAMERA'S BUSTED.
THAT'S TWO THIS MONTH. IT'S LIKE THE FRONTLINES ALL OVER AGAIN.
ポタ
ポタ
FOR SOMEONE THEY CALL A GODDESS, SHE DOESN'T SEEM TO KNOW MUCH.
UH...
ザザザ

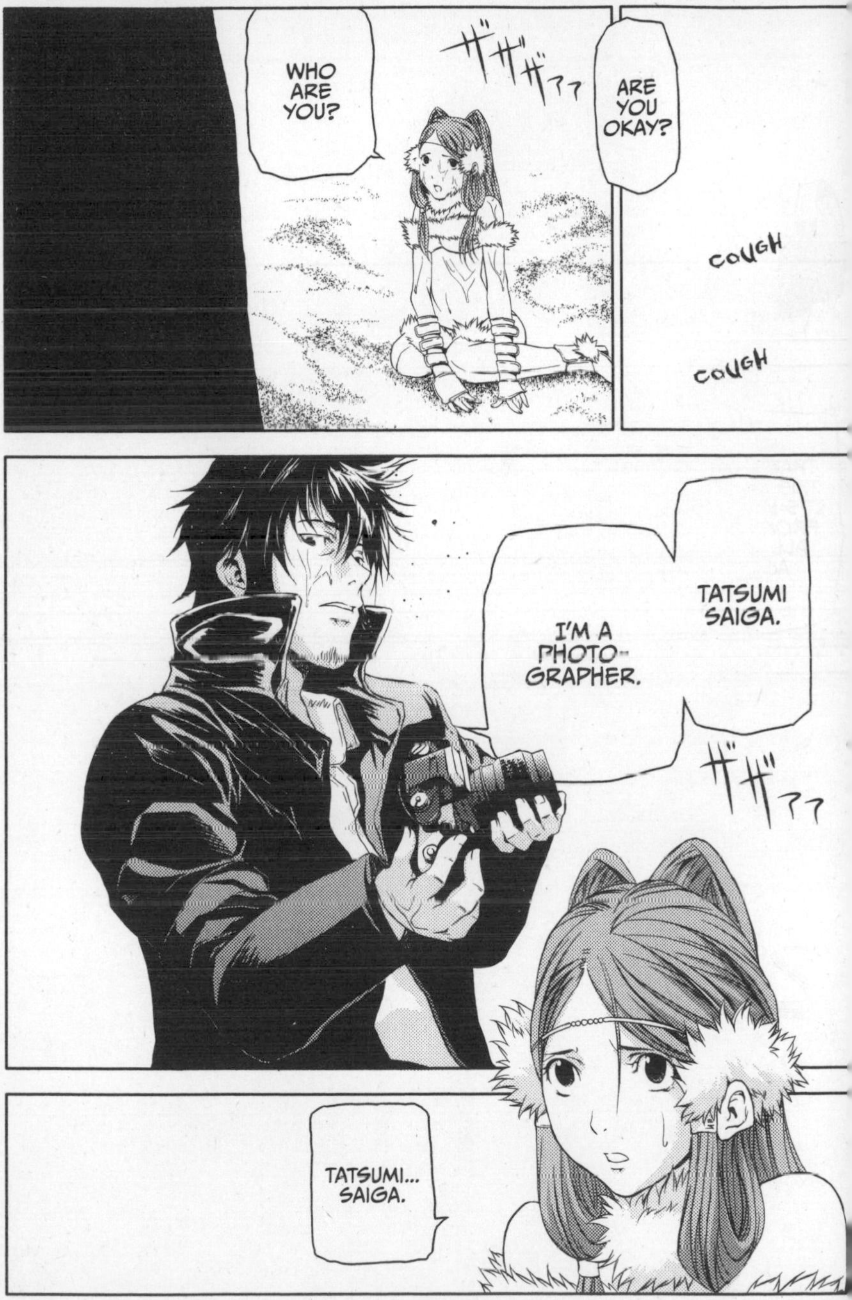
ARE YOU OKAY?
COUGH
COUGH
ザザザアァ
WHO ARE YOU?
ザザァァ
TATSUMI SAIGA.
I'M A PHOTO-GRAPHER.
TATSUMI... SAIGA.

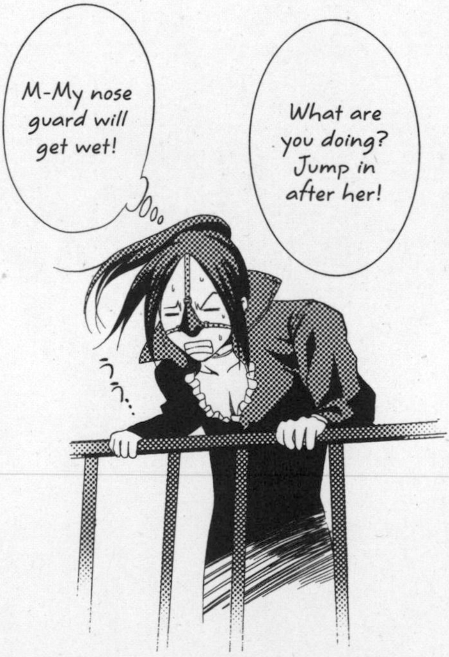
What are you doing? Jump in after her!
M-My nose guard will get wet!

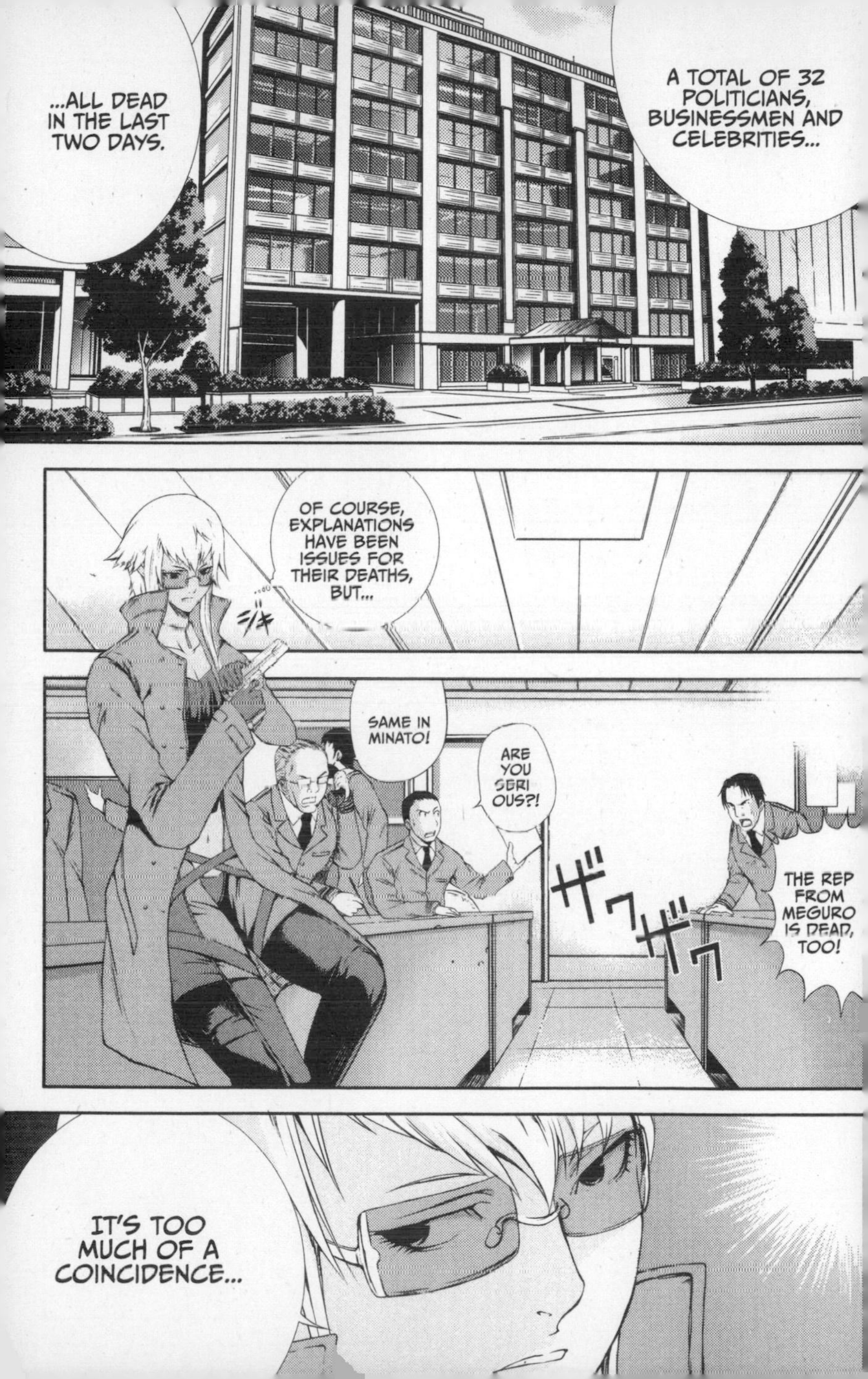
A TOTAL OF 32 POLITICIANS, BUSINESSMEN AND CELEBRITIES...
...ALL DEAD IN THE LAST TWO DAYS.
OF COURSE, EXPLANATIONS HAVE BEEN ISSUES FOR THEIR DEATHS, BUT...
THE REP FROM MEGURO IS DEAD, TOO!
ザワザワ
ARE YOU SERIOUS?!
SAME IN MINATO!
IT'S TOO MUCH OF A COINCIDENCE...

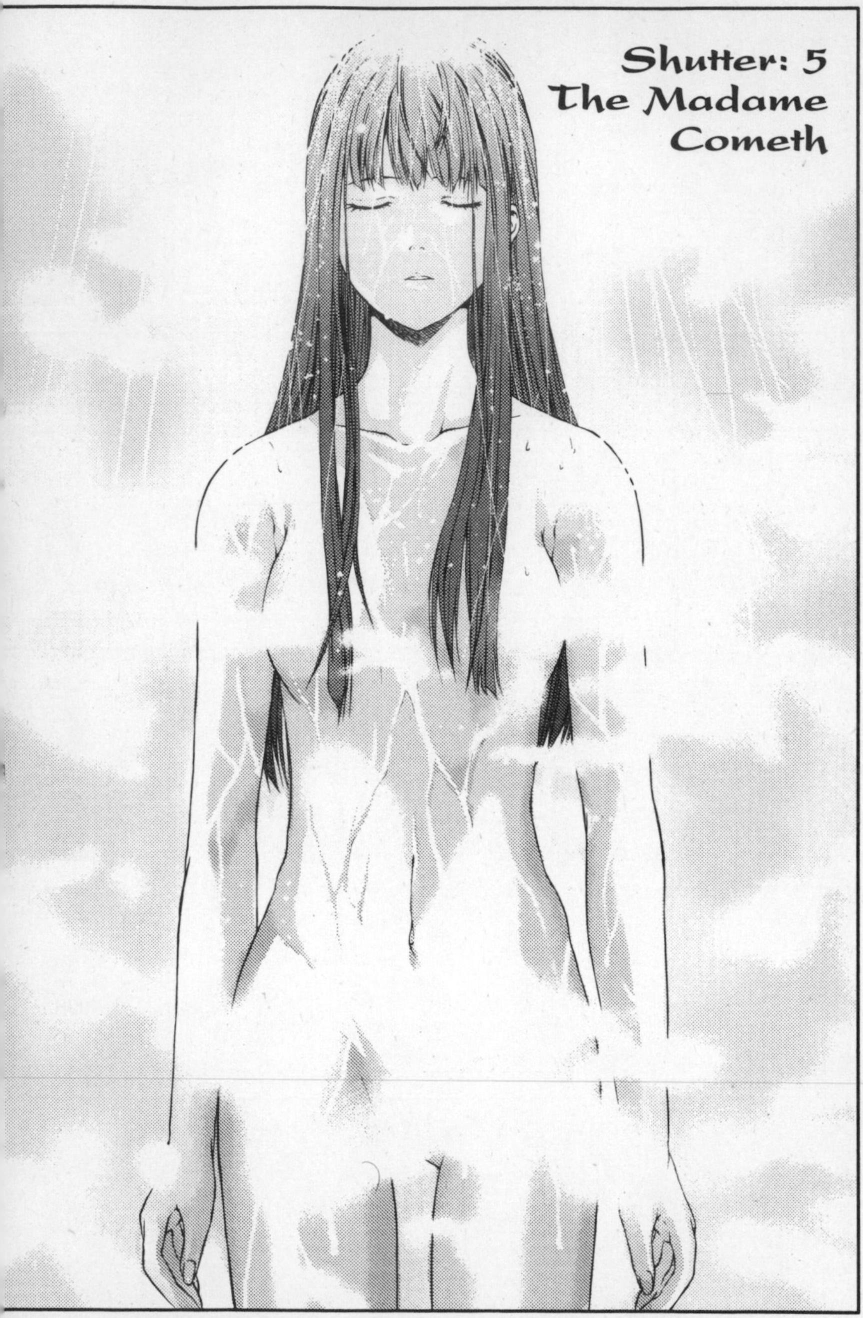
Shutter: 5
The Madame Cometh

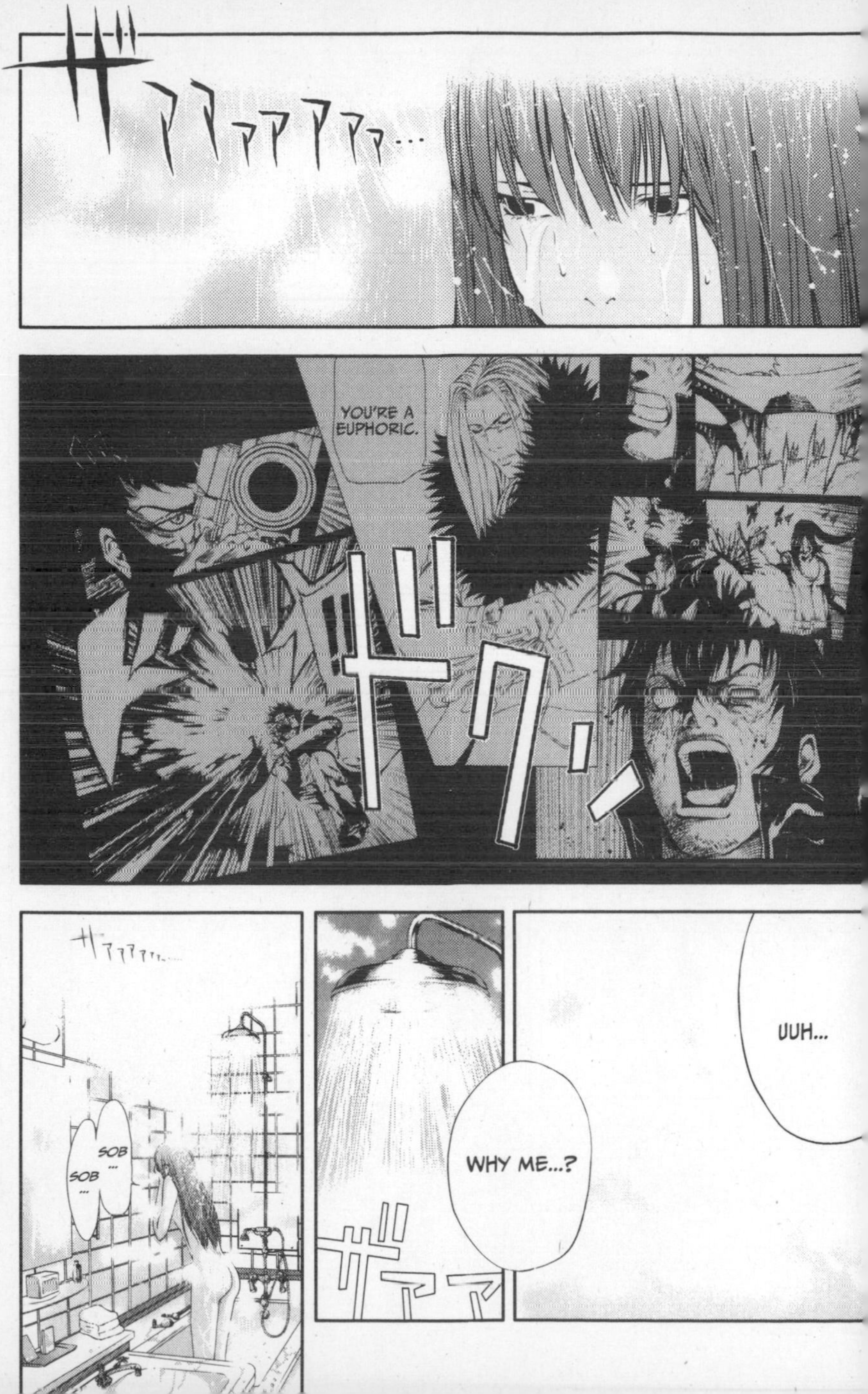
YOU'RE A EUPHORIC.
UUH...
WHY ME...?
SOB...
SOB...

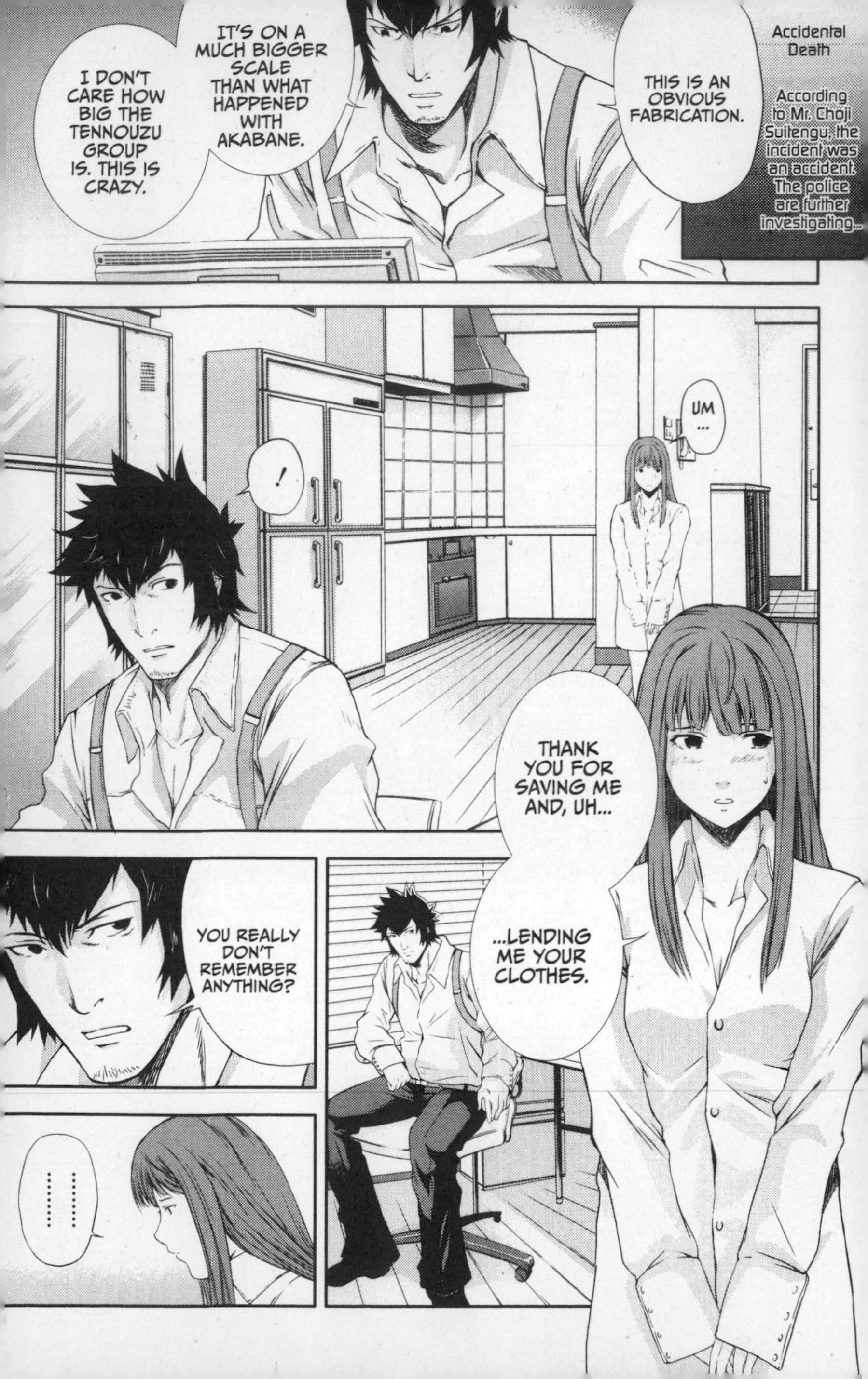
Accidental Death
According to Mr. Choji Suitengu, the incident was an accident. The police are further investigating...
THIS IS AN OBVIOUS FABRICATION.
IT'S ON A MUCH BIGGER SCALE THAN WHAT HAPPENED WITH AKABANE.
I DON'T CARE HOW BIG THE TENNOUZU GROUP IS. THIS IS CRAZY.
UM ...
!
THANK YOU FOR SAVING ME AND, UH...
...LENDING ME YOUR CLOTHES.
YOU REALLY DON'T REMEMBER ANYTHING?
......

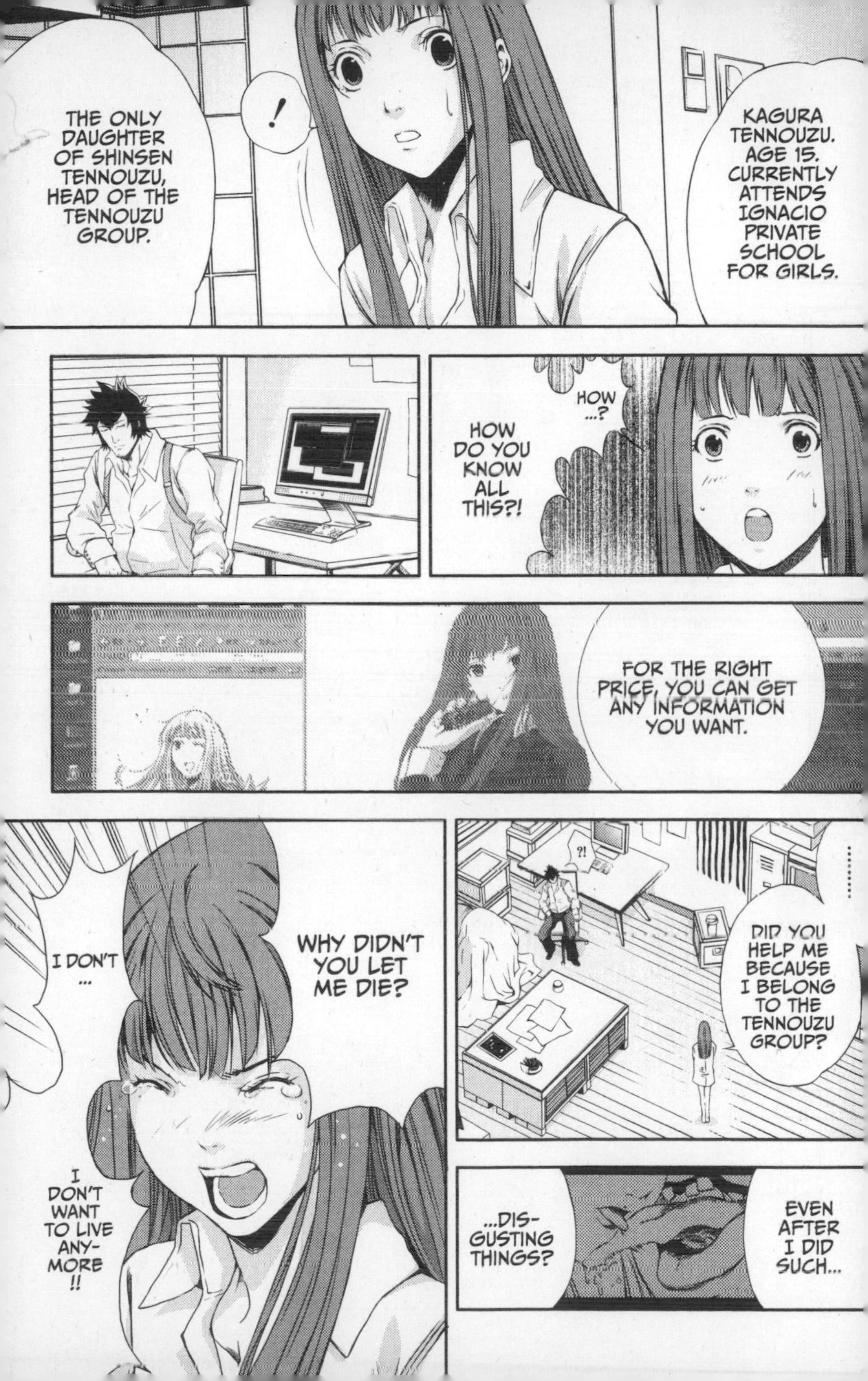
KAGURA TENNOUZU. AGE 15. CURRENTLY ATTENDS IGNACIO PRIVATE SCHOOL FOR GIRLS.
!
THE ONLY DAUGHTER OF SHINSEN TENNOUZU, HEAD OF THE TENNOUZU GROUP.
HOW ...?
HOW DO YOU KNOW ALL THIS?!
FOR THE RIGHT PRICE, YOU CAN GET ANY INFORMATION YOU WANT.
......
?!
DID YOU HELP ME BECAUSE I BELONG TO THE TENNOUZU GROUP?
EVEN AFTER I DID SUCH...
...DIS-GUSTING THINGS?
WHY DIDN'T YOU LET ME DIE?
I DON'T ...
I DON'T WANT TO LIVE ANY-MORE !!

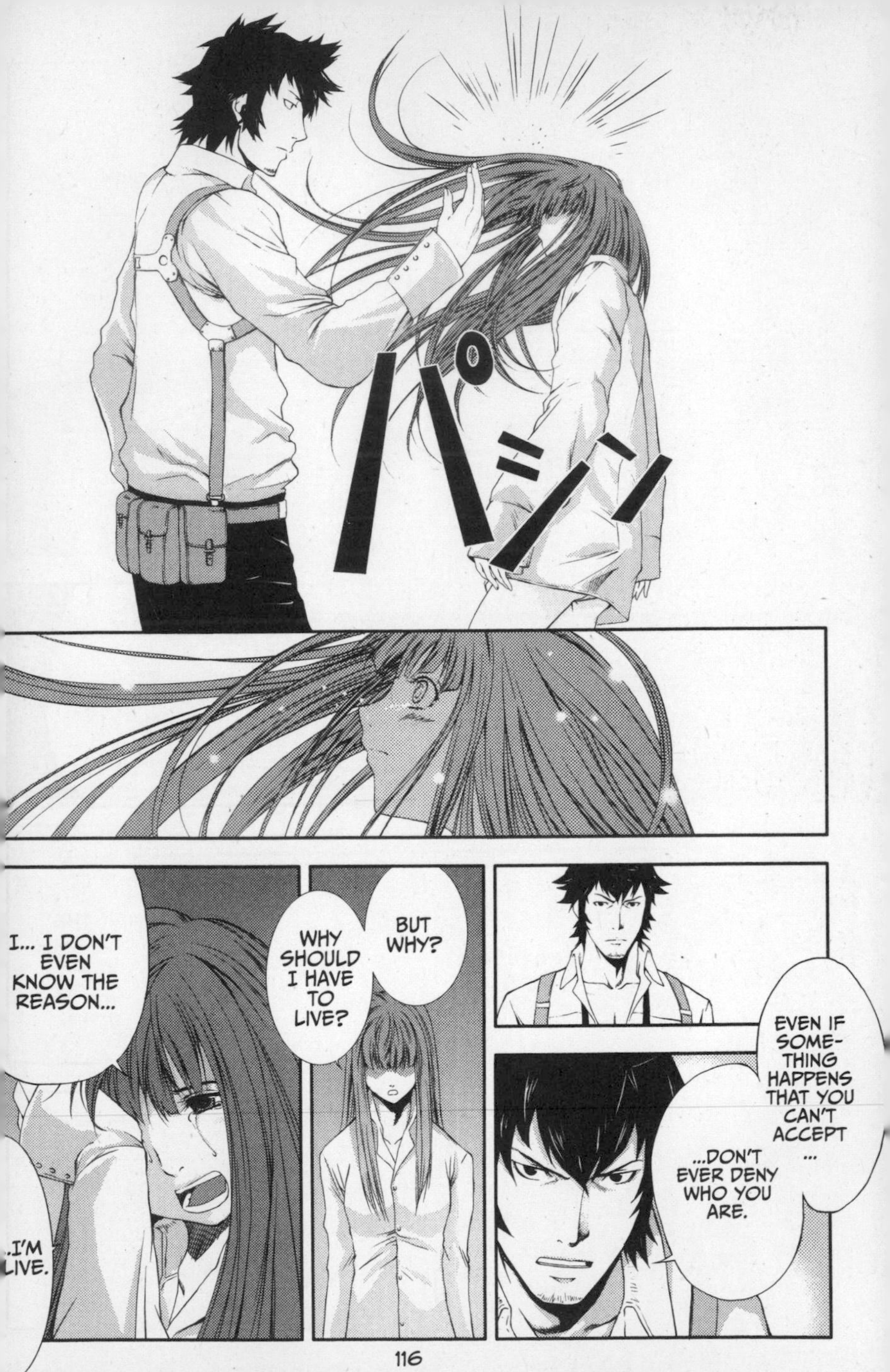
EVEN IF SOME-THING HAPPENS THAT YOU CAN'T ACCEPT ...
...DON'T EVER DENY WHO YOU ARE.
BUT WHY?
WHY SHOULD I HAVE TO LIVE?
I... I DON'T EVEN KNOW THE REASON...
.I'M LIVE.

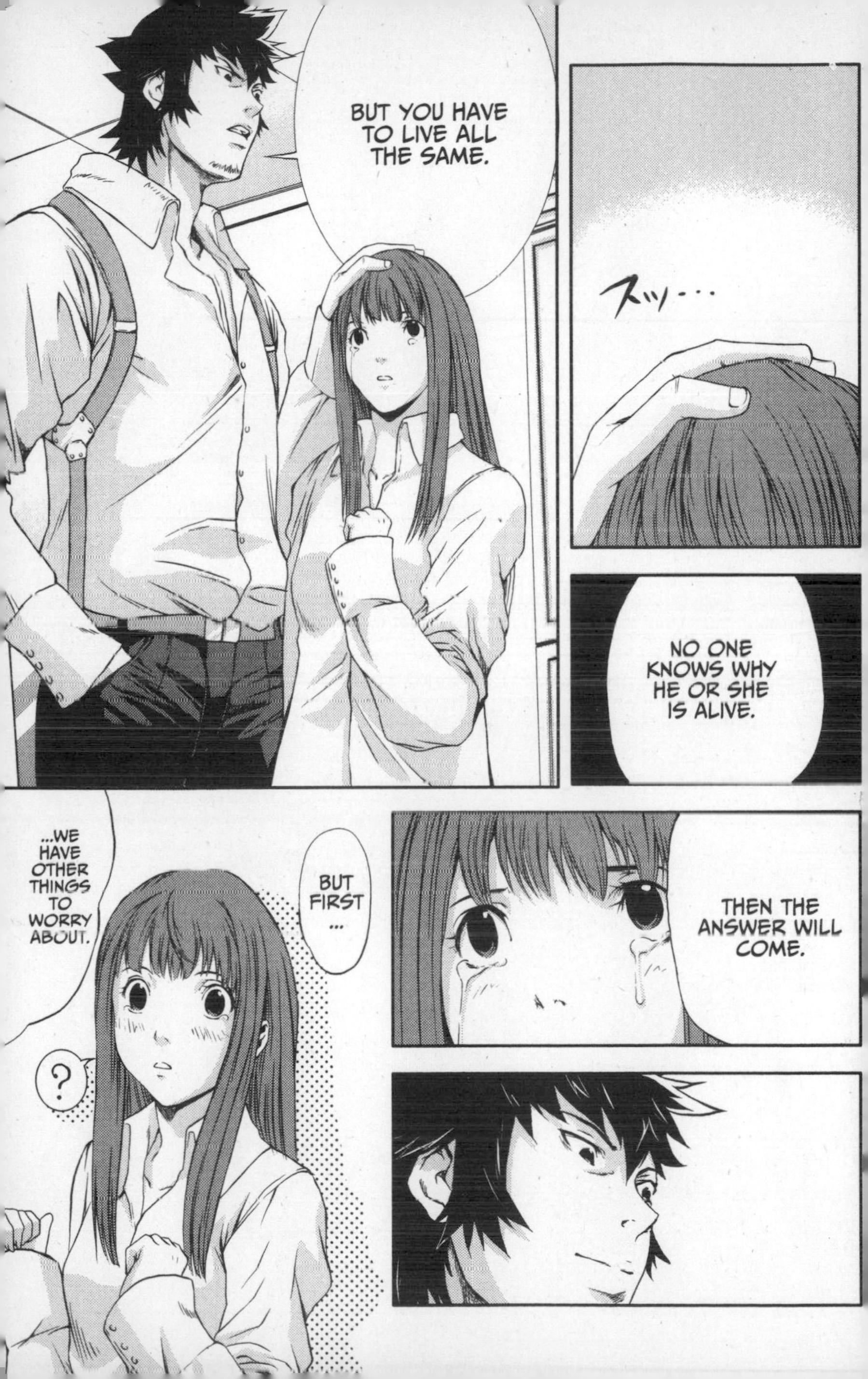

スッ・・・
NO ONE KNOWS WHY HE OR SHE IS ALIVE.
BUT YOU HAVE TO LIVE ALL THE SAME.
THEN THE ANSWER WILL COME.
BUT FIRST ...
...WE HAVE OTHER THINGS TO WORRY ABOUT.
?

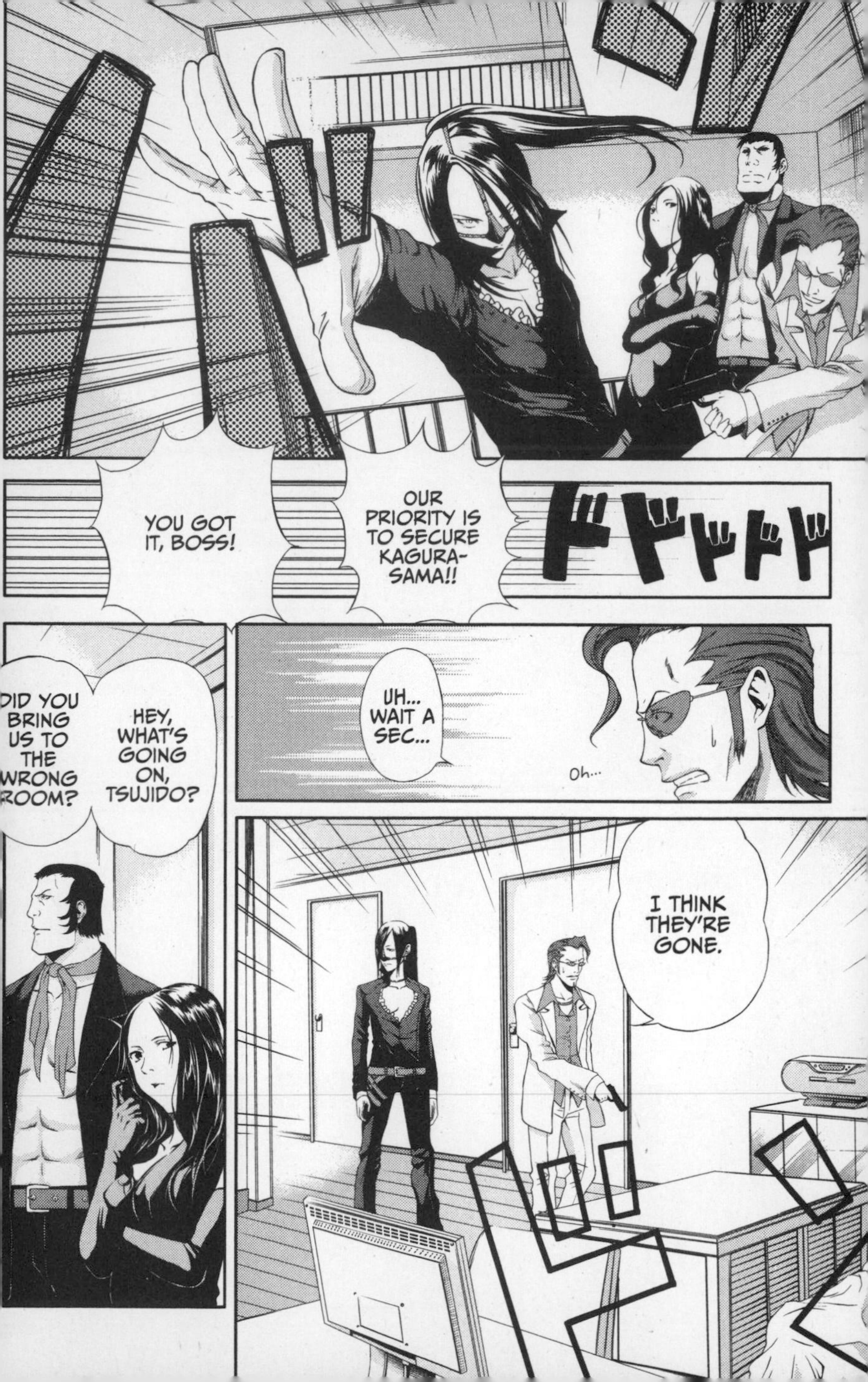
ドドドドド
OUR PRIORITY IS TO SECURE KAGURA-SAMA!!
YOU GOT IT, BOSS!
UH... WAIT A SEC...
Oh...
I THINK THEY'RE GONE.
HEY, WHAT'S GOING ON, TSUJIDO?
DID YOU BRING US TO THE WRONG ROOM?

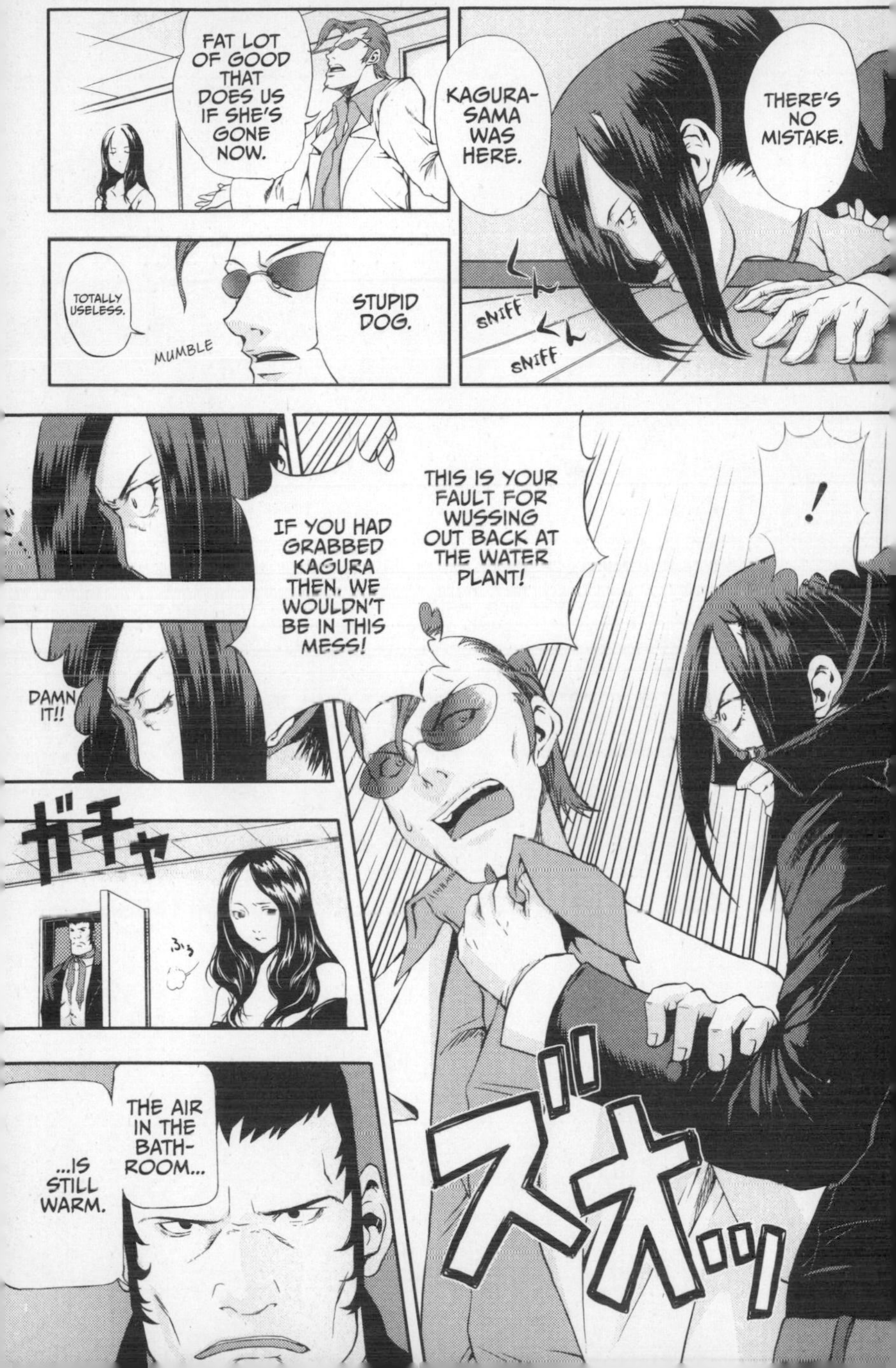
SNIFF
SNIFF
THERE'S NO MISTAKE.
KAGURA-SAMA WAS HERE.
FAT LOT OF GOOD THAT DOES US IF SHE'S GONE NOW.
STUPID DOG.
TOTALLY USELESS.
MUMBLE
!
THIS IS YOUR FAULT FOR WUSSING OUT BACK AT THE WATER PLANT!
IF YOU HAD GRABBED KAGURA THEN, WE WOULDN'T BE IN THIS MESS!
DAMN IT!!
ガチャ
THE AIR IN THE BATH-ROOM...
...IS STILL WARM.

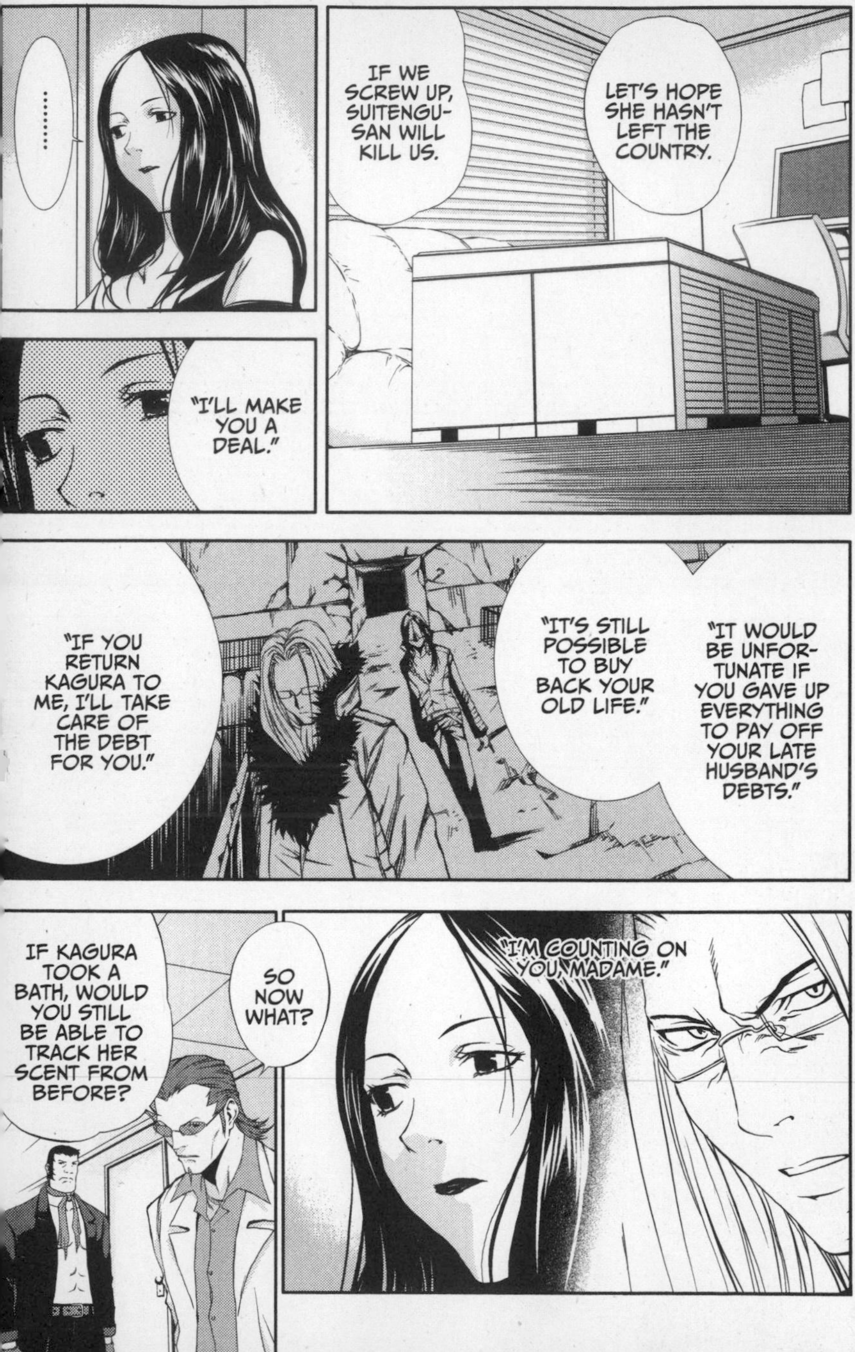
LET'S HOPE SHE HASN'T LEFT THE COUNTRY.
IF WE SCREW UP, SUITENGU-SAN WILL KILL US.
......
"I'LL MAKE YOU A DEAL."
"IT WOULD BE UNFORTUNATE IF YOU GAVE UP EVERYTHING TO PAY OFF YOUR LATE HUSBAND'S DEBTS."
"IT'S STILL POSSIBLE TO BUY BACK YOUR OLD LIFE."
"IF YOU RETURN KAGURA TO ME, I'LL TAKE CARE OF THE DEBT FOR YOU."
"I'M COUNTING ON YOU, MADAME."
SO NOW WHAT?
IF KAGURA TOOK A BATH, WOULD YOU STILL BE ABLE TO TRACK HER SCENT FROM BEFORE?

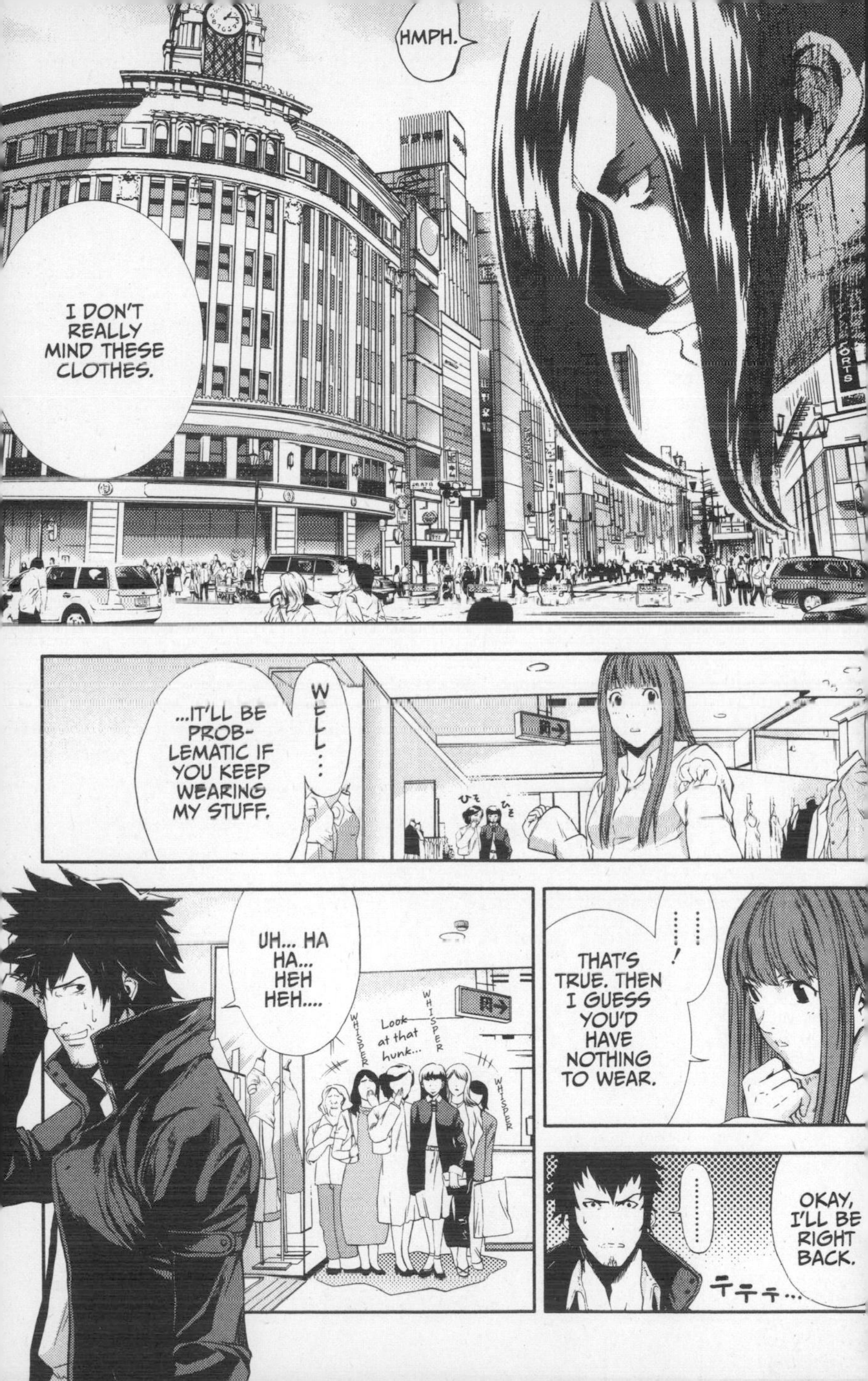
HMPH.
I DON'T REALLY MIND THESE CLOTHES.
WELL...
...IT'LL BE PROB-LEMATIC IF YOU KEEP WEARING MY STUFF.
ひそ ひそ
...!
THAT'S TRUE. THEN I GUESS YOU'D HAVE NOTHING TO WEAR.
......
OKAY, I'LL BE RIGHT BACK.
テテテ...
UH... HA HA... HEH HEH....
WHISPER
Look at that hunk...
WHISPER
WHISPER

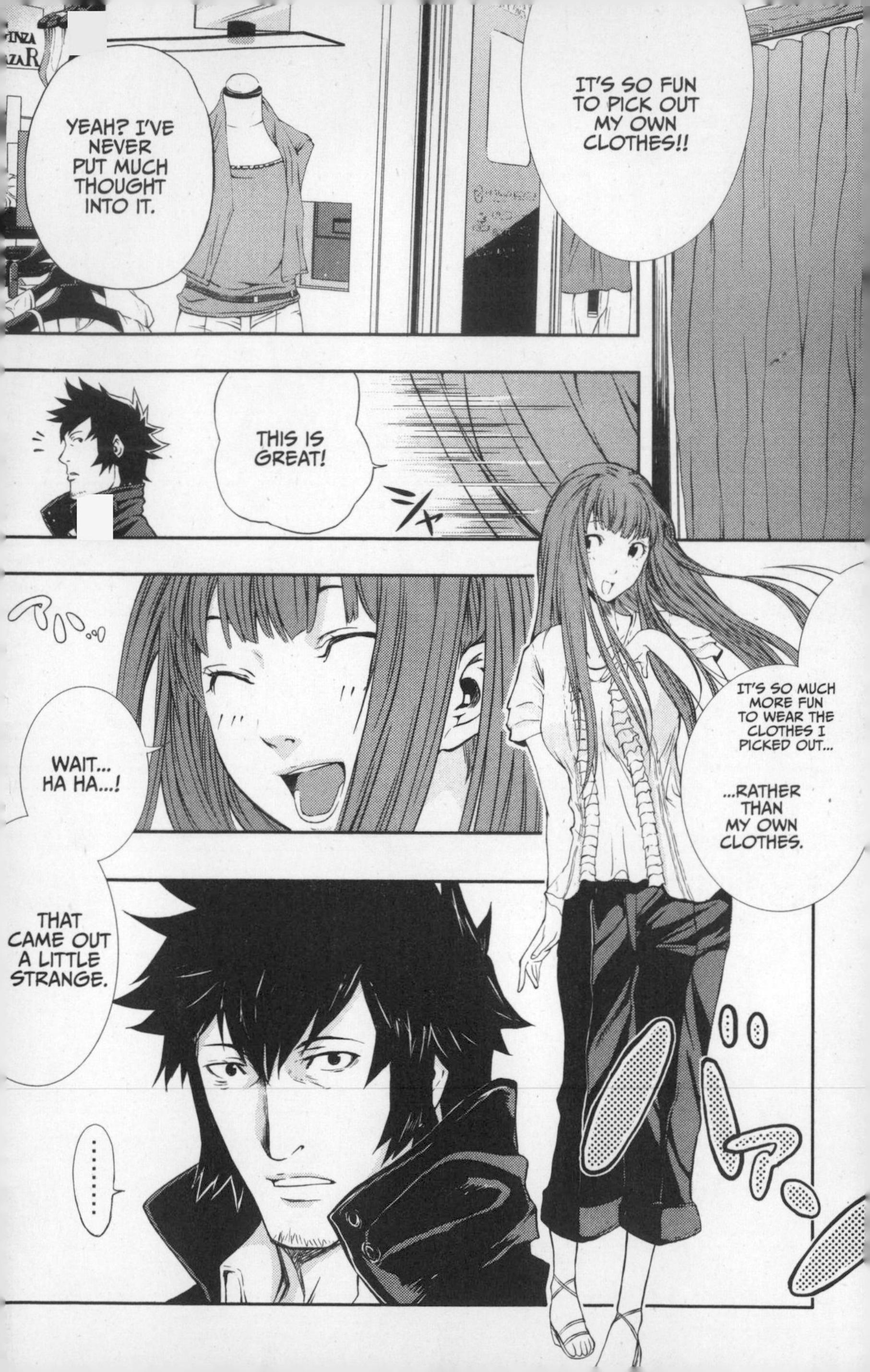
IT'S SO FUN TO PICK OUT MY OWN CLOTHES!!
YEAH? I'VE NEVER PUT MUCH THOUGHT INTO IT.
THIS IS GREAT!
IT'S SO MUCH MORE FUN TO WEAR THE CLOTHES I PICKED OUT...
...RATHER THAN MY OWN CLOTHES.
WAIT... HA HA...!
THAT CAME OUT A LITTLE STRANGE.
......

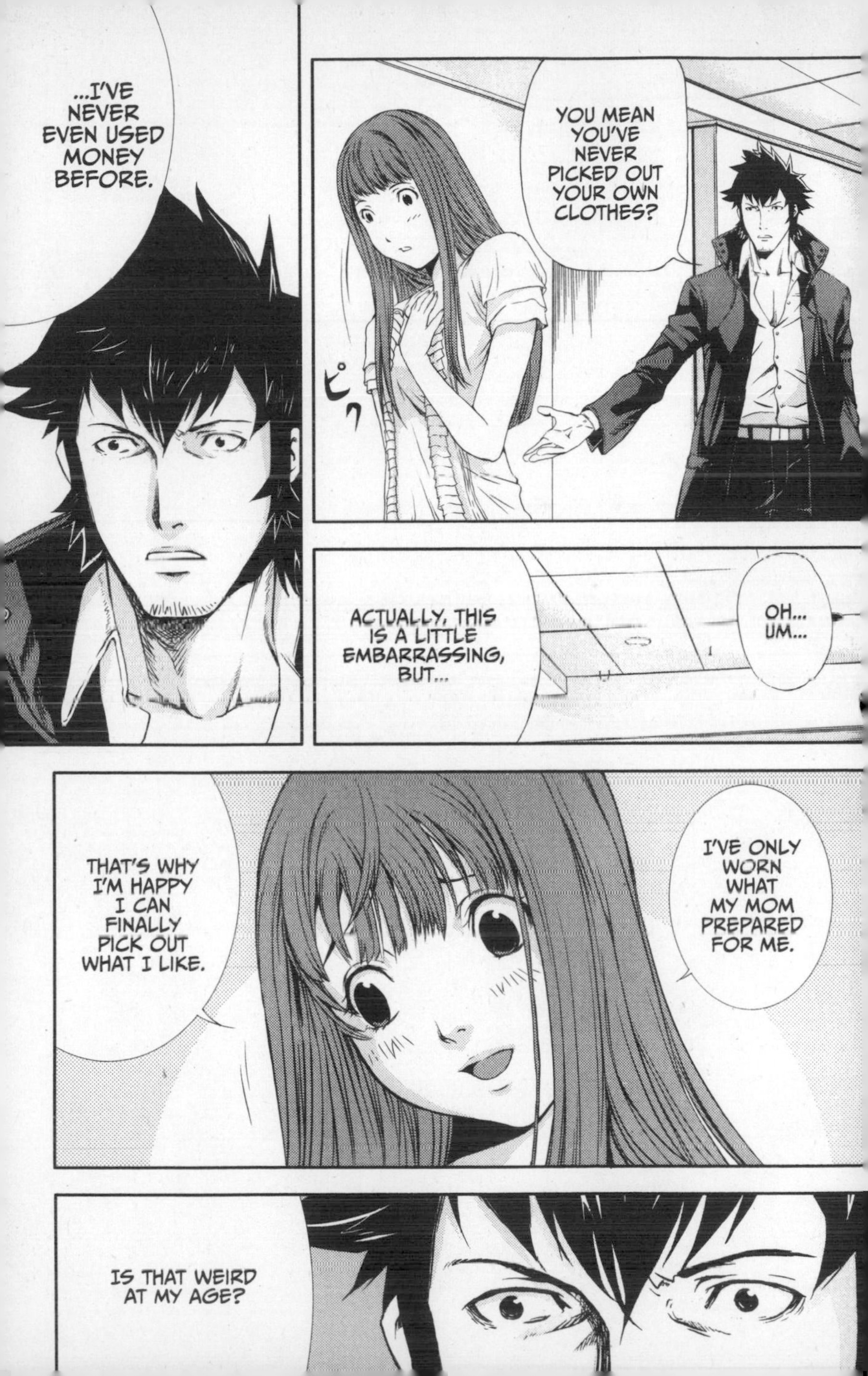
YOU MEAN YOU'VE NEVER PICKED OUT YOUR OWN CLOTHES?
ピク
OH... UM...
ACTUALLY, THIS IS A LITTLE EMBARRASSING, BUT...
...I'VE NEVER EVEN USED MONEY BEFORE.
I'VE ONLY WORN WHAT MY MOM PREPARED FOR ME.
THAT'S WHY I'M HAPPY I CAN FINALLY PICK OUT WHAT I LIKE.
IS THAT WEIRD AT MY AGE?

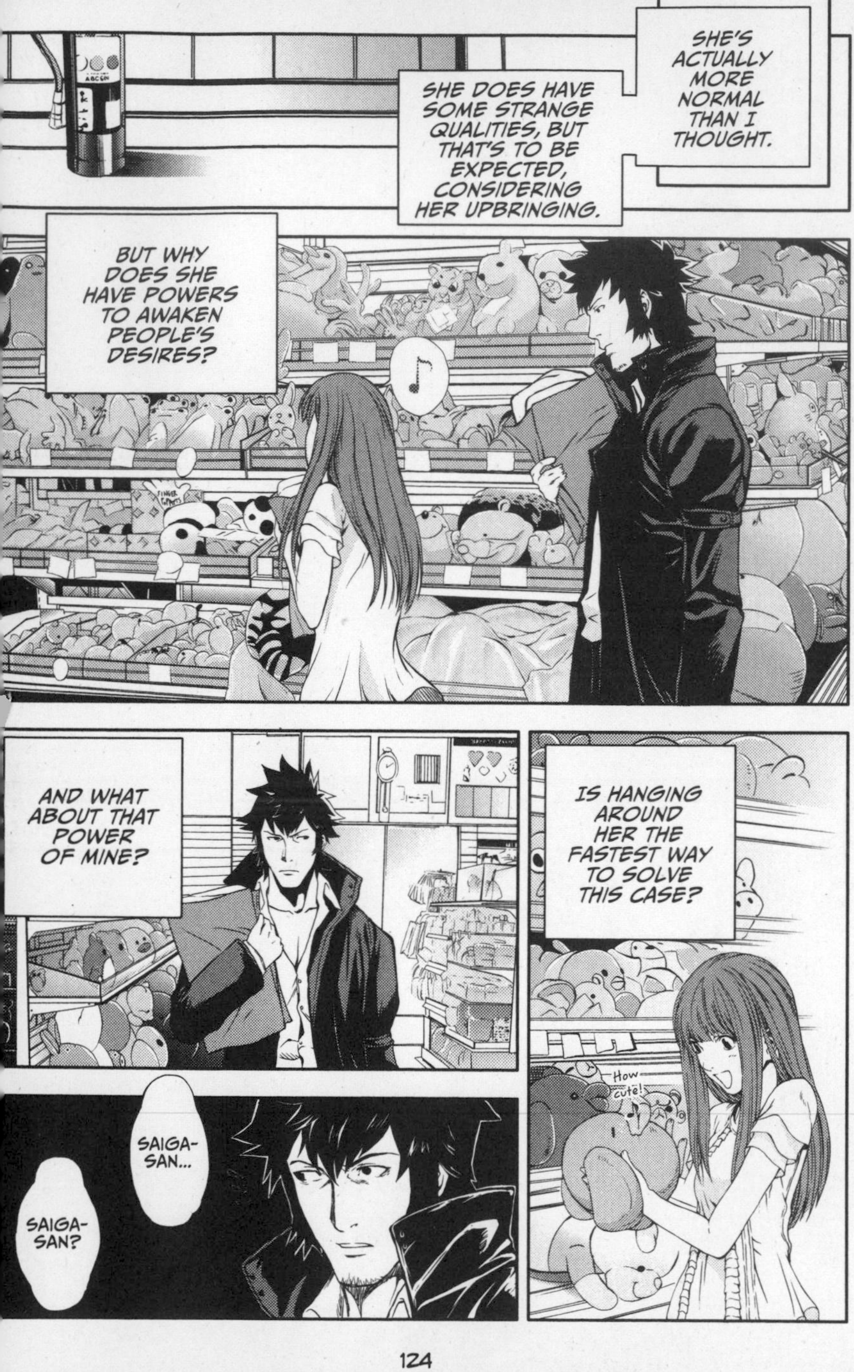
SHE'S ACTUALLY MORE NORMAL THAN I THOUGHT.
SHE DOES HAVE SOME STRANGE QUALITIES, BUT THAT'S TO BE EXPECTED, CONSIDERING HER UPBRINGING.
BUT WHY DOES SHE HAVE POWERS TO AWAKEN PEOPLE'S DESIRES?
♪
IS HANGING AROUND HER THE FASTEST WAY TO SOLVE THIS CASE?
How cute!
AND WHAT ABOUT THAT POWER OF MINE?
SAIGA-SAN...
SAIGA-SAN?

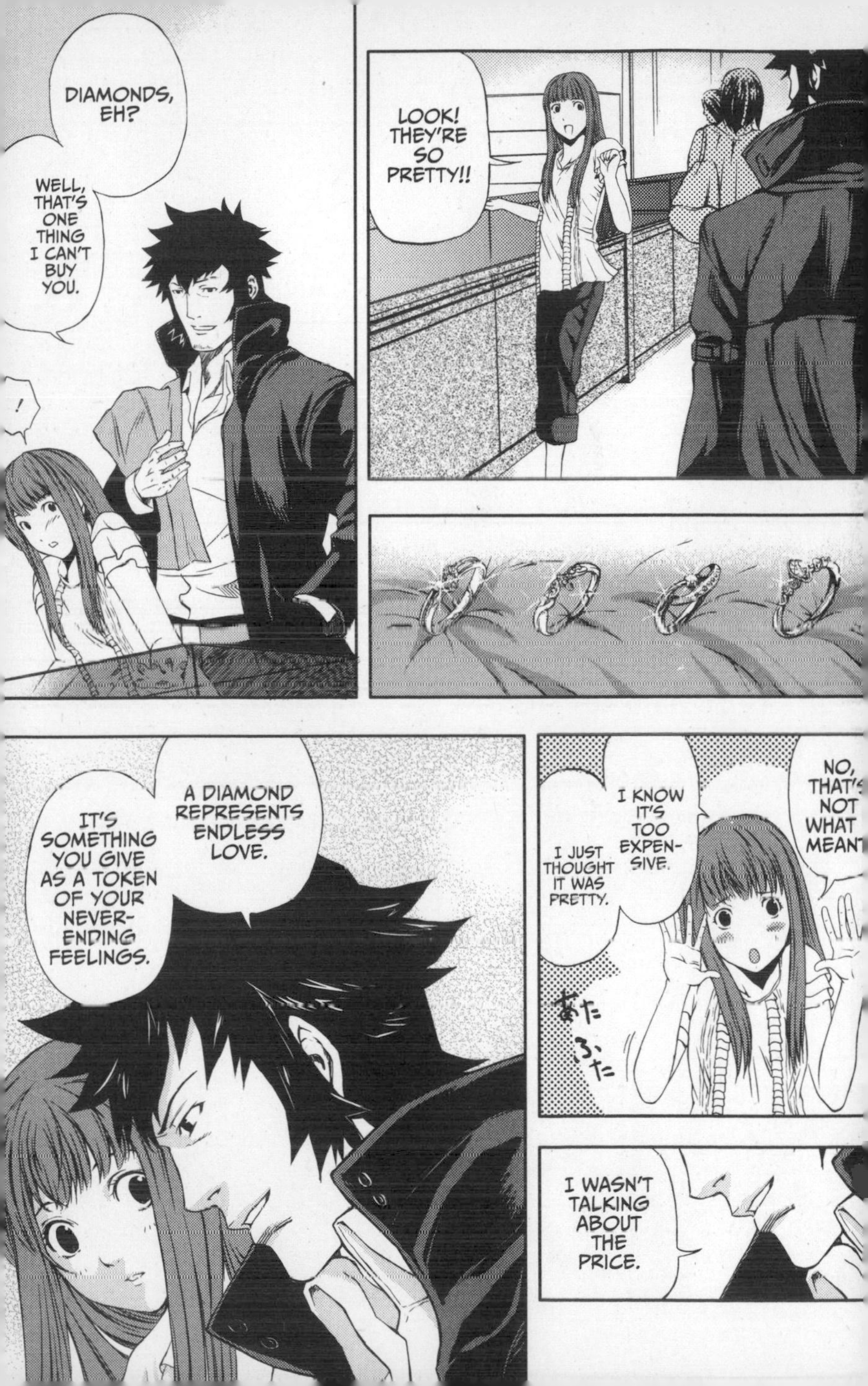
LOOK! THEY'RE SO PRETTY!!
DIAMONDS, EH?
WELL, THAT'S ONE THING I CAN'T BUY YOU.
!
NO, THAT'S NOT WHAT MEANT
I KNOW IT'S TOO EXPENSIVE.
I JUST THOUGHT IT WAS PRETTY.
あたふた
I WASN'T TALKING ABOUT THE PRICE.
A DIAMOND REPRESENTS ENDLESS LOVE.
IT'S SOMETHING YOU GIVE AS A TOKEN OF YOUR NEVER-ENDING FEELINGS.

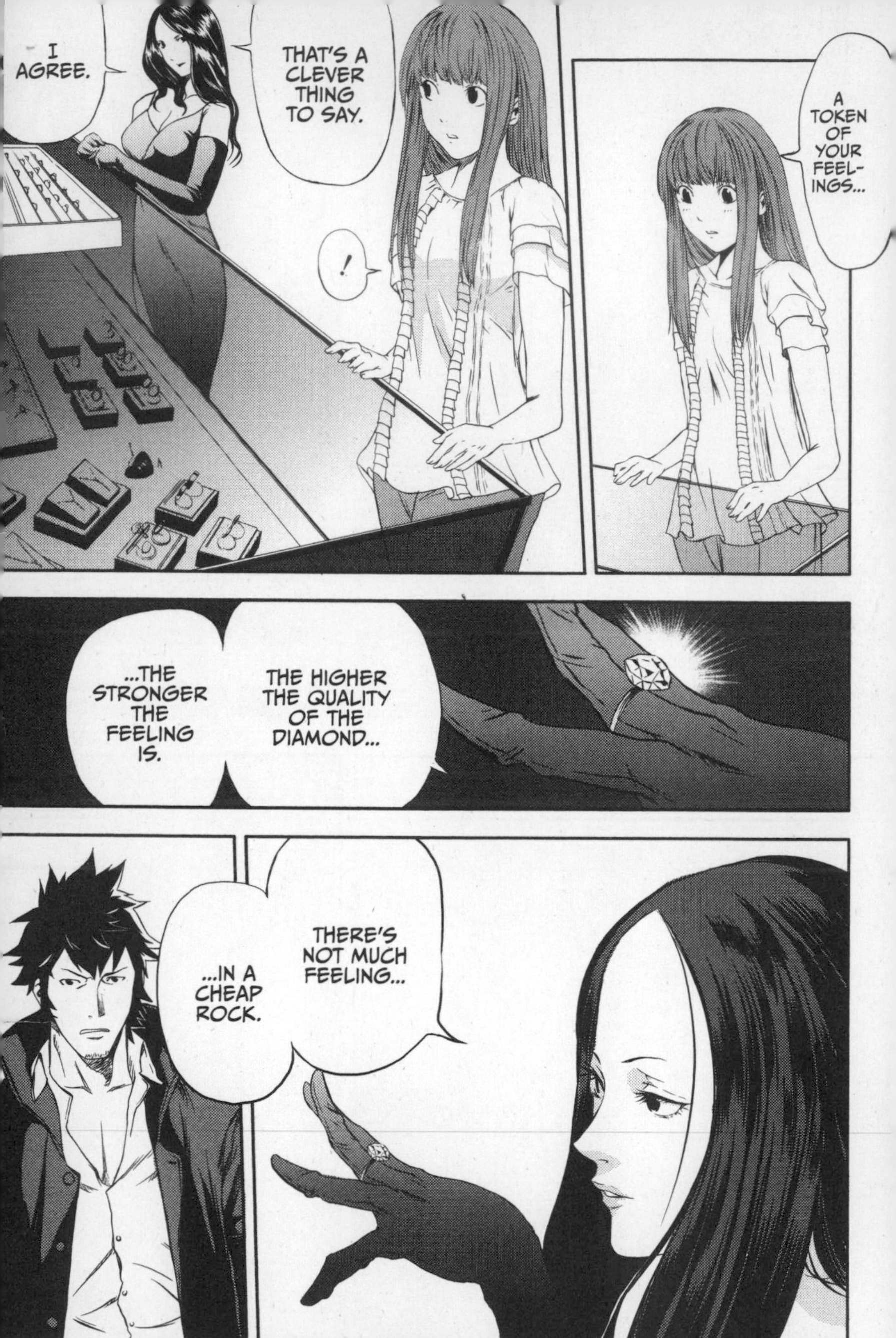
A TOKEN OF YOUR FEEL-INGS...
THAT'S A CLEVER THING TO SAY.
I AGREE.
!
THE HIGHER THE QUALITY OF THE DIAMOND...
...THE STRONGER THE FEELING IS.
THERE'S NOT MUCH FEELING...
...IN A CHEAP ROCK.

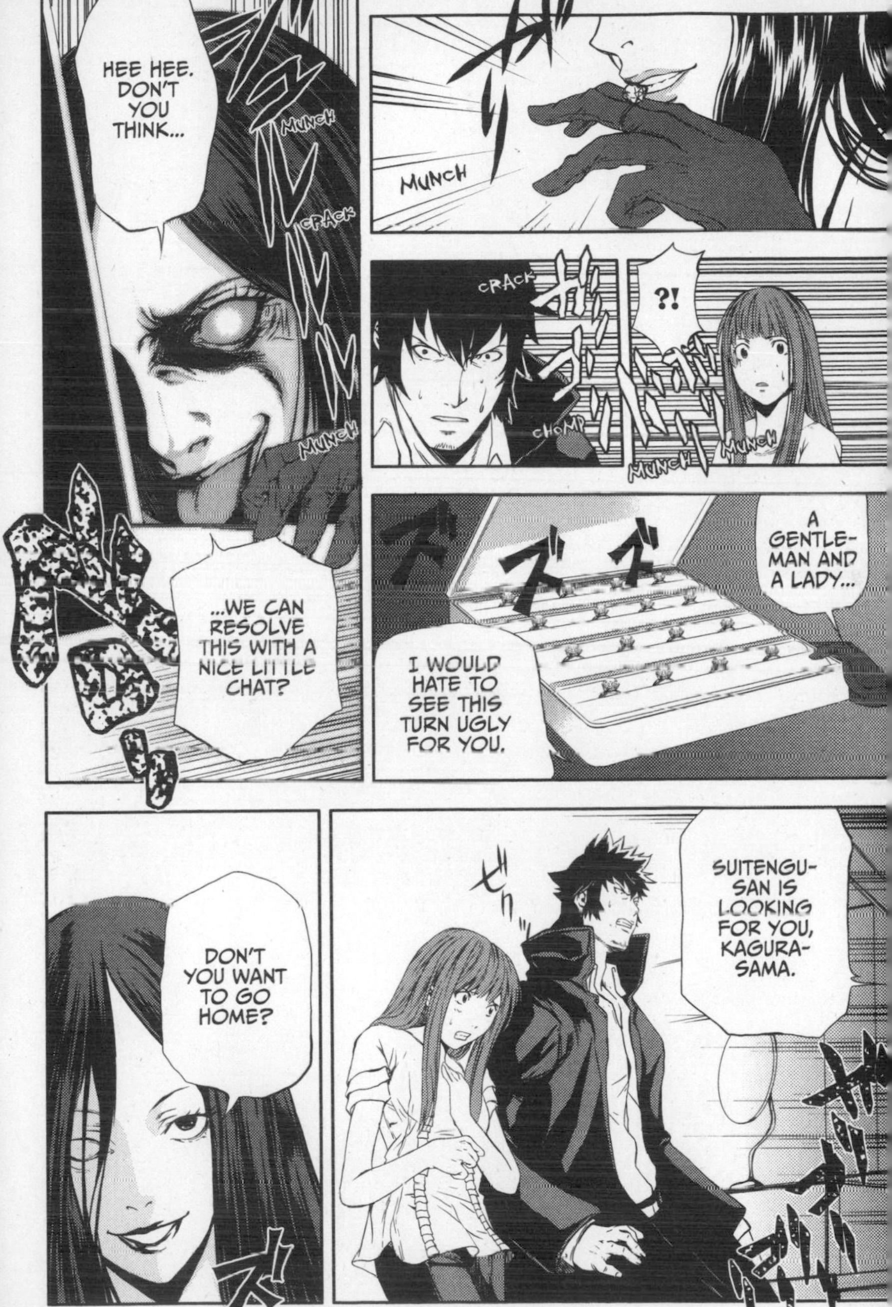
MUNCH
?!
CRACK
CHOMP
MUNCH
MUNCH
A GENTLE-MAN AND A LADY...
I WOULD HATE TO SEE THIS TURN UGLY FOR YOU.
HEE HEE. DON'T YOU THINK...
MUNCH
CRACK
MUNCH
...WE CAN RESOLVE THIS WITH A NICE LITTLE CHAT?
SUITENGU-SAN IS LOOKING FOR YOU, KAGURA-SAMA.
DON'T YOU WANT TO GO HOME?

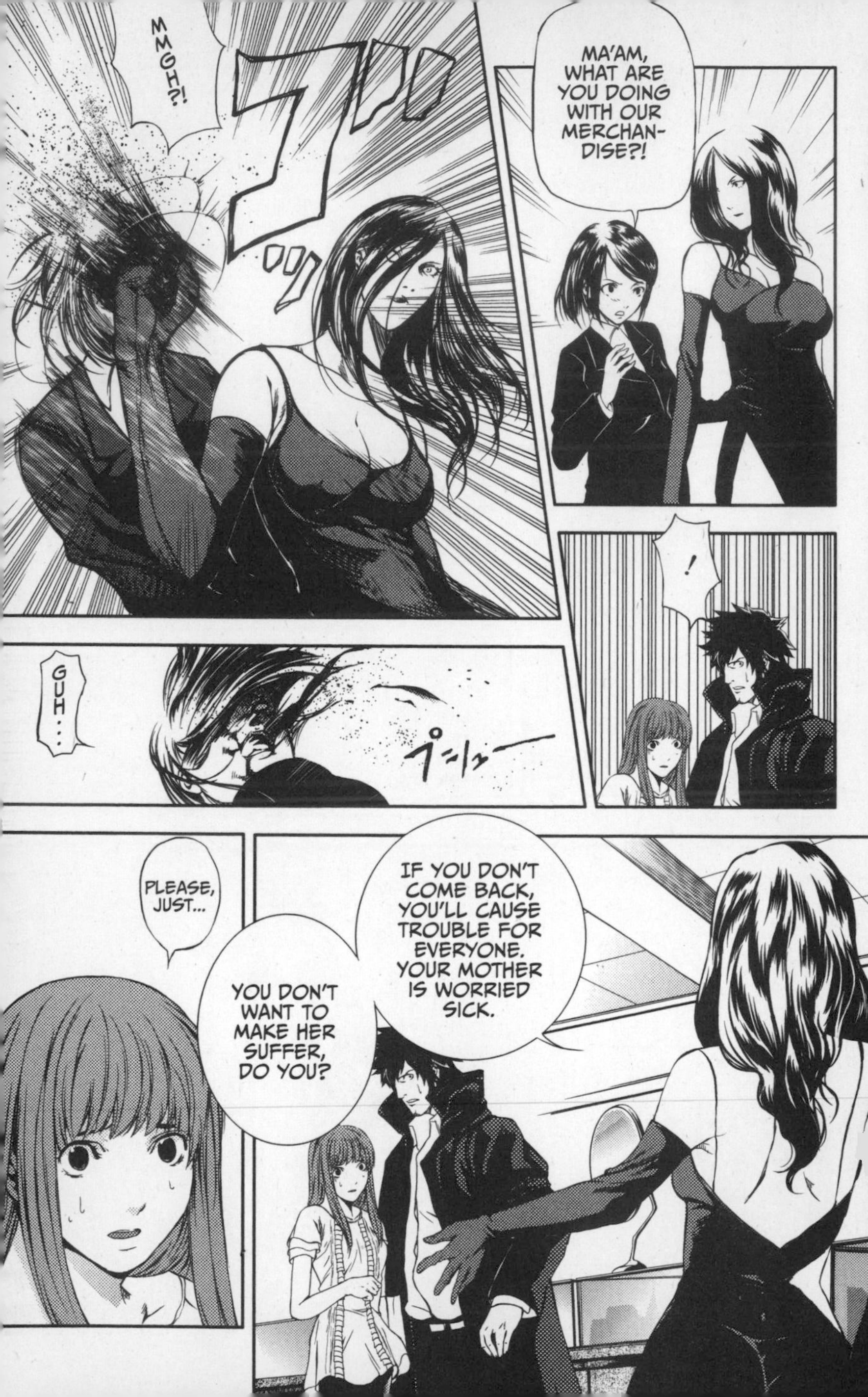
MA'AM, WHAT ARE YOU DOING WITH OUR MERCHAN-DISE?!
MMGH?!
!
GUH...
プシュー
IF YOU DON'T COME BACK, YOU'LL CAUSE TROUBLE FOR EVERYONE. YOUR MOTHER IS WORRIED SICK.
YOU DON'T WANT TO MAKE HER SUFFER, DO YOU?
PLEASE, JUST...

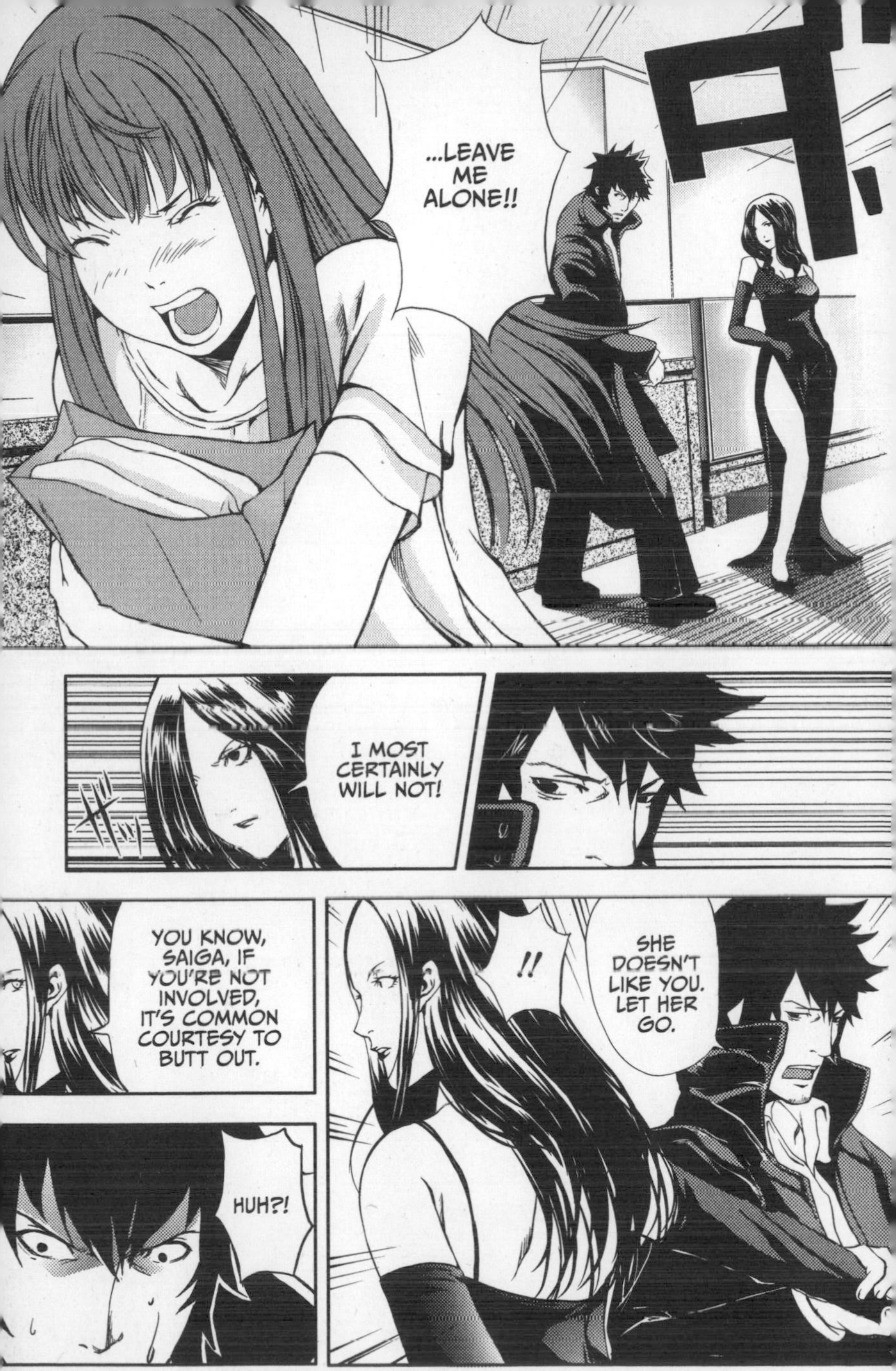
...LEAVE ME ALONE!!
I MOST CERTAINLY WILL NOT!
SHE DOESN'T LIKE YOU. LET HER GO.
!!
YOU KNOW, SAIGA, IF YOU'RE NOT INVOLVED, IT'S COMMON COURTESY TO BUTT OUT.
HUH?!

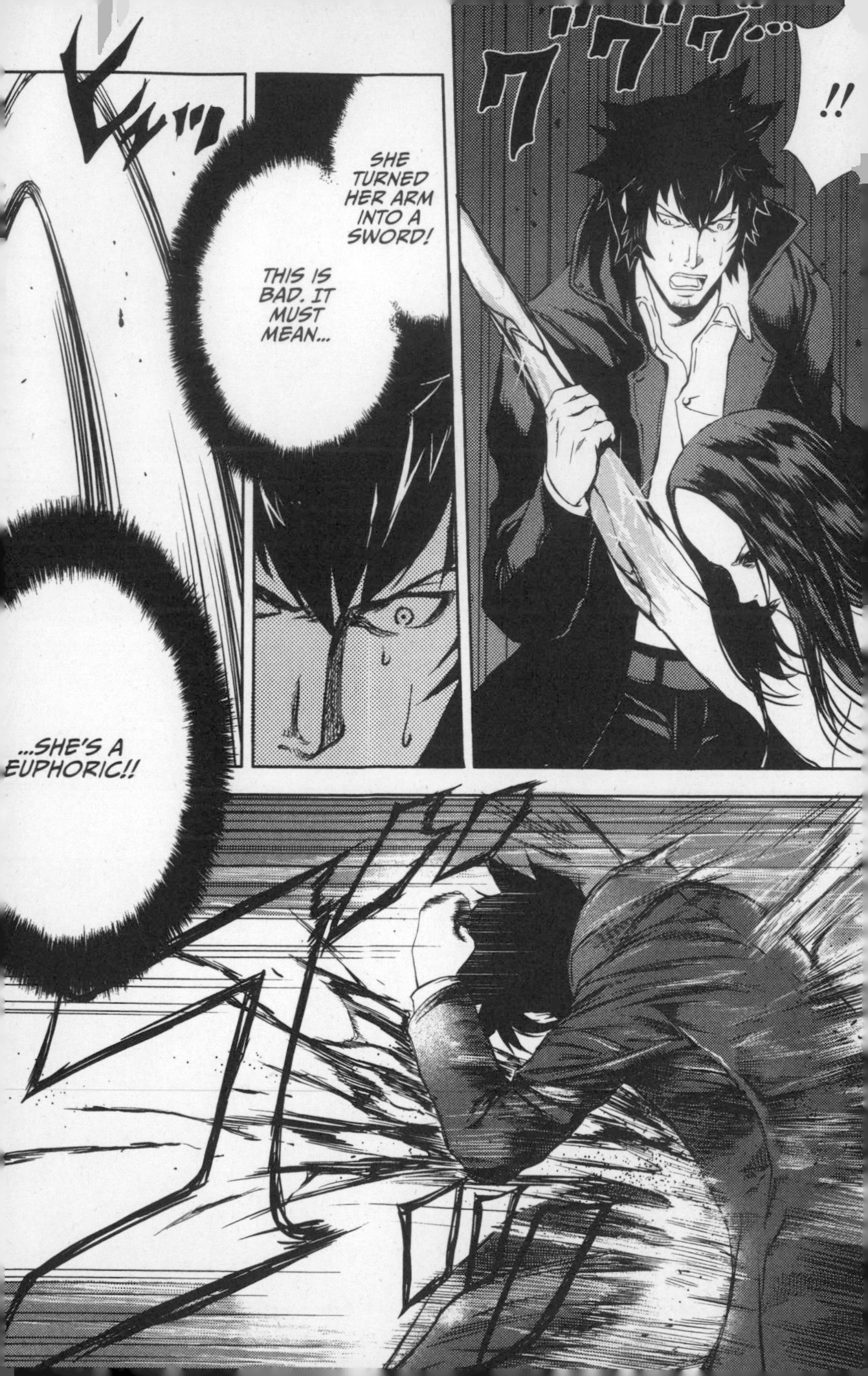
!!
SHE TURNED HER ARM INTO A SWORD!
THIS IS BAD. IT MUST MEAN...
...SHE'S A EUPHORIC!!

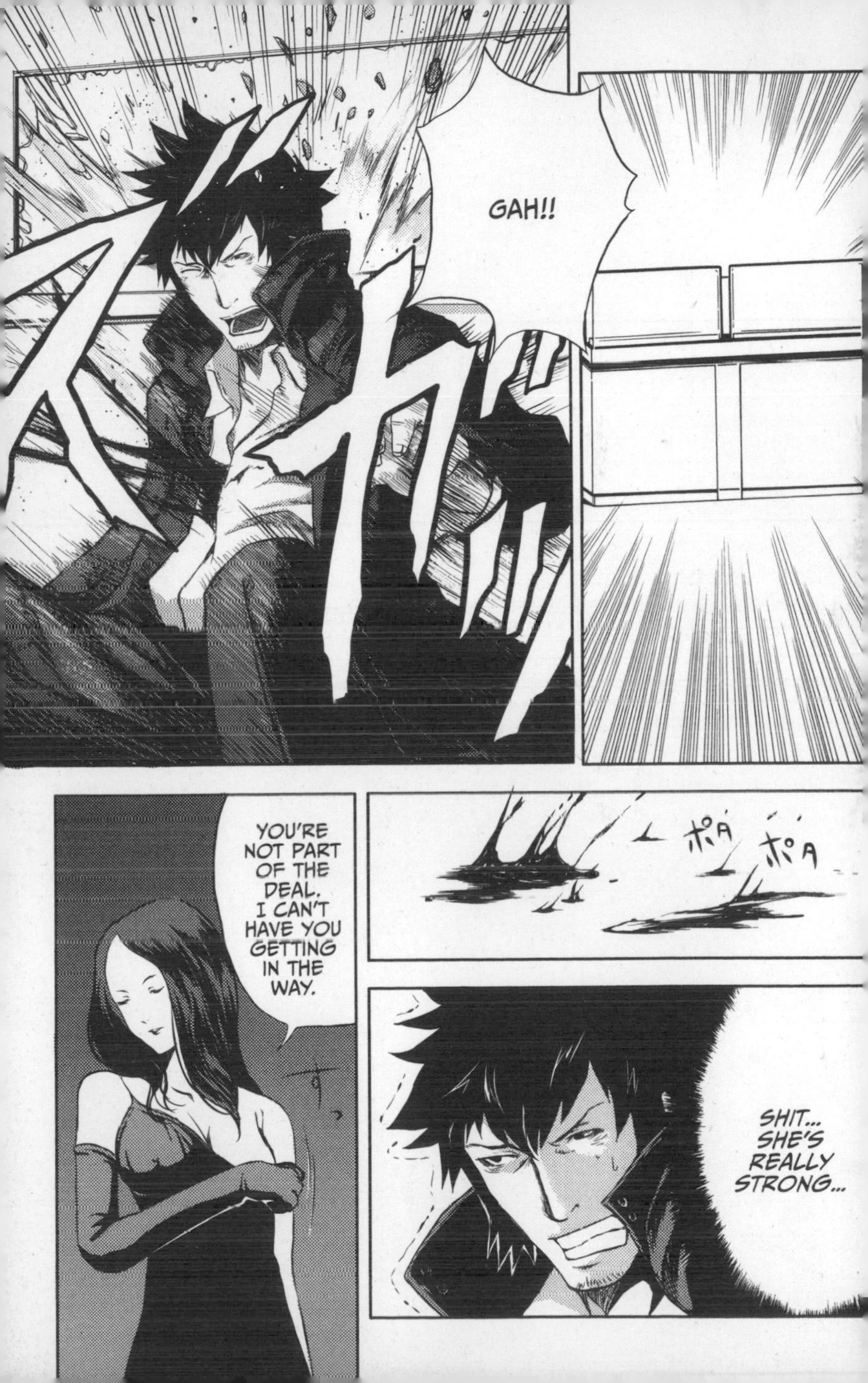
GAH!!
SHIT... SHE'S REALLY STRONG...
YOU'RE NOT PART OF THE DEAL. I CAN'T HAVE YOU GETTING IN THE WAY.

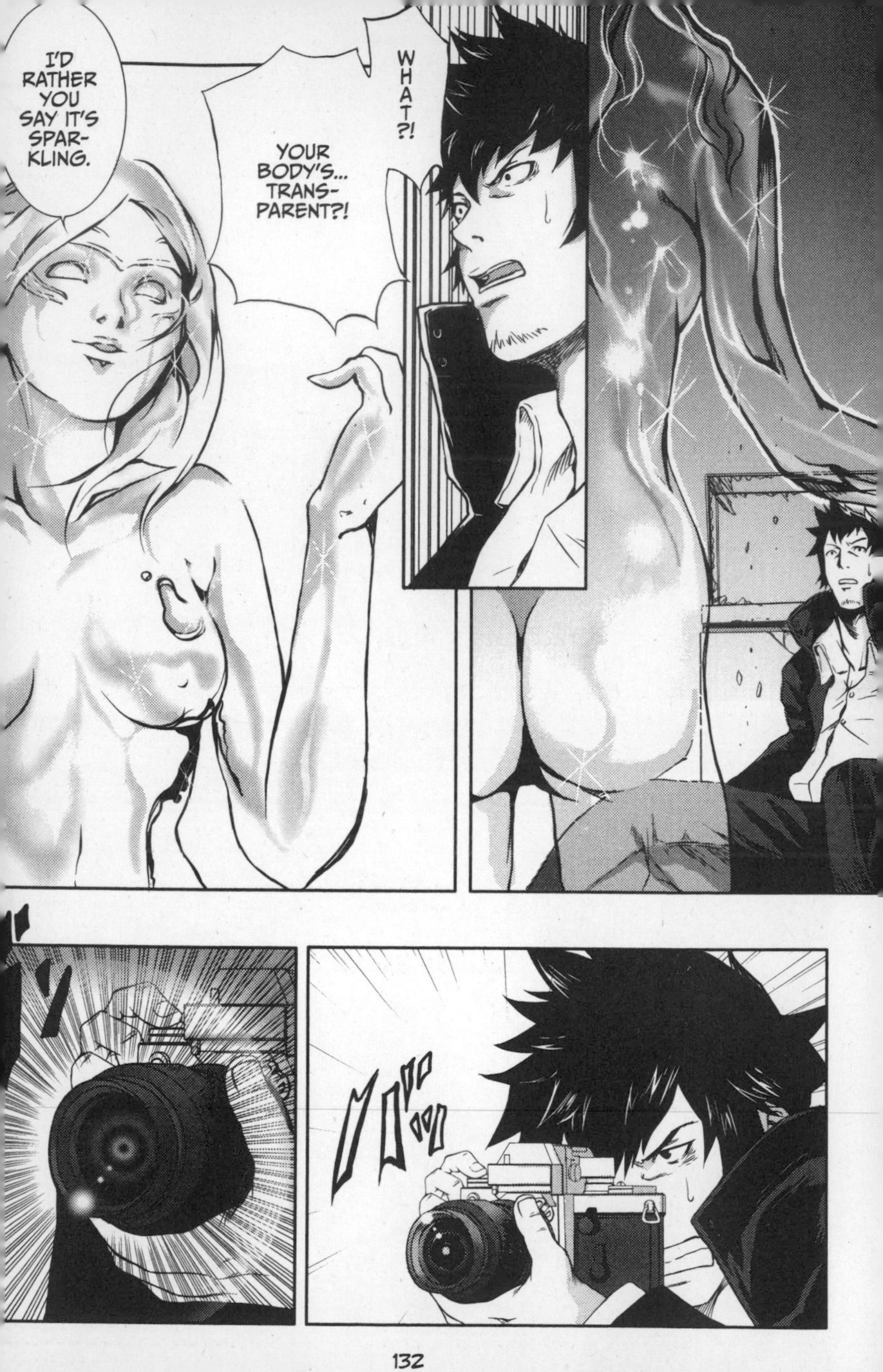
WHAT?!
YOUR BODY'S... TRANS-PARENT?!
I'D RATHER YOU SAY IT'S SPAR-KLING.

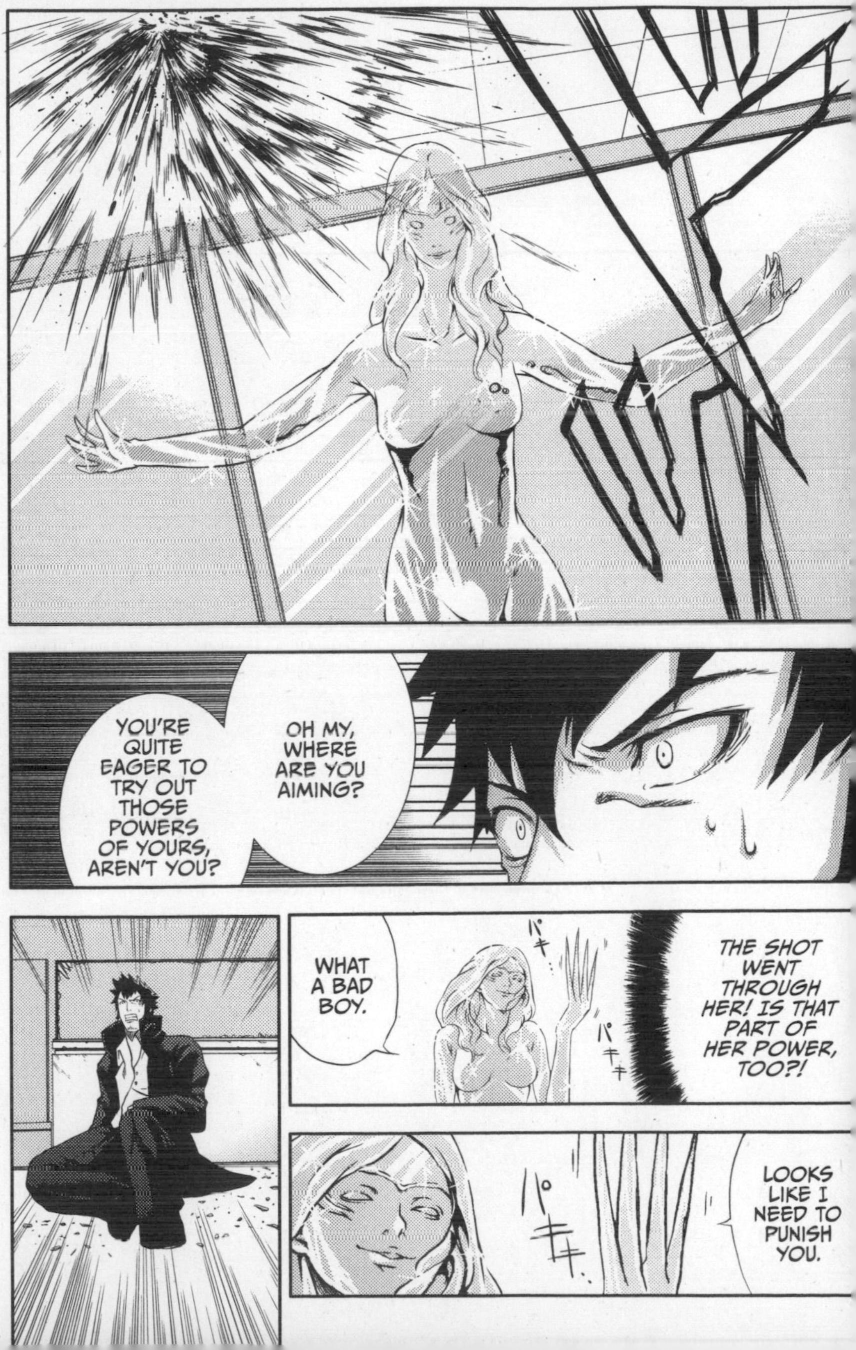
OH MY, WHERE ARE YOU AIMING?
YOU'RE QUITE EAGER TO TRY OUT THOSE POWERS OF YOURS, AREN'T YOU?
THE SHOT WENT THROUGH HER! IS THAT PART OF HER POWER, TOO?!
パキ…
パキキ
WHAT A BAD BOY.
LOOKS LIKE I NEED TO PUNISH YOU.
パキキ

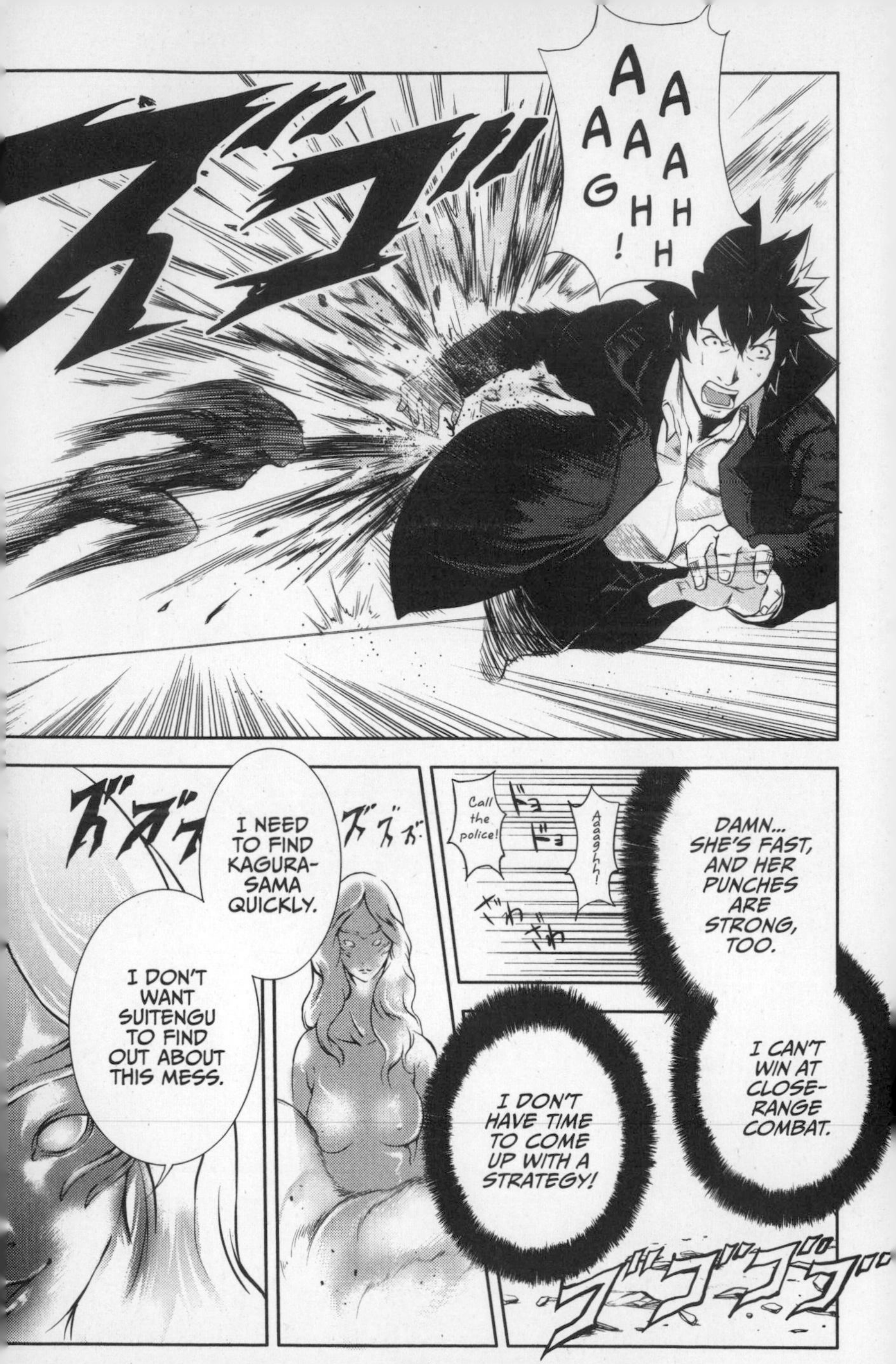
AAH
AAHH
AAG!
Call the police!
Aaaagh!
DAMN... SHE'S FAST, AND HER PUNCHES ARE STRONG, TOO.
I CAN'T WIN AT CLOSE-RANGE COMBAT.
I DON'T HAVE TIME TO COME UP WITH A STRATEGY!
I NEED TO FIND KAGURA-SAMA QUICKLY.
I DON'T WANT SUITENGU TO FIND OUT ABOUT THIS MESS.

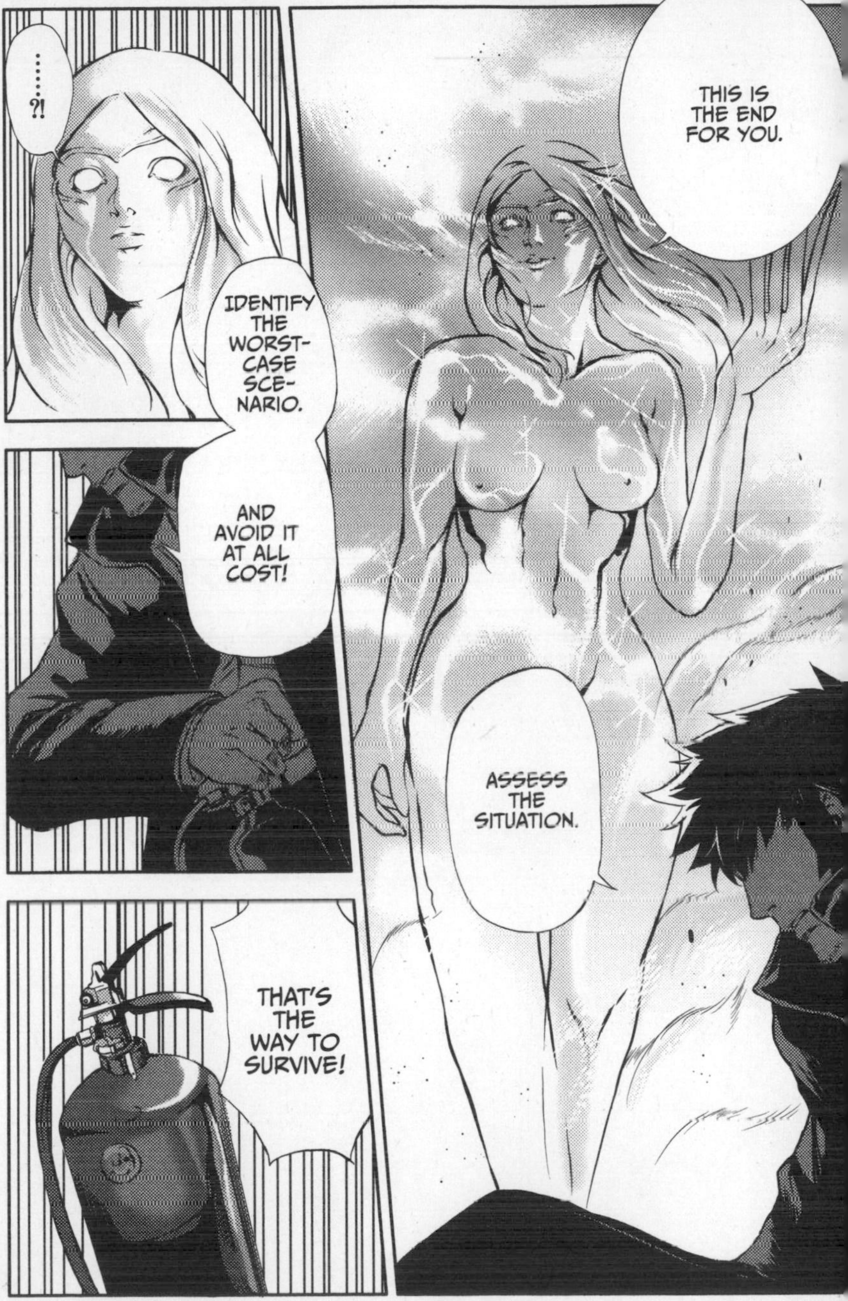
THIS IS THE END FOR YOU.
ASSESS THE SITUATION.
......?!
IDENTIFY THE WORST-CASE SCE-NARIO.
AND AVOID IT AT ALL COST!
THAT'S THE WAY TO SURVIVE!

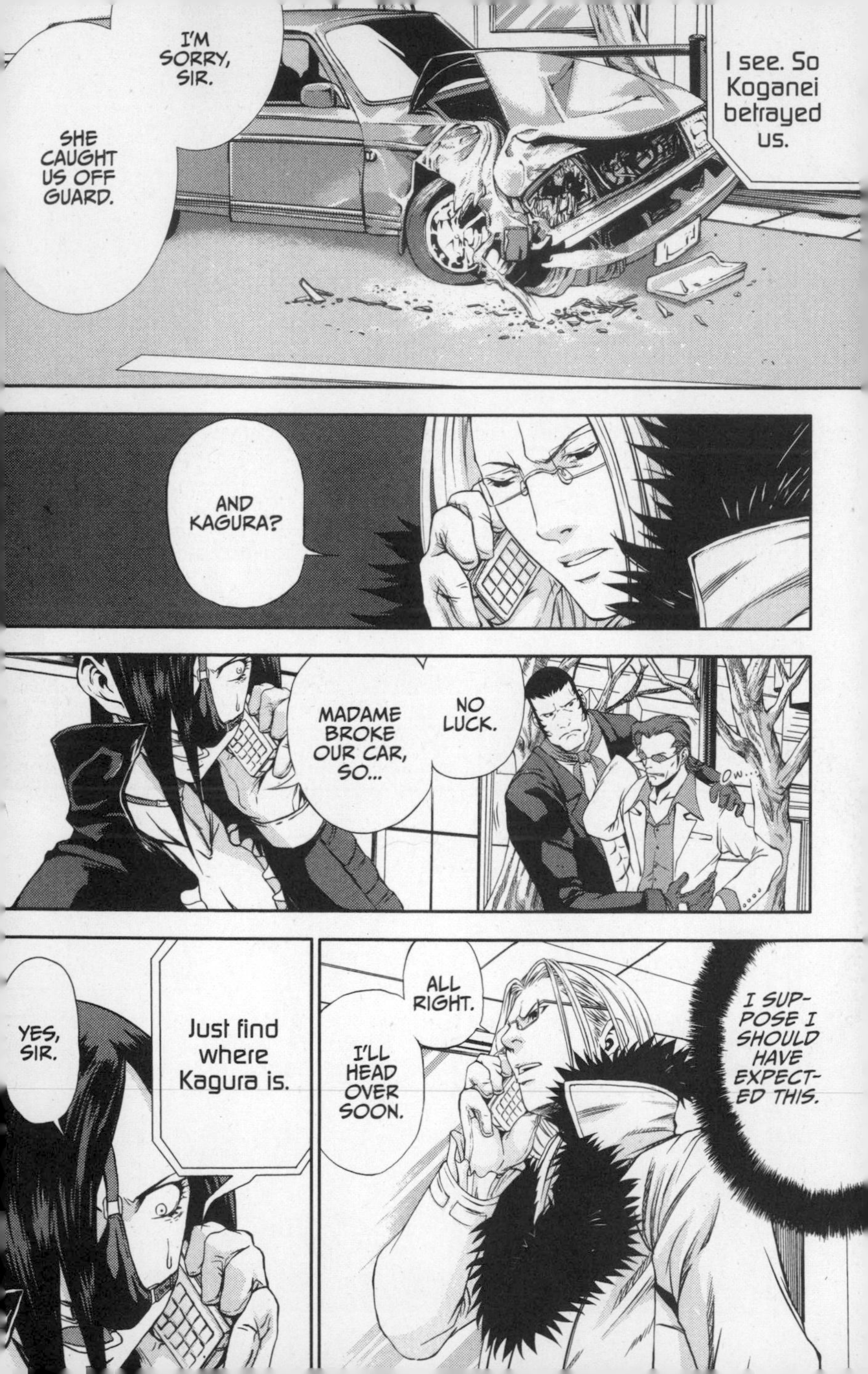
I see. So Koganei betrayed us.
I'M SORRY, SIR.
SHE CAUGHT US OFF GUARD.
AND KAGURA?
NO LUCK.
MADAME BROKE OUR CAR, SO...
Ow...
I SUP-POSE I SHOULD HAVE EXPECT-ED THIS.
ALL RIGHT.
I'LL HEAD OVER SOON.
Just find where Kagura is.
YES, SIR.

THE WORD "DIAMOND" IS DERIVED FROM THE GREEK WORD "ADAMAS."

IT MEANS "ONE WHO IS UNCONQUERED."

KOGANEI, IS THIS DUE TO YOUR RESENTMENT TOWARD ME OR YOUR OVERWHELMING DESIRE?

EITHER WAY, I MUST RETRIEVE KAGURA AS SOON AS POSSIBLE.

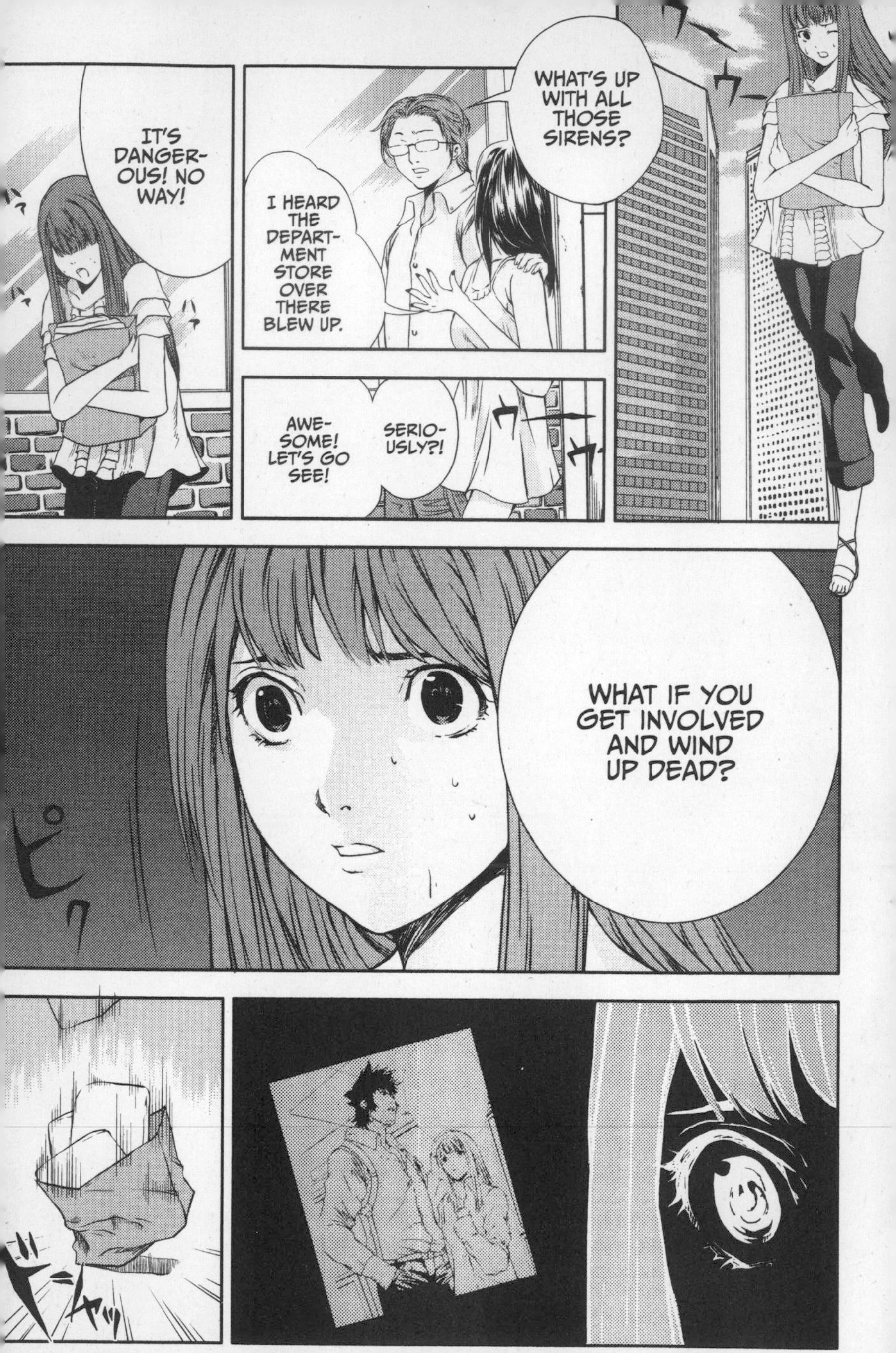
WHAT'S UP WITH ALL THOSE SIRENS?
I HEARD THE DEPART-MENT STORE OVER THERE BLEW UP.
SERIO-USLY?!
AWE-SOME! LET'S GO SEE!
IT'S DANGER-OUS! NO WAY!
WHAT IF YOU GET INVOLVED AND WIND UP DEAD?

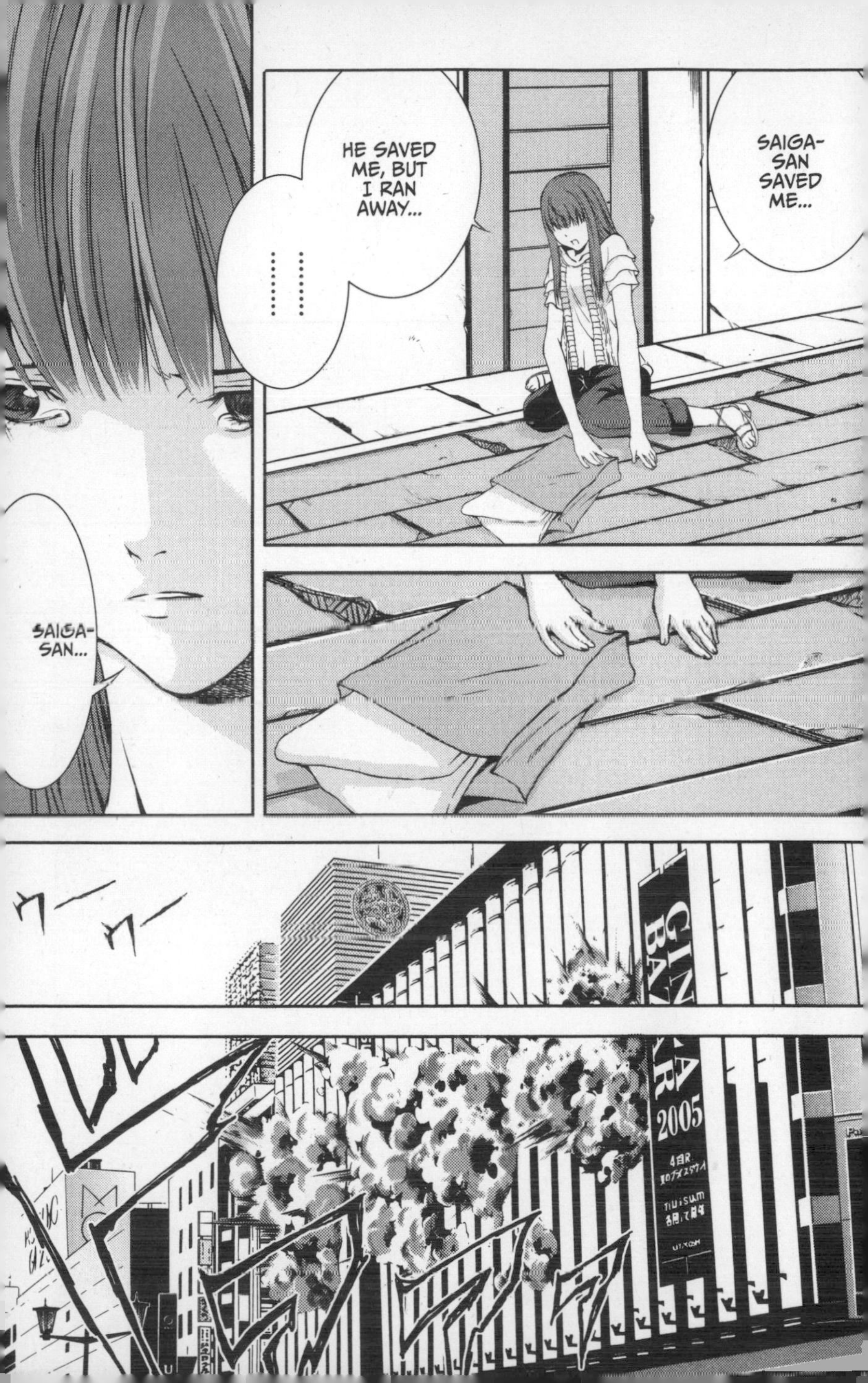
SAIGA-SAN SAVED ME...
HE SAVED ME, BUT I RAN AWAY...
......
SAIGA-SAN...
ウー ウー

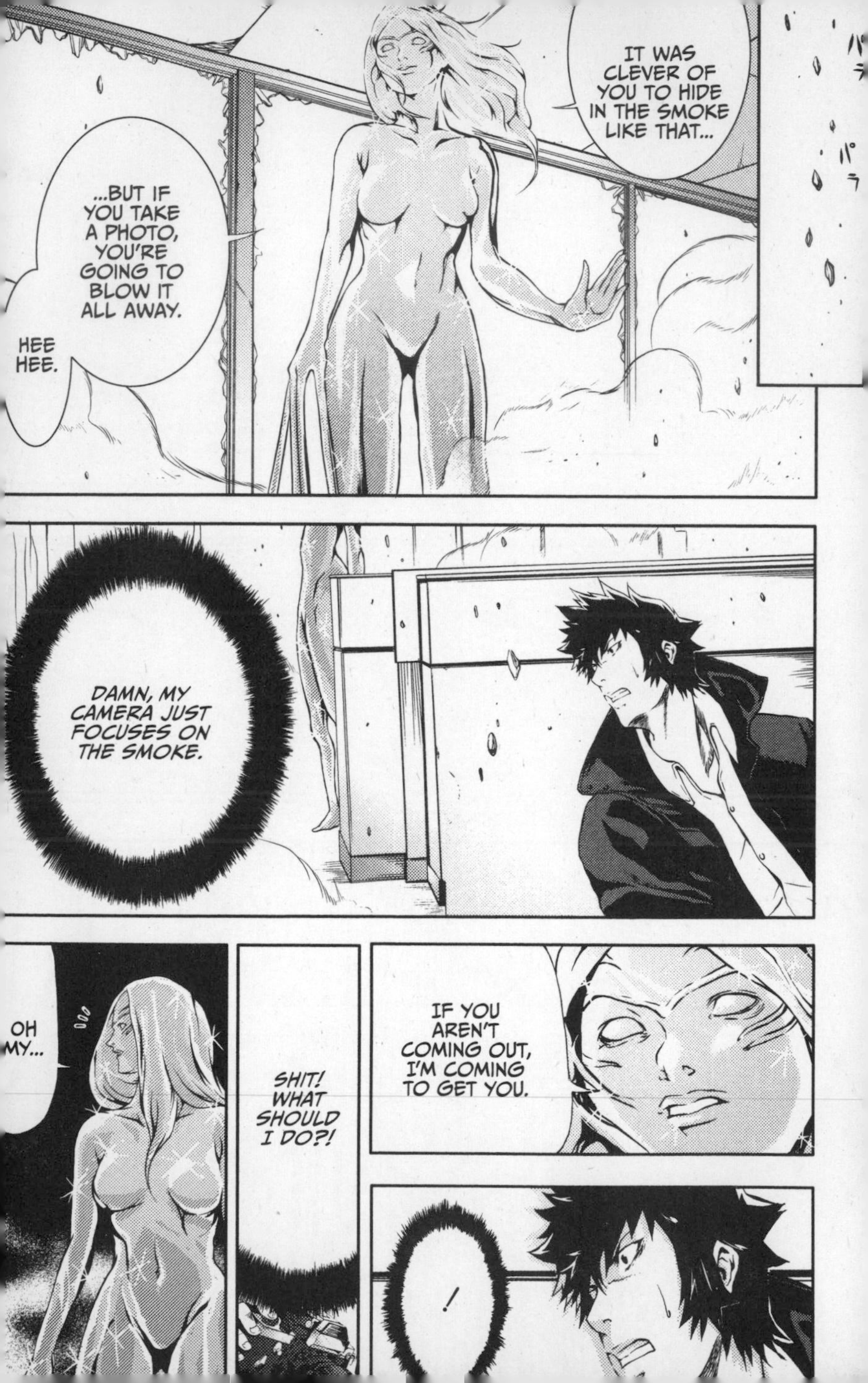
パラ
パラ
IT WAS CLEVER OF YOU TO HIDE IN THE SMOKE LIKE THAT...
...BUT IF YOU TAKE A PHOTO, YOU'RE GOING TO BLOW IT ALL AWAY.
HEE HEE.
DAMN, MY CAMERA JUST FOCUSES ON THE SMOKE.
IF YOU AREN'T COMING OUT, I'M COMING TO GET YOU.
!
SHIT! WHAT SHOULD I DO?!
OH MY...

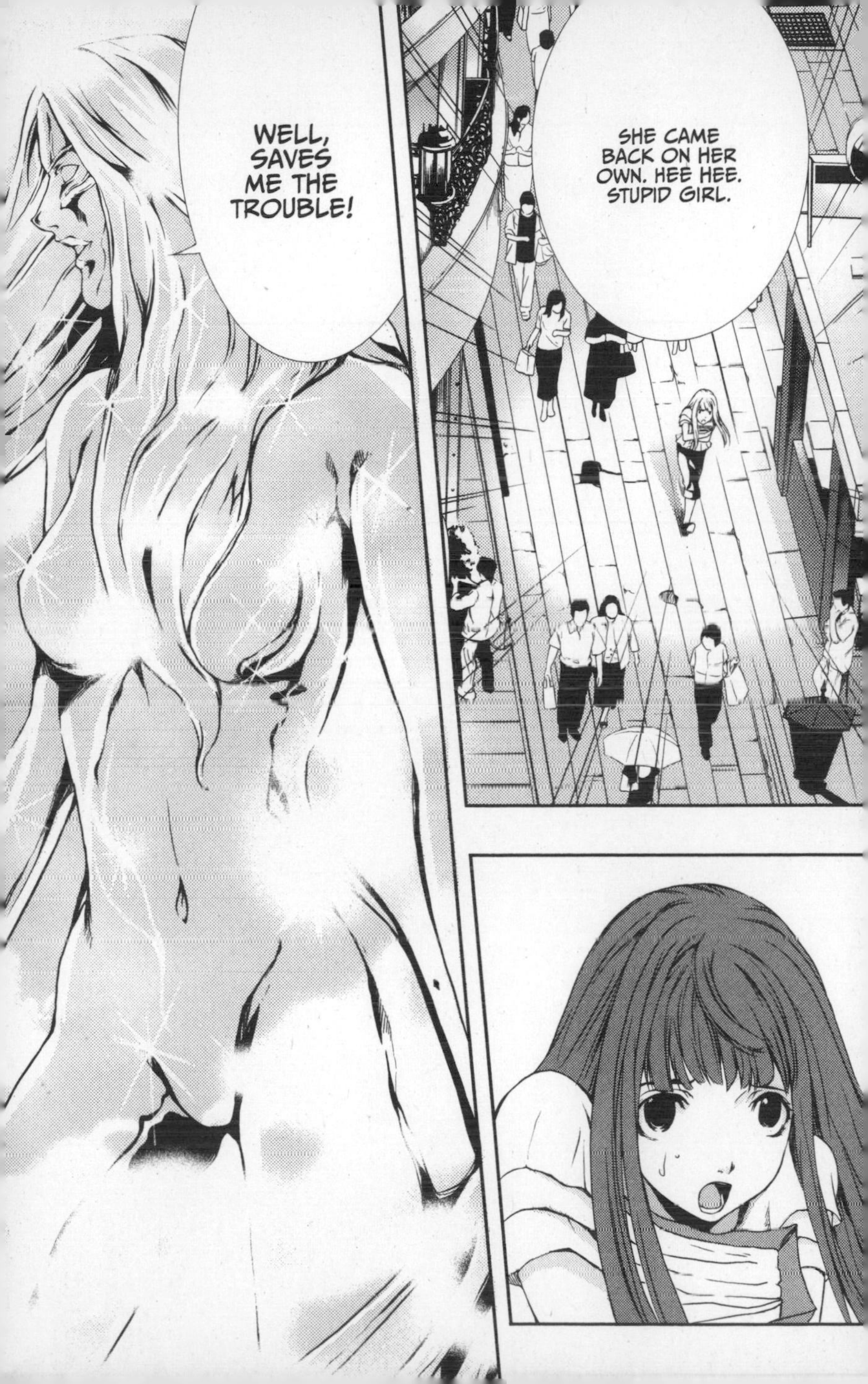
SHE CAME BACK ON HER OWN. HEE HEE. STUPID GIRL.
WELL, SAVES ME THE TROUBLE!

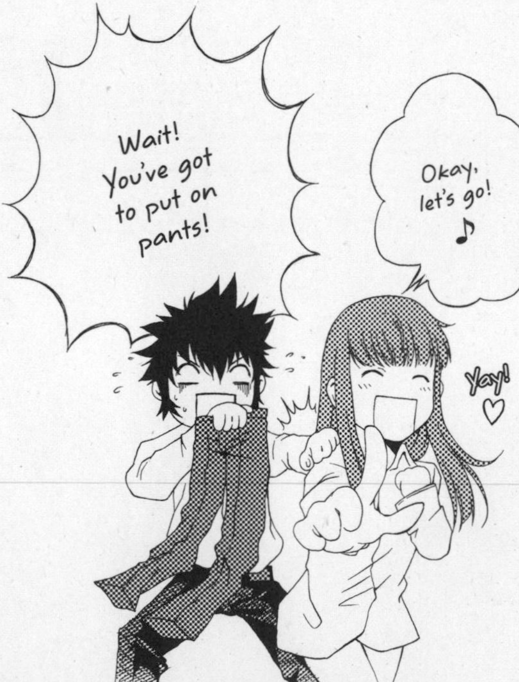
Okay, let's go! ♪
Wait! You've got to put on pants!
Yay! ♡

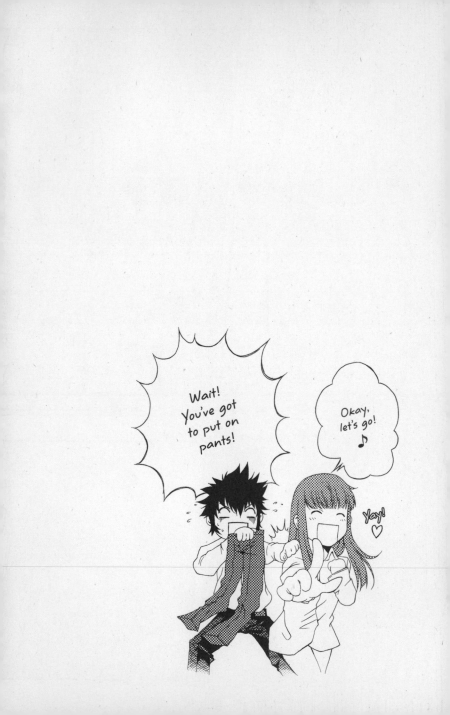

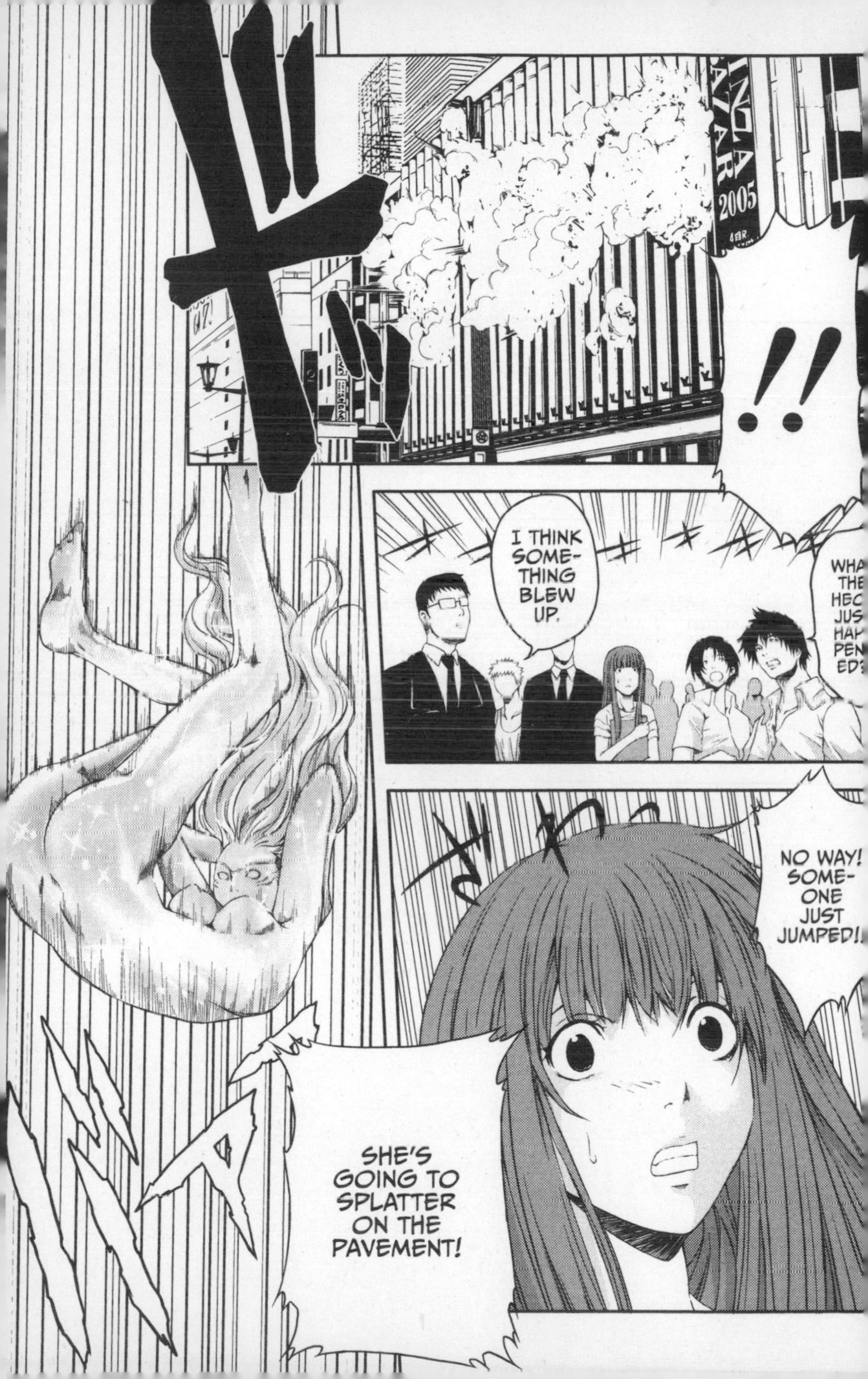

2005
!!
WHA THE HEC JUS HAP PEN ED?
I THINK SOME- THING BLEW UP.
NO WAY! SOME- ONE JUST JUMPED!!
SHE'S GOING TO SPLATTER ON THE PAVEMENT!

Shutter: 6
Goodbye, Lady Diamond

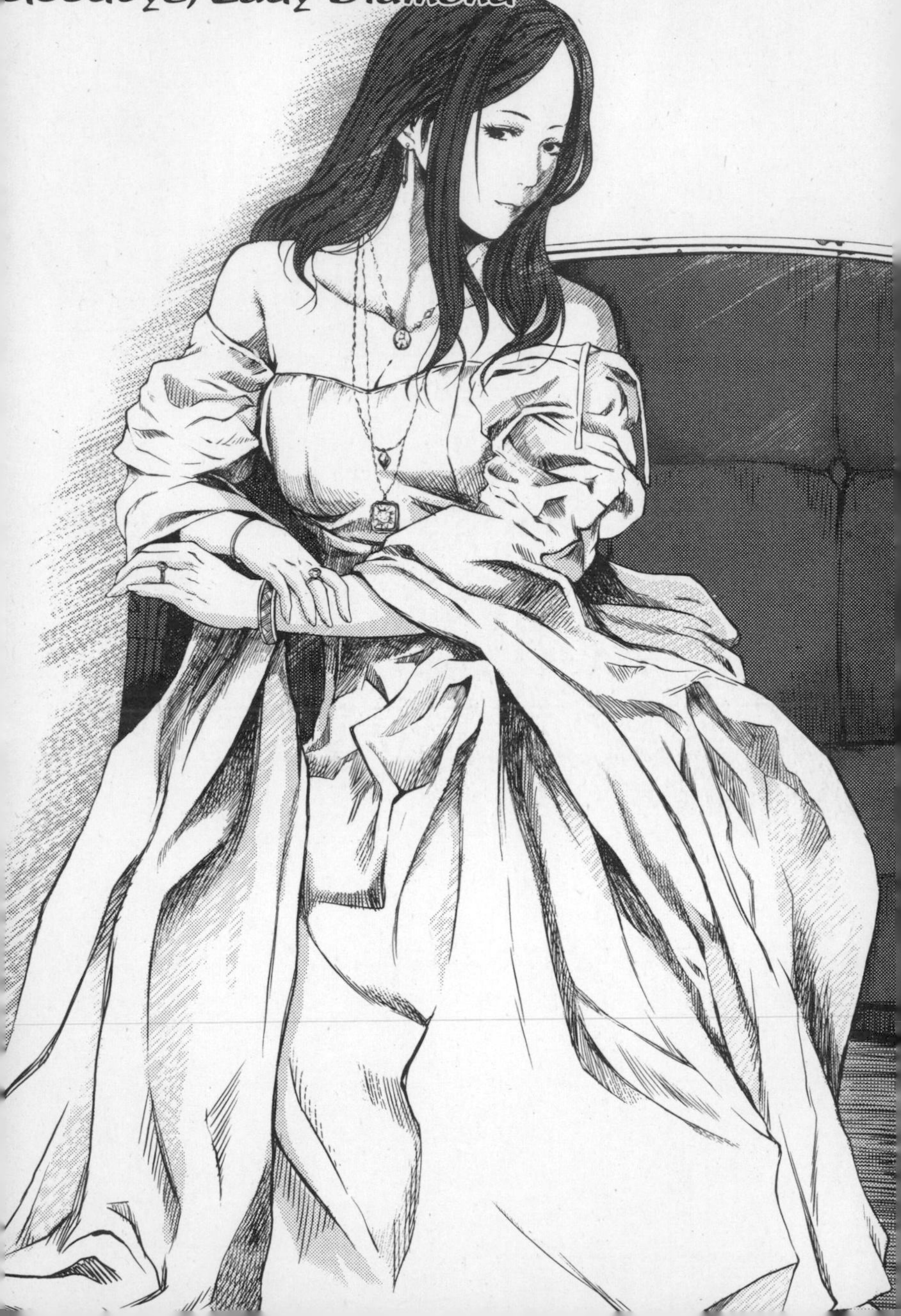

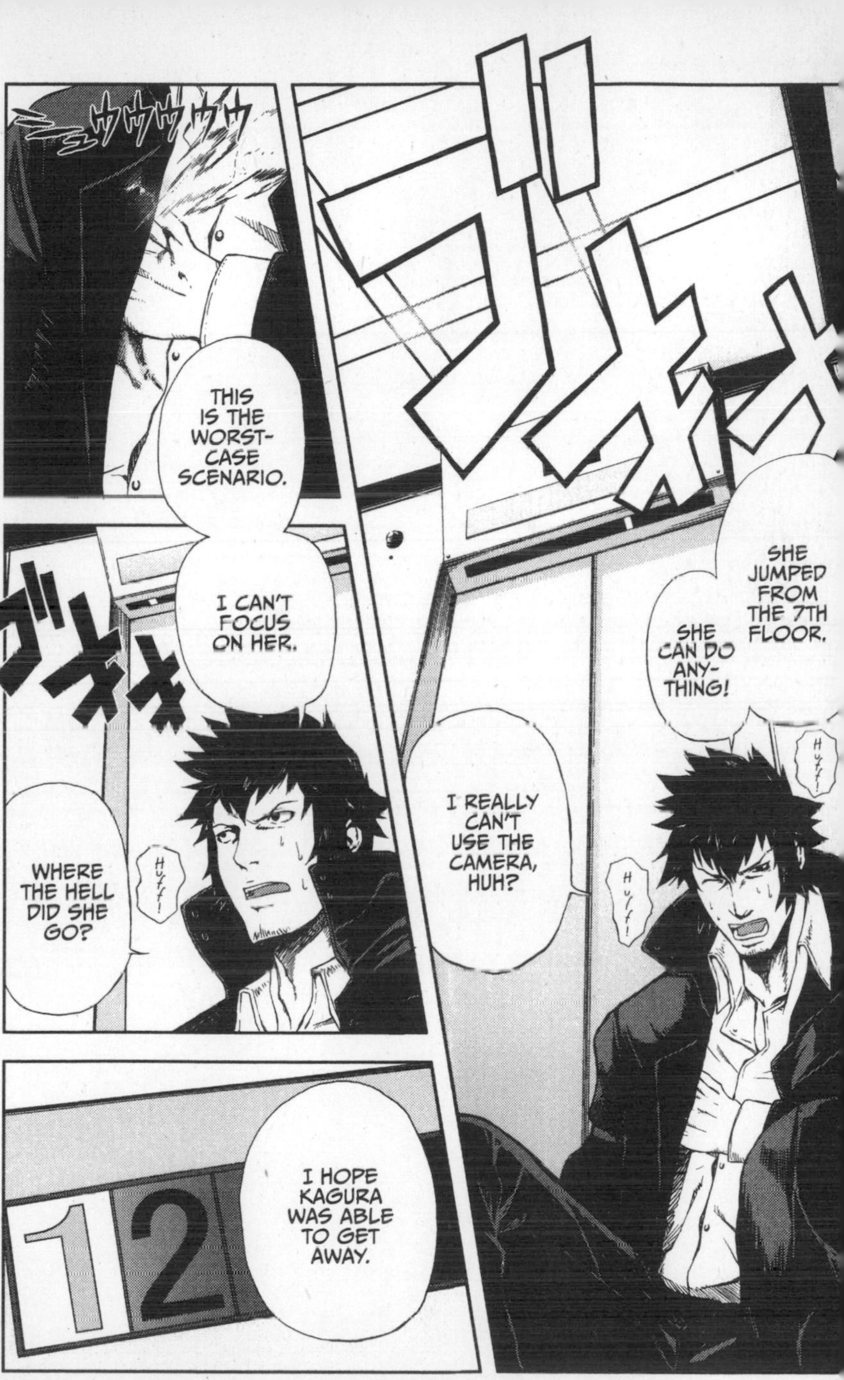
SHE JUMPED FROM THE 7TH FLOOR.
SHE CAN DO ANY-THING!
Huff!
I REALLY CAN'T USE THE CAMERA, HUH?
Huff!
THIS IS THE WORST-CASE SCENARIO.
I CAN'T FOCUS ON HER.
Huff!
WHERE THE HELL DID SHE GO?
I HOPE KAGURA WAS ABLE TO GET AWAY.
12

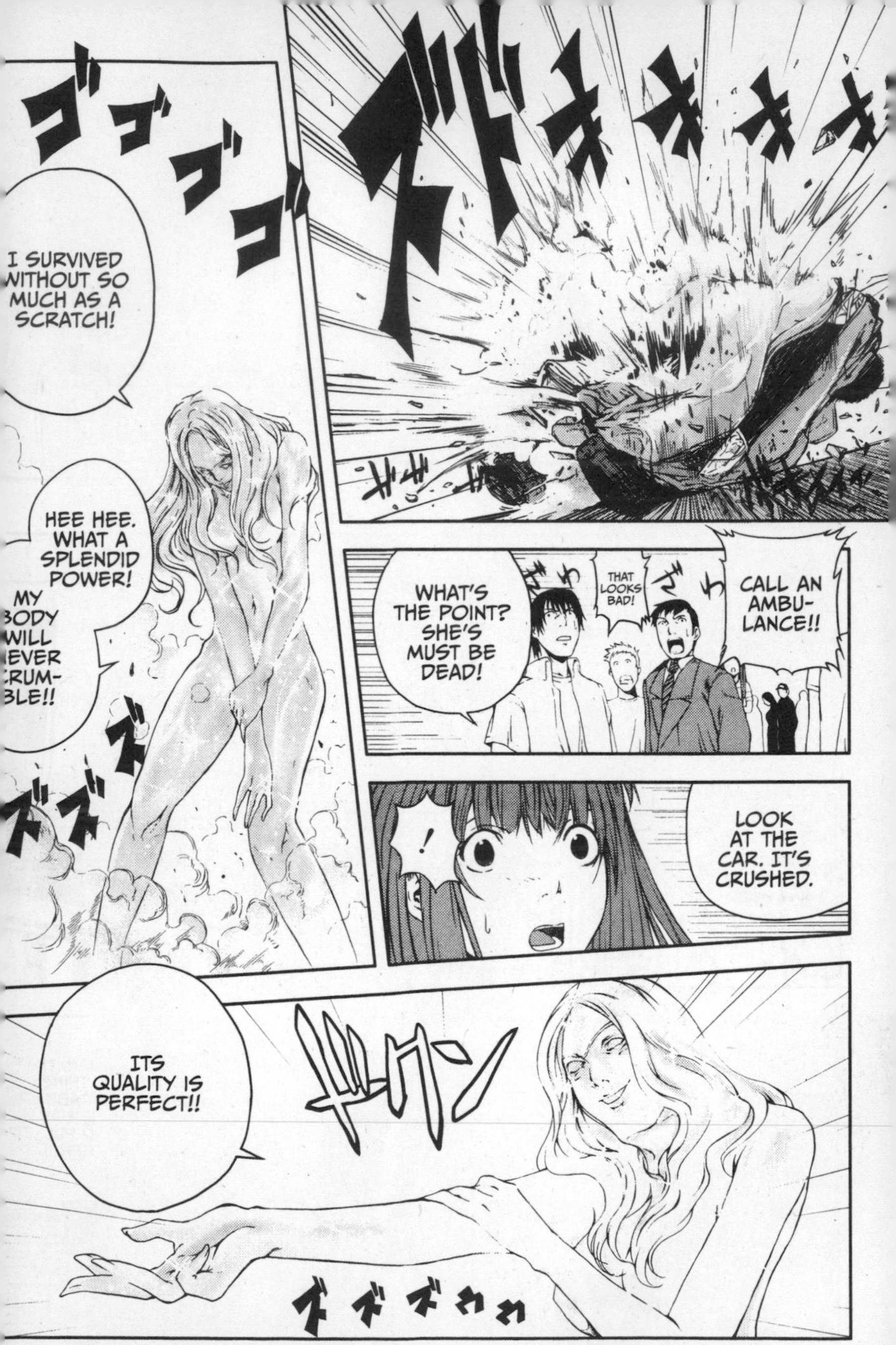

CALL AN AMBULANCE!!
THAT LOOKS BAD!
WHAT'S THE POINT? SHE'S MUST BE DEAD!
LOOK AT THE CAR. IT'S CRUSHED.
I SURVIVED WITHOUT SO MUCH AS A SCRATCH!
HEE HEE. WHAT A SPLENDID POWER!
MY BODY WILL NEVER CRUMBLE!!
ITS QUALITY IS PERFECT!!

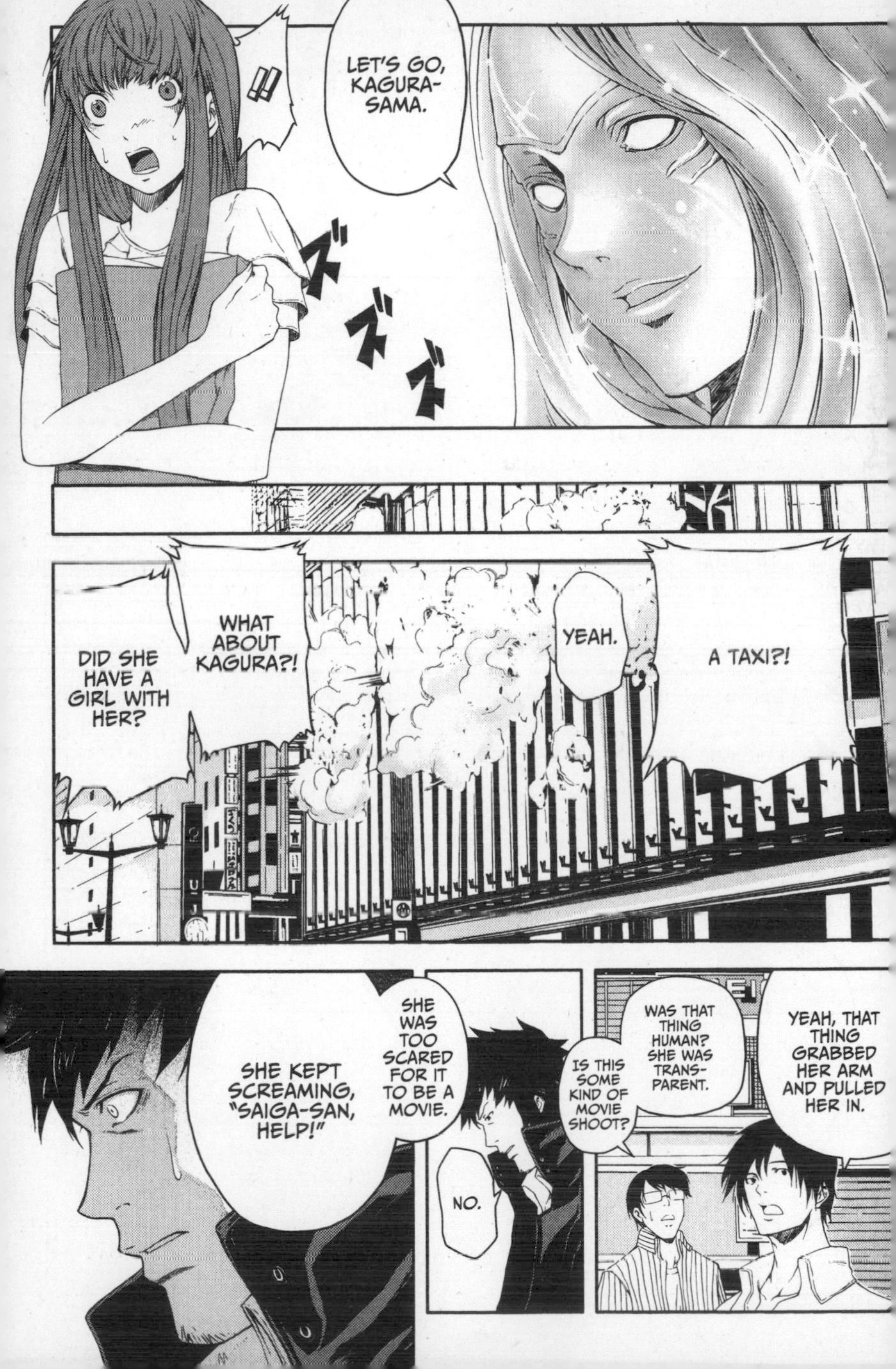
LET'S GO, KAGURA-SAMA.
!!
ズ ズ ズ
A TAXI?!
YEAH.
WHAT ABOUT KAGURA?!
DID SHE HAVE A GIRL WITH HER?
YEAH, THAT THING GRABBED HER ARM AND PULLED HER IN.
WAS THAT THING HUMAN? SHE WAS TRANS-PARENT.
IS THIS SOME KIND OF MOVIE SHOOT?
SHE WAS TOO SCARED FOR IT TO BE A MOVIE.
NO.
SHE KEPT SCREAMING, "SAIGA-SAN, HELP!"

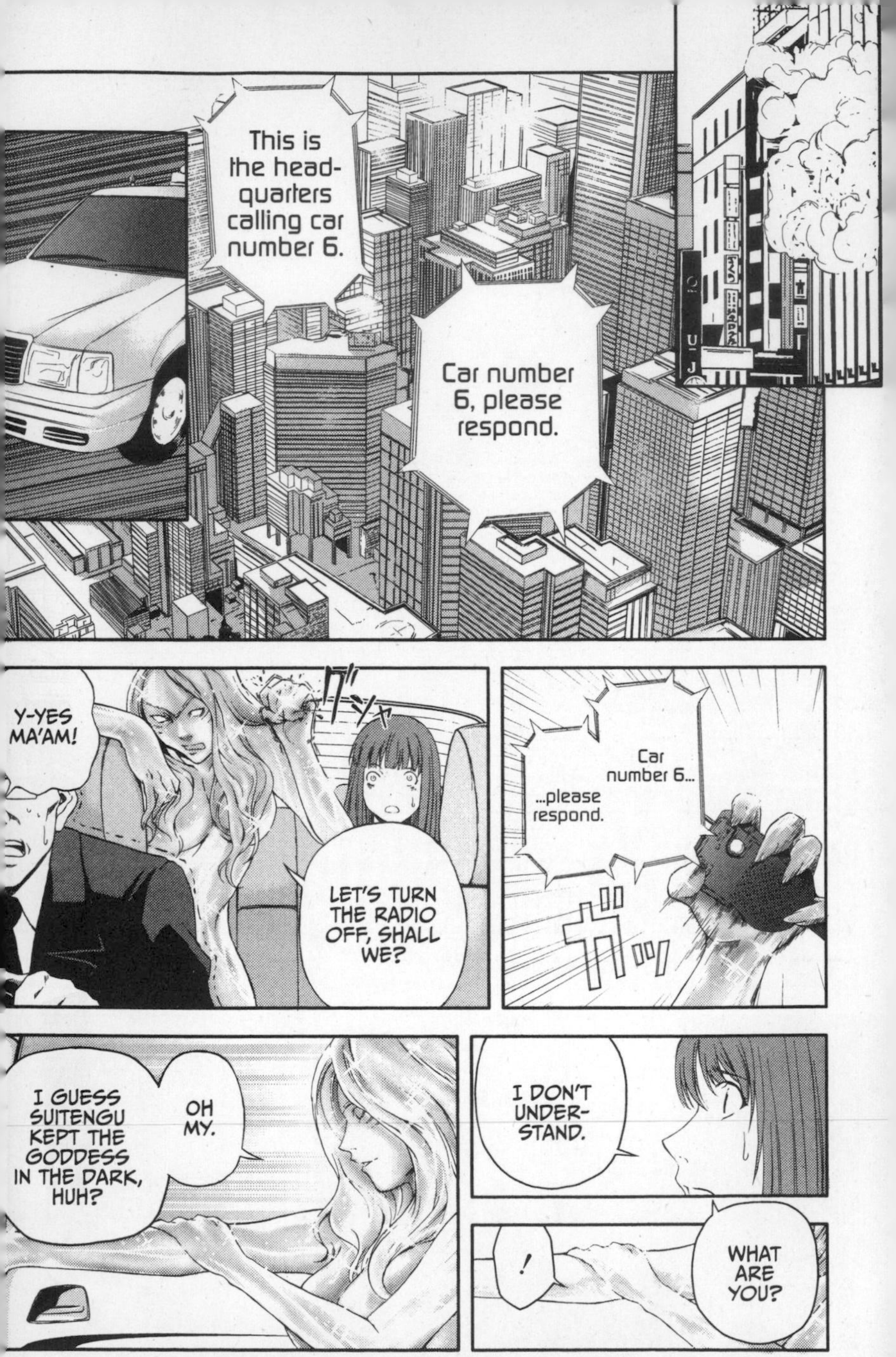
This is the head-quarters calling car number 6.
Car number 6, please respond.
Car number 6...
...please respond.
LET'S TURN THE RADIO OFF, SHALL WE?
Y-YES MA'AM!
I DON'T UNDER-STAND.
WHAT ARE YOU?
!
OH MY.
I GUESS SUITENGU KEPT THE GODDESS IN THE DARK, HUH?

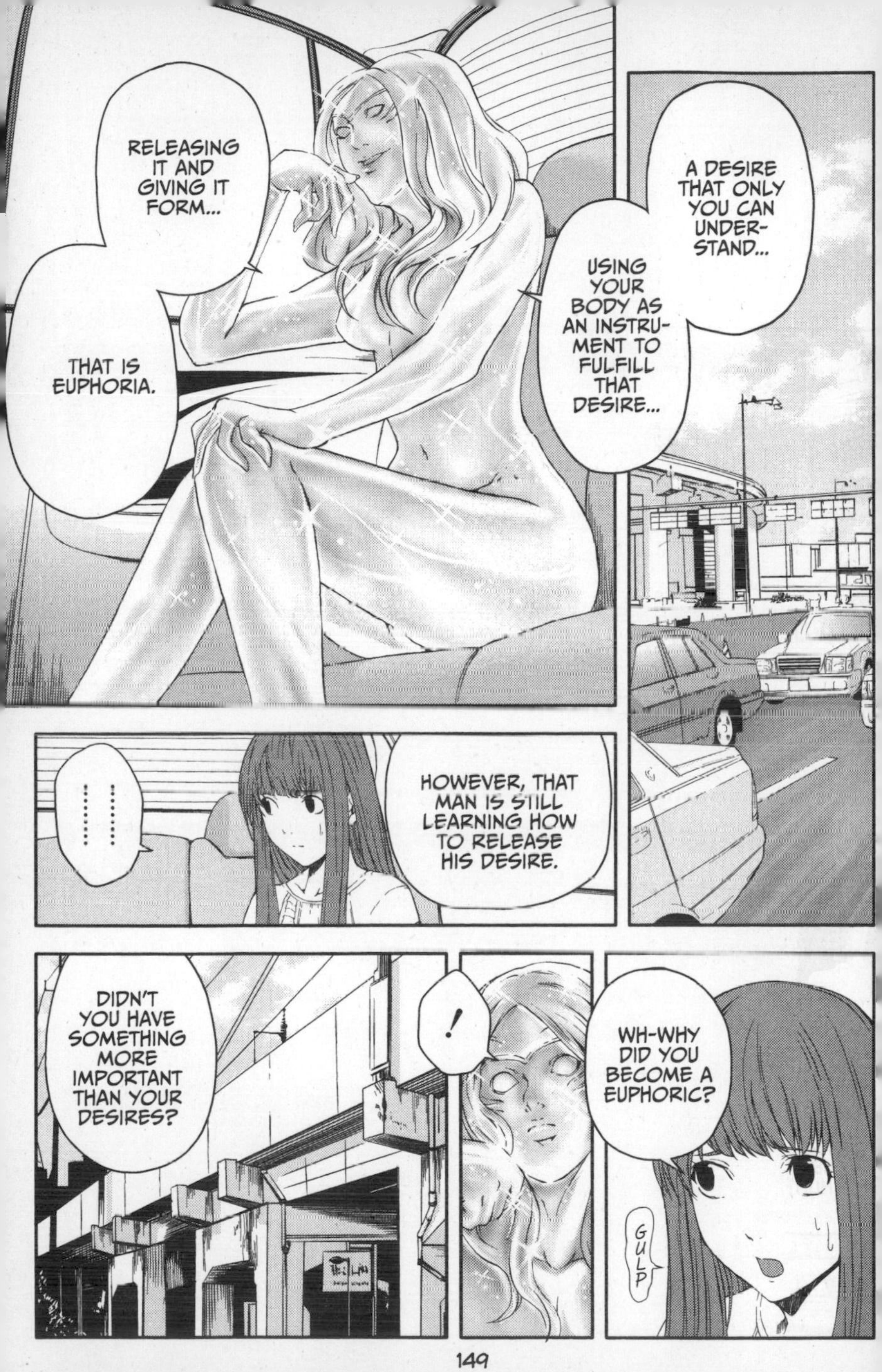

A DESIRE THAT ONLY YOU CAN UNDER-STAND...
USING YOUR BODY AS AN INSTRU-MENT TO FULFILL THAT DESIRE...
RELEASING IT AND GIVING IT FORM...
THAT IS EUPHORIA.
HOWEVER, THAT MAN IS STILL LEARNING HOW TO RELEASE HIS DESIRE.
......
WH-WHY DID YOU BECOME A EUPHORIC?
GULP
!
DIDN'T YOU HAVE SOMETHING MORE IMPORTANT THAN YOUR DESIRES?

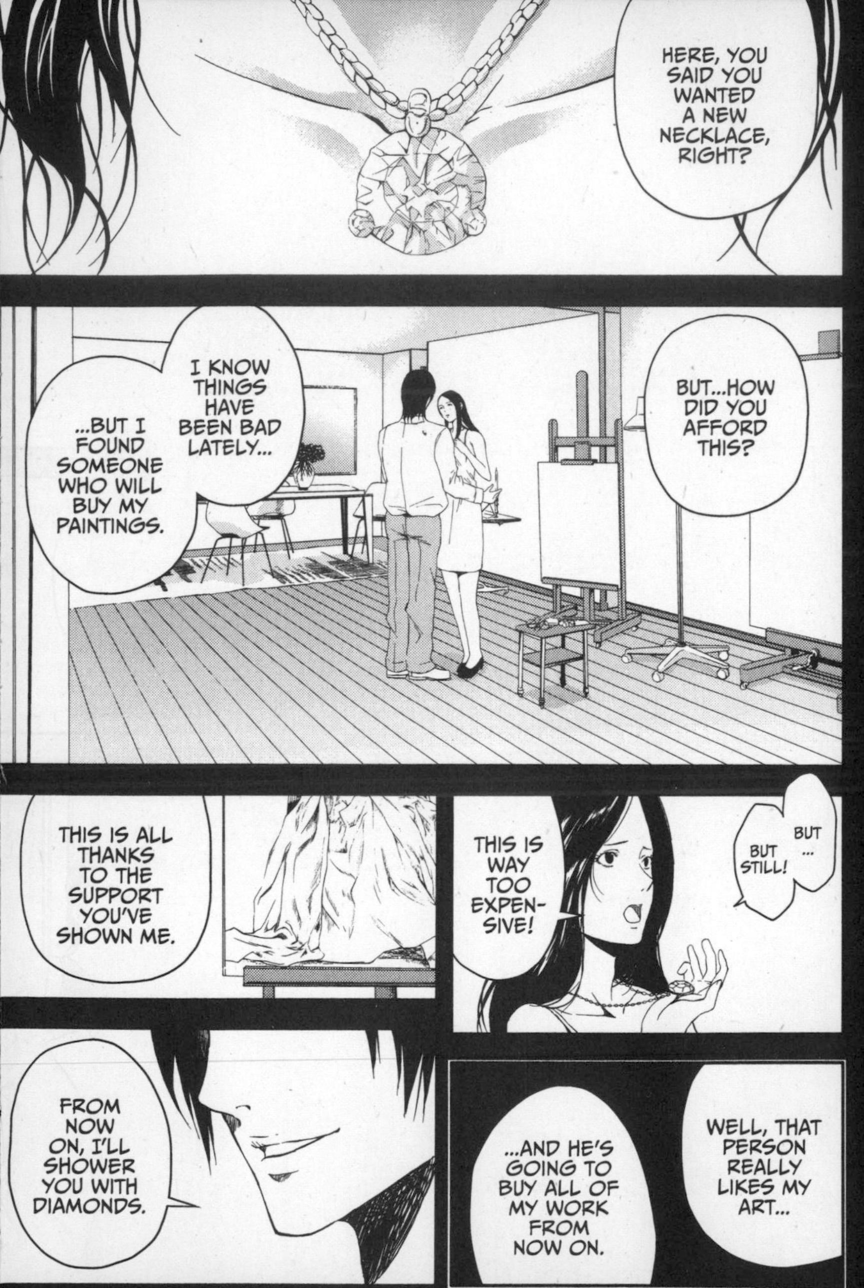
HERE, YOU SAID YOU WANTED A NEW NECKLACE, RIGHT?
BUT...HOW DID YOU AFFORD THIS?
I KNOW THINGS HAVE BEEN BAD LATELY...
...BUT I FOUND SOMEONE WHO WILL BUY MY PAINTINGS.
BUT ... BUT STILL!
THIS IS WAY TOO EXPEN- SIVE!
THIS IS ALL THANKS TO THE SUPPORT YOU'VE SHOWN ME.
WELL, THAT PERSON REALLY LIKES MY ART...
...AND HE'S GOING TO BUY ALL OF MY WORK FROM NOW ON.
FROM NOW ON, I'LL SHOWER YOU WITH DIAMONDS.

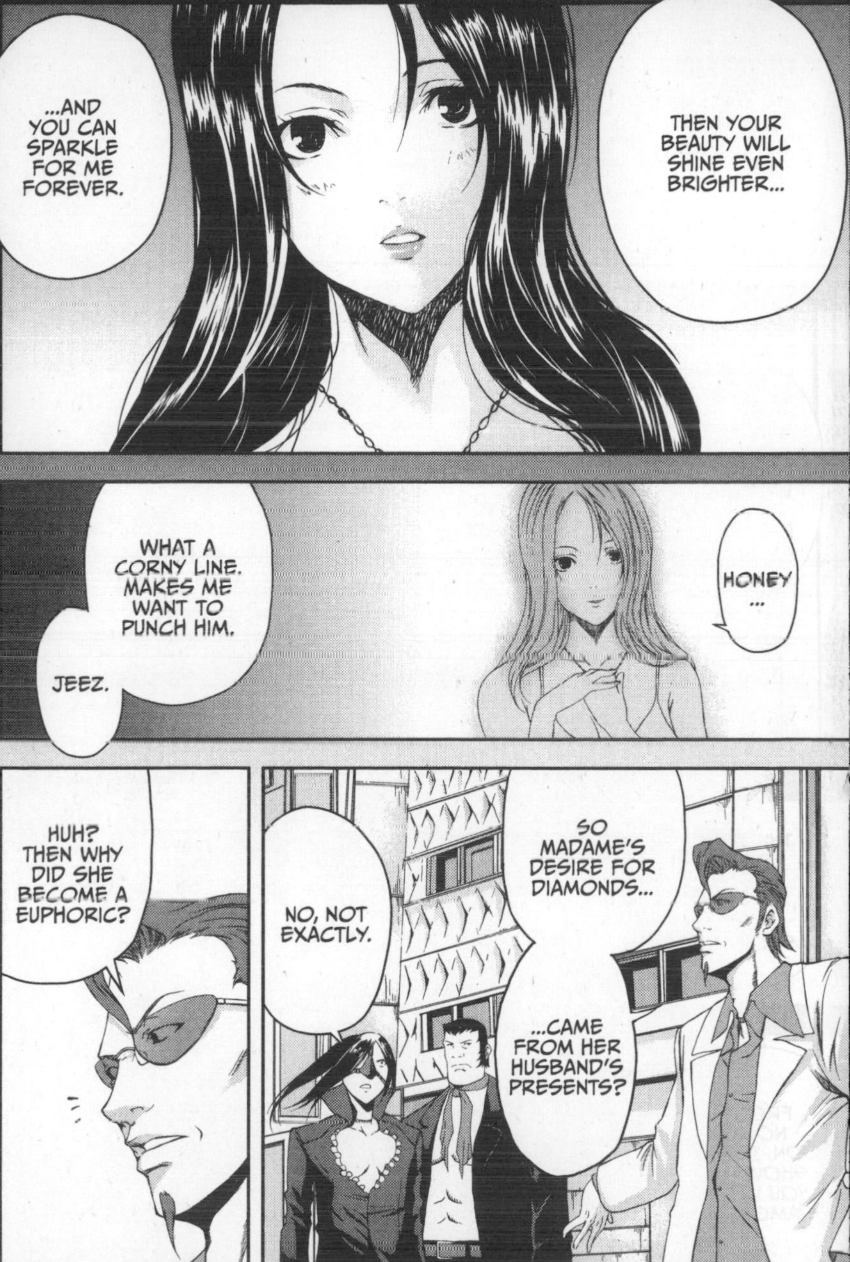
THEN YOUR BEAUTY WILL SHINE EVEN BRIGHTER...
...AND YOU CAN SPARKLE FOR ME FOREVER.
HONEY ...
WHAT A CORNY LINE. MAKES ME WANT TO PUNCH HIM.
JEEZ.
SO MADAME'S DESIRE FOR DIAMONDS...
...CAME FROM HER HUSBAND'S PRESENTS?
NO, NOT EXACTLY.
HUH? THEN WHY DID SHE BECOME A EUPHORIC?

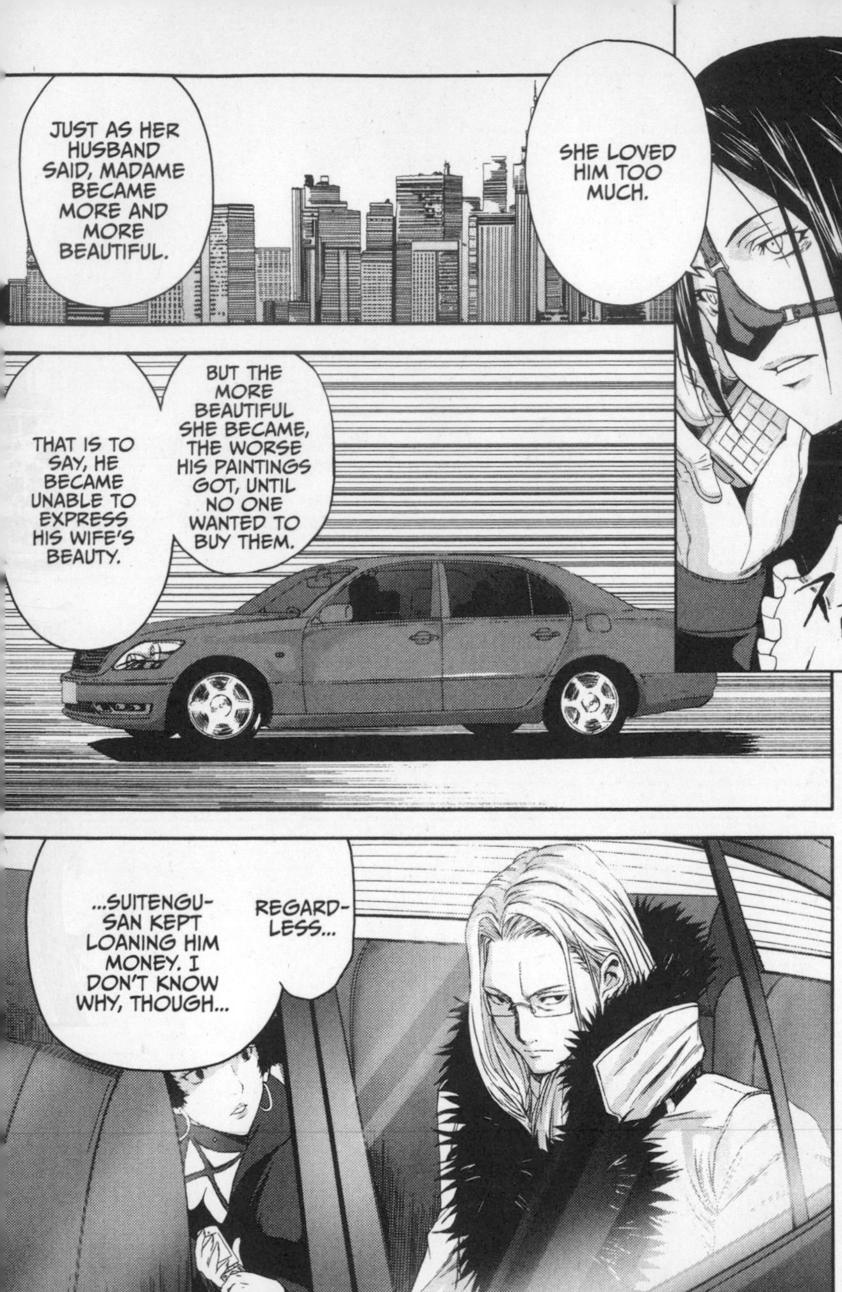
SHE LOVED HIM TOO MUCH.
スッ
JUST AS HER HUSBAND SAID, MADAME BECAME MORE AND MORE BEAUTIFUL.
BUT THE MORE BEAUTIFUL SHE BECAME, THE WORSE HIS PAINTINGS GOT, UNTIL NO ONE WANTED TO BUY THEM.
THAT IS TO SAY, HE BECAME UNABLE TO EXPRESS HIS WIFE'S BEAUTY.
REGARDLESS...
...SUITENGU-SAN KEPT LOANING HIM MONEY. I DON'T KNOW WHY, THOUGH...

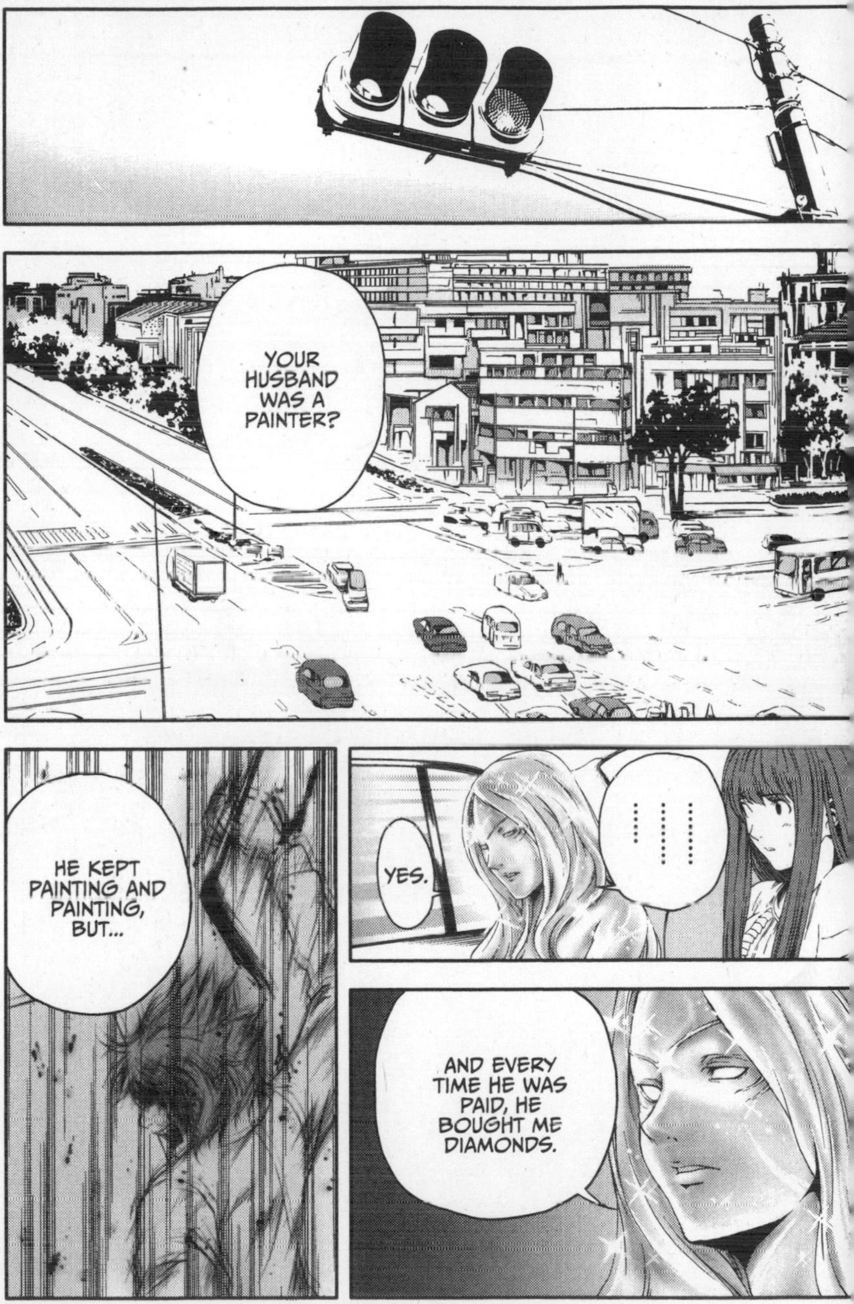

YOUR HUSBAND WAS A PAINTER?
......
YES.
AND EVERY TIME HE WAS PAID, HE BOUGHT ME DIAMONDS.
HE KEPT PAINTING AND PAINTING, BUT...

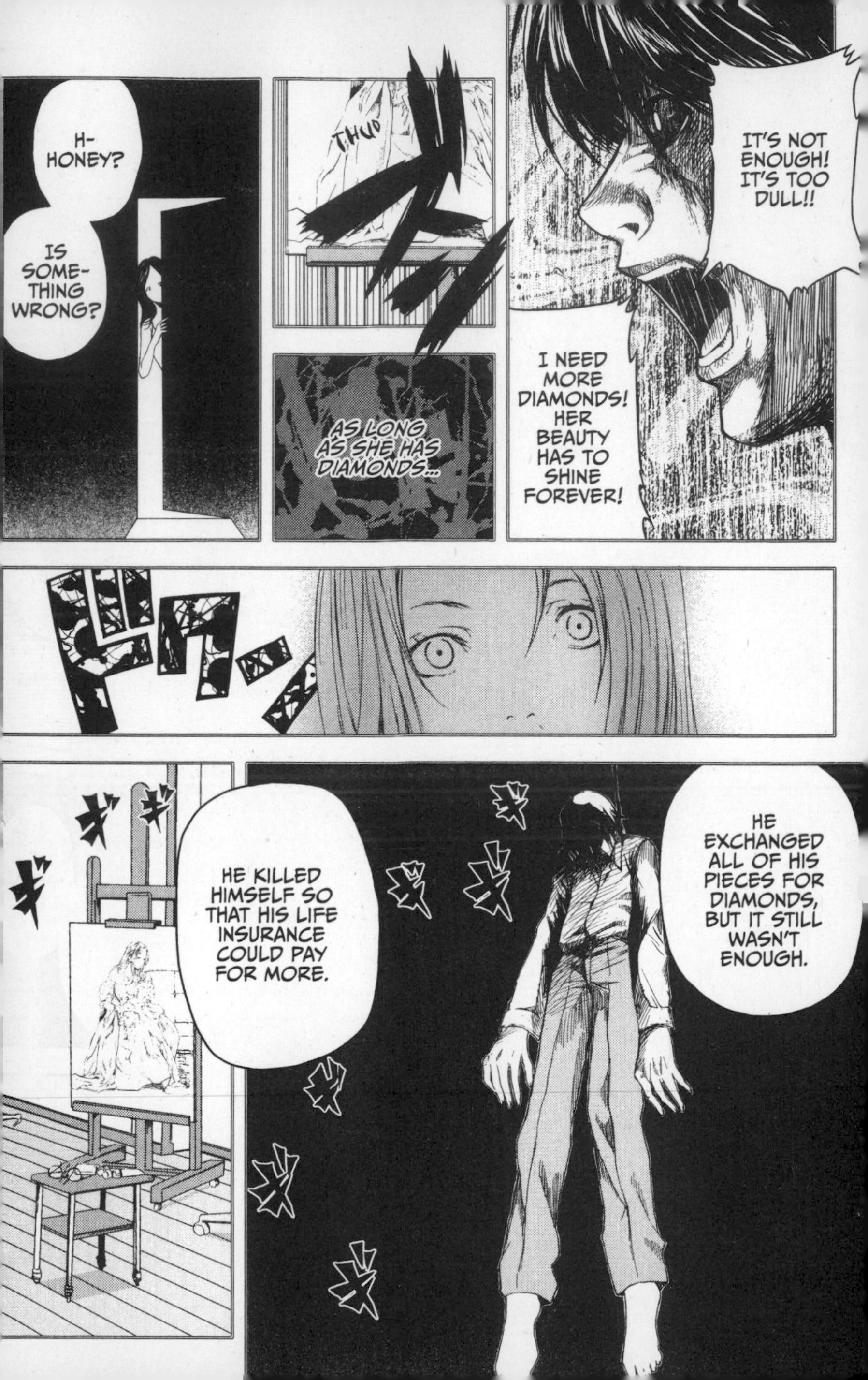
IT'S NOT ENOUGH! IT'S TOO DULL!!
I NEED MORE DIAMONDS! HER BEAUTY HAS TO SHINE FOREVER!
THUD
AS LONG AS SHE HAS DIAMONDS...
H-HONEY?
IS SOMETHING WRONG?
HE EXCHANGED ALL OF HIS PIECES FOR DIAMONDS, BUT IT STILL WASN'T ENOUGH.
HE KILLED HIMSELF SO THAT HIS LIFE INSURANCE COULD PAY FOR MORE.

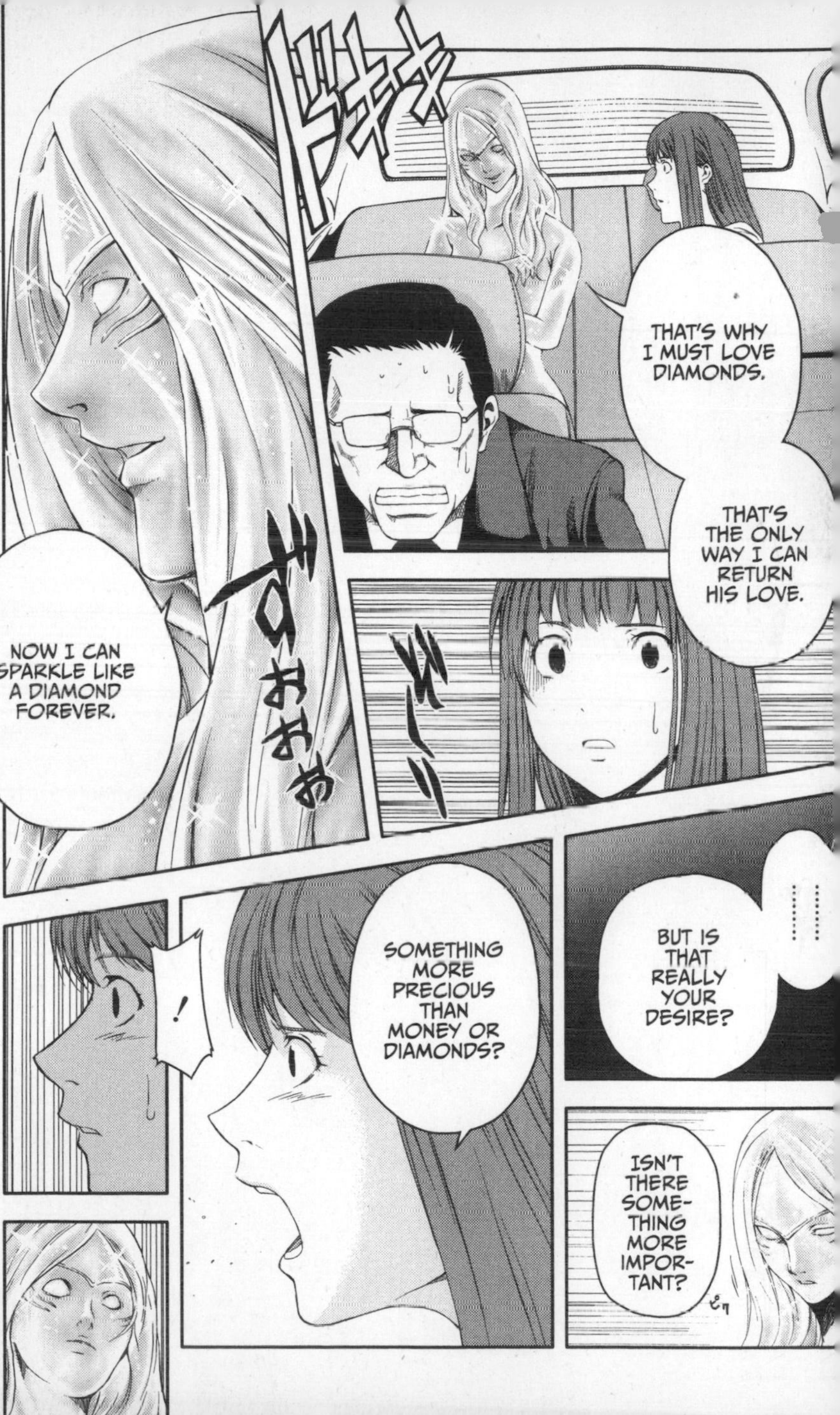
THAT'S WHY I MUST LOVE DIAMONDS.
THAT'S THE ONLY WAY I CAN RETURN HIS LOVE.
NOW I CAN SPARKLE LIKE A DIAMOND FOREVER.
......
BUT IS THAT REALLY YOUR DESIRE?
ISN'T THERE SOMETHING MORE IMPORTANT?
SOMETHING MORE PRECIOUS THAN MONEY OR DIAMONDS?
!

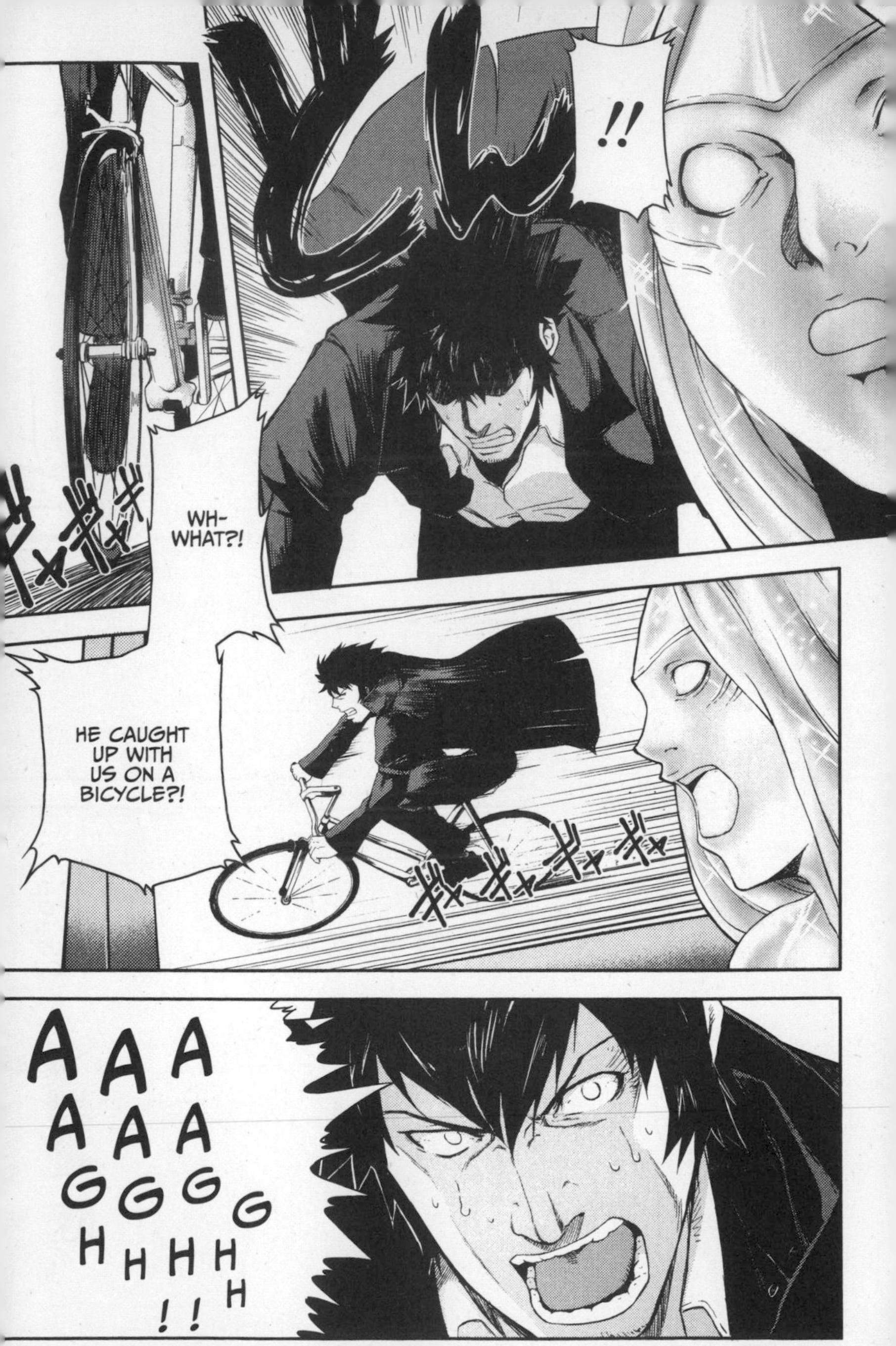
!!
WH- WHAT?!
HE CAUGHT UP WITH US ON A BICYCLE?!
AAAAAAGGGGHHHHH!!

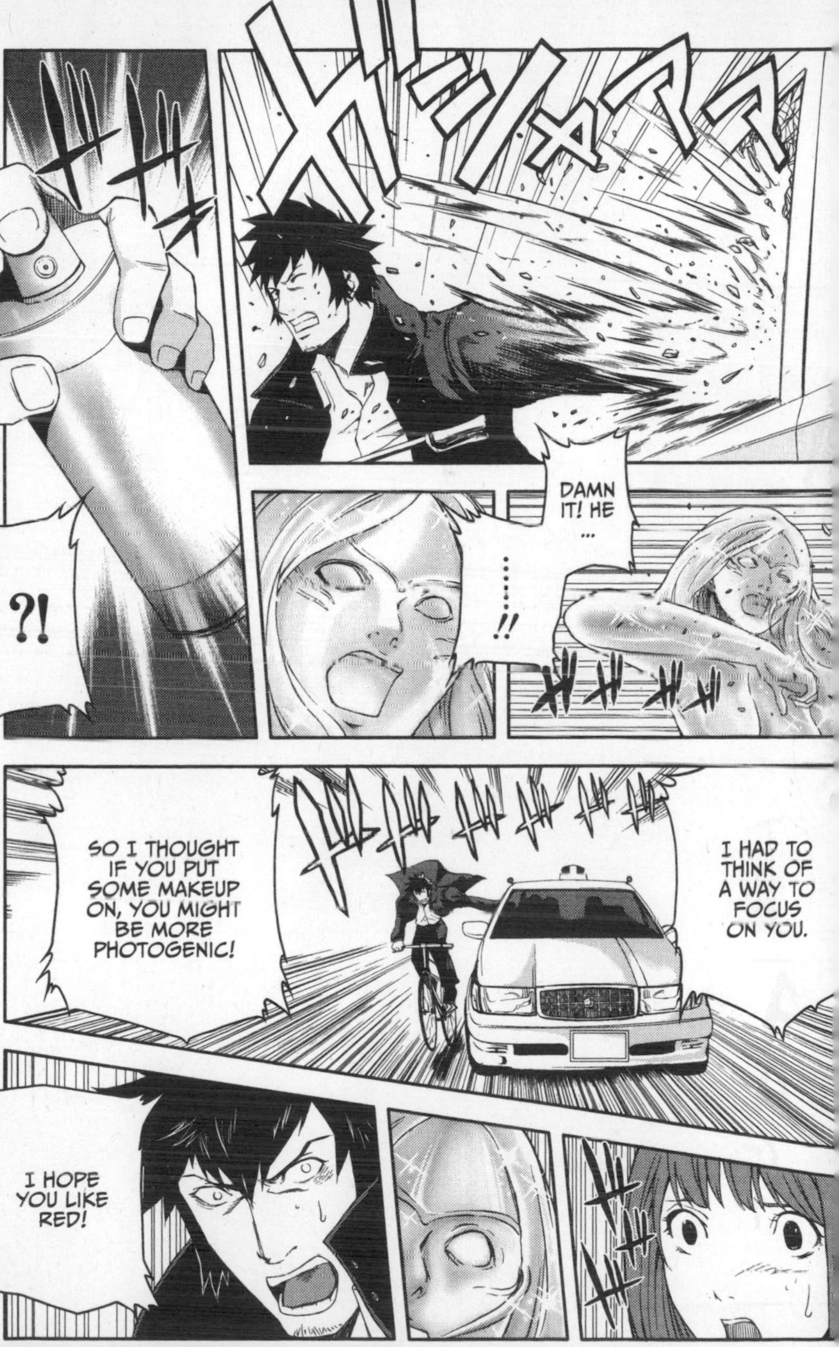
DAMN IT! HE ...
......!!
?!
I HAD TO THINK OF A WAY TO FOCUS ON YOU.
SO I THOUGHT IF YOU PUT SOME MAKEUP ON, YOU MIGHT BE MORE PHOTOGENIC!
I HOPE YOU LIKE RED!

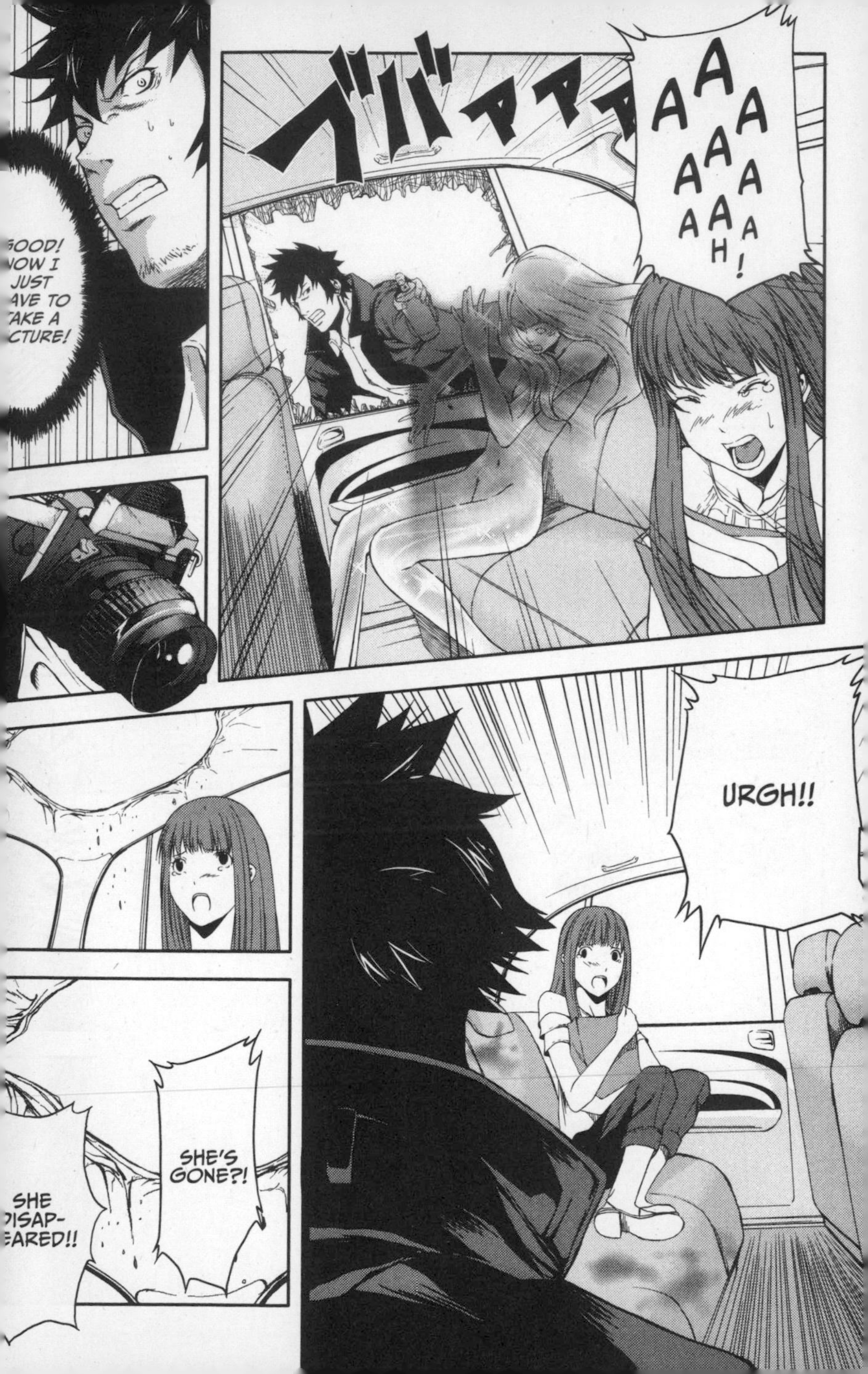

ブバァァァ
AAAAAAAAAAAH!
GOOD! NOW I JUST AVE TO AKE A CTURE!
URGH!!
SHE'S GONE?!
SHE ISAP-EARED!!

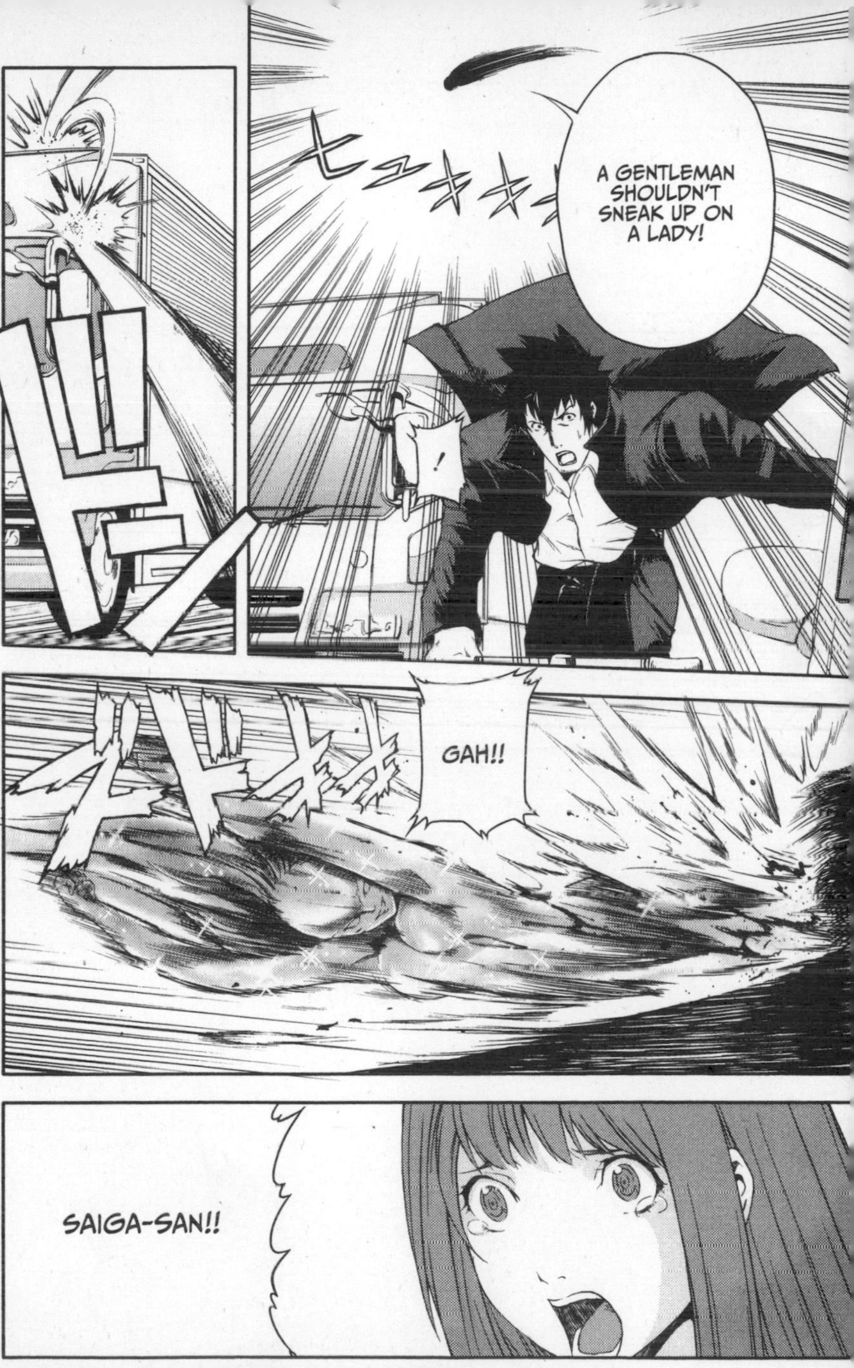
A GENTLEMAN SHOULDN'T SNEAK UP ON A LADY!
!
GAH!!
SAIGA-SAN!!

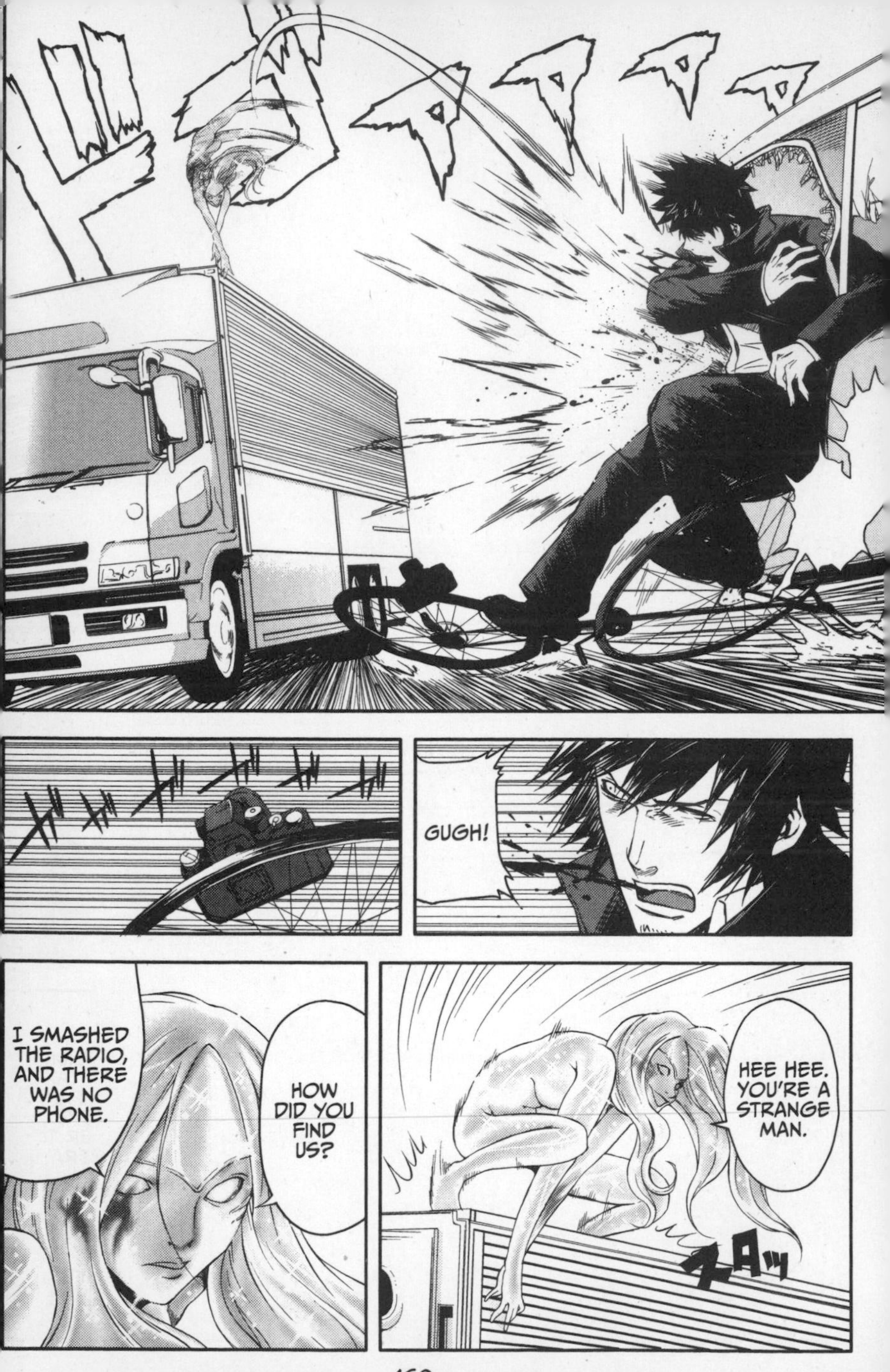
GUGH!
HEE HEE. YOU'RE A STRANGE MAN.
HOW DID YOU FIND US?
I SMASHED THE RADIO, AND THERE WAS NO PHONE.

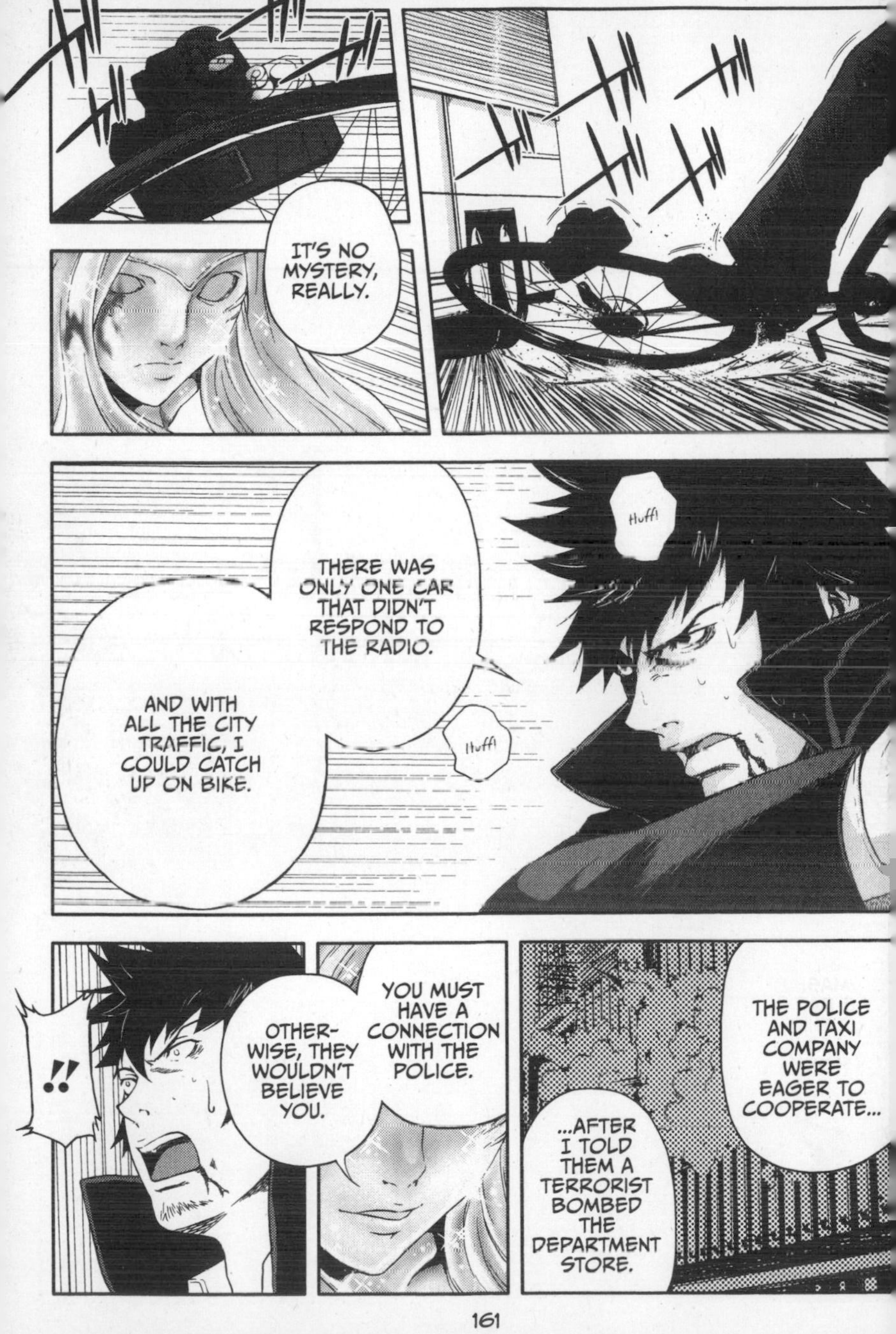

IT'S NO MYSTERY, REALLY.
Huff!
THERE WAS ONLY ONE CAR THAT DIDN'T RESPOND TO THE RADIO.
Huff!
AND WITH ALL THE CITY TRAFFIC, I COULD CATCH UP ON BIKE.
THE POLICE AND TAXI COMPANY WERE EAGER TO COOPERATE...
...AFTER I TOLD THEM A TERRORIST BOMBED THE DEPARTMENT STORE.
YOU MUST HAVE A CONNECTION WITH THE POLICE.
OTHER-WISE, THEY WOULDN'T BELIEVE YOU.
!!

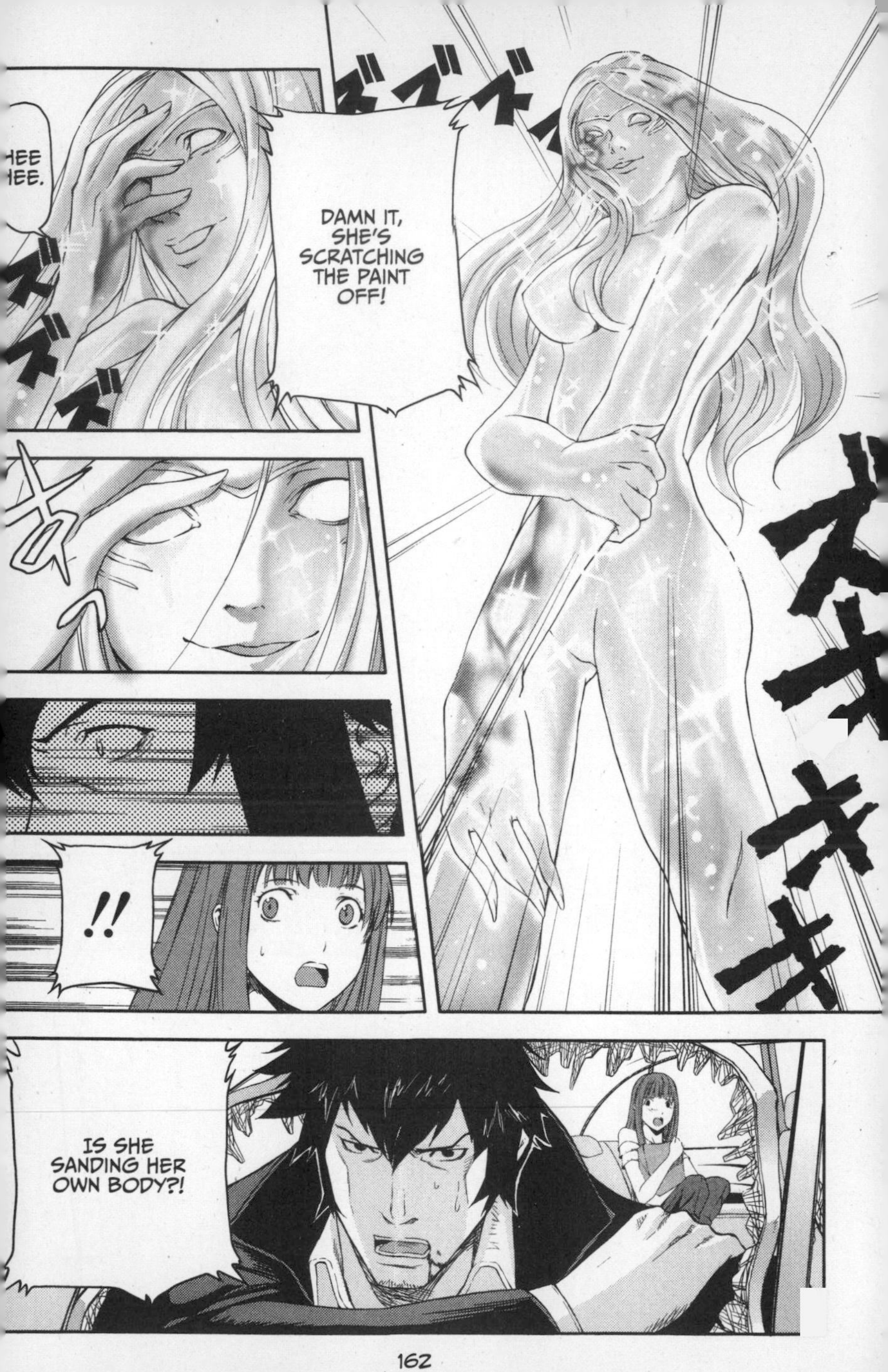
DAMN IT, SHE'S SCRATCHING THE PAINT OFF!
HEE HEE.
!!
IS SHE SANDING HER OWN BODY?!

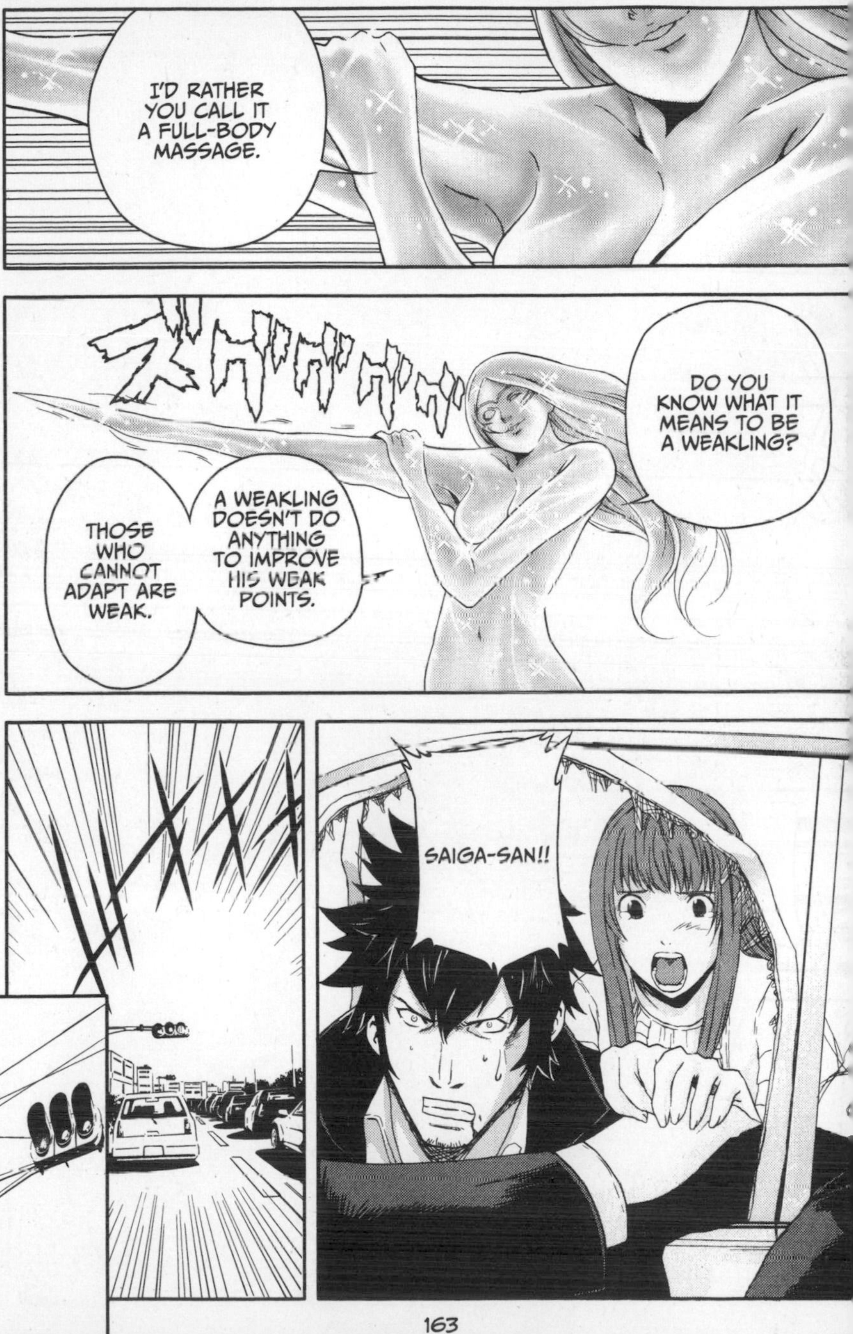
I'D RATHER YOU CALL IT A FULL-BODY MASSAGE.
DO YOU KNOW WHAT IT MEANS TO BE A WEAKLING?
A WEAKLING DOESN'T DO ANYTHING TO IMPROVE HIS WEAK POINTS.
THOSE WHO CANNOT ADAPT ARE WEAK.
SAIGA-SAN!!

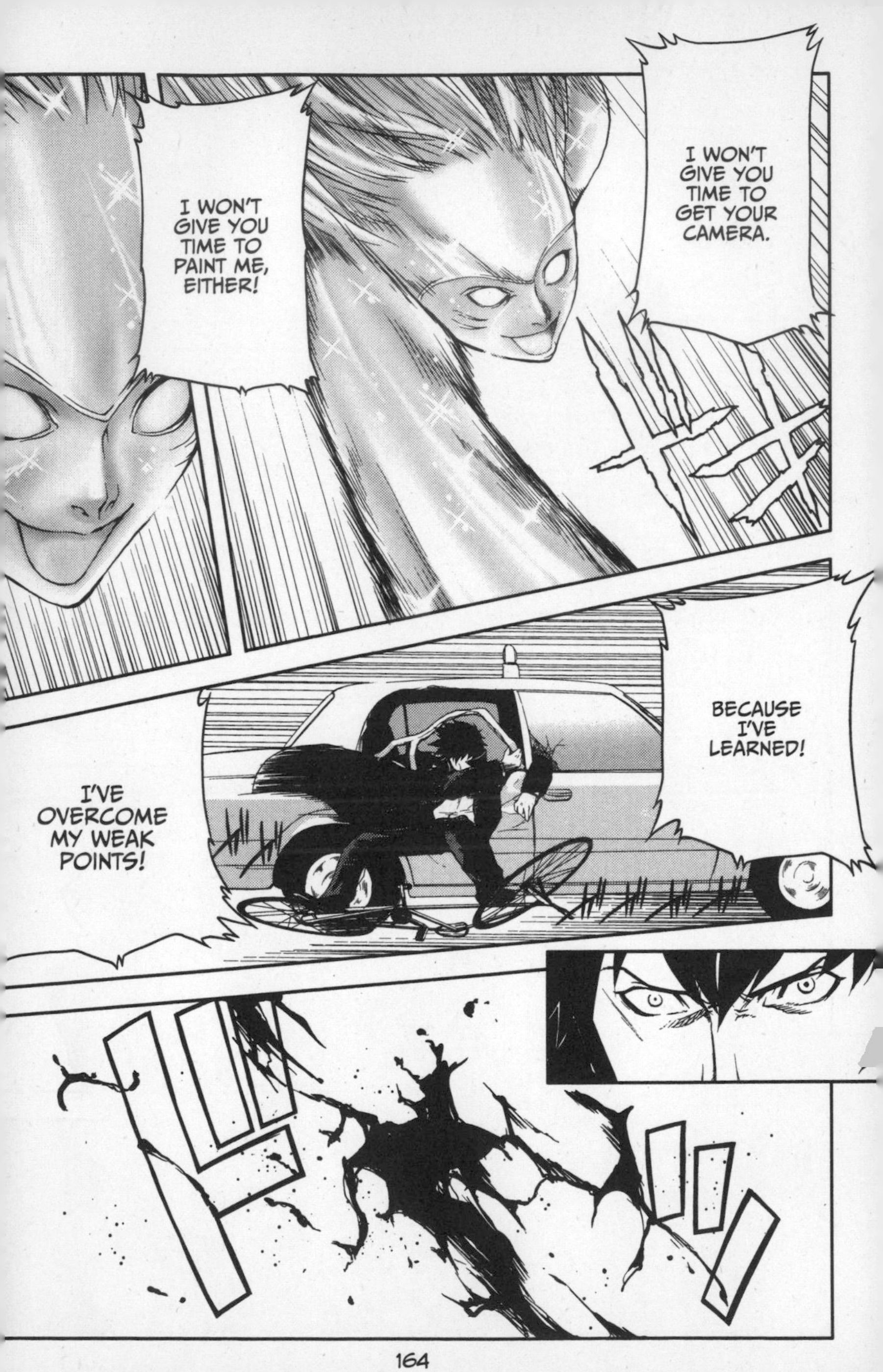
I WON'T GIVE YOU TIME TO GET YOUR CAMERA.
I WON'T GIVE YOU TIME TO PAINT ME, EITHER!
BECAUSE I'VE LEARNED!
I'VE OVERCOME MY WEAK POINTS!

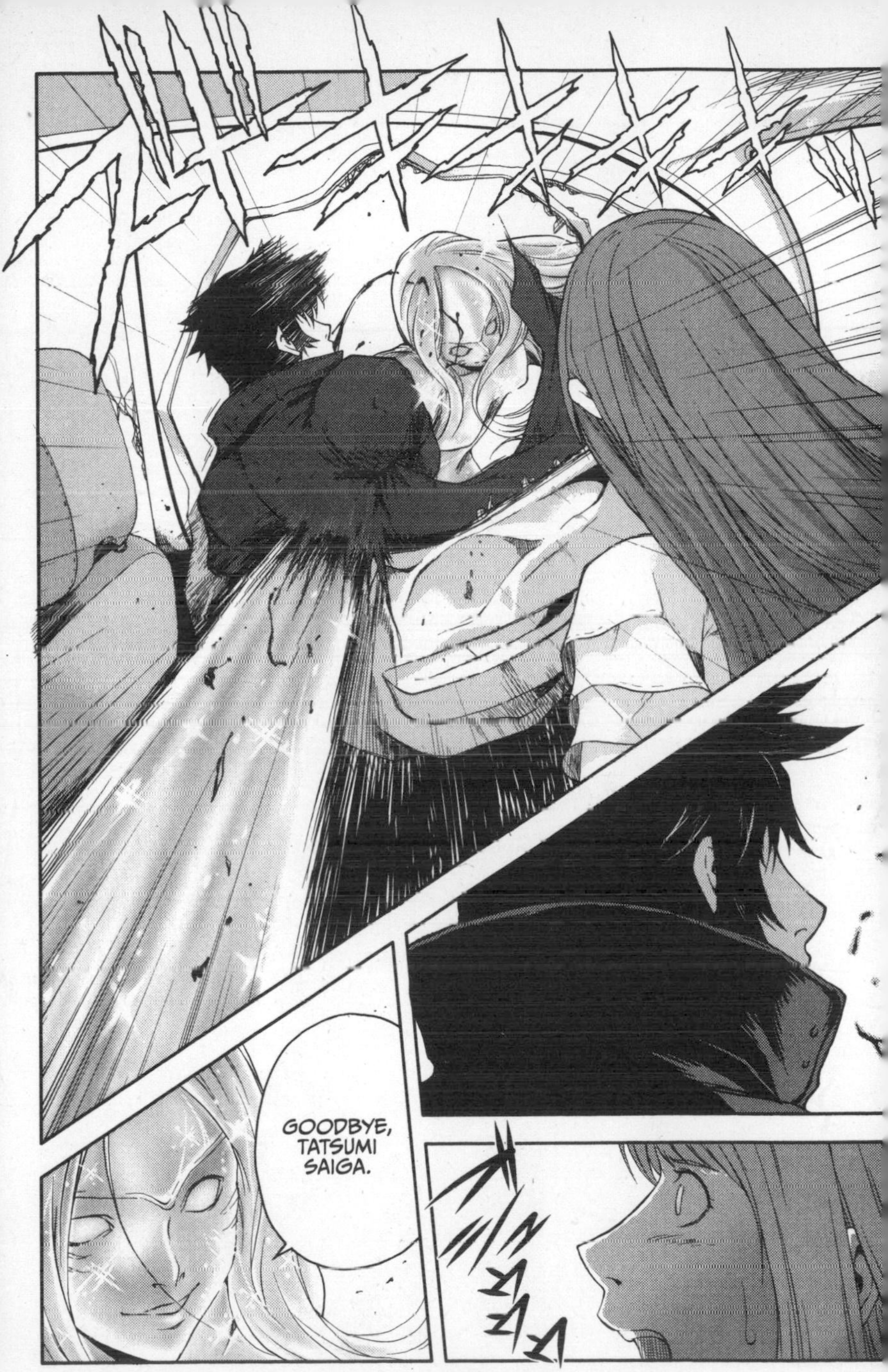
GOODBYE, TATSUMI SAIGA.

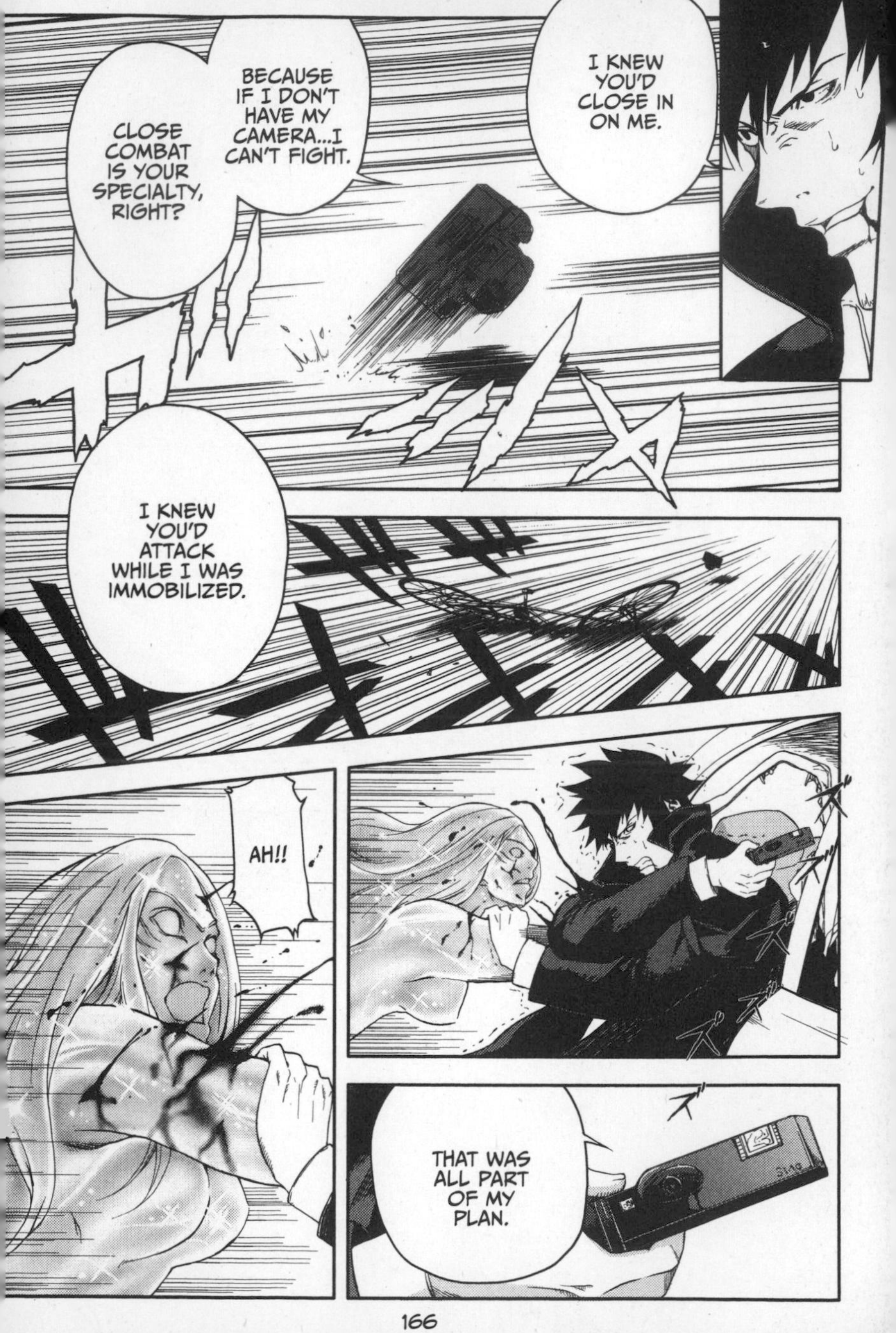
I KNEW YOU'D CLOSE IN ON ME.
BECAUSE IF I DON'T HAVE MY CAMERA...I CAN'T FIGHT.
CLOSE COMBAT IS YOUR SPECIALTY, RIGHT?
I KNEW YOU'D ATTACK WHILE I WAS IMMOBILIZED.
THAT WAS ALL PART OF MY PLAN.
AH!!

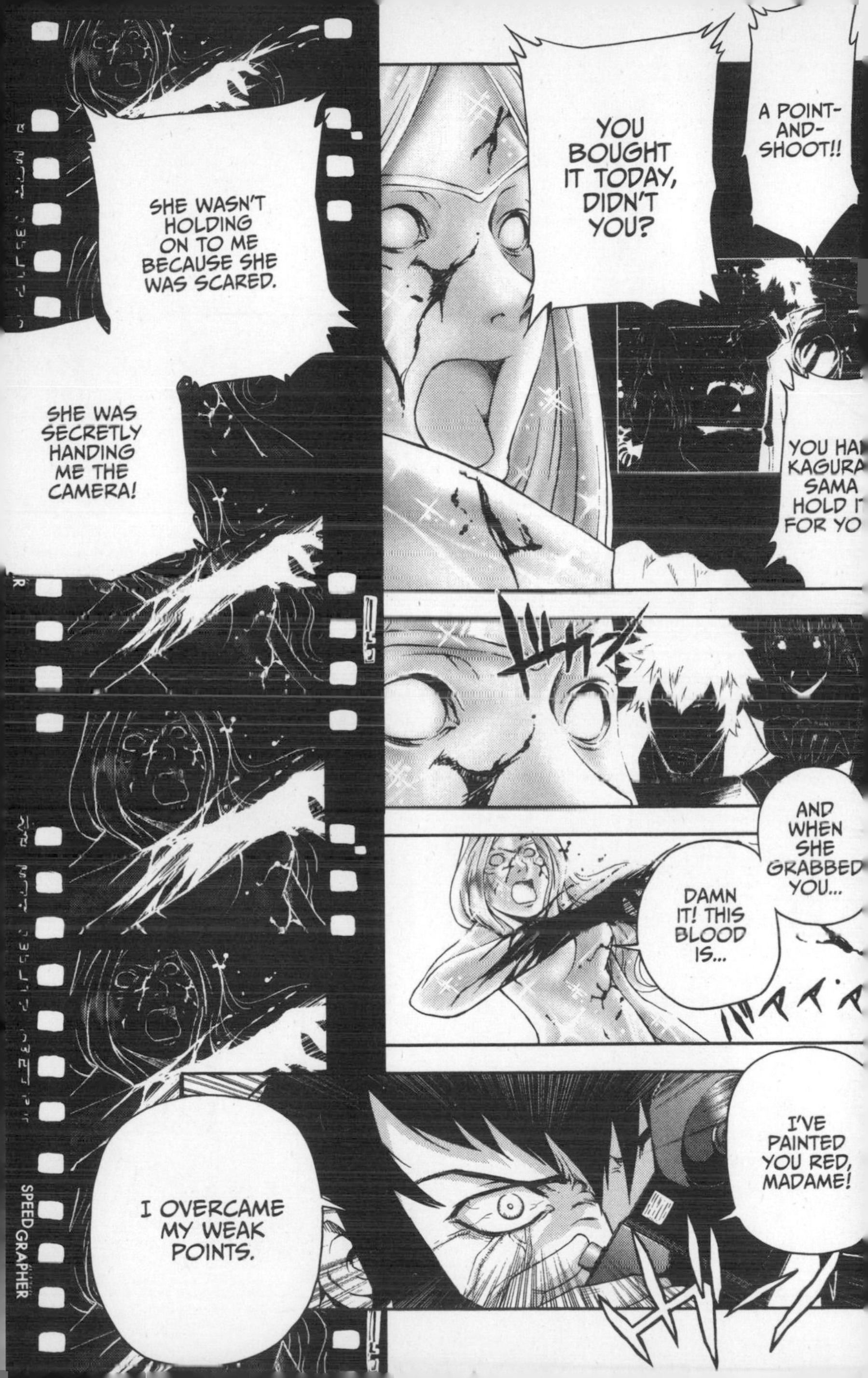
A POINT-AND-SHOOT!!
YOU BOUGHT IT TODAY, DIDN'T YOU?
YOU HA KAGURA SAMA HOLD I FOR YO
AND WHEN SHE GRABBED YOU...
DAMN IT! THIS BLOOD IS...
I'VE PAINTED YOU RED, MADAME!
SHE WASN'T HOLDING ON TO ME BECAUSE SHE WAS SCARED.
SHE WAS SECRETLY HANDING ME THE CAMERA!
I OVERCAME MY WEAK POINTS.
SPEED GRAPHER

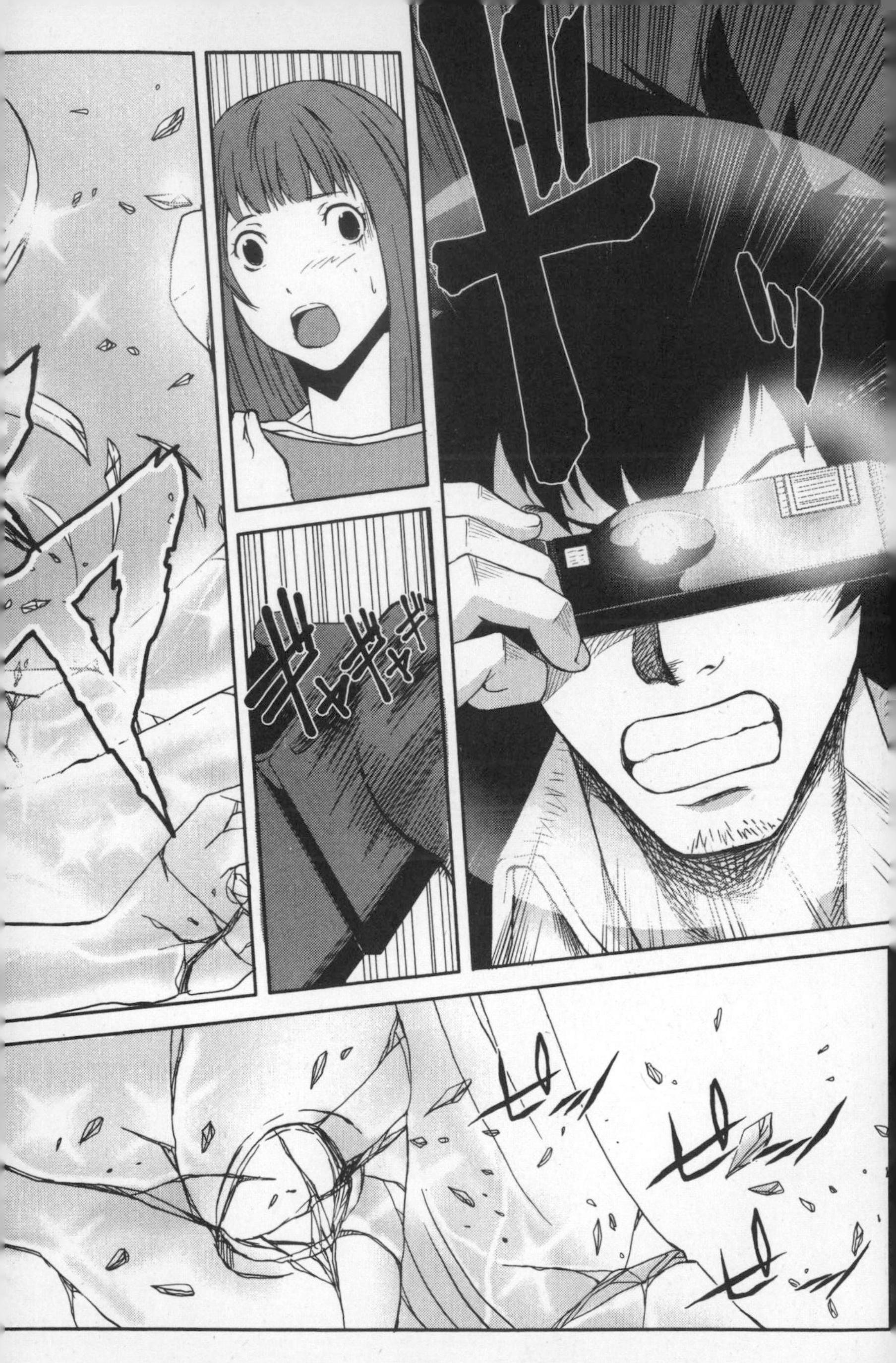
ギャギャギャ

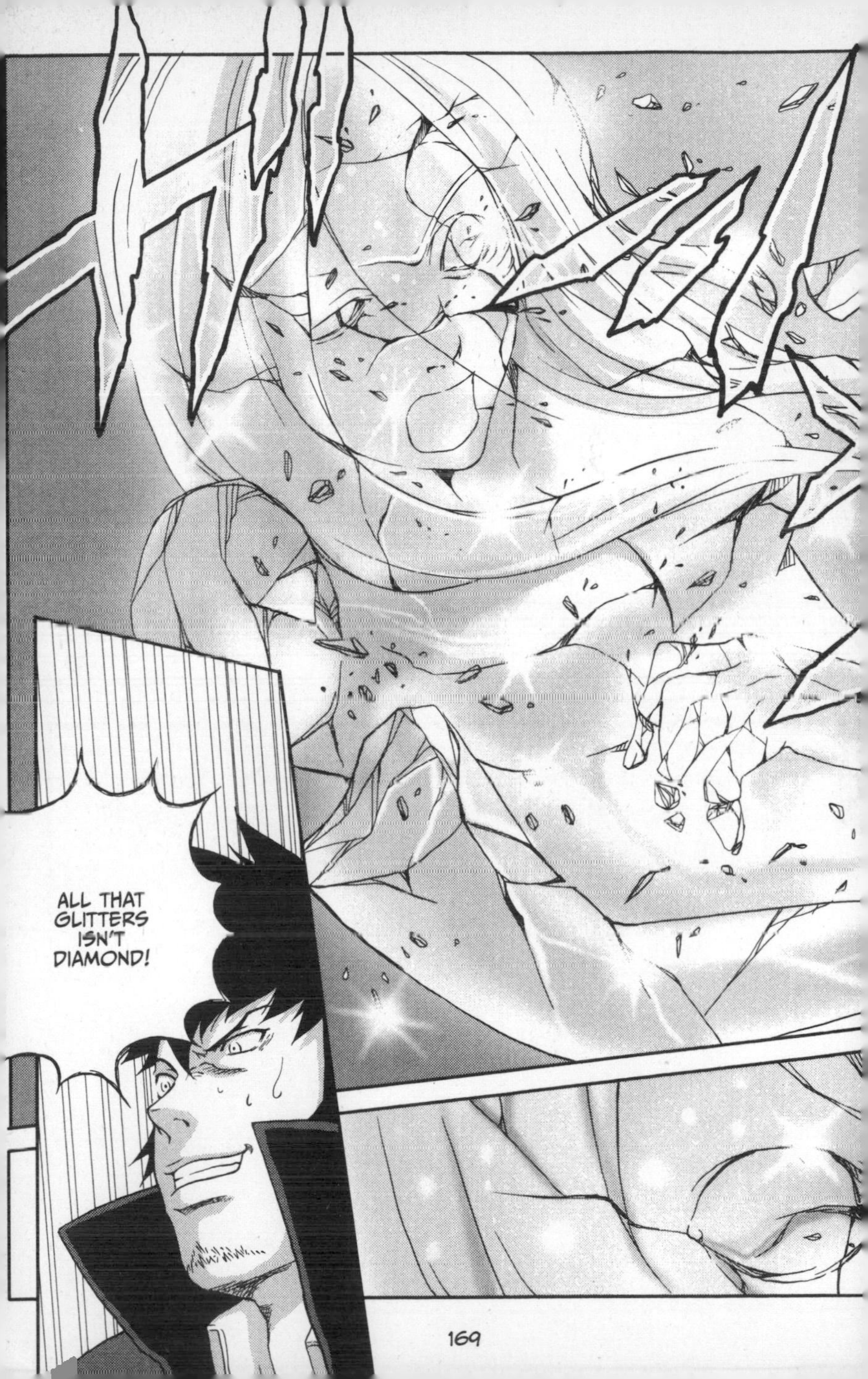
ALL THAT GLITTERS ISN'T DIAMOND!

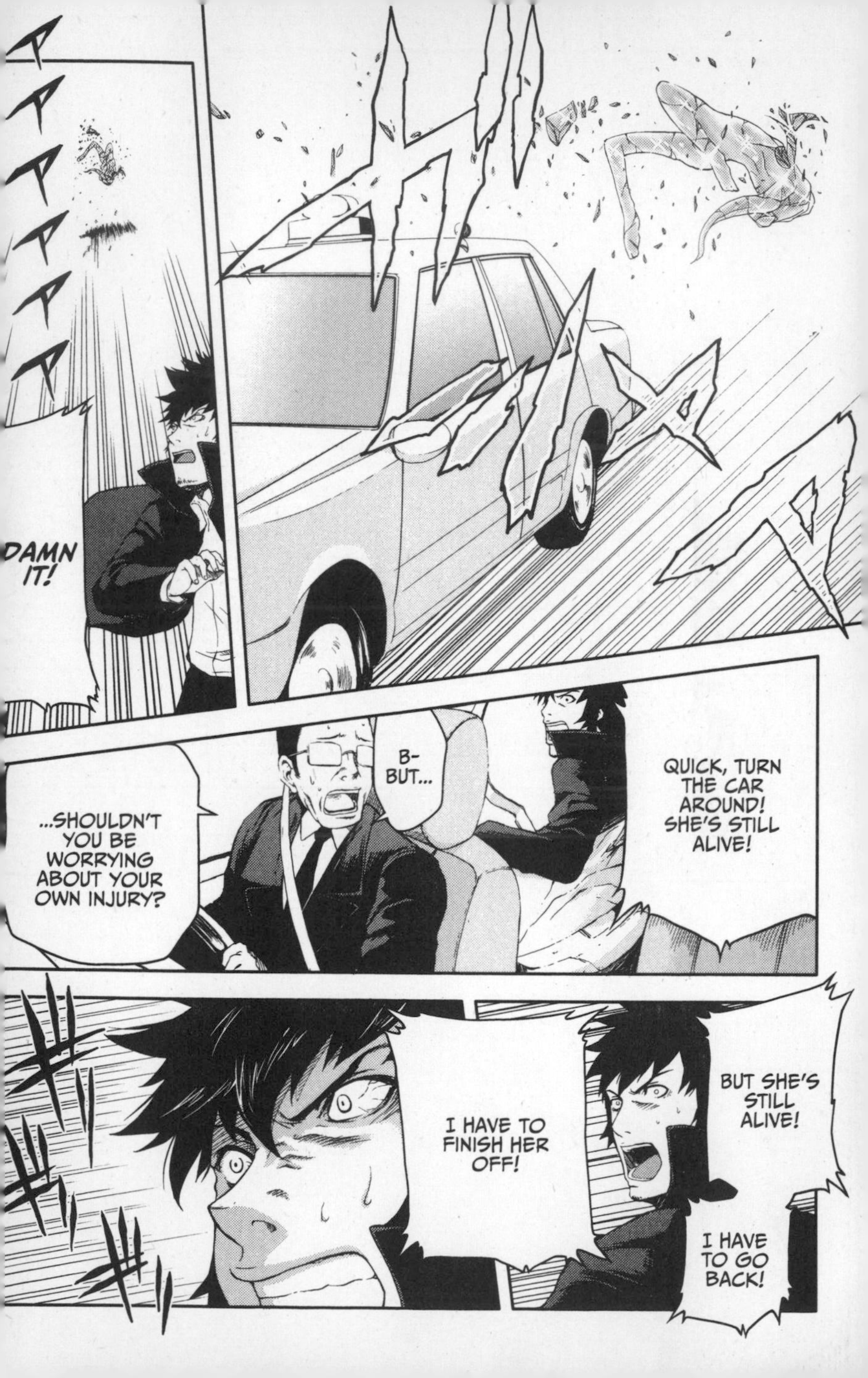
DAMN IT!
QUICK, TURN THE CAR AROUND! SHE'S STILL ALIVE!
B- BUT...
...SHOULDN'T YOU BE WORRYING ABOUT YOUR OWN INJURY?
BUT SHE'S STILL ALIVE!
I HAVE TO GO BACK!
I HAVE TO FINISH HER OFF!

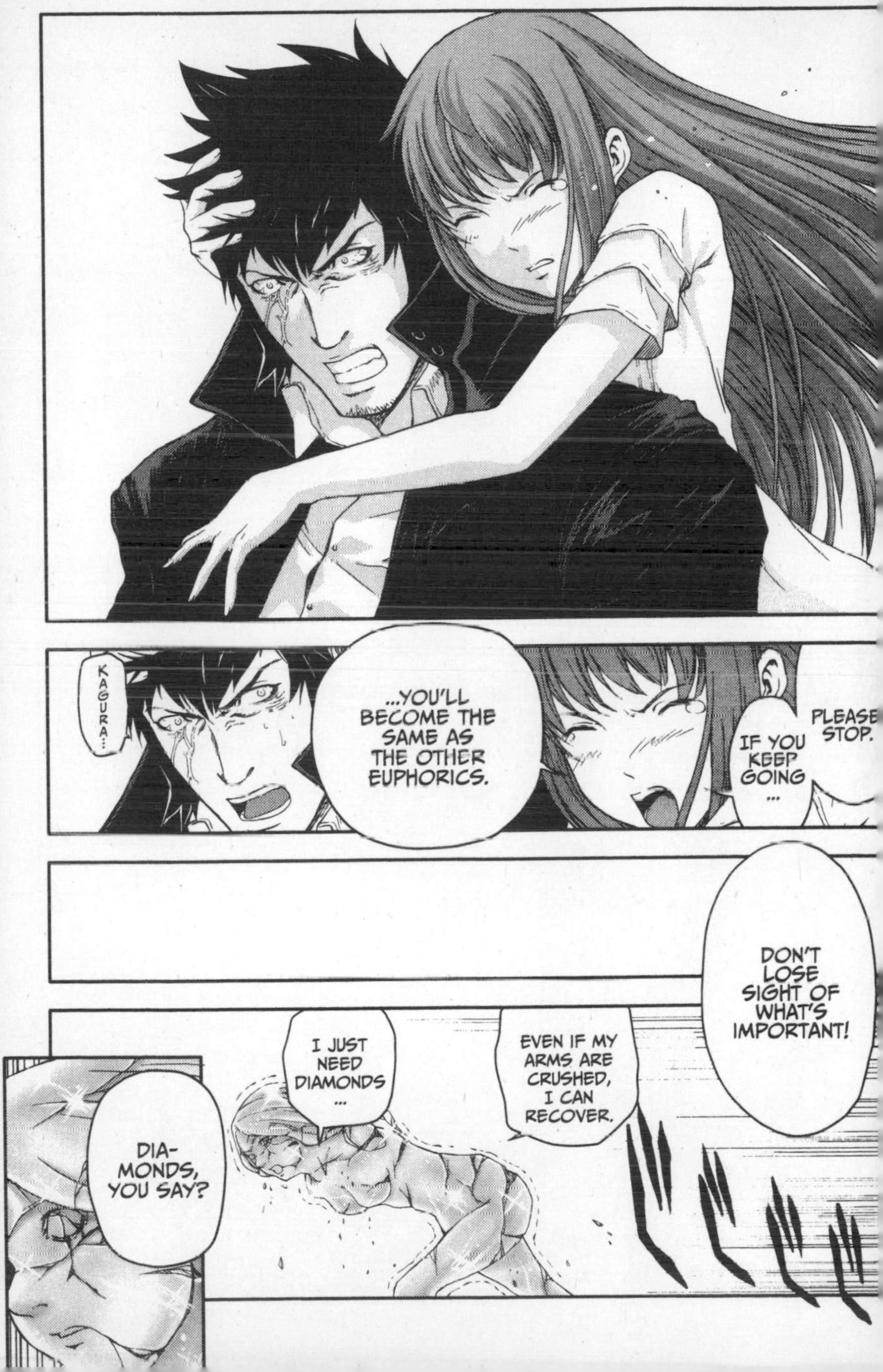
PLEASE STOP.
IF YOU KEEP GOING ...
...YOU'LL BECOME THE SAME AS THE OTHER EUPHORICS.
KAGURA...
DON'T LOSE SIGHT OF WHAT'S IMPORTANT!
EVEN IF MY ARMS ARE CRUSHED, I CAN RECOVER.
I JUST NEED DIAMONDS ...
DIA-MONDS, YOU SAY?

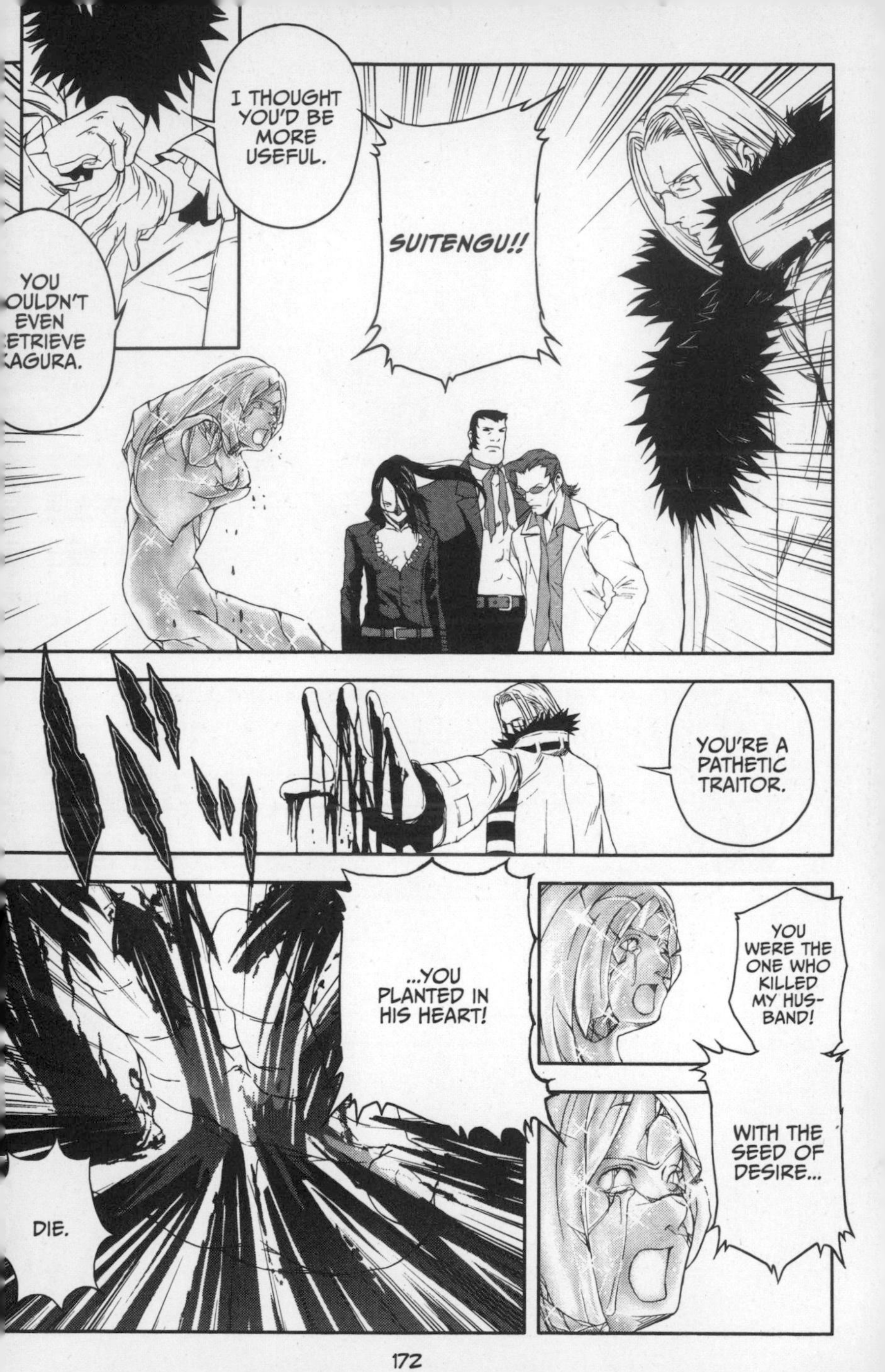
SUITENGU!!
I THOUGHT YOU'D BE MORE USEFUL.
YOU OULDN'T EVEN ETRIEVE AGURA.
YOU'RE A PATHETIC TRAITOR.
YOU WERE THE ONE WHO KILLED MY HUS-BAND!
WITH THE SEED OF DESIRE...
...YOU PLANTED IN HIS HEART!
DIE.

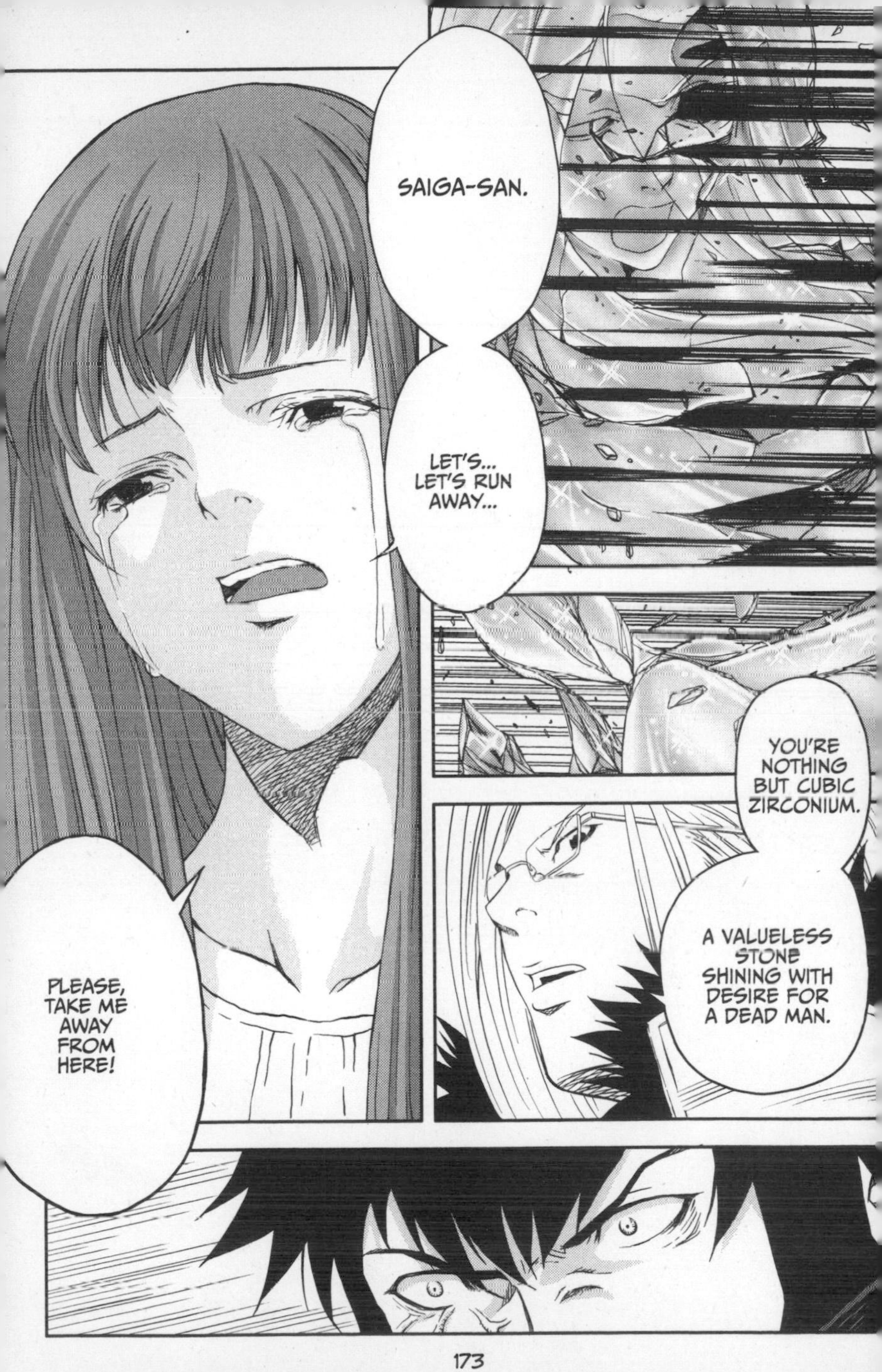

SAIGA-SAN.
LET'S... LET'S RUN AWAY...
YOU'RE NOTHING BUT CUBIC ZIRCONIUM.
A VALUELESS STONE SHINING WITH DESIRE FOR A DEAD MAN.
PLEASE, TAKE ME AWAY FROM HERE!

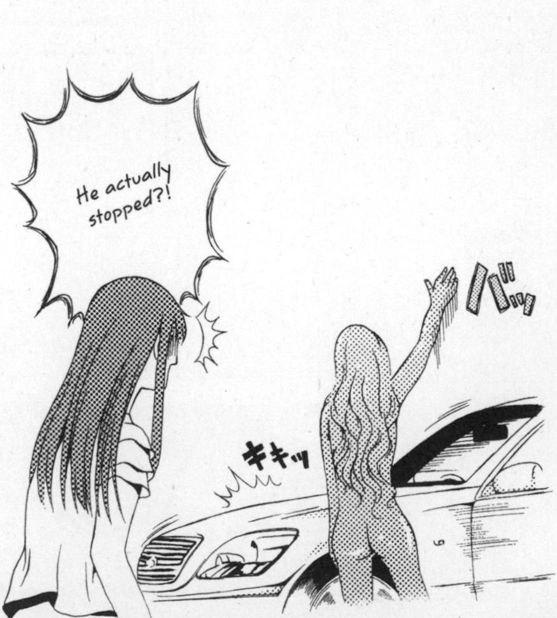
He actually stopped?!
バッ
キキッ

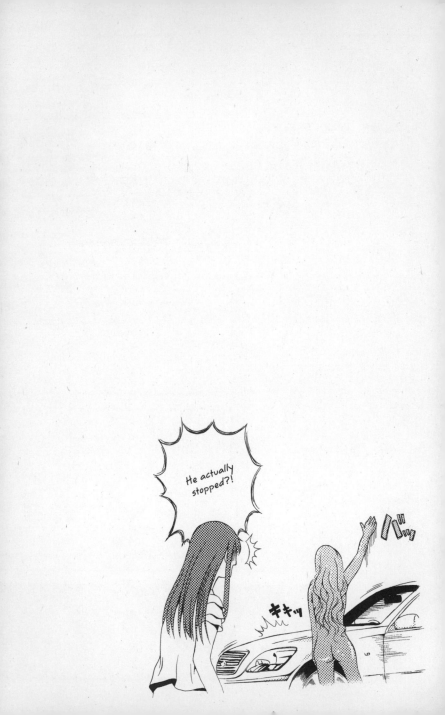

SPEED GRAPHER

スピードグラファー

Volume 1

END

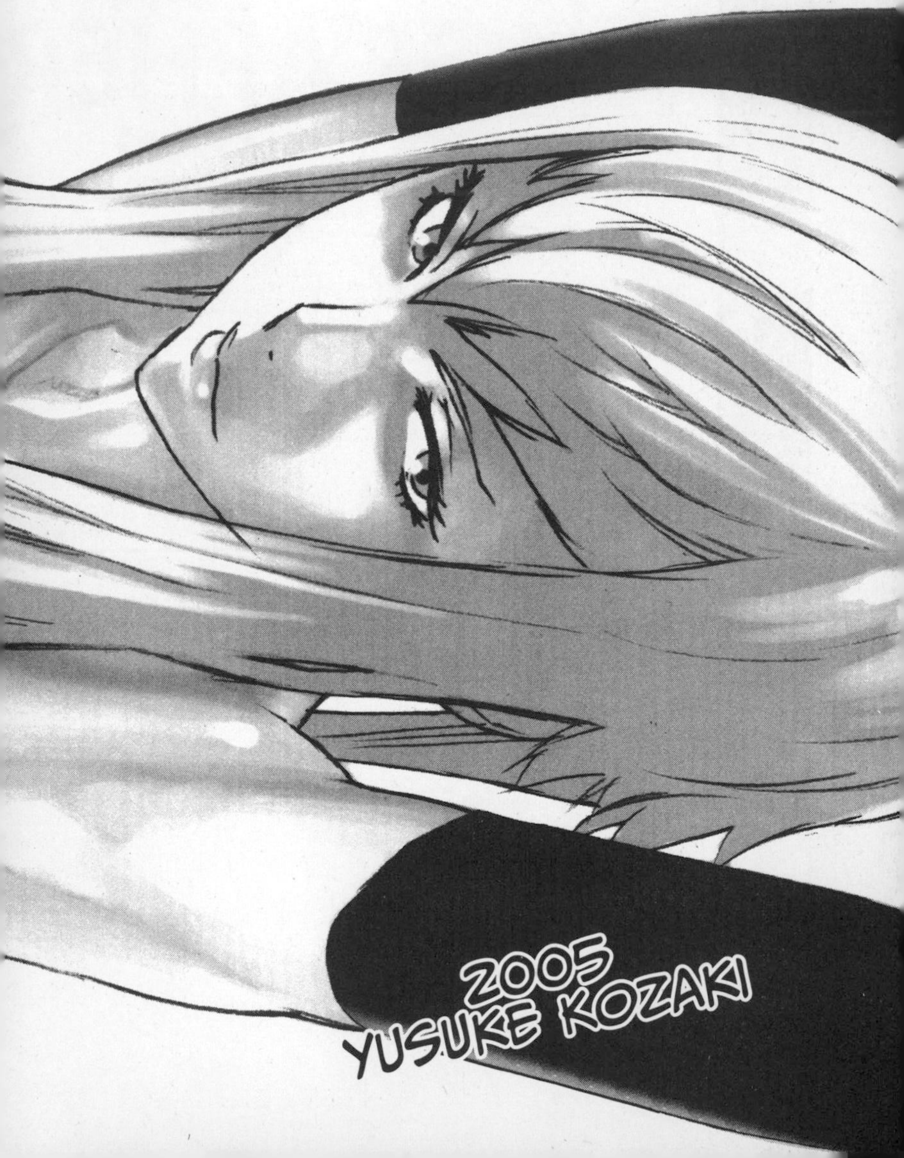
2005
YUSUKE KOZAKI

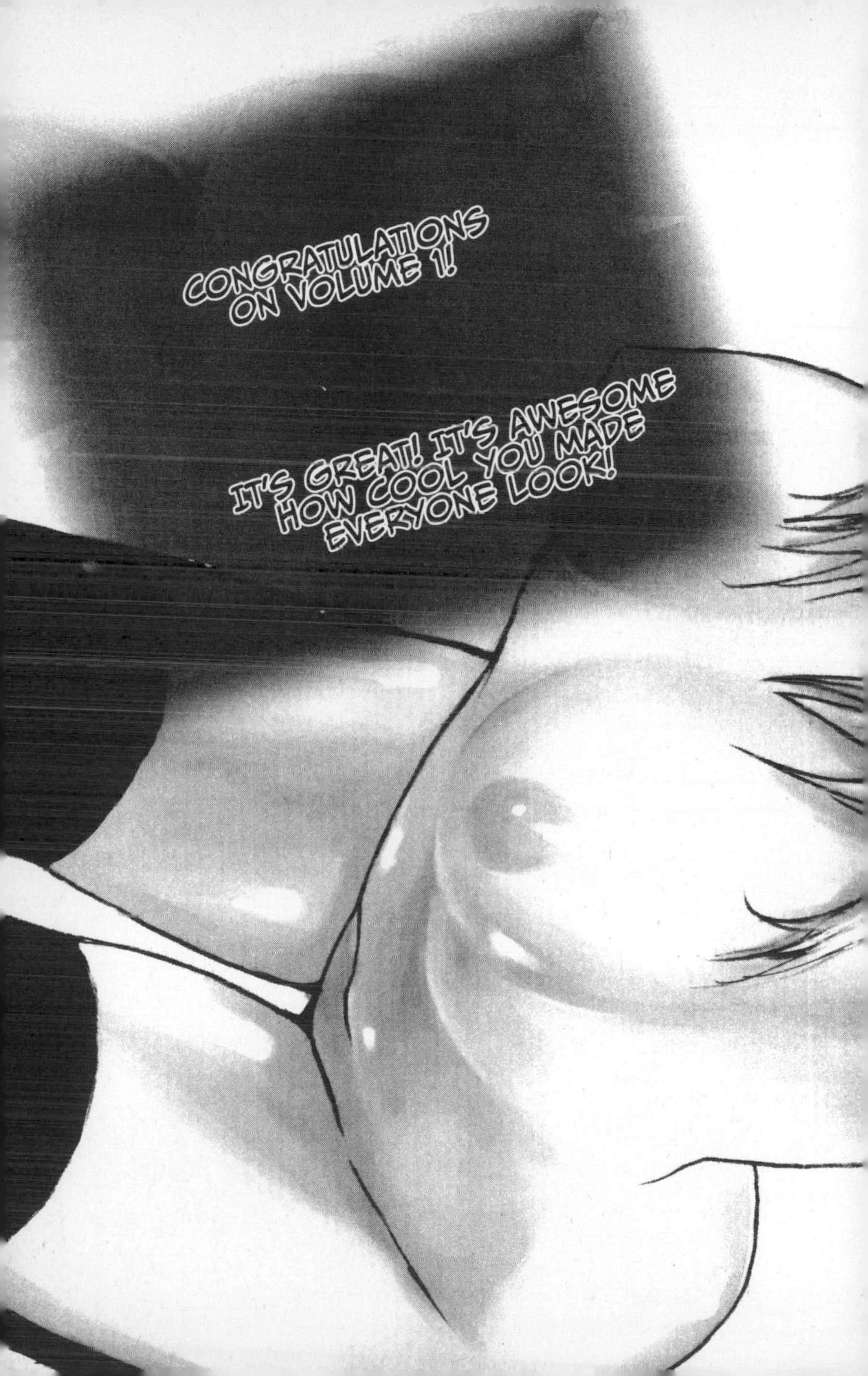
CONGRATULATIONS ON VOLUME 1!
IT'S GREAT! IT'S AWESOME HOW COOL YOU MADE EVERYONE LOOK!

Afterword

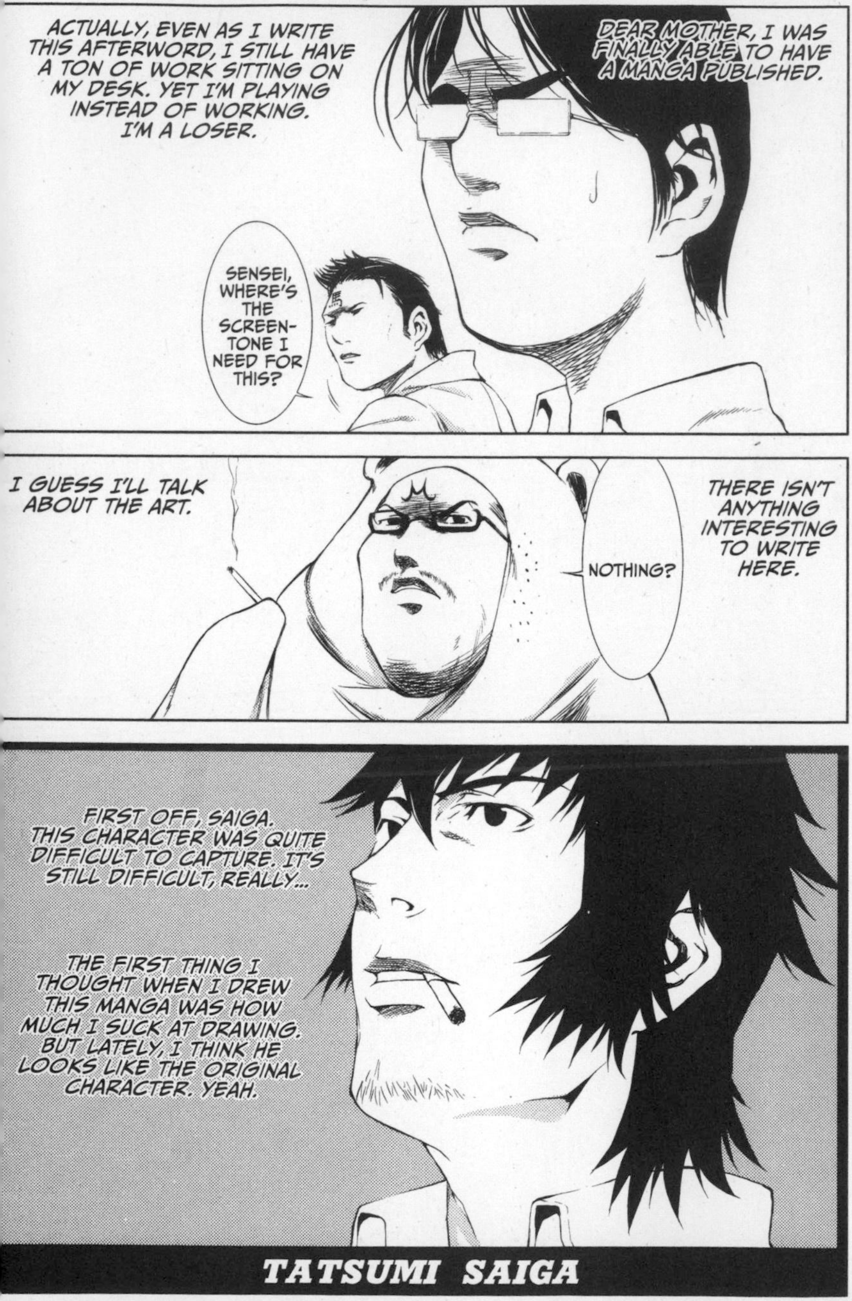
DEAR MOTHER, I WAS FINALLY ABLE TO HAVE A MANGA PUBLISHED.
ACTUALLY, EVEN AS I WRITE THIS AFTERWORD, I STILL HAVE A TON OF WORK SITTING ON MY DESK. YET I'M PLAYING INSTEAD OF WORKING. I'M A LOSER.
SENSEI, WHERE'S THE SCREEN-TONE I NEED FOR THIS?
THERE ISN'T ANYTHING INTERESTING TO WRITE HERE.
NOTHING?
I GUESS I'LL TALK ABOUT THE ART.
FIRST OFF, SAIGA. THIS CHARACTER WAS QUITE DIFFICULT TO CAPTURE. IT'S STILL DIFFICULT, REALLY...
THE FIRST THING I THOUGHT WHEN I DREW THIS MANGA WAS HOW MUCH I SUCK AT DRAWING. BUT LATELY, I THINK HE LOOKS LIKE THE ORIGINAL CHARACTER. YEAH.
TATSUMI SAIGA

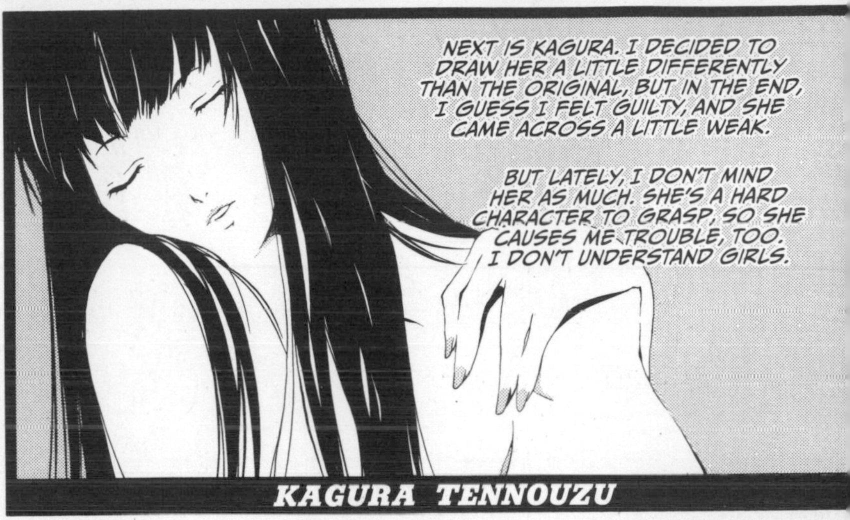
NEXT IS KAGURA. I DECIDED TO DRAW HER A LITTLE DIFFERENTLY THAN THE ORIGINAL, BUT IN THE END, I GUESS I FELT GUILTY, AND SHE CAME ACROSS A LITTLE WEAK.
BUT LATELY, I DON'T MIND HER AS MUCH. SHE'S A HARD CHARACTER TO GRASP, SO SHE CAUSES ME TROUBLE, TOO. I DON'T UNDERSTAND GIRLS.
KAGURA TENNOUZU

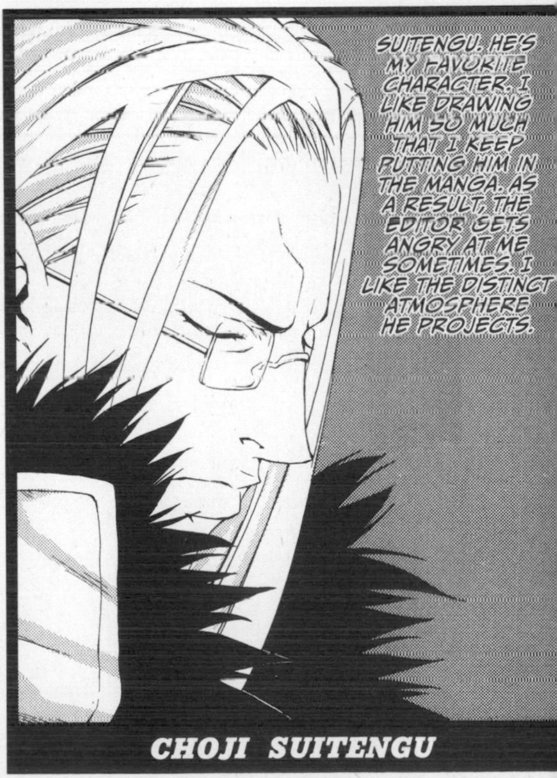
SUITENGU. HE'S MY FAVORITE CHARACTER. I LIKE DRAWING HIM SO MUCH THAT I KEEP PUTTING HIM IN THE MANGA. AS A RESULT, THE EDITOR GETS ANGRY AT ME SOMETIMES. I LIKE THE DISTINCT ATMOSPHERE HE PROJECTS.
CHOJI SUITENGU

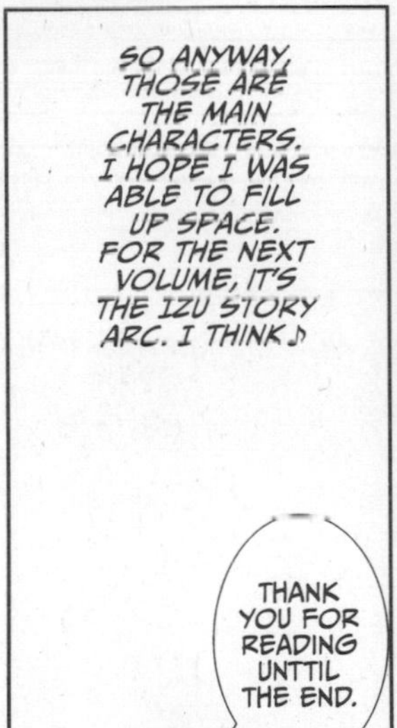
SO ANYWAY, THOSE ARE THE MAIN CHARACTERS. I HOPE I WAS ABLE TO FILL UP SPACE. FOR THE NEXT VOLUME, IT'S THE IZU STORY ARC. I THINK♪
THANK YOU FOR READING UNTTIL THE END.
BOW

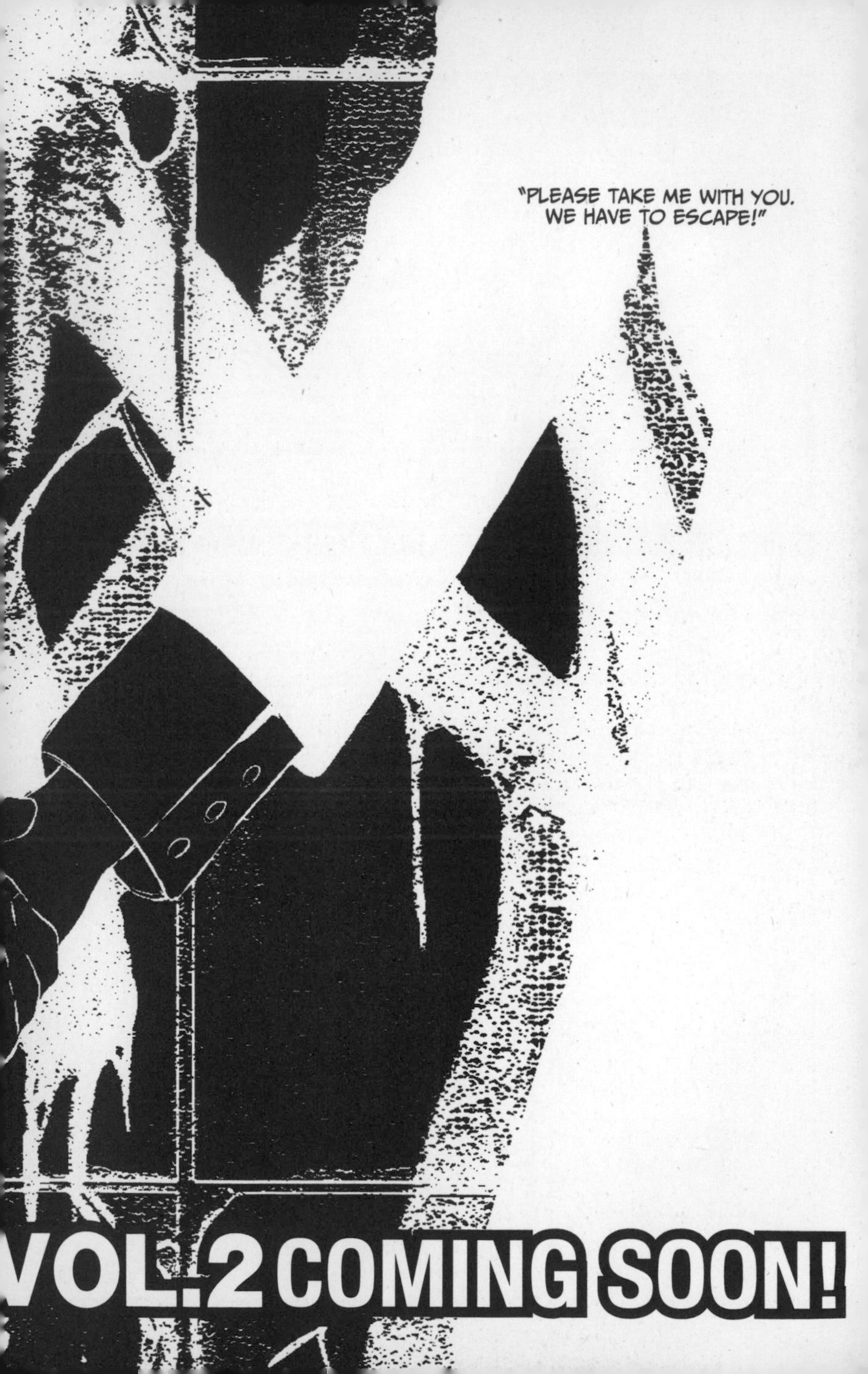
"PLEASE TAKE ME WITH YOU.
WE HAVE TO ESCAPE!"
VOL.2 COMING SOON!

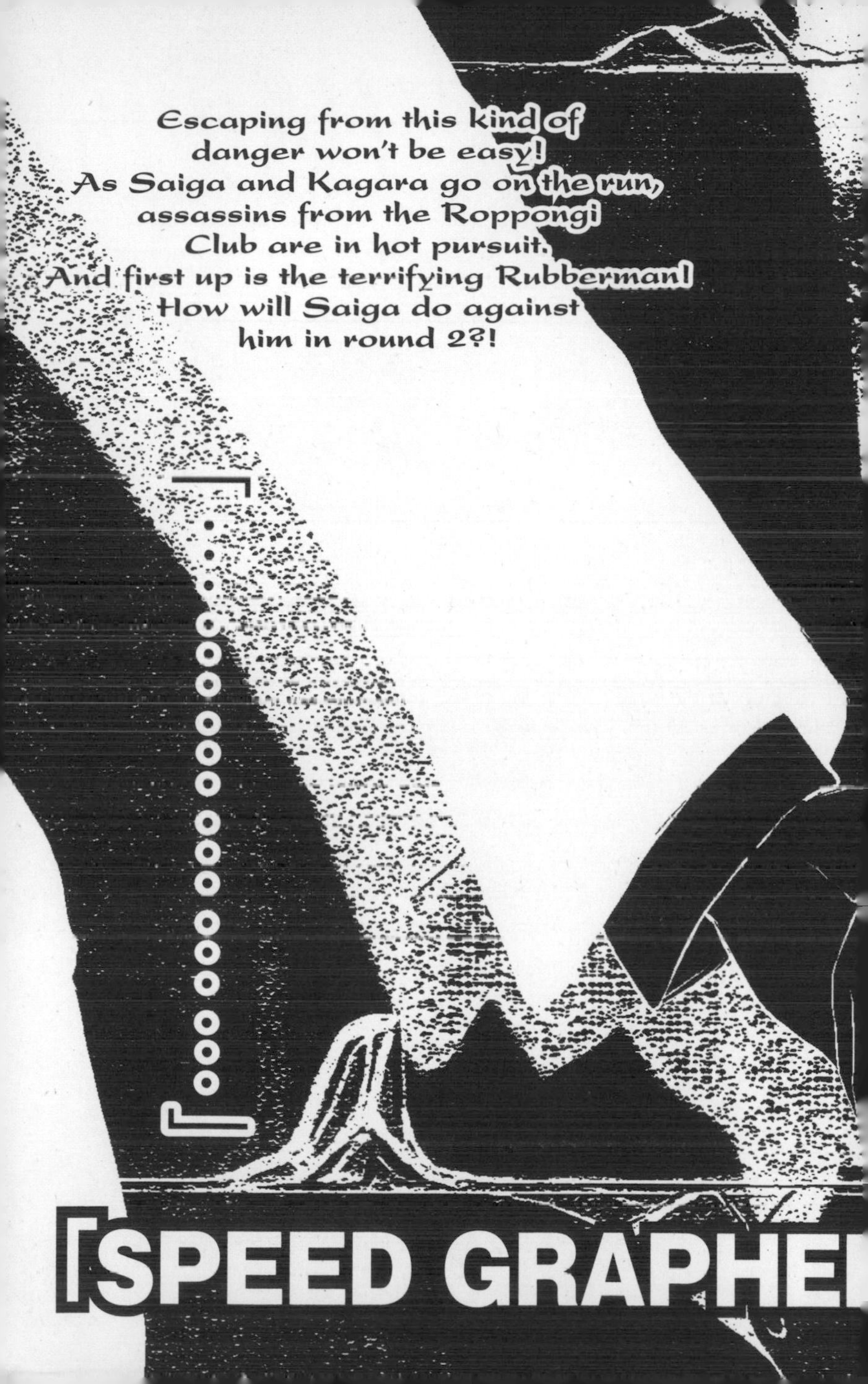
Escaping from this kind of danger won't be easy!
As Saiga and Kagara go on the run, assassins from the Roppongi Club are in hot pursuit.
And first up is the terrifying Rubberman!
How will Saiga do against him in round 2?!
「SPEED GRAPHE

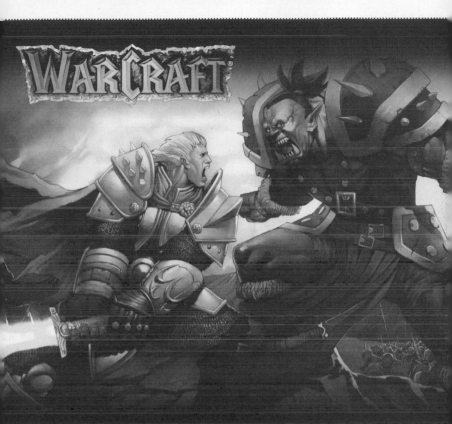

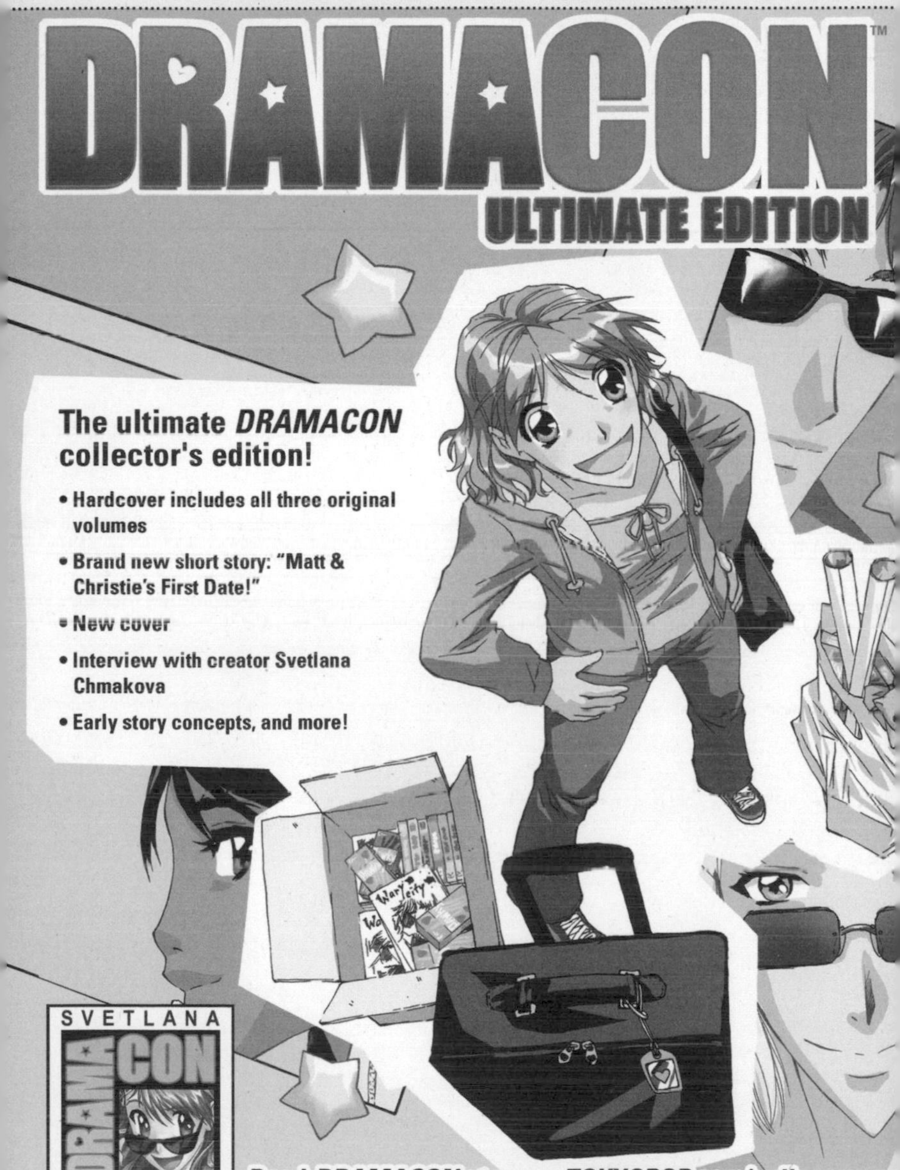

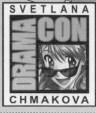

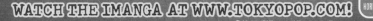

STOP!

This is the back of the book.
You wouldn't want to spoil a great ending!

This book is printed "manga-style," in the authentic Japanese right-to-left format. Since none of the artwork has been flipped or altered, readers get to experience the story just as the creator intended. You've been asking for it, so TOKYOPOP® delivered: authentic, hot-off-the-press, and far more fun!

DIRECTIONS

If this is your first time reading manga-style, here's a quick guide to help you understand how it works.

It's easy... just start in the top right panel and follow the numbers. Have fun, and look for more 100% authentic manga from TOKYOPOP®!

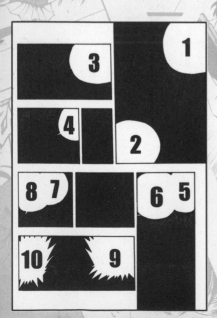